Advocates of Reform

General Editors

John Baillie (1886–1960) served as President of the World Council of Churches, a member of the British Council of Churches, Moderator of the General Assembly of the Church of Scotland, and Dean of the Faculty of Divinity at the University of Edinburgh.

John T. McNeill (1885–1975) was Professor of the History of European Christianity at the University of Chicago and then Auburn Professor of Church History at Union Theological Seminary in New York.

Henry P. Van Dusen (1897–1975) was an early and influential member of the World Council of Churches and served at Union Theological Seminary in New York as Roosevelt Professor of Systematic Theology and later as President.

THE LIBRARY OF CHRISTIAN CLASSICS

Advocates of Reform
From Wyclif to Erasmus

Edited by

MATTHEW SPINKA
PhD, ThD, DD

Westminster John Knox Press
LOUISVILLE • LONDON

© 1953 The Westminster Press

Paperback reissued 2006 by Westminster John Knox Press, Louisville, Kentucky.

Cover design by designpointinc.com
Published by Westminster John Knox Press
Louisville, Kentucky

This book is printed on acid-free paper that meets the American National Standards Institute Z39.48 standard.♾

PRINTED IN THE UNITED STATES OF AMERICA

United States Library of Congress Cataloging-in-Publication Data is on file at the Library of Congress, Washington, D.C.

ISBN-13: 978-0-664-23079-1
ISBN-10: 0-664-23079-2

GENERAL EDITORS' PREFACE

The Christian Church possesses in its literature an abundant and incomparable treasure. But it is an inheritance that must be reclaimed by each generation. THE LIBRARY OF CHRISTIAN CLASSICS is designed to present in the English language, and in twenty-six volumes of convenient size, a selection of the most indispensable Christian treatises written prior to the end of the sixteenth century.

The practice of giving circulation to writings selected for superior worth or special interest was adopted at the beginning of Christian history. The canonical Scriptures were themselves a selection from a much wider literature. In the Patristic era there began to appear a class of works of compilation (often designed for ready reference in controversy) of the opinions of well-reputed predecessors, and in the Middle Ages many such works were produced. These medieval anthologies actually preserve some noteworthy materials from works otherwise lost.

In modern times, with the increasing inability even of those trained in universities and theological colleges to read Latin and Greek texts with ease and familiarity, the translation of selected portions of earlier Christian literature into modern languages has become more necessary than ever; while the wide range of distinguished books written in vernaculars such as English makes selection there also needful. The efforts that have been made to meet this need are too numerous to be noted here, but none of these collections serves the purpose of the reader who desires a library of representative treatises spanning the Christian centuries as a whole. Most of them embrace only the age of the Church Fathers, and some of them have long been out of print. A fresh translation of a work already

9

translated may shed much new light upon its meaning. This is true even of Bible translations despite the work of many experts through the centuries. In some instances old translations have been adopted in this series, but wherever necessary or desirable, new ones have been made. Notes have been supplied where these were needed to explain the author's meaning. The introductions provided for the several treatises and extracts will, we believe, furnish welcome guidance.

JOHN BAILLIE
JOHN T. McNEILL
HENRY P. VAN DUSEN

CONTENTS

General Introduction

THE PRESENT VOLUME AIMS TO INTRODUCE THE reader to the principal advocates of reform within the Church from the second half of the fourteenth century to the beginning of the sixteenth century, and as such it is intended as a continuation of Volume XIII of this series, entitled *Late Medieval Mysticism*. For it must be kept in mind that ever since the breakup of Scholasticism, there existed various movements that strove to bring about a reform of the Church. Scholasticism reached its highest expression in the thought of Thomas Aquinas (1225-1274). After his death, his system became a target for determined attacks, and for a considerable period the nominalistic school dominated the scene. Thus "the medieval synthesis" (magnified out of its true proportion by the modern Neo-Thomists), which found its best expression in the *Summa contra gentiles* and the *Summa theologica* of the Angelic Doctor, was shattered by the resurgent nominalism of Duns Scotus and William of Ockham. Instead of sharing Aquinas' confidence in the capacity of human reason to fathom at least some of the divine truths which he classified as belonging to "natural theology," they tended to separate the functions of reason and faith and to make the entire divine revelation the exclusive province of faith. This signified the real collapse of the medieval and the rise of the modern period of Christian thought.

The reaction to the Scholasticism of Thomas Aquinas, to which were later added resentments against the abuses of the Avignonese papacy and of the Great Schism, took three-fold form: The first aspect was theological, as witnessed by the already mentioned systems of Duns Scotus, William of

Ockham, and other less prominent thinkers of the late Scholastic period. The principal tenet of nominalistic theology—the distrust of reason in matters of religion and the acceptance of revealed truth by faith alone—strongly affected the future Reformers. Luther was considerably influenced by the Ockhamist thought, for among his teachers at the University of Erfurt were two stanch adherents of that medieval thinker, Jodocus Trutvetter and Bartolomaeus von Usingen. He was likewise influenced by the writings of the former professor of theology at the University of Tübingen, Gabriel Biel (d. 1495), in his day the most prominent representative of the same nominalistic school. No wonder that Luther referred to Ockham as his "master." When he entered the Erfurt Augustinian monastery, he studied the works of Ockham, d'Ailly, and Gerson.

Another group of religious leaders of the post-Thomistic period was constituted of those who were convinced that what mattered supremely in Christian life was not mere fine-spun speculation but holy living. With Saint Hilary, they held that the Lord was not pleased to save his people by means of subtle points of theology. They were founders of the mystical movement which flowered most profusely, during the fourteenth and the fifteenth centuries, in the Rhine Valley and the Netherlands. For the greatest part, the mystics were not deficient in theological learning; in fact, some of them, like Meister Eckhart, were exceedingly profound thinkers. Gerard Groote, the founder of the Brethren of the Common Life, before his retirement from his brilliant academic career, had won for himself a widespread renown for his philosophical and theological learning. But, as he himself expressed it later, "What availeth it to reason high secret mysteries of the Trinity if a man lacks meekness, whereby he displeaseth the Trinity?" This and other similar insights into the true nature of Christian piety made that golden little book *The Imitation of Christ* (edited by Thomas à Kempis from the writings of Groote) one of the treasures of devotional life for the vast majority of Christians. Likewise, although aware of the corruptions that infected the contemporary Church, and sometimes victims of the persecutions of that Church, they did not regard it as their *primary* duty to strive for institutional changes (although Gerard Groote's denunciation of the vices of the clergy cost him dearly), but rather stressed the inner transformation and sanctification of one's life. Thus the unknown author of the *Theologia Germanica* never tired of insisting upon the supreme necessity of self-renunciation, the denial of the "I" and "mine." This element of emphasis upon holy life, the denial of one's will and its submission to the will of God, remained an integral part of the reform movement, although not always in its exclusive form, but more often in combination with other reform requirements. Thus, for instance, John Hus and the Czech Reform (particularly the Unity of Czech Brethren) placed a similar emphasis on holy living. Erasmus was strongly influenced in this regard by the Brethren of the Common Life. Luther gladly bore testimony to the strong impress which the *Theologia Germanica* had exercised upon his thinking; in fact, it was he who had rescued the little book from oblivion by twice publishing it.

In the third place, the reaction to Scholasticism, and particularly to that period of papal degradation known as the Babylonian Captivity (1309–1377) as well as to the subsequent Great Schism (1378–1417), when two and later three popes disputed with each other the supreme authority in the Church, took the form of a demand for institutional and moral reforms so radical that it would have produced a basic transformation of the papacy. This reform was represented mainly by John Wyclif and the Conciliarists. Wyclif, however, found it necessary, in order to secure for himself a *locus standi* in his radical criticism of the Church and the papacy, to ground his argument upon a solid theological basis. His theological speculation ultimately outweighed his practical reform. Since he had to find a higher authority for his tenets than the Church possessed in the papacy, he elevated Scripture to that supreme position. It may be pointed out that Hus and the later great Reformers were led to adopt the same conclusion and on similar grounds. The Conciliarists, on the other hand, for the greatest part anxiously sought to restrict themselves to institutional and moral reforms, without getting involved in a radical contradiction of the current scholastic theology. For that reason, Cardinal d'Ailly and John Gerson were determined to dissociate their cause from that of Wyclif and Hus, and hence were violently opposed to the latter at the Council of Constance. Similarly, Erasmus was by temperament closer to the Conciliarists than to Wyclif and Hus, not to say anything about Luther, although the reforms he advocated were different from those of the Conciliarists. Furthermore, it is important to note that the principle of representative government, advocated by the Conciliarists for the Church, was not without its influence upon the political thinking of later ages. Even more strongly may such an influence be traced to the *Defensor pacis* of Marsiglio of Padua.

The continuity and interdependence of the entire reform movement from the breakdown of Scholasticism to the Reformation of the sixteenth century is, therefore, obvious. Both Luther and Calvin [1] made the supreme authority of Scripture the cornerstone of their systems, as Wyclif and Hus had done before them. In the dispute with John Eck at Leipzig (1519), Luther acknowledged the essential identity of his position, as far as the supremacy of the pope and the infallibity of general councils were concerned, with that of Hus. He furthermore asserted that Hus had been unjustly condemned by the Council of Constance: "We are all Hussites!" he exclaimed. The Communion in two kinds, which has become the general practice of all Protestants, had been reinstituted and defended during the long, bloody wars waged by the Czech Calixtines, having been advocated as a part of the general reform of the Church by Jakoubek of Stříbro, a friend and successor of Hus. The second focal point of Calvin's system—his insistence upon a disciplined Christian life—is certainly reminiscent of similar emphases in the writings of the mystics, of Wyclif, Hus, the Conciliarists, and even of Erasmus. Perhaps one of the most direct links between the earlier advocates of reform and the sixteenth century Reformers is furnished by John Major, to whom Erasmus, Calvin, and perhaps Knox, were indebted. Although Major never associated himself with the Reformation, yet in a sense he was a forerunner of it by reason of his bold stand for the authority of councils against that of popes.

From this brief survey it is clear that, despite the necessarily selective treatment of the subject to which this volume is devoted, its four separate sections possess a real inner unity. Other advocates of reform could have been included had the scope of this work permitted. But those who have been selected, and the representative passages from their writings which have been made available, will, we hope, suffice to show that the demand for reform, sometimes in a surprisingly radical form, existed within the Church for some two and a half centuries prior to its culmination in the Protestant Reformation.

The space at our disposal did not allow the inclusion of the

---

[1] Selections from the works of Luther will be published in Vols. XV–XVIII; selections from the works of Calvin will occupy Vols. XX–XXIII.

complete texts of the works selected. While a judicious pruning
of the verbose and involved treatises of Wyclif may have served
to improve those texts which were included, the painful task
of deletion of much that was worthy of inclusion was perhaps
the hardest duty the editor was called upon to perform. In most
instances, the entire treatise has been translated, and the reduction then proceeded on the basis of the whole text. In every
instance where a reduction of the text was necessary, deletion
has been marked by the customary three dots, or by the inter-
ruption of the sequence of the numbered paragraphs.[2]

[2] Where the complete text had been translated, a typewritten copy of
it was deposited in the Case Library of the Hartford Seminary Foundation. The following works are available in this form: Wyclif's
On the Pastoral Office, together with substantial portions of *On the Eucharist*
and *On Divine Lordship*; furthermore, all the works included in the section
on the Conciliarists, and, in addition to these, Peter d'Ailly's *Tractatus
super reformatione ecclesiae* and John Gerson's *De potestate ecclesiastica*, all
of which are contained in James Kerr Cameron's thesis, "Conciliarism
in Theory and Practice, 1378–1418." Finally, the complete texts of Hus's
On Simony and of Erasmus' *Enchiridion*, are likewise available in the translation of Matthew Spinka and Ford Lewis Battles respectively.

JOHN WYCLIF

John Wyclif, Advocate of Radical Reform

I N PRESENTING THE MOST ESSENTIAL BIOGRAPHICAL
data concerning Wyclif's life we may follow Workman [1] in
accepting the year 1328 as that of his birth. Wyclif studied
at Balliol College, Oxford, but little is known of his student
years. He took his master's degree perhaps in 1358, and was
then or shortly thereafter elected Master of his alma mater;
but he held that office only for a year. In order to secure means
for continuing his studies, he was granted two benefices and,
what is even more remarkable, held them as a nonresident, not
even troubling himself to secure the bishop's dispensation for
one of them. After receiving his bachelor's degree in theology,
he continued his studies toward the doctorate, which he obtained in 1372. But he was disappointed in his expectations of
some lucrative office, which he had been promised by Pope
Gregory XI, and hence entered the service of the Crown. In
consideration thereof, King Edward III granted him the parish
of Lutterworth, which he held to his death.

Wyclif entered upon the public stage of his career in 1374,
when he was appointed a member of a commission sent to
Bruges to treat with papal representatives regarding the tribute
which the *curia* claimed as its feudal right ever since King John
had become a papal vassal, as well as regarding other disputed
matters. Even then he held theories about "lordship" which
logically and theologically justified, under certain conditions,
the seizure of ecclesiastical goods by the State. He adumbrated
them in his *Determinatio* (1374), but developed them fully in

---

[1] Herbert B. Workman, *John Wyclif* (London, 1926), 2 vols.; also for a
short summary, John T. McNeill, *Makers of Christianity*, II (Henry Holt
& Company, Inc., New York, 1935), 157 ff.

his *De dominio divino* (On Divine Lordship, 1375)[2] and *De civili dominio* (On Civil Lordship, 1376).[3] These two works represent the substance of his Oxford lectures delivered during the two years after he returned from Bruges, and with them Wyclif makes his formal debut as a major thinker. Lack of space, unfortunately, precluded the inclusion of the first-named work, although its translation was completed.

In the treatise *On Divine Lordship* Wyclif followed fairly closely in the footsteps of Archbishop FitzRalph,[4] who taught that God is the supreme Lord of all. "Divine Lordship is the basis of any lordship of the creature and not conversely."[5] Man, created in the image of God, is capable of lordship and has been placed over all things inferior to him. Natures inferior to man cannot exercise lordship. But since there are three sorts of rational natures, it is clear that correspondingly there are given three modes of lordship: divine, angelic, and human. Its species vary according to the bases of lordship, especially in man. For, just as there are natural law, evangelical law, and human law, correspondingly there are natural lordship; evangelical lordship, such as that of charity, or vicarious lordship, as when someone receives in Christ's name ministry from another; and finally coercive lordship, which varies according to the variation of the laws and of the rights of those founding it.

Nor is this primacy of the divine lordship abrogated, diminished, or nullified when God bestows an infinitesimal portion of it upon one of his human creatures. Such temporary "loan" of lordship then is neither permanent nor unlimited, and is suited to the conditions of the recipient. Hence, such a person "is improperly called a lord, but is rather a steward of the supreme Lord. It is clear from this that every creature is a servant of the Lord, possessing whatsoever he has of pure grace that he may husband it."[6]

Consequently, since all lordship is based on grace, Wyclif concludes, in his *De civili dominio*, that all possessions and all power, civil and ecclesiastical, are held righteously only as long as their possessors remain in grace. It follows, therefore, that a pauper, if he be in grace, has a better moral right to "lordship"

[2] R. L. Poole, ed., *Johannis Wycliffe De dominio divino* (London, 1890).
[3] R. L. Poole, ed., *Johannis Wycliffe De civili dominio*, I; Johann Loserth, II (1900–1904).
[4] Wyclif used FitzRalph's *De pauperie Salvatoris* (R. L. Poole, ed., appendix to Wyclif's *De dominio divino*).
[5] Battles' translation, I, ch. 3, par. 2.
[6] *Ibid.*, III, ch. 6, par. 4.

than a pope or an emperor in a state of mortal sin. To be sure, the unrighteous may, and frequently do, hold possessions, but only "naturally." Only the righteous hold them rightfully,[7] or, as Wyclif expresses it, "from dignity and merit." Applying this reasoning to the lords ecclesiastical, he argues that according to the gospel a Christian is "lord" only in so far as he is a servant of all.[8] In the last division of the book Wyclif turns to the relation of State to Church, and denies the lawfulness of any grants in perpetuity. The ecclesiastical lords can only declare what God has done, but have no right themselves to make a valid, perpetual grant. They are stewards, not masters.[9] Hence follows the chief conclusion that if they themselves are not in grace, they are not righteous possessors of property and may—nay, should—be deprived of it by the secular power.

Such a theory, if rigorously applied to all cases, whether civil or ecclesiastical, would have proved destructive of the political and social, as well as the ecclesiastical, order, for it would have overturned, or at least rendered uncertain, the possessions or rule of all who might be regarded as "not in grace." Moreover, who would be rightfully in a position to determine the state of a man's heart? Would not this lead to a fantastic increase of the power of the Church, a premature declaration of the dogma of papal infallibility? Fortunately, Wyclif did not choose to be consistent, and did not push the logic of his revolutionary principle to its obvious conclusion, by applying it to the State as well as the Church. He explicitly forbade the use of force against the existing civil order, even when it was frankly tyrannous,[10] and tamely advised the subjects to submit to it. Since, then, a righteous subject might have to submit to an unjust lord, the statement of this principle later figured among his "heretical" conclusions that "God must in this matter obey the devil."

But as for the rule and property of ecclesiastical persons "not in grace," that was, as we have already seen, an altogether different matter. He had long held the doctrine propounded by earlier reformers, that Christ gave the Church authority over only the spiritual, not the temporal, realm. He professed himself to be a disciple of Marsiglio of Padua, William of Ockham, William of St. Amour, and Richard FitzRalph.[11] Furthermore, he had long sympathized with Saint Francis' insist-

---

[7] *De civili dominio,* I, ch. 3.   [8] *Ibid.,* I, ch. 11.
[9] *Ibid.,* I, ch. 35.   [10] *Ibid.,* I, ch. 28.
[11] *De ordinatione fratrum,* in *Die lateinische Streitschriften,* ed. by R. Buddensieg (1883), 92.

ence upon apostolic poverty as obligatory upon all priests,
and with the notion that the chief cause of the Church's ills
is found in the great wealth of prelates, monks, and priests.
It is for that reason that he found cordial support among many
members of the mendicant orders. [12] Along with others of the
time, he traced the corruption of the Church to the time of
Constantine, when that emperor had allegedly endowed the
papacy with temporal possessions and thus had "poured poison
into the Church." "The first plot of the devil began in the
time of Sylvester." The unworthy priest or prelate, then, who
manifests in his life lack of grace should be deprived of his benefice. Such disciplinary action belongs, in the first place, to the
Church itself, and the Church should deprive its unworthy
servants of both their office and their income. But in view of
the notorious corruption of the Avignonese papacy and the
subsequent period of the Great Schism, such an expectation
would have been naïve and futile. A crow would not peck out
the eyes of its fellow crow, as the proverb says. Hence, Wyclif
called upon the State to perform the function. It is indeed the
divinely appointed duty of the State to deprive unworthy clerics
of their possessions, since the State has the responsibility for
the temporal order. Not only should the clergy pay taxes, but
all ecclesiastical income beyond the actual need of the incum-
bents should be used by the State for the relief of the very strin-
gent economic conditions caused by the war with France.
"Believing that the priesthood had become corrupted through
wealth and power, he held that it was the king's duty to dispossess the 'Caesarean' clergy, disendow the 'delinquent'
Church, and restore a priesthood of grace." [13] No wonder
that the secular lords—and particularly the unscrupulous and
rapacious John of Gaunt, who utilized the senility of his father,
King Edward III, in order to exploit the political scene for his
own and his henchmen's interest—afforded Wyclif not only
"moral" support, but even very effective protection. Since
John of Gaunt "made the scheme of disendowment peculiarly
his own," [14] he only furthered his own selfish interests in pro-
tecting Wyclif. One is forcefully reminded of the disgraceful
scene in St. Paul's (1377) when Archbishop Sudbury cited

---

12 Cf. Aubrey Gwynn, *The English Austin Friars in the Time of Wyclif* (Oxford
University Press, London, 1940), *passim*.
13 John T. McNeill, "Some Emphases in Wyclif's Teaching," *The Journal
of Religion*, VII (1927), 461.
14 G. M. Trevelyan, *England in the Age of Wyclif* (New York, 1906), 41.

Wyclif to appear before him for examination of his views: the latter appeared, accompanied by the generally hated Duke of Lancaster and his then marshal, Lord Henry Percy, and by overawing the ecclesiastical court frustrated the proceedings. This is an eloquent example of how unscrupulous politicians of all ages are prone to make use of convenient theological doctrines! Had Wyclifite views of lordship then prevailed, they would have resulted in delivering a venal priesthood into the hands of equally venal politicians. For that matter the measures advocated by Wyclif in *De officio regis* (On the King's Office)— the principle of a territorial Church governed by the king— were actually realized in the days of Henry VIII and his successors (except Mary).

Before we proceed to the next phase of Wyclif's activity, his much more important and better conceived radical reform of the concept of the Church, we must examine his *On the Pastoral Office*, a substantial portion of which, in translation, is likewise included in this volume. Since no English translation of the two works of Wyclif chosen in this volume has hitherto been available, the inclusion of Ford Lewis Battles' version is a valuable contribution. As is generally known, Wyclif's writings are both linguistically and stylistically exceedingly involved and difficult. Reginald Poole, who edited a number of them, expressed himself feelingly when he wrote, "Wycliffe's Latin is base even as compared with that of such of his predecessors as Ockham; there is a gulf between it and that of Thomas Aquinas." [15]

Lechler dates the treatise not later than 1378. In it Wyclif furnishes a positive definition of pastoral duties, which he asserts to be twofold: purging the Church of all moral stain, and feeding Christ's sheep spiritually on his Word. In dealing with the former, Wyclif again stresses the duty of the clergy to live frugally, in accordance with Paul's instruction, "Having food and wherewith to be clothed, let us be content." [16] They should live exclusively upon the support furnished them by their parishioners. All other possessions they should distribute among the needy. When a priest is deficient in his pastoral duties, parishioners should withdraw their "alms" from him in order to avoid fostering wickedness, and should not even attend upon his ministrations. [17] Such a denial of support should

[15] R. L. Poole, ed., *De civili dominio*, I, xviii.
[16] Battles' translation, I, ch. 2 (I Tim. 6:8).
[17] *Ibid.*, I, ch. 8.

particularly be resorted to in regard to the "four sects"—
bishops, monks, canons, and friars.

As for the second part of the treatise, the duty of the priest
to feed his flock spiritually, this is his supreme task. It is to be
performed, not merely by preaching, but by a living example
as well. "Evangelization [preaching the gospel] exceeds prayer
and administration of the sacraments to an infinite degree." [18]
Wyclif then attacks friars because their preaching is "not
founded in the entire gospel," and is done "in hope of temporal
gain." [19] He calls their monasteries "castles of Cain," and
asserts that Christ never intended religious folk to hide in
cloisters.

Into this text of the Latin version was incorporated Chapter
XV of the Middle English version, devoted to a spirited
defense of the translation of the Bible into the vernacular.
Although this version is perhaps not Wyclif's own (Workman
regards it as the work of one of Wyclif's assistants in Bible
translation[20]), yet it reflects the Reformer's own opinions.

This phase of Wyclif's reform activity is only preliminary
to his much more radical later reform, when John of Gaunt
washed his hands of the uncompromising theologian. Moreover,
during this latter phase one hears but little about his concern
with the State. This change was occasioned by the Great
Schism (1378), which ultimately led him to denounce the pope
as the Antichrist, to repudiate the whole papal system, and to
advocate theological reforms that shocked and alienated the
contemporaneous world.

The basic principle upon which he sought to ground his
reform was the supreme authority of the Scriptures. This
doctrine, which more than anything else links him with the
Reformation, was carefully worked out in *De veritate sacrae
Scripturae* (On the Truth of the Holy Scriptures), published in
the very year in which the schism broke out. Wyclif asserts and
defends therein the absolute superiority of the Scriptural
doctrine over scholastic theology or the current assertion of
papal supremacy in all matters of faith and practice. For him,
"Holy Scripture is the highest authority for every Christian
and the standard of faith and of all human perfection."[21] The
Bible alone is the supreme organ of divine revelation; the

---

[18] *Ibid.*, II, ch. 2.   [19] *Ibid.*, II, 4.
[20] Workman, *op. cit.*, II, 329.
[21] R. Buddensieg, ed., *De veritate sacrae Scripturae* (London, 1905–1907),
Introduction, 25.

Church's tradition, pronouncements of the councils, papal decrees, and all other expositions of Christian doctrine must be tested on the Scriptural touchstone. All truth is contained in the Scriptures.[22] They are divinely inspired in all their parts, hence, equally authoritative throughout. As such, they alone are a sufficient guide in all matters, religious and secular. Every Christian must know them and read them in his own language. This explains Wyclif's interest in procuring a Middle English version of the Bible.

This doctrine was basic to all Wyclif's subsequent thought, and furnished him with a *locus standi* from which he could judge the monstrous abuses of the existing ecclesiastical practice. Basing himself on this bedrock of Biblical doctrine, Wyclif initiated his restatement of Christian theology by a thoroughly Augustinian doctrine of the Church. In his *De ecclesia* (On the Church) (completed toward the end of 1378) he defined the Church as the *universitas fidelium praedestinatorum*, comprised in the three traditional states—the Church triumphant, consisting of saints in heaven; the Church militant, of those still on earth; and the sleeping Church, of those in purgatory.[23] Outside this body of the predestinate there is no salvation; the reprobate, even though they be members of the institutional Church, do not belong to the real Church, the Church invisible. Of this timeless, spiritual company of believers Christ alone is the head, as it is his body. Hence, merely formal membership in the ecclesiastical organization, the Church visible, is no proof of salvation. No ecclesiastical office, no matter how exalted, guarantees it. Hence, even the pope and his cardinals need not necessarily, merely ex officio, be members of the Church invisible. In fact, no pope can rightfully claim to be the head of the communion of saints, for at the most he is the head of the Roman portion of the Church visible. After 1380, Wyclif reached the radical conclusion that the pope is the Antichrist and his claims are blasphemous.

The visible Church, then, by contrast, consists of both the predestinate and the reprobate. The latter form a body, just as the predestinate do, but it is the *"corpus diaboli."* There is no sure and infallible method of distinguishing between the wheat and the tares, although a life of piety and obedience to the will of God is a presumptive evidence of predestinate status, while on the contrary a life of open wickedness and revolt against

---

[22] *Ibid.*, 47. He repeats this assertion throughout his later writings.
[23] Johann Loserth, ed., *De ecclesia* (London, 1886), 8.

God's will is indicative of reprobate status. For "by their fruits ye shall know them."

The radical criticism of the papacy formulated under the terrific impact of the Great Schism was further extended and sharpened in *De potestate papae* (On the Power of the Pope),[24] which is dated 1379. In this bitter attack on the papacy he denies the divine institution of that office—that cornerstone of the Roman Church then and now. Following FitzRalph, Wyclif acknowledged Peter's primacy among the apostles, but ascribed it to his pre-eminent personal qualities, and above all to his exceptional love for Christ. No election to papal office can automatically confer these qualities; hence, no successor of Peter possesses Peter's authority unless he has the same qualities of devotion, faith, and love. Thus primacy is a matter of character, not of office. Pre-eminence depends on outstanding gifts of the Spirit. Wyclif enumerates twelve proofs in support of his contention, and asserts that a pope who fails to follow Christ in simplicity and poverty is the Antichrist.[25] Hence, as an office, the papacy is of human origin, its founder being Emperor Constantine, or, rather, Emperor Phocas.[26] A pope may be a heretic, as Pope Liberius was. In true Marsiglian spirit Wyclif declares that the pope's administration of the Church is limited to spiritual concerns; these are, nevertheless, superior to the temporal; but Christ did not grant him jurisdiction over temporalities, since his "Kingdom is not of this world." Both spiritual and temporal rules are from God, who is the supreme Lord of all; but they are exercised co-ordinately by Church and State.

In his later works, Wyclif advocates the abolition of the papal office altogether: the pope, instead of being "quasi-divine or god on earth," who has the right to dispense men from laws human and divine, and to offend whom is a graver trespass than to offend Christ,[27] is in reality the Antichrist.

Following hard upon this major attack, Wyclif arrived at his most flagrantly radical conclusion (or so it seemed to his contemporaries) by rejecting the dogma of transubstantiation. He had adumbrated this idea as early as 1379 in his treatise *De apostasia*. He wrote then that the sacrament of the altar consists "in nature of the substance and body of bread and wine, and

---

[24] Johann Loserth, ed., *De potestate papae* (London, 1907).
[25] *Ibid.*, 176–179.   [26] *Ibid.*, 177–178.
[27] R. Buddensieg, ed., *John Wyclif's Polemical Works* (London, 1883), II, 674–676, 691.

in significance and figure in the body and blood of Christ; it is impossible to impugn this definition."[28] In his treatise *On the Eucharist*[29] Wyclif repeats many of the arguments used previously, but presents them in greater detail and formulates them in a sharply antitransubstantiationist fashion. Although this treatise is written in his accustomed ponderous style, full of repetitions, logical hairsplitting, and verbal infelicities, it is an important contribution to Christian thought (particularly from the Reformation point of view), and as such it has been deemed worthy of inclusion (in part) in this volume.

Wyclif claimed no originality in his formulation of this doctrine: hence, he was conscious of no heresy. In fact, Wyclif was, in his own estimation, restating and defending the doctrine of the ancient Church as against the innovations introduced by the "modern doctors." He appeals to "the triple witness" of Augustine, Ambrose, and Anselm. He likewise repeatedly cites "the blessed decretal of Nicholas II, *Ego Berengarius*" (1059), which to him represents an authoritative statement of the doctrine of the ancient Church, from which the later church- men like Pope Innocent III, Thomas Aquinas, and Duns Scotus have erroneously departed. Hence the opinions of these "modern doctors" are "frivolous; for they scarcely grasp the shell of the words of the saints before them. And for that reason, inasmuch as they lack intelligence, these later doctors deny and erroneously impose their folly upon the saints. And they fashion glosses quite foreign to the Fathers, to the display of their own greater folly, as is clear from the gloss of the Common Doctor [Thomas Aquinas] to the sayings of Augustine on the powers of the soul: how the memory, reason, and will are not qualities inseparable from the essence of the soul. But Augustine assumes an opposite view in both cases.[30]

"The modern Church proposes transubstantiation of bread and wine into the body and blood of Christ; but the primitive Church did not hold this; therefore, they disagree in opinion."[31]

How does Wyclif substantiate his view? What, according to him, was the true doctrine concerning the Eucharist during

[28] M. H. Dziewicki, ed., *Tractatus de apostasia* (London, 1889), 119.
[29] Johann Loserth, ed., *De Eucharistia* (London, 1892). Workman (*op. cit.*, II, Appendix M, p. 408) dates it 1379; it is far more probable that it was published in 1380. Additional treatment of the Eucharistic contro- versy will be found in Vol. IX of THE LIBRARY OF CHRISTIAN CLASSICS, entitled *Early Medieval Theology* (edited by George E. McCracken), in the section on Ratramnus.
[30] Battles' translation, III, par. 37.   [31] *Ibid.*, II, par. 29.

the first millennium of the Church's history? He asserts that the ancient faith held the consecrated elements of bread and wine to be efficacious signs and symbols of Christ's body and blood. Hence, the latter are figuratively, *sacramentally*, effectively, but not materially, carnally present. "Thus we agree that we do not see the body of Christ in that sacrament with the bodily eye, but rather with the eye of the mind, that is, in faith, through a mirror darkly.[32] When we see the host, we ought to believe, not that it is itself the body of Christ, but that the body of Christ is [sacramentally] concealed in it.[33]

"Therefore, the faithful can gather that the sacrament of the Eucharist is really bread and wine, or (as others understand it) the sacrament is an aggregate of that substance and the body of Christ (as Augustine hints [in *De consecratione*, dist. 2, *Hoc est*]); this aggregate is effected by God's blessing or power, so that neither the bread nor the wine is destroyed."[34]

Since, then, the consecrated host is "not the Lord's body, but an efficacious sign thereof," to worship it would be sheer idolatry whereby "a creature . . . is worshiped as [if it were] God [himself]."[35] Hence the doctrine of remanence, for the bread and wine as material substances remain, even after consecration, what they were before.

This concept of Wyclif's, resting basically on his realist philosophy, which could not conceive of any accidents of a substance as existing by themselves apart from that substance (for so was the dogma of transubstantiation defined at the Lateran Council of 1215 held under Innocent III), is commonly referred to as consubstantiation, although he never uses the term. But this suggests that the "substances," bread and wine and body and blood, are coequal. That is not the case: bread and wine are and remain material substances, but the body and blood are present symbolically, sacramentally. Hence, the term "consubstantiation" may be misleading, as if two coequal substances coexisted in the sacrament. For, after all the body of the Lord is not to be thought of in carnal terms, but as "glorified," "transformed," or in the Pauline phrase, a "spiritual body." Consequently, it would be better to speak of Wyclif's view as sacramental, in the only proper sense of the word, namely, as a material substance symbolizing a spiritual content or, as Augustine phrased it, an outward symbol of an inner grace. Wyclif himself, refuting the "pagan" notion that "a

32 *Ibid.*, I, par. 7.   33 *Ibid.*, I, par. 11.
34 *Ibid.*, V, par. 21.   35 *Ibid.*, I, par. 9.

hog, a dog, or a mouse can eat our Lord," declares that "such beasts can eat the consecrated host, . . . not the body or blood of Christ. When a lion devours a man, he does not also devour his soul; yet his soul is present in every part of the body. Thus should one believe concerning the body of Christ in the sacrament of the altar. For this is whole, sacramentally, spiritually, or virtually, in every part of the consecrated host, even as the soul is in the body." [36]

This radical departure from the orthodoxy of the day cost Wyclif the support of many of his former adherents, among them the friars who were formerly, before he embarked upon his theological reforms, his supporters. John of Gaunt and the royal court party, as well as many of his Oxford friends, hastened to dissociate themselves from him. The offending views exposed Wyclif to prosecution by the Archbishop Courtenay, who convened, in 1382, a synod at the Blackfriars Convent and condemned ten of his conclusions, including three from *De Eucharistia*, as heretical. But Wyclif himself was not summoned or cited by name. His Oxford disciples, however, were summoned, and one by one they recanted. One of them, Repyngdon, later became a cardinal. Wyclif himself retired to his parish of Lutterworth and remained there until his death, two years later.

During those last years he devoted his strength to the building up of a body of "poor preachers," practically itinerant evangelists, whom he trained in a kind of work similar in manner to that of the friars, although very dissimilar in aims and practices. Since the knowledge of the Scriptures was basic to the whole program, Wyclif was exceedingly eager to have the Bible translated into the vernacular and made the core of preaching by the "Lollards." He himself is not known to have contributed directly to the work of translation, although his English writings abound in Biblical quotations of his own translating. [37] He also gave attention to the training of his own missioners by producing volumes of sermons in English, for the principal work of the "poor priests" consisted in preaching rather than in administering the sacraments. This is the burden of his unfinished *Opus evangelicum*, in which he reiterated the principle of the all-sufficiency of the Scriptures. It was while engaged in these labors that he died on the last day of 1384.

[36] *Ibid.*, I, par. 1–2.
[37] M. Deanesly, *The Lollard Bible* (Cambridge, 1920), 238–240.

On the Pastoral Office

THE TEXT: PART I

I

The office of a Christian,[1] to which the faithful should diligently attend, ought to be twofold: to purge the Church Militant of false shoots not bedded in the highest Pastor, who is the vine of the entire Church; and to dispose its branches that they may better bear fruit for the blessing of the Church. One should mention in passing the four "sects"[2] which are obviously harmful to the edification of the Church. Let us then look for a moment into the pastoral office, that through the grace of God and this purpose of mine the three parts of the Church Militant may be more fruitful. Now there are two things which pertain to the status of pastor: the holiness of the pastor and the wholesomeness of his teaching. He ought to be holy, so strong in every sort of virtue that he would rather desert every kind of human intercourse, all the temporal things of this world, even mortal life itself, before he would sinfully depart from the truth of Christ. This is clear: "He who loves his father and mother more than me is not worthy of me; and he who loves son and daughter above me is not worthy of me."[3] In Luke, seven things are mentioned which Christ,

[1] The text from which this translation has been made is that of G. V. Lechler, *Johannis de Wiclif tractatus de officio pastorali* (Leipzig, 1863). A Middle English version, with considerable differences, is to be found in F. D. Matthew, *The English Works of Wyclif Hitherto Unprinted* (Early English Text Society, Original Series, 74 [1902]). This version, M. Deanesly, *The Lollard Bible* (Cambridge, 1920), 266, 268, 378, states, was probably translated from the Latin original of John Wyclif by John Purvey. Chapter XV of the Middle English version is herein printed as Chapter 2a of Part II.

[2] "The four sects": bishops ("Caesarian clergy"), monks, canons, friars. See *De officio pastorali*, c. X, ed. Lechler, 18. On the nickname "sect," see Workman, *op. cit.*, II, 93 ff.   [3] Matt. 10:37.

because love is held in little esteem, teaches us to hate.[4] So it is necessary for any pastor or curate especially to be instructed in the three theological virtues, faith, hope, and charity, which are in their essence the Lord Jesus Christ. Otherwise he would not have the likeness of Christ whereby he might lay down his soul for the sheep, and teach them faithfully. . . .

2

From this principle of faith, which can signally be called by the faithful "golden," plainly is derived the rule which the apostle has handed down, "Having food and wherewith we are clothed let us be content." [5] This is clear: each one ought, to the limit of his ability, to follow Christ in his manner of life. But each priest, curate, or pastor has the ability so to follow Christ in his manner of life; therefore he should do it. This moved the apostles and the other priests of the Lord after them to imitate Christ in this evangelical poverty. The apostle understands by the word *alimenta* food and drink sufficient for nourishment. He did not mean splendor or superfluity of food, but simply said *alimenta*, meaning what agrees with the nourishment of the body for the service owed to God. And he means by the word *tegumenta* both the vestments of the body and also suitable houses which are to protect the faithful, according to their service, from storm and heat.[6] * * * What, I ask, of these temporal things would most benefit the pilgrim? And since we have received this pilgrimage from God for the blessedness which is to come, it follows that all things which are in excess will be superfluous and will be sin.[7] . . . From this principle it is clear to the faithful how notoriously these four "sects," together with others, have departed from this principle of faith. For all these four "sects" heap up for themselves superfluous goods by exceeding too far that apostolic rule, and this is clear from the withdrawal of their service in the labor of the people. For this reason they exceed this apostolic rule. . . .

3

But against this it is objected, first, that the secular arm would not be approved by God, since it is necessary that they

---

[4] Luke 14:26.   [5] I Tim. 6:8.

[6] A word is missing at the end of this sentence in the MS.

[7] Wyclif, *De simonia*, 16 f., calls the priests' possession of more temporal goods than they need "simony."

A.O.R.—3

possess lordship beyond food and clothing for the carrying out
of their office. Secondly, the apostles chose seven deacons for
the distribution of material alms from the people;[8] it is permitted therefore to priests, lesser as well as greater, to give
material alms prudently to the needy. Thirdly, the apostle
teaches that a bishop ought to be hospitable and well provided
with a good house,[9] which could not be unless he possessed
goods beyond mere necessary food. Therefore it is permitted to
the bishop both in food and in clothing to exceed what is strictly
necessary. And more or less on the same basis this is permitted
to pastors or curates; hence it is impossible to apply the rule of
the apostles.

As to the first objection, it is said that Christ ordained that
there be temporal lords and adapted secular lordship to them,
as is clear in the treatise concerning servants, and evidently
from the fact that Christ gave the didrachma to Caesar.[10]
Christ, therefore, knowing all things, would not so act, nor
permit that damnable sin, unless the status of secular lordship
were approved by him for the advantage of the Church. It is
clear that the inference assumed ought to be denied. But to
make plain what has been assumed above, it ought to be noted
that it seems to many that the apostle spoke in the aforesaid
rule especially concerning priests and bishops, including himself among them. But by extending the words of the apostle to
individual Christians it seems probable that one might say
that through clothing and shelter [tegumenta] are understood
all things for the pilgrim beyond what is necessary for the
carrying out of the duty of his station. Thus it is necessary that
secular lords with moderation possess temporal goods to this
end. Because often a lapse in such things takes place, the
apostle prudently added "shelter" [tegumenta], meaning by the
word tegumenta all things necessary for the duties of his station.
For this reason just as there are three steps in renunciation of
temporal goods, thus likewise are there in the possession of
them. But the first step of renunciation is to renounce the im-
moderate love of them, necessary for anyone who is to be saved,
as Christ says, "Unless one renounce all that he possesses, he
cannot be my disciple." [11] The second renunciation (which also
is universal) is the relinquishment of temporal goods in so far
as they are useless for the fulfillment of one's station. Thus the
priest and any person of the Church ought not to aspire to

8 Acts 6:3 f.   9 I Tim. 3:2, 4.
10 Cf. Matt. 17:24 ff.   11 Luke 14:33.

the possession of a superfluous amount of temporal goods. But the third renunciation is more strictly concerned with the priest, namely, the relinquishment of treasure or of temporal goods beyond what is necessary for the fulfillment of his holy office. Thus it is irrelevant for the priest to have secular lordship or temporal goods on a permanent basis for the carrying out of his office. Let us see how the apostles have renounced these temporal goods according to Christ's example, and let us do likewise. Yet it is conceded that . . . secular lords . . . repeatedly draw back in this renunciation of temporal goods while they abuse them for the sake of carnal lust or worldly excellence or slothful retention of them with respect to the office for which they were divinely granted; for God has granted secular lordship that man might powerfully defend the law of Christ and compel the lesser ones to enter into the Lord's sect. . . .

4

As to the second argument, of the office of deacons, it is certain that it does not savor of secular lordship among them, since they all were poor, not having possessions individually. Therefore also he does not say that they gave these alms, but that they were wont to minister at table, and gave to each according to his need.[12] The evidence is too slight from this to conclude that priests ought to heap up wealth in order to give material alms.[13] . . .

As to the third argument, it is said that the apostle wished the bishops, whom he called curates, to reside in their parishes when there was opportunity to minister faithfully to their flocks in things spiritual, and to support the faithful by their office, the wandering poor by their hospitality, for whom a simple board would be a banquet. But now our prelates are perverted on the side of the devil, not so sustaining the poor by hospitality, but rather secular lords and tyrants, who do not need such alms, but are commonly gorged with inhuman and gluttonous feasts, and yet are satiated sumptuously without a qualm from the goods of the poor. And thus, the place of the gluttons, from such a misguided comparison, deceives these governors: as if just because Paul gave the precept that the bishop should receive such poor folk in his house to feed them,

12 Acts 6:2; cf. ch. 2:45.
13 Cf. Wyclif, *Sermons*, I, 314.

our prelates ought to receive such outrageous fellows [14] in
their house to feed them, in order to acquire the honor of the
world and to starve their soul in many ways. . . .

5

On this basis one assumes that all curates ought according
to the law of the Lord to be induced to live solely upon the
material alms of their subjects. For if they possess sufficient
revenues or worldly wealth, they ought to relinquish them in
favor of the material alms of their flock. [15] When food is elsewhere lacking, they ought in recompense of charity to live
from such alms of their subjects, and thus to distribute more
worthy alms (because they are spiritual). [16] Thus should the
word of The Acts of the Apostles be wisely understood: that
"it is more blessed to give than to receive." [17] For it is more
honorable for a priest to give such spiritual alms than to receive material alms. Yet both are honorable, since Christ gave
both as an example for us. As to spiritual alms it is clear that
he taught the entire Church how it ought to live, as is evident
from the method [ex processu] of the gospel; nor can a curate
attain to this doctrine, but ought humbly to follow Christ in
this. And as for bodily alms, it is clear that Christ received them
from devoted men and women. For Luke states: "Mary Magdalene, out of whom he cast seven devils, and Joanna the wife of
Cusa, steward for the procurator of Caesar, and Susanna,
and many others who ministered unto him of their substance." [18] There is no doubt that, just as Christ receives our
miseries and poverty, he thus receives these under the title of
alms. . . .

6

From these principles one concludes that a curate ought
not to extort tithes from his subjects through excommunication or other censures, and it is clear therefore that a curate

---

14 Outrageous fellows: the Latin has *discolos*. This is from the Greek
δύσκολος, found in I Peter 2:18, and there translated as "froward."
The word means "bad-tempered," "peevish," "irritable," "hard to
satisfy," "troublesome," "harassing." Derivatives found in *On the
Pastoral Office* include *discolivi* ("troublemakers," I, chapter 7) and
discolia ("frowardness," I, chapter 17).

15 Cf. *De officio regis*, 59; also *Sermons*, I, 290 f.

16 Cf. *De officio regis*, 260; also *De blasphemia*, 180.

17 Acts 20:35.   18 Luke 8:2 f.

ought not to quarrel with his subjects concerning such matters. Christ and his apostles indicated this by not so exacting tithes,[19] being satisfied instead with needful food and clothing. In the new law we rarely read of tithes being levied. If, however, a curate should exact tithes on the basis of the old law, let him realize that he is bound to other needful observances by such tithing. Such a conclusion is clear, first, because no one would excommunicate a subject or persecute him through other censures unless, entitled by love, he intends to remove his ignorance like a physician. But to achieve this end Christ's teaching is easier: to remit such injury to the subjects and to live under stricter penalty in such office. Therefore the prelate ought to act after the example of Christ. . . . And it is true, if excommunication or persecution for tithes is not found here, it should have no basis anywhere else. . . .

7

From this the faithful infer that a curate ought not through censures or other temporal threats to give to his lord prelate tribute from the alms of the people subject to him, which cannot be established from the law of the Lord. For if pope, cardinal, bishop, or archdeacon require such tribute from a subject curate, it is certain that such requisition is unjust, for it is not founded in the law of the Lord;[20] and the whole business ends in the spoliation of the poor subjects. But, according to the original statement, the curate ought not to consent to spoliation of this sort on account of the infliction of punishment or any worldly good. Hence the conclusion.

And this rule ought to be observed in order that false prelates might mitigate their transgression . . . receiving from their subjects few or no temporal goods. Prelates say in effect today, "Despoil your poor sheep and simple ones of so much money, else I will thoroughly excommunicate you and I will suspend them from entering the church and from divine service." Would such great blasphemy and infidelity prevent any really faithful priest from observing justice? . . . Alas, the Church is so much occupied with outrageous fellows that when one faithful curate persists in his appointed task there are a thousand troublemakers of the devil who freely accept this despoiled office so that they may be able more boldly to despoil the devoted people of the Lord according to their own vulpine

[19] *De officio regis*, 63.   [20] *De blasphemia*, 175.

vow. While a single true pastor (or none) goes forth, a thousand foes sally out to despoil the simple folk in countless ways . . . [to] the nourishment of sin. Curate and faithful people would rather desert the office [of pastor] than consent to such exactions, else they would love shameful gain of temporal goods more than their own soul's salvation.

8

From these considerations the faithful conclude that when a curate is notoriously negligent in his pastoral office, they as subjects should, yea, ought, to withdraw offerings and tithes from him and whatever might offer occasion for the fostering of such wickedness.[21] For proof we note first that John commands that such, even on account of a lesser deviation in doctrine, ought not to be greeted as sons of God by the faithful.[22] Therefore much more ought the negligent curate not to be applauded for these transgressions. And this confirms our view: that for the lesser sin of lechery the faithful ought not to hear the Masses of such priests.[23] This many papal laws make clear.[24] How, therefore, will the subjects sustain the office of such priests which it is not worthy for them or anyone else to obey? Similarly, such people sustaining a curate thus notoriously give alms imprudently against Christ. No one should do this; therefore people should not support such a curate with alms. For Christ commands, "Beware of false prophets who come to you in the clothing of sheep, yet inwardly are ravenous wolves!"[25] How therefore does he beware of them, who gives them temporal assistance in order to perpetrate such a great crime so harmful to curate, prelate, and subjects? There is no doubt that it is contrary to the rules of charity. . . .

9

From this opinion just now set forth these new orders would have been provided with new colleges, through which by a novel device churches are appropriated. Now there are three ecclesiastical classes to which such appropriation is forbidden, namely, monks, canons, and collegiate churches. And the collegiate churches[26] fall into three classes: the *greatest*, which

---

21 Cf. Wyclif, *Sermons*, I, 244; also *De veritate sacrae Scripturae*, c. XXV; *De officio regis*, 165, and xviiif.   22 II John 10.
23 Cf. *On the Eucharist*, chapter 1, par. 14.
24 Cf. *Decretum magistri Gratiani*, Aemilius Friedberg, ed., *Corpus iuris canonici* (Leipzig, 1889), pars I, dist. XXXII, c. 5, I, 117.   25 Matt. 7:15.
26 On collegiate churches, see Workman, *op. cit.*, II, 115.

are called cathedral churches, as is especially true of prebends; the *middle*, which are the chapels of princes, for which (by the same scheme but without the authority) churches are commandeered; the *least*, which are colleges of studies.[27] Tithes are appropriated for all these and the work of the pastoral office suspended. But just as temporal lords ought to take away lordship from priests who, against the law of the Lord, are richly endowed,[28] thus tithing people ought to take away their offerings and tithes from such appropriated churches while the pastoral offices are notoriously and habitually withdrawn from them. For thus could a lay person and manifest devil be constituted as pastor among the people in order to seduce them through the broad way that leads to Tartarus. And the same, moreover, is the reason for withdrawing alms from such falsely appointed curates or pastors and from other simple persons who do not labor faithfully in that office, to whom that statement of the apostle could be applied, "He who toils not let him not eat."[29] . . . In like manner those giving alms to clerks through such offerings and tithes ought prudently to beware lest, against Christ, they nourish the sons of Antichrist. But this happens often in these three appropriations; therefore tithers ought more diligently to beware this. If, moreover, these two sects or these colleges are alienated by their wickedness from the Lord, would it not be the stupidest sort of presumption against Christ to suppose that there would be alms so to nourish them? . . . In like manner, by pride of the princes of the world, and of other foundations, these colleges, which are the nests of the devil, are overflowing with those who consent to, and nourish, this pride. While, therefore, when he gives tithes to his sons, they participate in this pride, it seems that this would draw them back from consent, for any one of us has because of his own sin a burden already too heavy, even though he does not heap up for himself participation in the sin of another. Such evidences should move the faithful to destroy customs not founded in Christ.

10

. . . God abundantly teaches [30] to what persons such alms ought to be paid. Otherwise a stolid servant of the Lord could, out of stupid participation, excessively stir up his church

[27] On appropriated churches, see *ibid.*, II, 410f., Appendix O.
[28] Cf. *Opus evangelicum*, I, 5.   [29] II Thess. 3:10.   [30] Luke 14:12 ff.

by giving to the froward the gifts of God, and by despoiling the faithful and simple ones of the necessaries of life. This often happens. And on account of such anxiety to gain riches it is believed that Christ and his apostles more readily distributed spiritual rather than material alms. For Peter says, "Silver and gold I have none, but what I have I give thee." [31] And in this excess of spiritual alms over material alms many governors have been blinded; therefore the servant apportioning such alms ought to beware of such blind pride, since the servant of the Lord is merely apportioning his goods to other servants. Secondly, what does he apportion out? To the needy the very goods of the Lord, to the weak poor, to the blind poor, or to the lame poor, because God has apportioned out of his spiritual work his assistance to such. . . .

II

But to this Antichrist replies, finding an excuse for sin. Perhaps such a curate may not reside in his own parish, yet he provides for a suitable vicar, and busies himself in prayers and contemplation, a task more excellent and more useful to the Church. And thus Holy Mother Church is the queen, standing at the right hand of Christ in gilded clothing surrounded with variety. [32] Moreover, on divine authority it is fitting that one member of the Church be occupied with one office and another with another office. For out of this the utility of the Church of Christ and the usefulness of its servants shines forth, and thus it is said that the curate resides through the vicar. This is equivalent to the residence of curates. . . .

If that curate therefore tends toward contemplation and prayer, let him lay aside the office and name; for no reason exists why he should thus falsely bear the name of pastor, unless as spiritual vicar of Antichrist. . . .

If, moreover, such a sect, whether monk or canon, desires to live contemplatively and to pray, let him lay aside this false office or name, and let him contemplate and pray, just as the fathers did in the primitive Church. For if he wishes these temporal goods, and with this to possess secretly the name of holiness, let him know that he is inconstant in all his ways. [33] It would be more useful for the Church to go without such prayer, rather than to possess it with things like these. [34] For

[31] Acts 3:6.
[33] Cf. James 1:8.
[32] Ps. 44:10, 14, Vg.; 45:9, 13, E.V.
[34] Cf. *De officio regis*, 112.

the prayer of such a double-minded man commonly leads into sin.[35] If therefore the solicitude of the vicar suffices for the office of pastor, let him efface from the Church of God the superfluous one, and let the given vicar remain the curate in full of his sheep, alongside Christ. . . . But it would be far better for the Church of Christ that there not be such religious in the Church Militant, since they bear as it were superfluously the name of pastor, indeed the name of true Christian, since they are spurious offshoots not rooted in the vine of the Church. Just as is borne out from the deceptions in England, it might happen that a cobbler or any kind of sinner could be a curate in name and for the spoliation of the temporal goods of the flock. Therefore, just as Jesus "began to do and to teach," [36] so should such curates begin to do, when they freely receive from the fountain of the pastors their various goods, and they are enjoined to give freely of the same from this very fountain.[37] Therefore, just as private religious are in their several ways a spring bitter and putrid, thus their prayer or contemplation is of little or no benefit to the Church. And just as they share their goods, so ought they to share in the works of merit. For in the day of judgment such a curate will not be excused through a vicar appointed by himself or by his family. For this reason such a sophistry of the devil stinks before the eyes of the Redeemer.

12

But Antichrist interposes the objection that such curates have their appropriation and confirmation from the supreme pontiff. Who, therefore, would argue about their acceptance of the income of such a church? Therefore one must either deny the pope or approve the occupation of such a benefice and office. . . .

As to this it is often said that the confirmation of the Roman pontiff is not valid except to the degree that it is in conformity with the will and ordination of God, who is the highest Lord. Nor is it a matter of faith (since the opposite often happens) [to believe] that God who is the highest Priest and Lord authorizes whatever the pope may do, since then the pope would be incapable of sinning and also be God upon earth. If on account of the lust and authority of a lord of this sort, license were given for anything, it is not more than the license of Antichrist. . . .

---

35 James 1:8.   36 Acts 1:1.   37 Cf. Matt. 10:8.

13

Certain of the faithful . . . neither contemn nor damn the Roman pontiff in this, but out of faith they set the Lord Jesus Christ as God before all; and when the notorious defect has been taught and made manifest, they boldly say, "Because either the pope or someone else has established this, this establishment is evil." In case he thus presumptuously continues in error, it would be good for the Church that there not be such a pope, who thus falls away from the narrower path of Christ and his vicar Peter. But that man, namely, the pope, on account of peril ought especially to stand within the limits of the law of Christ, lest through the novelties that have been introduced he seduce the Church. But certain ones call him Antichrist and the first patron of the sect which has been introduced without the permission of Christ. Thus with respect to the division which has been made,[38] it is conceded that the error of the pope and the presumption of his dignity ought to be denied rather than that he thus presume against the best interest of the Church. Nor would such permission of the pope move the faithful to confer their alms upon such sophistically called curates, since the pastoral office is lacking, and the faithful well know for this reason that these false curates are unworthy to receive alms. . . .

14

Here are further evidences to be examined why the subject ought not to hold back tithes unjustly. And it seems that especial evidence, exceeding papal bulls, excommunications, and other censures, is the humble ministration of priests. Suppose it is definitely known that priests faithfully minister to their parish, and that they are in need: any subject would be "worse than an infidel"[39] who in this case held back the pay due them, and protested loudly that the tithe belongs to the Lord, with which in a measure any faithful pastor is content. But there are many reasons why they persuade the faithful that the tenth part ought by the active ones to be given by each individually to God, as they say, because the works of the six days are wholly the

---

[38] Cf. chapter 12 above: "Therefore one must either deny the pope or approve the occupation of such a benefice and office."

[39] I Tim. 5:8.

goods of God, of the angels of heaven also (although they are not mentioned in Genesis), and common things [40] are things seven and eight, and above this the humanity of Christ is the ninth thing, and above it is his divinity as the tenth. . . . Such are the many reasons; but let it suffice for the faithful to derive from Scripture the conclusion that God has appropriated to himself the tenth part.

15

. . . I do not see why all clergy ought not to be content according to the rule of the apostle with food and clothing. However justly they may be come by, tithes ought prudently to be shared with the poor.[41] Therefore it is permitted to curates following the poverty of Christ to receive moderately from tithes. Moreover, it is commonly practiced—a custom which I do not praise but reprove according to the evil arising from it— when curates have offerings and tithes in their entirety, that laymen are more and more clearly excused from remorse of conscience. Now curates ought to live from tithes and offerings, observing the rule of the apostle. But in case part of these remain to be distributed, they ought to distribute them to the poor of Christ and use it prudently for other purposes in accordance with the will of the Lord. On top of this rule, by human ordination, numerous laws have been piled. Some of these are false, e.g., that the income of the curate ought to be divided into four parts. First, the clerics ought to take moderately something for themselves. Second, they ought to distribute prudently another part to the outside poor and needy. The third part they should give to the upkeep of the church. The fourth, to the repair and proper maintenance of their house. And in this human law lurk very many subtleties of the serpent. Moreover, there are other infinite difficulties, as from which things tithes ought to be given, if from an orchard or other growing things of the earth, if of fishes and wild beasts, if of the pay of those laboring, even through filthy lucre, as for example the harlot's pay or usury, or other illicit income. Such are the many fabulous difficulties concerning human traditions, about which it would seem the cleric is basely occupied. Therefore let the curate have necessary food and clothing for his office, and let him lay aside these frivolous and harmful traditions. . . .

40 *Res communes*: i.e., *universalia sive ideae* [Lechler].
41 Cf. Wyclif, *Sermons*, I, 315.

16

It remains [for us] to examine the roots of sin, which have grown up out of this [human] law and of the devil's subtlety.[42] Now certain curates feed themselves out of the superabundance of temporalities too elegantly; they are unsuited to preaching the gospel, and to beseeching God for their subjects. Since it ought to be accepted almost as a matter of faith that such curates are obligated to the pastoral office more than other officials, they ought to recognize themselves to be poor and needy, and that they receive their income from the meager gifts of widows and poor subjects. In so far as they depend upon the collections of the needy, they should recognize that they are going to answer individually for each one of those in the day of judgment. Where, then, is there a more straitened condition of miserable poverty? The Luciferine sign of pride is that the prelate is proud of the fatness of his benefice, which nevertheless he is able to spend each year. . . . To repress this pride one should recognize carefully that God expressly grants to each his part. Since the prelate is the bailiff of such a great Lord, he ought more especially to ponder that it behooves him to give a faithful account of the part due to God, how he has faithfully managed that part. And this would be a checkrein for rectors, not to play the wanton in banquets or to misappropriate for their own personal use the meager alms of their subjects. . . .

This same ought to be applied to the four sects, namely, the bishops, the monks, the canons, and the friars, because all these wantonly spend in banquets and ornaments (contrary to the life and rule of Christ) the alms of their poor subjects. In matters such as these the poor prelate would blush if he were not blinded by devilish pride.

The third reason which should move the conscience of pastors of this sort consists in this, that the bishop of souls appoint the curate himself, not as the guardian of excrements for thus playing the wanton in his body, but as the guardian of souls which were made in the image and likeness of God. For this reason ought he to fatten the souls spiritually in the pasture of virtues; and he will follow the highest Pastor in morals, who attends to the feeding of the spirit and not to the feeding of the body, unless there is grace in this. . . . And if in this state perchance he become needy, as for example blind or

42 Law: i.e., the "human law," mentioned in the previous chapter.

lame or stricken with some other bodily infirmity, the provider of the necessaries of the soul for his subjects ought according to the rule of the apostle to be sustained by their alms. . . .

17

. . . How ought the curate to exemplify to his subjects the struggle against the three enemies of the soul? As for lust, many so-called curates are not content with a parish church unless they have a chapel attached thereto, or a wife sojourning with them or living sumptuously apart, yet near enough to be supported by parish funds. Yet they live outside of matrimony in open adultery, and it is clear how this sin ought to be detested by subjects and by curates alike. For subjects ought not to hear the Mass of such priests, nor as a consequence in other pastoral offices to participate in his wickedness, since prayer and whatever else he does are notoriously sinful in the eyes of God; as a consequence they ought not to give to him offerings or tithes lest they seem to be consenting to such a notorious crime in curates. . . . He would then not be a protector, but a plunderer of Antichrist, who would not blush, were his many sheep to perish out of hunger, and withal he would sustain his darling that she might go about in sumptuous raiment and in silver or gold net. Where, I ask, could be the conscience of such a pastor but rather more truly of a ravisher, not fearing to seize the tithes of his poor parishioners in order to wallow with such a prostitute in lust, and with this to set himself up as worthy to exercise any pastoral office for the salvation of his own soul or of the souls of his subjects? Surely such a one seems to be not only a rapacious wolf but even a strangler of his simple sheep for salvation both of body and of soul. And the same seems to be true concerning a curate lingering in the Roman *curia*, seeking after other benefices or privileges, who secures the alms of his poor subjects, or living in London or other places of wantonness outside his own parish on what he has taken from them, however such sojourning of the Antichrist might be cloaked. . . . Thus in every respect ought curates engaged in human studies, law (as for example, civil or papal), to be detested, also those concerned with medicine or the teaching of Aristotle, although from such studies some good might proceed.[43] In all such cases it is permitted to the parishioners

---

[43] Wyclif expresses a more lenient attitude toward absence of curates from their livings in *De blasphemia*, 178. See also in the present treatise Part II,

wisely to withdraw their alms, lest they seem to defend and foster the frowardness of such a so-called pastor. . . .

18

. . . How are certain rectors born of the will of the flesh and of the will of man and not of God? [44] Christ has not granted them the power to become sons of God, but rather are they the sons of the king of pride, who from that very pride, holding the law of the Lord in contempt, enrich their own legacies from the goods of the poor. One cause of this is that they seem noble men or illustrious to the world. For thus many persons from a truly humble level are elevated to worldly heights. And this sophistry is colored by a more subtle deceit of the devil, saying that mercy and natural affection lead to this end; for who is not naturally inclined more to love his own parents and his relatives than other brothers in the Lord? This moves many in a simoniac fashion to seek many ecclesiastical offices. . . . Such folk, putting more weight on parentage of this sort, in their love esteem Christ less than their own parents according to the flesh. However, it seems to many that any Christian ought more to be loved because he is a neighbor or a carnal brother, since spiritual kinship is nothing less than for a Christian to have Christ directly as father, and His spouse the Church as mother.[45] For this reason he sins in no mean fashion, who through illicit means gives preference to this lesser good. We ought individually to follow Christ under pain of heavy punishment. Christ, the supreme and almighty Pontiff, did not so enrich his carnal mother or his own relatives, but ordained that they endure in open poverty; it seems then that to do the opposite through the means now current would be a manifest condition of the Antichrist. . . .

19

Let us see how such prelates are infected by the splendor of the world and by avarice. Certain ones presume to feed the

8, and *De officio regis*, 163. In *ibid.*, 177, Wyclif upholds "the strict interpretation of the decree of Pope Honorius, ordering all 'religious' persons attending lectures on law or physic to return to their convents within two months under pain of excommunication" (Introduction, xix).
[44] Cf. John 1:12.
[45] An echo of the well-known phrase of Cyprian.

reprobate from the goods of the poor, so that they become rich men in the world's eye, actors, who proclaim publicly that those curates are generous providers. . . . The king of pride has broken forth to such an extent in superfluous expenditures that he moves priests in five ways to have hunting dogs, fat horses, superfluous ornaments, furnished from the goods of the poor. . . . Even though these five are damnable in a mere rector, they are even more damnable in a bishop or abbot, not only because they exceed simple rectors in these five ways, but because from greater obligation and hypocrisy they do these things more openly before the world. And—to increase the gravity of the crime—they take joy in these sins, as if they were confirmed in the service of the devil. . . . Nor does it matter that such curates have at the same time many benefices transformed into another use, so that they may not bring forth sin with manifold reason. Suppose that an abbot or a bishop has many so-called perpetual alms, and the pope allows him to transform them into another kind, giving him permission to misuse them—in spite of the fact that these "alms" would make it possible for many to serve God more in conformity with this law than do all these. These are indeed hypocritical excuses which increase the gravity of sin. . . . But it is necessary to note that he who serves God and his lord faithfully thus does not burden the people, from whom he receives such income, which Paul calls spoils.[46] But this seems Luciferine cupidity, that the curate for whom the other things given by his subject poor are sufficient exacted his pay in advance through censures. And, thirdly, it is clear that Paul fled, nor would he allow himself to become a burden to any people. He is a burden, too, upon the people who takes from them his pay and does not render back more good. . . .

PART II

I

We have touched superficially on the first part of the priestly office, holiness of life. . . . Now the second part pertaining to the pastor, that is, wholesomeness of teaching, remains to be looked at. While Jesus Christ "began to do and to teach," [47]

46 In a portion omitted just before this, Wyclif quoted II Cor. 11:8 f.
47 Acts 1:1.

the curate, who ought to be his vicar, ought to shine with
sanctity in his own person, and, secondly, ought to be resplendent with righteousness of doctrine before his sheep. Otherwise
his preaching would be useless, since it is written: "But to the
sinner God has said, 'Why do you declare my justices, and take
my covenant in your mouth? You have hated discipline and
have cast my words behind you!' " [48] Therefore the first condition of the pastor is to cleanse his own spring, that it may not
infect the Word of God. [49] And as for the second condition,
which is very manifold, the first and particular function of the
pastor remains to be seen. The pastor has a threefold office: [50]
first, to feed his sheep spiritually on the Word of God, that
through pastures ever green they may be initiated into the
blessedness of heaven. The second pastoral office is to purge
wisely the sheep of disease, that they may not infect themselves
and others as well. And the third is for the pastor to defend his
sheep from ravening wolves, both sensible and insensible. In
all these the especial office of the pastor seems that of sowing
the Word of God among his sheep. God ordains for a good
reason that by the teaching of the pastor and his own manner
of life his preaching to his sheep may be made efficacious,
since this acts more effectively than mere preaching. . . . The
life of a good pastor is of necessity a mirror to be imitated by his
flock. The highest Pastor could not depart from righteousness
in deed or word; for this reason his life and moral example are,
as it were, a vital spirit to be attended by individual Christians and especially by pastors, who say that they are the vicars
of Christ. As a sign of this, because life and work ought to precede word in the pastor, righteousness of life is necessary in
anyone who would be saved, but eloquence of preaching is
especially necessary in curates. For "no one," either an infant
or a feeble person, "can be saved unless his life according to
the righteousness of Christ be found just through His
grace." . . .

2

"Among all the duties of the pastor after justice of life, holy
preaching is most to be praised," [51] for Christ, the Primal

48 Ps. 49:16 f., Vg.; 50:16f., E.V.   49 Cf. *Opus evangelicum*, I, 7.
50 On the threefold office of pastor, cf. *Select English Works*, I, 140.
51 Among the many passages in Wyclif's works which deal with preaching
one may note: *Sermons*, II, 277–285, 447–452; III, 384–386; IV, 256 ff.
There is a discussion in G. R. Owst, *Preaching in Medieval England*, 132–135,
et passim.

Truth, . . . said to the woman commending the one who bore
him in the womb and nourished his body, "They are blessed
who hear the word of God and keep it." [52] There is no doubt
but that preaching the Word of God is as great as hearing it.
Moreover, in Christ there were these three things: the highest
was the preaching of the Word, [then] the hearing of it, and
[finally] the keeping of it in deed. Yet in others preaching is
more commendable than hearing, just as action is superior to
being acted upon. In like manner, Christ, in highest wisdom,
commanded his apostles when he ascended into heaven to
preach the gospel to every creature; [53] indeed the wisest Master
would not have done this unless such preaching were more to
be praised in apostle or curate. Hence, among his duties
such an activity is more worthy [than the rest]. It is evident
that preaching the gospel is the special work of the curate, for
Christ advances more in his apostles by preaching to the people
than by doing any miracle which in his own person he did in
Judea. . . . Preaching the gospel exceeds prayer and administration of the sacraments, to an infinite degree. [54] . . . Spreading the gospel has far wider and more evident benefit; it is
thus the most precious activity of the Church. [55] Just as the
judges of the kings handing down their judgment to the people
are especially designated next to the kings in honor, thus those
preaching the gospel truly are to be set apart by the authority
of the Lord.

2a

The friars with their followers say that it is heresy thus to
write God's law in English and make it known to ignorant
men. [56] . . .

It seems first that the knowledge of God's law should be
taught in that language which is best known, [57] because this
knowledge is God's Word. [58] When Christ says in the Gospel

---

52 Luke 11:28.   53 Matt. 28:19.   54 Cf. *Sermons*, I, 110, 377.
55 Cf. *Opus evangelicum*, I, 42 f.
56 Wyclif's advocacy of the translating of the Scriptures into the vernacular
   may be studied from the references to his Latin works gathered in
   Deanesly, *op. cit.*, 240–249. Miss Deanesly speaks of this chapter (XV
   in the middle English Version) as "inserted in the English *De officio
   pastorali*," 270, 378.
57 Cf. *De Eucharistia*, ch. IV, pars. 11 f.
58 Matthew, *op. cit.*, 530, gives the following note: "For the language,
   whether it be Hebrew, or Greek, or Latin, or English, is as it were the
   vestment of the Lord's law. And through whatever vestment the meaning

that both heaven and earth shall pass away but his words shall not pass away,[59] he means by his "words" his knowledge. Thus God's knowledge is Holy Scripture that may in no wise be false. Also the Holy Spirit gave to the apostles at Pentecost knowledge to know all manner of languages to teach the people God's law thereby; and so God willed that the people be taught his law in divers tongues. But what man on God's behalf should reverse God's ordinance and his will? For this reason Saint Jerome labored and translated the Bible from divers tongues into Latin that it might after be translated into other tongues. Thus Christ and his apostles taught the people in that tongue that was best known to them. Why should men not do so now? And for this reason the authors of the new law who were apostles of Jesus Christ wrote their Gospels in divers tongues that were better known to the people. Also the worthy kingdom of France, notwithstanding all hindrances, has translated the Bible and the Gospels with other true sentences of doctors out of Latin into French.[60] Why should not Englishmen do so? As the lords of England have the Bible in French, so would it not be against reason that they have it in English; for thus, with unity of knowledge, God's law would be better known and more believed, and there might be more agreement between kingdoms. In England the friars have taught the Lord's Prayer in the English language, as men see in the play of York,[61] * * * and in many other counties. Since the Lord's Prayer is part of Matthew's Gospel, as clerks know, why may not all of the Gospel be turned into English as is this part? This is especially so since all Christian men, learned and ignorant, who should be saved might always follow Christ and know his teaching and his life. But the common people of England know it best in their mother tongue and thus it is the same thing to prevent such knowledge of the Gospel

[of Scripture] is most truly known by the faithful, that is the codex most reasonably to be accepted." *De contrarietate duorum Dominorum*, c. II, MS. Ashburnham, lf. 44.

59 Mark 13:31 and parallels.

60 Matthew, *op. cit.*, 530, mentions the fact that the MS. of the oldest complete French Bible in the Royal Library at Paris was executed in England in the fourteenth century. "A revised translation was undertaken by a contemporary of Wyclif, Raoul de Presles (d. 1383)."

61 *Ibid.*, 530 f. "Once on a time a play, setting forth the goodness of the Lord's Prayer, was played in the city of York, in which play all manner of vices and sins were held up to scorn and the virtues were held up to praise." The popularity of this play led to the formation of a guild to keep up its performance.

and to prevent Englishmen from following Christ and coming
to heaven. I well know that there may be faults in unfaithful
translating as there might have been many faults in turning
from Hebrew into Greek and from Greek into Latin, and from
one language into another. But let men live a good life,
and let many study God's law, and when errors are found
let them who reason well correct them.[62] Some say that the
friars and their followers labor in this cause for three reasons;
God knows whether they be so. First, the friars would be
thought so necessary to the Englishmen of our kingdom that
solely in their knowledge lay the knowledge of God's law, and
to tell the people God's law in whatever manner they please.
And the second reason is: Friars would lead the people in teaching them God's law and thus they would teach some, hide some,
and cut off some parts. For then faults in their life should be
less known to the people and God's law should be less truly
known both by clerks and by common people. The third cause
that men notice consists in this, as they say: All these new
orders are afraid that their sins should be known and how
their entry into the Church had no divine sanction. Thus
out of fear they do not desire that God's law be known in
English, for they could not put heresy upon men if English told
what they said. May God move lords and bishops to stand up
for the knowing of his law.

3

. . . Furthermore, Christians must heed how the devil,
especially envying these preachings of the Gospel, spreads
sophistries through the priests of Belial, "salubriously preaching
to the people." [63] Nor is this wile of the devil of recent origin,
since in the days of the apostles out of envious displeasure he
was wont to seduce the people through this. But all sin arising
out of this office can be reduced to three points. Certain ones
devilishly exalt their own fame in adulterated words which
are called subtleties, by which they diabolically extol themselves. And this can be reduced to the saying of the apostle,
"For we are not as many others adulterating the Word of God
but with sincerity as from God we speak in Christ." [64] For these

---

[62] Deanesly, op. cit., 378, points out the close similarity of these two sentences to the General Prologue to the Old Testament of John Purvey, c. XV.
[63] Cf. G. V. Lechler, John Wycliffe and His English Precursors, tr. Lorimer
(London, n.d.), 197.   [64] II Cor. 2:17.

are adulterers of the Word of God who in prostitutes' robes
and colored veils observe the Word of God for the people.
But those who hold their conscience sincere exclude all pomp
of the devil or self-honor; inasmuch as the subject matter of
their speaking is God, so do they speak in his presence, since
all our thoughts are in their bare state known before him. And
in all of these things we ought to speak in exemplary fashion
in Christ, because he himself of his own free will is the Lord of
the Word. Who therefore would not fear to speak a word in
the presence of God which would not be pleasing to his ears?
This word of the apostle would plainly instruct the faithful
to promulgate the Word of God among the people. Secondly,
some spread sophistries drawn from the words of the Lord in
order to nourish carnal sins. And in these hues the devil is much
less content with one crime, but entangles us in many according
to the form by which he tempted the Lord Jesus Christ. And
to that can be added what the apostle says: "They wish you
to be circumcised that they may glory in your flesh. But God
forbid that I should glory but in the cross of our Lord Jesus
Christ, by whom the world is crucified to me, and I to the
world." [65] . . .

4

. . . Often the faith of the gospel points out how one cannot
be a disciple of Christ unless he love Him more than any other,
next to himself. [66] And it is certain from faith that no one can
come to heaven unless he be a disciple of Christ and, what is
the same thing and more, his member.

But the friars [67] corrupt and hate this way of evangelizing,
because they are afraid that they cannot base in the whole
gospel the amassing of temporal goods through preaching the
gospel; for Christ teaches, "Freely receive, freely give." [68] It
is certain that such preaching of the friars in hope of temporal
gain is in the sight of God notorious simony. The Antichrist is
afraid that such ludicrous falsehoods and heresies concerning
spiritual support, which have been spread abroad by the friars,
will be publicly exposed, and they will not have as much booty
from the Church as they are wont.

Other sons of the devil hinder this evangelical manner of
preaching, because they wish their own false words to be held

[65] Gal. 6:14.   [66] Matt. 10:37 ff.; Luke 14:26.
[67] Wyclif's opposition to the friars grew slowly but steadily after 1381.
    See Lechler, op. cit.; 322 f.   [68] Matt. 10:8.

in high esteem among the people, and, because of pride, their
own fame to be exalted among the people. But there are a
thousand stratagems by which these three parties of the devil
act privately or publicly against Christ. The bishops with
their satellites impose heresies upon the faithful by preaching.
Thus they prevent [faithful priests] from preaching in their
own diocese, or, unless God graciously prevent them, through
false friars they stir up feeling that such priests be burned. . . .

5

Let us see how the devil introduces this traitorous deception
little by little. Thus the principal ministry which Christ
instituted in his Church is lulled to sleep. One stratagem is the
endowment or secular donation of priests, on account of which
it is necessary for them to live in a secular manner like lords.
But this is utterly alien to the spreading of the gospel and the
humble following of the Lord Jesus Christ. The second stratagem is more extensive, that curates are not content with the
rule of the Saviour that having food and clothing they be
humbly content with these, and on this account they must
needs wallow in worldly cares; nor do they savor of gospel
preaching, but of that which confers gain of temporal goods
upon them, for they are not led by Christ, that they may
acquire for themselves and for their sheep the Kingdom of
God, but that they may live more lavishly according to the
flesh and the desire of this world. . . . The third cause of the
laying aside of the preaching of the gospel is the appropriation
of churches of five sorts, which appropriation the glebed curates
esteem little in such churches. Monks and canons, chapels of
kings and dukes, colleges of universities, and appropriations of
cathedral churches defraud parishes of lawful preachers of
the Word of God. The fourth cause on the devil's behalf, frus-
trating such preaching, is the broadcasting of the false friars,
who in the provinces weigh down the poor parishioners,
craftily filching temporal goods to the limit of their ability.
And their every solicitude is not to propagate the words of the
gospel, useful to the salvation of the souls of the subjects, but
jesting, lying frauds,[69] through which they are able more easily
to despoil the people. . . . The fifth cause (for a round number)

---

[69] Against telling of stories in sermons instead of preaching God's Word,
see also *Opus evangelicum*, I, 3 f. This is a common theme also in Wyclif's
sermons.

is the aforesaid authority of the Roman *curia*, which the simple-
minded folk recognize as the gospel so that whatever it decrees
is to be taken as the faith of the Church.[70] . . .

6

Let us consider how the lords temporal hinder Christ's
ordinance. This is a sin of supreme ingratitude after such benefits of Christ have so freely been given to them. For first they
found the "castle[s] of Cain," [71] and thus would hinder
Christ's offshoots from fructifying the Church. This clearly
hinders the ordinance and advancement of Christ, according
to which the faithful ought to labor in the Church. Surely because Christ knew nothing of the founding of such castles, a
fraud against true merit, no one of Christ's sect can have recourse to them. For after his ascension he scattered his apostles
with the greatest degree of freedom, and did not permit them
to conceal themselves as cloistered folk, and not without good
reason. To such a degree certain ones seem to be dead wood,[72]
because nodding their heads they seem to say to God, "Damn
all faithful poor and needy, who follow you in life and morals,
and bless us rich in the world who build castles against your
ordinance, in which are nourished so many gluttonous disciples of Antichrist!" For the faithful ought to recognize that
if merit lurks in such edifices, God, who is the Universal
Lord, wishes to reward all his servants who have served him
as sons here on earth. For they ought not to hope for the riches
of this life, thinking that they will have suitable merits by virtue
of such castles or new foundations of Antichrist, but rather
to attend to the ordinance of their God. These religious, blind-
ing secular lords, to such an extent wish in their own persons
to exemplify false charity among others, who, however rich
they are, do not wish another sect to build such castles. Since
therefore charity seeks not its own,[73] but exemplifies in life
and work that which it would see fulfilled, . . . it seems
evident that the hypocritical heresy of these new orders blinds

[70] Cf. *De blasphemia*, 2 ff.

[71] *Castra Caimitica*: Wyclif means cloisters, abbeys, and the like. His persistent spelling of Cain as C A Y M is an acrostic for *C*armelites, *A*ugus-
tinians, *I*acobites (= Dominicans), *M*inorites (= Franciscans). Cf.
Selected English Works, III, 348, 368. For further references see Workman, *op. cit.*, II, 103, and n.3.

[72] Lifeless trees: cf. Jude 12, "autumn trees that bear no fruit."

[73] I Cor. 13:5.

these temporal lords. Surely they are of the college of Pharisees, who "say and do not." [74] For this reason they ought to attend to the mirror of the faith of Christ and to recognize that such newfangled fabrications are of little or no value for the assistance of souls. For Christ has made easy the way of man in this life and has not taught him to build such castles ; but his ordinance has very often been set at nought and despised. Secular [lords], indeed, who have to be occupied with temporal matters, can lawfully construct for themselves such edifices with moderation. But it is not so with priests, who ought to follow Christ more closely. For this reason let worldly persons know how much these are dominated here in the world, that they are not permitted, except for a brief hour by Christ's leave, so to enrich and build up so-called priests, but really disciples of Antichrist. Secondly, moreover, secular lords erect their own power against Christ in this respect, that against their own interest they hinder parish priests in their ministry. And thus such high and mighty betrayal is often said to be against Christ. They invest such a one to be Christ's priest, and as a consequence [state] that he is fitted to minister on Christ's behalf, as if Christ himself had instituted him. They have established him in this service, incompatible with the service of Christ; how they appoint him in this chief office, that of the cure of souls, cannot be hidden from Christ. Thirdly, secular lords more damnably, although apparently remotely, fail in the service of Jesus Christ; for they ought to destroy such spongy spots of sin, since this function belongs to the power of secular lords conferred by God. Yet they do not destroy but rather defend this [abuse], [saying] that such abbeys or [some other sort of] groundless novelties claim these patrons. And the faithful, hiding in such cloisters, who wish to assert the law of God, they imprison as heretics or robbers. . . .

7

. . . Who ought to be appointed curate over the people according to God's law and reason? There is no doubt but that a curate, intellectually and emotionally [75] instructed for the exercising of the curate's office, ought to be set over a given

---

[74] Matt. 23:3.
[75] *In intellectu et affectu:* Wyclif is wont both to differentiate and to join *intellectus* and *affectus* [ed. Lechler, 39n.].

flock. And while there is no contention about burdensome temporal things, the chief occasion for contention is checked. Then there would be free election by the parishioners and the choice of the curate would be limited by merit alone. I care little for the appointment by the pope or his bishop, to the glebe [76] of a church, the office of curate, and other things belonging (according to the world) to him. . . . For Christ chose his apostles as bishops, and the apostles after his ascension chose others; yet they were not endowed, but were in every respect utterly alien to traditions now current. . . .

8

Let us examine the supplying of a vicar for the office of pastor. Although many so-called curates have vicars, they usually explain the appointment of the vicar as being intended for this purpose: to collect (either by himself or through another) money or income, vulgarly called "the fruits of the benefice." Granted that it is not an inherited office, yet it seems that it is contrary to the law of God and reason for any such curate thus to fulfill his function through a vicar,[77] for any such curate is personally held not only responsible to God for the sheep entrusted to him, but to the Church Militant, according to his merit. Since it is necessary that he answer for the sheep entrusted to him, it is therefore also necessary that he personally feed them. And since all the merit of the curate ought to be directed to God, it would seem exceedingly difficult for an absent curate spiritually to aid his sheep more than one bodily present. Yet it is known that the necessary spiritual works of mercy require a local relationship between pastor and flock. But to preach such works of mercy these pastors care little. In like manner no curate can satisfy God through a vicar without in his own person incurring sin. Although he were to institute a thousand vicars, yet he cannot thus excuse the leprosy of sin in his own spirit. For this reason it seems that this human tradition savors of heresy against the apostle's "Each one will carry his own burden." [78] And in the creed of Athanasius it is said, "Every man will render account for his own actions." . . . In like manner before the tradition of paying such a curate

---

[76] Glebe: The land belonging to, or yielding revenue to, a parish church or ecclesiastical benefice.
[77] See I, chapter 11; also Workman, *op. cit.*, 2:410 f., Appendix O.
[78] Gal. 6:5.

with tithes and offerings was invented, that curate was required
to aid the subjects given into his care as much as he was able;
nor ought he to be lax or tardy on account of that human
tradition; therefore he is still bound to aid spiritually the people
given into his care as much as he is able. . . .

9

Now we should investigate how the electors and the elected
incur God's indignation upon these livings and the more often
damn themselves. For the electors often stupidly consent, even
authorize or initiate, pastoral wickedness; and when they have
agreed to such a crime, they ought to fear God and the devil
out of consent. Even though many err more often out of consent,
yet this ignorance seems crass and supine on account of the
illicit pretended temporal reason, as when electors or procurers
elect a curate for him to reimburse them with temporal gain,
which often causes the devil to draw the soul into the whirlpool
of sin. What therefore moves these electors to entangle themselves in such a crime? Moreover, this ignorance, on account
of their rudeness and the gain of temporal advantages, is said
by some to be crass stupidity. The elector lies down prostrate
before the devil, opposing no more resistance to him than a
dead man. . . . Hence such electors often originate such
crimes in this world. . . . Therefore, what wisdom or basis in
Christ or reason is there to elect a person whom the electors
either suspect or doubt as worthy? Indeed, [judging] from what
commonly happens, they ought to flee from him as unworthy. . . . A certain devoted people, mindful of the salvation
of the soul, choose a skilled and suitable priest, who will not
be burdensome to them on account of baseless novelties. But
when the people quarrel in this, or decline from the rectitude
of truth, it behooves temporal lords to hold them in the path of
justice.[79]

10

We need now to scrutinize the means by which the one
elected to such a prelacy ought to stand within the limits of
reason. It is indeed agreed as a matter of faith that just as
it is necessary for one to be subject to God, so it is necessary
for one to be subject to God's law. Moreover, God's law obliges
one to deserve as much as one can of each and every one of
one's subjects, before such spiritual care of the sheep is entrusted.

[79] Cf. Marsiglio of Padua, *Defensor pacis*, II, 8.

But just as before it had sufficed to merit well of those sheep, so afterward, therefore just as before he was obligated with respect to God, so afterward he is obligated. . . . And if this reason, together with its additions, were well understood, no one would receive temporal goods here except those necessary to life, for any ministry of spiritual goods here administered. As Christ says, "They have received their pay," [80] where it is taught that remuneration sought after by men, either through vain praise or through temporal gain, while one sojourns here, detracts from the reward of merits in heaven. And this is the reason why man ought to acquire merits secretly, as, for example, alms or other things in this life. This is demonstrated by the rule, . . . "But having food and wherewith to be clothed, with these let us be content." [81] Nor do I see for what subjects this command is of benefit, unless it be limited to bodily circumstances, through which it appropriately commends itself to the people; for although our merits are fully in God's hand, it is in his power according to the prerogative proper to him to distribute these merits to those whom he pleases. . . . The priests of Christ here on earth should not lay claim to more than food and clothing, and not as reward, but as means leading to reward. But the curate who puts his reward or goal in such things is on the threshold of damnation.

II

Let us examine how so many curates infected with these sins can honorably satisfy God and the Church Militant. It seems to me that I and perchance others like me have lapsed in this matter in many ways. There are three degrees to which clerics have lapsed from the poverty of Jesus Christ. The first degree is in occupying secular lordship. In this degree are the pope, bishops, abbots, and others in many ways disguised. In the second degree are those having only slightly anxious possession of so-called temporal movable goods. In the third degree are the clerics burning with desire for temporal goods, and others who have cast aside anxiety for the cure of souls and thrust their anxiety too much into the quest for the temporal goods of this world. As to all these matters it seems that one ought to say briefly that Scripture commands that old offenses be not admitted, and that those committed be wept over effectively, according to the statement spoken to the

[80] Matt. 6:2.   [81] I Tim. 6:8.

adulterous woman, "Go and sin no more."[82] Moreover, this
saying seems to savor of sanity from the fact that it is founded
in the faith of Scripture and arouses one to the following and
the imitation of our Lord Jesus Christ. But who stands scrupu-
lous of conscience in this? Especially should the three endowed sects be exhorted that, following Christ, they should
abandon those gifts which have craftily been attached to them.
For so long as affection of soul remains completely occupied
with these things, it seems certain that the ones so occupied
are involved in a hog wallow of sins. Thus, they do injury to
God and to the whole Church: to God indeed because they ought
(according to the law of Christ) to carry out what they fail to do
for him; and to the remaining part of the Church, according
to the example of Christ's poverty and the law which he
himself gave. For this reason, while all their merit depends
upon the gratitude or grace of the Saviour, it seems true that
such clerks are stubbornly ungrateful toward Christ, very much
indisposed toward being deserving of him and of the people.
In like manner no one doubts but that clerks by thus stripping
off these gifts are unburdened of the cares of temporal goods
and more disposed to minister to the people according to the
standard of Christ's law.[83] Who doubts that this will be better
and more pleasing to Jesus Christ? Who denies what has been
assumed in the life and teaching of our Lord Jesus Christ?
Why therefore are the clerks turned from winged creatures of
heaven into snakes, and the disciples of Christ into Pharisees,
straining out a gnat and swallowing a camel?[84] For marriage
permitted to them according to the law of Christ they hate as
poison, and secular lordship prohibited to them by Christ[85]
they with great avidity embrace.[86] Just as according to the
faith that Paul exemplifies, and the experience of the devout,
clerks ought especially to hate these earthly things as vile, and
to converse with things celestial. But to this end especially
secular lordship indisposes; therefore clerks ought to expunge
this rule or lordship. . . . Happy therefore will be the conversion of them through Christ, supposing that they freely relinquish to secular lords all these lordships and fruitfully cling
to poverty, which Christ taught his apostles. . . . Either let
them remain purely clergy in the image of Christ or purely

[82] John 8:11.
[83] On the secularization of church revenues, cf. *Trialogus*, 310. See also
  Lechler, *op. cit.*, 327.   [84] Cf. Matt. 23:24.   [85] Cf. Luke 22:25 f.
[86] *De officio regis*, 29; cf. *De civili dominio*, II, 13 [Lechler, *op. cit.*, 309 f.].

secular lords, since Christ hates such duplicity in possession and affection, on account of the falsity which it implies. . . .

12

Even though work of merit ought to be voluntary, yet it happens, as befell Paul, that the work due is at first involuntary, and grace is infused together with the compulsion of works. Indeed, extrinsic good works are not so much excommunicated or foreign to God that he cannot thereby infuse grace upon the pilgrim. And for this reason it seems that the clergy in all these four sects ought to be compelled in every respect to return to the religion of the Lord. But I speak concerning the compulsion of charity as the Gospel speaks,[87] and as Christ exemplified in Paul.[88] . . . If the secular arm shrinks from communicating with a traitor known to an earthly king, even applies diligence in order to capture him, and to punish him fiercely, what will it do with him who on the basis of faith of Scripture is a notorious traitor of the heavenly King, who brings upon the Church continuously such great loss? Surely faith, hope, and charity seem in this matter too much to falter. . . . Thus also as a matter of charity, he could be induced to leave off the following of the devil. In the first book of the *Decretals*,[89] they point out to Caesar how other princes yield preference to Caesarian prelates,[90] and give them the place of honor. . . . For this reason princes ought faithfully to note the decree of Isidore where the opinion is advanced that whether the Church increases or decreases, Christ will require a reckoning from them in the day of judgment, of how they have exercised in this ministry the power which he gave them.[91] . . . Surely he would be worse than an infidel who would esteem carnal affection or carnal advantage more than the salvation of his soul, or a perpetual damnation in Gehenna. Who therefore, sober of mind, will be offended toward the secular arm because he is reasonably charged with the perpetual salvation of himself and of the people, whose government God entrusted to him? And he who dissuades the king or princes from the perfection of this work teaches himself to be the betrayer of temporal kings and of the King of Kings, our Lord Christ.

Here endeth the second part of the *Treatise on the Pastoral Office.*

[87] Luke 14:23.   [88] Acts, ch. 9.
[89] *Decretales Gregorii IX*, I, t. XXX, c. 6, Friedberg, *op. cit.*, II, 196–198.
[90] *Caesariis praelatis.* See note 2.
[91] *Decretum*, pars II, C. XXIII, q. 5, c. 20, I, 937.

On the Eucharist

THE TEXT

I

(1) In dealing with the Eucharist[1] it is necessary to set forth the more commonly known facts, and first to consider whether the sacrament of the altar is the real body of Christ. On this topic I have often said in public[2] that there are three aspects of the sacrament of the altar to be considered, namely, the bare sacrament, apart from the matter of the sacrament,[3] as the consecrated host; second, the sacrament and the matter of the sacrament as the true body and blood of Christ; and third, the matter of the sacrament, apart from the sacrament itself, as the union of Christ with his mystical body the Church. This is nowhere comprehensible by the senses, and consequently is not anywhere a sacrament. From this belief arise the objections of the pagans. For they argue that a hog, a dog, or a mouse can eat our Lord, because they can eat the body of Christ, that is, God.

(2) But we reply to them in accordance with this belief. Their assumption is false; beasts can eat the consecrated host, but it is the bare sacrament and not the body or blood of Christ. When a lion devours a man, it does not also devour his soul; yet his soul is present in every part of his body. Thus should one believe concerning the body of Christ in the sacrament of the altar. For this is whole, sacramentally, spiritually,

[1] The text used is that edited by J. Loserth for the Wyclif Society (London, 1892), from which edition most of the footnotes to the present translation have been derived. Citations of this work by the original Latin title refer to sections not included in the present translation; citations of Wyclif, *On the Eucharist*, are from the translation as printed. Paragraph numbers have been assigned by the translator to the Latin text as printed.

[2] Cf. Wyclif, *Trialogus*, ed. Lechler (1849), 248.

[3] *Res sacramenti*: "matter of the sacrament."

or virtually in every part of the consecrated host, even as the soul is in the body.

(3) Secondly, they object on this account, that we priests break the body of Christ, and thus the head, neck, arms, and other members; this would be an utterly horrible thing to do to our God.

(4) But we reply according to the prior belief that they falsely assume this. We break the sacrament or consecrated host, but not the body of Christ, which is something different, just as we do not break a ray of the sun, even though we break a glass or a crystal stone. And this view is upheld by a hymn of the Church which sings,

> "When they this sacrament dismember,
> Without the slightest doubt, remember
> He lieth hid in every member
> As in the very whole." [4]

(5) Since, therefore, we cannot deny that the sacrament is broken, as the custom of the Church teaches (the senses will otherwise be led astray, through false reasonings based upon the truth), and the body of Christ is not broken, it is clear that the sacrament which is broken is not the body of Christ, because otherwise to the inquirer what is broken would be less truly spoken of as the body of Christ: what indeed he seeks is the substance of the thing.

(6) The third objection they make is this, that unless the consecrated host is the body of Christ, we would not see nor eat the body of Christ, that is, we do not bite it with the teeth, and thus we would not receive it. Such a conclusion would be embarrassing for Christians.

(7) But here we reply by distinguishing two kinds of seeing, of eating, and of digesting: namely, corporeal and spiritual. [5] Thus we agree that we do not see the body of Christ in that sacrament with the bodily eye, but rather with the eye of the mind, that is, in faith through a mirror darkly. And just as the image is perfect in every part of the mirror, so that it can be seen either in part or completely by any bodily eye placed anywhere, so also should one believe in part concerning

---

[4] From the Sequence attributed to Thomas Aquinas, *Lauda Sion salvatorem*, lines 55–58. See Daniel, *Thesaurus hymnologicus* (Leipzig, 1841–1856), II, 98. My translation.

[5] Cf. John Hus, *De corpore Christi*, in *Joannis Hus . . . historia et monumenta* (Nüremberg, 1558), I, fol. 174a, 15.

the body of Christ in the consecrated host as in a mirror. And in the same manner it is said that we do not physically touch or seize the body of Christ, just as we do not eat it corporeally. And this is the meaning of the hymn of the Church which sings,

> "What thou canst not take nor see,
> Faith yet affirms courageously,
> Beyond the things of sense."[6]

(8) Nor do we crush the body of Christ with the teeth, but rather we receive it in a spiritual manner, perfect and undivided. And so we understand the same hymn in which we sing,

> "The thing within sustains no tear;
> The sign alone is broken there;
> No loss the state or size doth bear
> Of this, the Signified."[7]

(9) But at this point certain folk object concerning our views that these ideas should not be mentioned to laymen who cannot understand or observe them, since from such ideas they might lose their former faith. But nothing is more absurd than such an objection; for entirely too many laymen as well as clergy are so unfaithful in this matter that they believe, worse than pagans, that the consecrated host is their God. Then, of course, they arrive at the aforesaid pagan arguments. Therefore, he who does not understand these matters ill understands the belief in the Trinity or the incarnation. Nor is the above-mentioned lay belief a belief that is pleasing to the Lord of Truth, but the vilest disbelief because it is a form of idolatry whereby a creature, cast down rather than lifted up, is worshiped as God. So according to this stupidity any error in faith would never be taught or argued, but lest worse things come to pass, the Christian, teachable though he might be, would wallow in unbelief, as if he were to be told that he ought not to take a thorn out of his foot, a spear out of his flesh, or to remove some deadly poison, the cause of illness in his body, lest perchance things might grow worse. Therefore it is the duty of bishops to destroy these heresies; otherwise they would become heretics themselves by condoning such views.

---

6 Daniel, *op. cit.*, II, 97, lines 34–36. My translation, with assistance of Professor J. T. McNeill.

7 *Ibid.*, II, 98, lines 59–62. My translation.

(10) Their second objection is that if this idea were spread among the laity the honor and devotion of the people to this venerable sacrament would thereby be destroyed or at least lessened.

(11) But this fiction involves the same falsity. For just as the apostle says . . . , "Why not do evil that good may come?",[8] one might much more faithfully say, "Why not commit idolatry that the people might be the more completely seduced out of false and faithless devotion?" For certainly it might lie a little less open to popular belief that the cup in which is the blood of Christ and the wood through which, crucified, he is worshiped are really our God. Just as when the cup is seen we break forth into profound worship, so also when the consecrated host is seen we do the same, not on account of the fact that that very cup has been consecrated by the priest, but because of the excellent sacrament hidden in the vessel. Thus when we see the host we ought to believe not that it is itself the body of Christ, but that the body of Christ is sacramentally concealed in it.[9] And this is the meaning of the Church when it sings,

> "Beneath these many forms we see
> Signs only, not reality;
> The wonder lies concealed." [10]

(12) And it is clear that when this error of idolatry has been destroyed, we can worship God more purely than we now worship him, because we ought to believe that Christ, present, is hidden in these sacraments. Why therefore should we not worship Christ when the host is seen just as we do when the cup is seen, and just as the faithful more devotedly worship the divine Majesty when any creature whatsoever is seen by them? Therefore, when this meaning is understood, the true worship which is due to God will be pleasing to him, just as now the worship of falsehood is indeed abominable to God. And this is the true meaning even though it may be displeasing to the priests of idols.

(13) Their third objection is this: that priestly authority would be damaged if the privilege of making the blood and body of Christ were not admitted to exist. . . . But who then

---

[8] Rom. 3:8, slightly altered.
[9] On the belief that Christ lies hidden in the elements, see also Wyclif, *De Eucharistia*, 29; *Wycket*, 12. Cf. Wyclif, *Sermons*, IV, 344, where the Eucharist is called the "tomb of Christ." Workman, *op. cit.*, II, 37n.
[10] Daniel, *op. cit.*, II, 97, lines 37–39. My translation.

would hear the Mass? Who would devotedly hire Masses to be said? Or who would receive the sacrament according to the custom of the Church?

(14) Here it is said that the first does not follow, but when the error of blasphemy has been destroyed, the priestly authority would be kept and comprehended within its proper limits. Nothing can be more awful than that any priest can daily make or consecrate the body of the Lord by saying Mass.[11] For our God is not a God newly made; nor is his body, since it is supremely holy and everlasting, thus sacramental or freshly to be created. But we priests make and bless the consecrated host, which is not the Lord's body, but an efficacious sign thereof. . . . Hence, because the priest does not have the power of making this sacrament except when God is the principal minister thereof, so the priest is said to complete, not the body of Christ, but the bare sacrament. And so because of sanctity of life, and not for that reason, ought he to be praised. So the Mass of the holy priest ought the more devotedly to be heard, and the Mass of the notorious sinner ought to be shunned.[12] We do not buy the approbation of priests as if it were money; but without civil agreement we render to them the necessaries of life just as the apostle teaches us to do with respect to preachers.[13] . . . Yet note that just as we bless God and our Lord because they are worthy of praise, not because of what they do, so also do we bless the body and blood of Christ, not by making it blessed or holy, but by praising and spreading abroad its holiness and blessedness which God has instituted in his body, and thus we sacrifice Christ and offer him to God the Father.

(15) Note also further with respect to the spiritual receiving of the body of Christ that it does not consist in bodily receiving, chewing, or touching of the consecrated host, but in the feeding of the soul out of the fruitful faith according to which our spirit is nourished in the Lord. And on account of ignorance of the eating of the body of Christ and drinking of his blood, many disciples have turned aside . . . : "Hard, they say, is this word, and who can hear it?"[14] For nothing is more horrible than the necessity of eating the flesh carnally and of drinking the blood carnally of a man loved so dearly. Therefore Christ speaks to

---

[11] Cf. G. V. Lechler, *op. cit.*, 347.
[12] See also chapter 4, pars. 43f., of the present treatise, where Wyclif's donatism is even more pronounced. Cf. also *On the Pastoral Office*, I, chapter 8.   [13] I Cor. 9:14ff.   [14] John 6:61.

the apostles, who, over and above the unworthy disciples who turned back, were worthy to be instructed in the life-giving sense because the carnal meaning of this will not benefit. But it is the spirit, that is, the spiritual meaning, which gives life,[15] while the other sense brings scandal when it is taken in evil part. Therefore, the faithful person must believe that that upon which his soul feeds in an objective sense is the spiritual food of the soul, and thus ought the flesh of Christ and his blood for sinners in dire straits to kindle in our spirits that love which is the food of the soul in order that we may in some measure willingly make recompense. . . . Augustine says . . . : "This it is therefore for a man to eat that meat and to drink that drink, to dwell in Christ, and to have Christ dwelling in him. Consequently he that dwells not in Christ, and in whom Christ dwells not, without any doubt neither eats His flesh spiritually nor drinks His blood, although he may press the sacrament of the body and blood of Christ carnally and visibly with his teeth. But rather does he eat and drink the sacrament of so great a thing to his own judgment." [16] And thus in the words of Christ and of his disciple Augustine three notable things ought to be pointed out: First, it is customarily supposed that the body and blood of Christ are eaten only in a spiritual sense, for God has ordained eternally that "his Holy One shall not see corruption" [17] in any of his members. Secondly, it is clear that neither a beast nor a man eternally foreknown to be reprobate eats Christ's body with his teeth, although he corporeally chews the sacrament. And thirdly, the wonderful subtlety of the words of the doctor is clear in which he says not that an unworthy person visibly presses the body of Christ with his teeth, but that he visibly presses the sacrament of the body and blood of Christ with his teeth. For that sacrament ought especially to be distinguished from the body of Christ which is the matter of the sacrament thereof.

(17) We ought to mark well the difference which Augustine posits between carnal and spiritual eating;[18] for in carnal eating that which is eaten changes into nourishment for the eater when it is taken in by his members. But in spiritual eating it is otherwise. When one eats the body of Christ spiritually, one is thereby incorporated into the members of

15 John 6:64, Vg.; 6:63, E.V.
16 Augustine, In Joannem, XXVI, 18, in Migne, Patrologia Latina (hereafter PL), 35:1614.
17 Ps. 15:10, Vg.; 16:10, E.V..   18 Augustine, op. cit., PL, 35:1614.

the Church, and thus into Christ. The act of spiritual eating then exceeds mere carnal eating. . . .

2

(1) The common opinion concerning this venerable sacrament being set forth, it remains to consider what it really is. In this matter there are three opinions: The first seems to be the view of Saint Thomas [19] and his followers that the Eucharist is magnitude of a quantitative sort, for since it must needs be an accident [20] and quantity is the first accident after the class of substance, it is necessary that that sensible sacrament be a continuous, permanent quantity in which such and such an amount of the bread already formally existed.

(2) The second opinion seems to be that of Scotus,[21] who disproves the previous view on the ground that this sacrament can be expanded or condensed, and hence cannot coincide with quantity; for this reason, since an accident is here appropriate, it seems to point to quality, inasmuch as it is necessary that accident be absolute. Hence some of this sect say that it is a figure, some that it is a primary quality, and others that it is a secondary quality, as color, taste, or some other sixfold quality of this sort, or gathered from many accidents. The third opinion is that of Berengarius, which seems to be the decree of the Holy Synod. It is established indeed from the public and solemn confession of Berengarius . . . that by correcting his prior error he confesses this sacrament perceivable by the senses to be bread and wine. For (as I have recounted above) his confession is inscribed there under these words: "I believe that the bread and wine which are placed upon the altar are, after consecration, not only a sacrament but also the true body and blood of our Lord Jesus Christ, perceivable by the senses not only sacramentally but in truth grasped and broken by the hands of the priests and crushed by the teeth of the faithful." [22]

19 Thomas Aquinas, *Summa theologica*, III, Q. 76; *Super IV sententiarum*, dist. X, Q. 1, art. 2. See Workman, *op. cit.*, II, 31 f.
20 "Accident": "A property or quality not essential to our conception of a substance; an attribute. Applied especially in Scholastic theology to the material qualities remaining in the sacramental bread and wine after transubstantiation; the essence being alleged to be changed, though the accidents remained the same." N.E.D.
21 John Duns Scotus, *De Eucharistia* (Lugd., 1639), Scholium III. See Workman, *op. cit.*, II, 33.   22 *Decretum* pars III, dist. II, c. 42, I, 1328 f.

There it is clear that he understands that the same bread and wine which were placed before the Mass upon the altar remain after the consecration both as sacrament and as the Lord's body. That, moreover, this was then the opinion of the Roman Church is clear for the three following reasons: First, because in the same decree we have from the words of the notary the following: "Having read and reread this, I have freely subscribed to it. This confession of his faith concerning the body and blood of our Lord Jesus Christ was made by Berengarius at Rome in the presence of 114 bishops."[23] From this it is clear that the Church through such a great synod would not permit the revocation of prior heresy and its reproof without vituperation in these words unless it approved his faith to be Catholic. Secondly, it is confirmed by the same decree that this was then the opinion of the Roman Church. For in the same place it is written as follows: "Pope Nicholas sent word through the cities of Italy, Germany, Gaul, and to various other places which Berengarius' reputation of depravity might already have reached, that the churches which before sorrowed concerning this opponent and schismatic afterward rejoiced over this penitent and convert."[24] From these words it is abundantly clear that the Church then understood the above opinion of Berengarius to be Catholic and the opinion contrary to it to be heretical.

(3) Thirdly, Berengarius' opinion is confirmed likewise by what he had professed in his first revocation under these words: "I consent moreover to the Holy Roman Church and to the Apostolic See and profess both by mouth and heart concerning the sacrament of the Lord's Table, that I hold the same faith which the venerable lord Pope Nicholas and this Holy Synod teach, by the authority of the gospel, and of the apostles, to be held and have confirmed to me."[25] And after this he confessed the opinion quoted above. From these words it is gathered that he had received from the pope and synod that opinion which he was to confess; and it is clear that it was once the meaning of the Church, as an article of faith, that bread and wine remain after consecration of the Eucharist just as before.

(4) From this evidence it is gathered that the latter Church erred in faith or equivocated in logic or expression or, thirdly, that variety of belief followed after a time, so that what was then an article of faith today is false.

(5) But it is agreed with regard to this third point that with

23 *Decretum*, pars III, dist. II, c. 42, I, 1328f.   24 *Ibid.*   25 *Ibid.*

equal reason it would be true that in the Eucharist bread and wine remain after consecration ever true and ever to be believed; for this reason, since ambiguity in matters of faith is no excuse, it would appear that the latter Church has erred.

(6) From this it is clear that the Roman Church can err in articles of faith, since it has so done.[26] Secondly, it is clear that it is not necessary to believe that, if the Roman Church declares anything Catholic or heretical, it therefore does so truly. Thirdly, it seems probable that the earlier Church believed wisely in this and that the latter Church was in error. For very great authority, very great sanctity, and very great wisdom or even greater, shone in this Pope Nicholas II, according to the chronicles, and in these 114 bishops, as well as in him who composed the decretals. For this reason therefore should not this opinion all the more be believed than the weaker opinion that followed it? Then the Church advances by deteriorating with respect to faith in Scripture. And again, the earlier opinion agrees more with sense, reason, the holy doctors, and Scripture; therefore, since it was not later abrogated or disproved, it seems that the Church ought still to believe it as at first.[27]

(7) That this agrees more with sense and reason will be evident below, and that it agrees more with the views of the holy doctors is evident from three authorities: First, from the statement of Saint Ambrose . . . : "Although the figure of bread and wine is seen, nevertheless after consecration nothing other than the flesh and blood of Christ ought to be believed."[28] Note that bread and wine ought to be believed to be the flesh and blood of Christ.

(8) Secondly, this same opinion is confirmed by blessed Augustine's statement . . . : "What is seen is the bread and the cup which the eyes renounce; but what faith demands to be taught is that the bread is the body of Christ and the cup is his blood. These are called sacramental elements for this reason that in them one thing is seen and another is understood.

26 See S. H. Thomson, "Three Unprinted Opuscula of John Wyclif," *Speculum*, III, 2 (April, 1928): *Errare in materia fidei quod possit Ecclesia Militans*, 250.

27 Wyclif consistently maintains in this treatise the contrast between the rectitude of the earlier Church and the error of the later Church in Eucharistic doctrine. Elsewhere he actually divides the development of the doctrine into historical periods. See *De apostasia*, 108 f., 130, 148, 174, 178; also, *De Eucharistia*, 287.

28 *Decretum*, pars III, dist. II, c. 74, I, 1344 f. Cf. Wyclif, *De apostasia*, 64.

What is seen has bodily appearance, what is understood has a spiritual fruit."[29] Note that this saint states that the visible sacrament is bread and wine.

(9) Thirdly, it is confirmed by Hilary's statement . . . : "The body of Christ which is taken from the altar is a figure, while bread and wine appear outwardly, yea, truly, while the body and blood of Christ are believed in truth to be within." [30] The words spoken by the three saints are to a great extent similar to those of Berengarius, and express the same opinion as he confessed.

(10) As to Scriptural witness [31] . . . it is related that Jesus took bread and said concerning it, "This is my body." For Luke . . . states, "And taking bread he gave thanks and broke it and gave it to them saying, 'This is my body.' " There it is clear (but not to a shameless man) that he afterward demonstrated that bread which he then took. And it is certain that so long as that bread remains it is not really the body of Christ, but the efficacious sign thereof. From these words it is gathered that the confession of Berengarius and the ancient decree of the Church are in every respect more in agreement with the truth. [32]

(11) But it is objected that the second part of the decree disagrees with the first and with Catholic truth, and consequently the whole decree is made void; for it posits that bread and wine not only are a sacrament after consecration, but the true body and blood of Christ which is broken and experienced by the senses as bread, which is a contradiction.

(12) Here I say (as above) that the second statement must be utterly ambiguous, since neither the substance of the bread nor that which was its accidental form are really the body of Christ, as both ancients and moderns must agree. For this reason the *Glossa ordinaria* [33] says that the confession of Beren-

---

[29] *Decretum*, pars III, dist. II, c. 58, I, 1336.   [30] *Ibid.*, c. 79, I, 1346.
[31] Mark 14:22; Luke 22:19 f.; I Cor. 11:24; Acts 2:46; John 6:59.
[32] Cf. *De apostasia*, 68.
[33] Cf. *Glossa ordinaria*, "Dentibus": "Nisi sane intelligas verba Berengarii, in maiorem incides haeresim quam ipse habuit et ideo omnia referas ad species ipsas, nam de Christi corpore partes non fecimus. . . ." The *Glossa ordinaria* was the great medieval commentary on the Vulgate, consisting of extracts from the Fathers and from other sources, accumulated over a period of many centuries, and assembled by Anselm of Laon (d. 1117) and his pupils. It was once legendarily credited to Walafrid Strabo (d. 849). For a brief account of the development, see B. Smalley, *The Study of the Bible in the Middle Ages* (Oxford University Press, London, 1941), 31 ff.

garius ought sanely to be understood, for otherwise the latest error would be worse than the prior one, damned by the Church as heretical. For today the prior opinion of Berengarius would be approved in its three parts which the Church then damned as heretical, namely, that that white thing remains after consecration only as the sacrament; secondly, that that is not the body of Christ; and thirdly, that through sensual perception of it the body of Christ is not broken or perceived by the senses. On these three points, according to the decree of the Church, he has corrected himself; and surely now to maintain that that Church then erred in faith as though by erroneous reasoning which was corrected through the wiser Church would be to impose the suspicion of calumny upon our entire conclusion as to matters of faith; or, to put it in other words, Scripture as well as the holy doctors failed in these respects. But who then would believe our words, since we could vary faith at will for the sake of gain? Therefore the statement of both Churches ought to be glossed according to the rule of faith of Scripture; and this is more in agreement and more honorable in all respects to both in order to understand Scripture, the holy doctors, and the confession of Berengarius, which was the decree of the Church.

(13) In this matter we must especially note (as above) the distinction between identical and figurative predication. It is identical (as I have said), when a predicate is identically asserted concerning a subject, as "Christ is man." But it is tropic or figurative predication when one extreme is noted to be figured through the remainder, as I have explained before: "The rock was Christ." Whence I adduce three examples to illustrate this meaning; the first is the saying of the apostle . . . : "I do not want you to be ignorant, brethren, since all our fathers were under a cloud, and all crossed the sea, and all drank the same spiritual drink. For they drank from the spiritual rock following them: and the rock was Christ." [34] And it is clear with respect to the meaning of this Scripture and those like it that it is necessary to note whether the sense is figurative or tropic; in this sense this saying is equally true as any other part of Scripture; for all the patriarchs were under divine protection, according to which the heat of God's vengeance was put to flight; all traversed the peril of the world and of all the opposing peoples; and since faith is not varied on account of passage of time, it is clear that they were nourished

[34] I Cor. 10:1, 4.

by the same faith by which the Christians were afterward nourished. And all this was figured through the forty years of wandering toward the Land of Promise, so that nothing happened to the travelers from Egypt which was not a future figure for their successors in their journey to their fatherland. For just as the people drank of the water flowing from the rock which Moses struck twice[35] . . . , so the Christian people drank spiritually the subtlety of the faith of Jesus Christ after the Jewish people thus infamously struck Christ; and just as he was followed by the opprobrium of reproof as a result of this striking, so does opprobrium follow the Jews, because they struck Christ thus on the gibbet. He says, "The rock was Christ," that is, that rock mystically figured Christ. Yet it ought to be noted that such expressions can be understood sanely in two ways, namely, that such a figure figured the thing figured, or by dismissing the literal sense to understand figuratively the thing ambiguously figured, and in either case there will be Catholic sense without any scruple of falsehood.

(14) . . . Another example is . . . : "This cup is the new testament in my blood"[36]; for the new testament figures the wine in the cup just as the blood of the bullock was the sign of confirmation of the old testament.[37] . . . Thus it is seen that the saints of the primitive Church and their sons after them figuratively understood through the bread and wine the body and blood of Christ. . . . The apostle related[38] how the Corinthians agreed to the partaking of the Lord's Supper and each one took with him his own bread and wine, so that *one* was *sated* and the *other hungry* after this meal. He chided them gently in this matter and added instruction as to this sacrament, which then sufficed for the Church, namely, that the partakers in an orderly manner gather in the church or else the sick partake at home; nor should others give occasion for scandal to the brethren in their bountiful, sumptuous, and elegant preparations of bread and wine. Whence for full instructions as to this sacrament he speaks as follows . . . : "For I have received of the Lord that which also I delivered to you, that the Lord Jesus, the night in which he was betrayed took bread, and giving thanks, broke and said: Take ye and eat: this is my body which shall be delivered for you: do this for the commemoration of me. . . . For as often as you shall eat this bread and drink this chalice, you shall show the death

---

35 Ex. 17:6.   36 Rev. 19:8 (in omitted portion); I Cor. 11:25.
37 Ex., ch. 24.   38 I Cor. 11:21.

of the Lord until he come."[39] Here it is clear that he speaks in fourfold fashion concerning the material bread and wine and consequently says that this is his body and blood in a figure, just as he says this cup to be the new testament and that this is to be done in remembrance of him. . . .

(29) But the third main point is answered on this ground: . . . The modern Church proposes transubstantiation of bread and wine into the body and blood of Christ; but the primitive Church did not hold this; therefore they disagree in opinion. The assumption of the First Book of the *Decretals* . . . is clear: "The body and blood of Christ under the appearance of bread and wine in the sacrament of the altar are truly contained by the transubstantiated bread in the body and by the wine in the blood through divine power."[40] But if bread and wine remain whole and unaltered after consecration, how are they transubstantiated through the words of the priest?

(30) In this matter, our Catholics, even the decretalists, taught that the above-mentioned term be described thus: Transubstantiation is the passage of one substance according to its entirety into another, with the whole multitude of accidents remaining, so that neither matter nor substantial form which were in the bread and wine remain after consecration, but all material or formal substance which was in them is destroyed. The body of Christ succeeds through conversion under the same accidents, and thus there is no annihilation of any substance, both because of the conversion of the entire substance into a better one, and also because the accidents that were previously in the bread and wine remain; for idolatry would be committed toward those remaining accidents by adoring bread and wine as the Lord's body, and thus as God.

(31) It seems to me that the primitive Church did not teach this, but the modern Church does, as certain ones indulging in faithless and baseless imaginings have baptized the term and have fancied many things falsely to the burden of the Church. First, therefore, it seems that the aforesaid decretal or its authors ought not to be believed in preference to the decree of the Church on Berengarius. As has been said above, in this the pope and his synod (which is more worthy of our belief) excel in sanctity and knowledge. For they spoke more in conformity with Scripture and with the opinions of

[39] I Cor. 11:23f., 26.
[40] *Decretales Gregorii IX*, I, t. I, c. 1, par. 3, Friedberg, *op. cit.*, II, 5.

the holy doctors, and more in agreement with reason, and, beyond this, explained more accurately and easily what was to be believed. Since "to be transubstantiated" is a schoolman's term, which a believer may interpret in any particular Catholic sense, it seems to signify ambiguously and incompletely the faith of the Church concerning the Eucharist. But the other decree explains how the pope and synod decreed against Berengarius how the bread and the wine which are placed on the altar remain after consecration not only as a sacrament but also as the true body and blood of Christ. Accordingly, the pope blithely announced to divers churches that this opinion was to be believed as an article of faith. Since therefore the material sign of the decretals or decrees has no bearing upon the faith to which the Church instinctively clings and a considerable or even greater authority shone forth in the earlier Church, it seems that the evidence taken from the decretal of the Church concerning transubstantiation, which upholds that the nature of bread and wine remains after consecration of the host, is held up to scorn.[41] . . . What inevitably follows, howsoever rude the logic, is confirmed first through this, under the form of bread and wine the body of Christ exists sacramentally. Therefore that bread and that wine constitute the substance for that form, and consequently, since that accidental form exists, the bread and wine remain in that form of greater permanence.[42] Secondly, it is confirmed through this that 114 bishops would not gather together to discern that bread and wine which are placed on the altar remain after consecration if they held to the opposite view that the bread and wine do not remain after consecration as that sacrament of the altar, but as accidents which once were bread and wine. For they would not deceive the people, saying contrary to custom that accidents exist independently, intending a statement contradictory to what they said. . . . Often the words of a decree

---

[41] A pun on *tollitur* and *tolleret*, which I have rendered as "upholds" and "holds up."

[42] "Sub forma panis et vini est corpus Christi sacramentaliter, ergo ille panis et illud vinum sunt substancia illi forme et per consequens illa existente forma accidentali panis et vinum remanent maioris permanencie illa forma." On this doctrine of remanence see *Fasciculi Zizaniorum* (London, 1858), 105, "Conclusiones Wycclyff de Sacramento Altaris," no. 3: "Formerly the faith of the Roman Church was expressed in the Confession of Berengarius, that the bread and wine which continue after the benediction are the consecrated host" (translation from Lechler, *op. cit.*, 368). See also Wvclif. *De blasphemia*, 247 f.

agree more with Scripture, with the holy doctors, and with reason and sense; for this reason, most mature and holy bishops either clearly take it on faith or express its meaning in some other way. For thus the decree frequently explains how the fact that bread is the body of Christ, that is, its sacramental sign, ought to be understood. This method of speaking was well known in Scripture and then accepted by the people, but afterward declined to identical predication.

(32) Hence today one must needs speak in conformity to the meaning as expounded, and to the scandal underlying the faith; nay, Christ did not refrain from so speaking on account of scandal[43] . . . but he subtly explains himself, as the decree of Augustine . . . teaches: "Spiritually understand what I have spoken: you are not about to eat this body which you see, nor are you about to drink the blood which they who crucify me are going to pour out. I have commended a sacrament to you; spiritually understood, it will quicken you."[44] Whence in order to understand that not by that means by which they think does He expend His body, "He says He is going to ascend whole into heaven. When you see," he says, "the Son of Man ascending, where was He before? It is the Spirit who quickens." It ought to be believed rather according to the ancient decree of the fathers . . . : "Howsoever much discordant opinion is found in the acts of the councils, the opinion of that council ought rather to be held, whose authority is older and more powerful."[45] Since therefore the opinion of the decree is closer to the fountain of Scripture, it seems that it ought preferably to be held to in matters of faith.

(33) Furthermore, as to the description of transubstantiation, it seems that it undergoes misrepresentation by supposing (as our opponents confess) that that conversion does not imply annihilation or identification of the bread with the body of Christ. For every accident must have a subject, and all such transubstantiation is an accident; therefore all such transubstantiation ought to have a subject. Even though, moreover, they claim an accident can exist without a subject, yet they say that it must have a subject at the outset. On the contrary (as

[43] John 6:61, 67.
[44] Wyclif credits this passage from the *Decretum* to Augustine's exposition of Ps. 4. This Ivo's edition gives; Gratian credits it to Augustine's exposition of Ps. 44. Friedberg (I, 1330) indicates that the whole chapter (44) has been taken from various places: Augustine's interpretation of Ps. 54 and 98, and *In Joannem*, XXVII, XXX.
[45] *Ibid.*, pars I, dist. L, c. 28, I, 190.

they say in their impossible way), because it is a subject at each point thereof, it is not therefore without subject. Each respective accident of whatsoever sort is a mutation. They concede that it cannot be without its subject; therefore it must be given something which is subjected to passive transubstantiation. This is not an accident, for it remains untransubstantiated; nor is it bread or wine, for since that transubstantiation must have a foundation (lest we are forced to agree that the body of Christ or the host is successively fashioned), it is clear that at the instant of transubstantiation neither the transubstantiated bread nor wine exists in any part thereof. As a consequence no accident then underlies it. That fact is deduced in the treatise *De annihilatione* [46] to have moved the philosophers to posit a primal matter subject to generation, for to imagine anything previously unheard of and without foundation would be an illusion; positing therefore transubstantiation, it tells what it is, where it is, and in what manner it is sustained. Since indeed there is form, it is necessary that some subject impart form and beauty, when it is so miraculously produced. Whence, although once I labored to describe transubstantiation in harmony with the meaning of the earlier Church, yet now it seems to me that they contradict one another and that the later Church is in error. [47] For if transubstantiation is the yielding of one substance in favor of another with respect to place, so that one transubstantiated substance remains through the same place as before, and a more worthy substance exists sacramentally through that place to which the prior substance is subordinated as a sign, then it follows that bread is transubstantiated at the instant at which it is not changed, but remains bread subject to accidents after consecration. This is said to call in question the viewpoint of the *Decretals*. For this reason I now dismiss the agreement of these principles and I call transubstantiation the conversion of one substance into another, as seed is converted into a living body, as man is converted into earth, and thus generally when one body is begotten from another.

---

[46] *Tractatus de annihilatione.* Perhaps a reference to the work, a portion of which, as the "Fragmentum *De Annihilatione*, ex tractatu de Potencia productiva Dei ad extra excerptum," was published in the *De ente* (ed. Dziewiecki, Wyclif Society, 1909); see 289 of this work. For Wyclif's realist repudiation of annihilation, see Workman, *op. cit.*, I, 137, 140; II, 33, where the requisite references to Wyclif's other works are given.

[47] Cf. Matthew, "The Date of Wyclif's Attack on Transubstantiation," *English Historical Review*, April, 1890.

(34) Furthermore, as to idolatry,[48] it is clear that the people ought to be instructed not to believe that the accident which they perceive by the senses is identical with the body of Christ; and this is necessary according to every opinion of this matter because the later Church admits that there remains something white, round, and hard which cannot be the body of Christ. Thus in reality since that is sensible of itself and consequently the people are thus more or less prone to believe that to be the body of Christ as bread, it is clear that for them no particle of color remains, compelling them to think that the bread ceases to exist according to any of its parts, lest by adoring bread as the body of Christ one commit idolatry. For the same reason whatever sensible [49] accident might be withdrawn, only illusion concerning the subject and its accident is added thereto; and the greater part of the people believe unfaithfully and quite irreverently that that remaining thing which they posit as an accident is identical with the body of Christ. Indeed it is evident that the accident is more extraneous to the nature of the body or blood of Christ, than to the nature of bread or wine. Concerning transubstantiation it will be made clear at length later on.

3

(3) . . . Since neither the matter nor the form of that which is transubstantiated remains, lest the body of Christ would be too much encumbered with new matter, there seems according to the consensus of opinion to be a possibility of annihilation, i.e., that the transubstantiated nature is simply [50] annihilated. For it is possible, according to the modern doctors, that both the bread and the wine are annihilated and the body and blood of Christ succeed sacramentally under these accidents, as we now see, but whatever it will then be, the matter is in part bread and wine; therefore it is now irrevocably annihilated in consecration. There is a well-known assumption among them that the substance can be annihilated while the accidents are preserved, and vice versa, as they say, nor does it prevent Christ's being able at the same instant to multiply his body under those accidents, since the movements would in every respect be separate.

[48] On the "worship of the elements" as "idolatry," see also *On the Eucharist*, chapter 3, par. 14; *Trialogus*, 248 f., 261 f., 263; *De blasphemia*, 20; *Fasciculi Zizaniorum*, 107. Lechler, *op. cit.*, 347 f.

[49] Sensible: i.e., perceptible by the senses.

[50] *Simpliciter*: i.e., absolutely, unconditionally.

(4) Likewise, annihilation, according to those speaking, is distinguished from the being of the parts of that which is annihilated, and ends simply in nonbeing. This is what happens in all transubstantiation according to them. . . . What difference, I ask, is there between annihilation A of bread, when the body of Christ follows it under the same accidents at the instant of annihilation, and transubstantiation B of bread into the body of Christ under its accidents sacramentally following at the same instant? For cessation and destruction of substance are exactly the same thing; for this reason it seems that there is complete conformity as to the process of destruction. For the destruction of the bread is the same thing whether matter will more quickly return or the body of Christ will forever remain under a subject perceivable by the senses.

(5) Nor is this fiction of transubstantiation or conversion of bread into the body of Christ valid, since the body of Christ receives neither matter nor substantive or accidental form from corrupt bread. Therefore it seems no more to be converted into the body of Christ than day is changed into night or vice versa. Therefore either bread is not irregularly converted into the body of Christ in the performance of the Eucharist or it is doubtful just when such conversion takes place. A description of it will not be attempted. And it is clear, even though the Church sings,

> "This dogma Christians all receive:
> The change from bread to flesh believe,
> And from the wine to blood," [51]

that even the theologians seem ignorant of the nature of that passage of bread into the body of Christ and of wine into his blood. For they posit a complete cessation of substance according to itself and know not where any bread remains or whither it goes. By separating that movement from the others it seems according to them that annihilation takes place. Otherwise it could be imagined concerning any movement that it was not annihilation on account of any other postulated concomitant movement; for it seems that bread is turned into nothing. Just as it is true of grace which is not turned into sin, so neither is the thing annihilated turned into a body which occupies its place. For nothing is turned or changes into something else unless it underlies the turning or the change even to the end

[51] *Lauda Sion salvatorem*, lines 31–32. My translation. See Daniel, *op. cit.*, II, 97.

to which the movement goes. One cannot call [this] a marvelous mutation from the being of bread to its nonbeing, since there is no underlying matter, just as there is not in annihilation. It seems that they should say that it is annihilation, since they know not how to explain this embarrassing conversion; for (as they say) afterwards, the first matter is produced according to itself and according to each part of itself; in no respect, therefore, in its cessation has annihilation taken place. . . .

(7) Likewise, according to Augustine . . . : "My flesh is truly meat, and my blood is truly drink: In those things God commended to us this sacrament, which from many are reduced to one. For from many grains bread is fashioned, and from many clusters wine flows together." [52] Now according to my opponents this would be heretical, since it plainly implies that the bread and wine remain in the host after the consecration; for this reason they say we receive the body of Christ not in those things but in accidents of which they know nothing. . . . Hence we say accidents remain that the senses may be rendered immune from deception; but the inner senses judge concerning material substances, since they are perceivable by the senses through the accident; for this reason it would be more evil to be deceived in them. Since therefore both the inner and outer senses of man judge what remains to be bread and wine identical with the unconsecrated thing, it seems that it would not be fitting for the Lord of Truth to incorporate such an illusion in graciously communicating such a worthy gift. . . .

(9) Saint Thomas [53] . . . glosses Saint Ambrose: "This means," says Thomas, "what is under the appearance of bread first was bread and wine and afterward the body of Christ." [54] But the Master of the Sentences . . . better glosses these words of the saints: "Because they use a certain figure of speech by which they are wont to choose words as signs of the things they signify." [55] For before consecration that bread was not thus the body of Christ, but by virtue of the words of Christ it becomes the efficacious sign thereof. Thus it is understood that bread is changed into the body of Christ; it is transubstantiated or is expressed by some term or other of mutation. . . .

(10) Likewise, it clearly seems according to these [modern]

---

52 John 6:56. Augustine, *In Joannem*, XXVI, 17, *PL*, 35:1614. Wyclif has made some minor changes in this quotation.
53 Thomas Aquinas, *Super IV sententiarum*, dist. XI, art. 2.
54 *Decretum*, pars III, dist. II, c. 55, I, 1334 f.
55 Peter Lombard, *IV Libri sententiarum*, IV, dist. X, par. 3, *PL*, 192:860.

doctors that in the conversion of the host are postulated two movements prior in nature, namely, the complete cessation of the bread according to itself and the complete beginning of the presence of the body of Christ according to itself. That conversion either is those two movements or is formally consequent to them. . . . Since therefore the subject of that conversion ceases to be, and is not of the number of accidents which were able to exist of themselves, but is a corrupt nature that can be changed, it seems that that conversion is the sum of those two movements. . . . Conversion is a positive movement, requiring the existence of the essence of the subject, for otherwise it itself would no more be converted than an essence (to which a new body were to succeed) would be annihilated. . . . For the conversion [of the bread] or the acquisition of the presence of the body of Christ . . . would be accidental to the cessation [of the bread], and hence would not remove appearance or quiddity therefrom. Those who think thus deny composition to be continued on the basis of nonexistent quantities, yet admit as possible the cessation of the bread at a particular instant and the conversion following immediately thereafter. Otherwise . . . at the instant at which either movement took place bread not yet converted would remain, and as a consequence the conversion would yet be in the future. But this implies that there are two immediate instants. . . . But the greatest difficulty is to explain in intelligible fashion how the bread undergoes passage, is converted, or gives way to the body of Christ, when (according to this), as they agree, it is possible for the substance of the bread to be annihilated either with or without its accidents. Hence, over and above the cessation of the bread and the beginning of the presence of the body of Christ, they posit a conversion separate in every way; but all those so teaching do not know how to explain it, nor is it taught in the faith of Scripture or the creed of the Church. . . .

(13) Likewise, according to my opponents it would be possible for the body of Christ to remain sacramentally under the guise of bread, just as it now remains under the bare accidents. Yet neither Holy Scripture, nor reason, nor revelation teaches anyone what such a transubstantiation may be. Therefore it would be foolish to induce such a meaning. For since according to Augustine . . . all truth is in sacred Scripture,[56] it would have bearing on the views set forward to

[56] Augustine, *De doctrina Christiana*, III; cf. *De baptismo contra Donatistas*, II, c. 3, *PL*, 43:128 f.; cf. *Trialogus*, 240.

examine carefully their foundation, lest out of falsity they deceive and burden the Church more than they ought. And this moves many, since no one ought to believe even the pope in matters of faith except to the extent that his pronouncements are founded upon Scripture. But neither upon Scripture nor reason nor revelation can the Avignonese Church base the said transubstantiation. Therefore we are not any more obliged to believe this than was the primitive Church. Thus also could the Church be burdened by a thousand falsities as if by faith; and the law of Antichrist could, through the passage of time, be introduced. . . .

(14) Since therefore the subtler modern doctors see and assert that nothing forces one to believe this except the above-quoted passage from the *Decretals*, and the same passage would not give, through itself, faith to the faithful, it seems that the foundation of this faith is lacking in this regard. How fitting it is for legists so solemnly founding a new festival, after they have set aside Baptism, to force upon us something new and wonderful! Accordingly all legists and their expositors do not know how to describe transubstantiation and how to distinguish it from annihilation, together with related difficulties in which the Church for this reason is involved. Yet it is granted that those accidents which some call bread and wine are to be honored as the sign of the blood and body of Christ. But just as much as the fathers of the old law warned against worshiping idols as if they were God, as is clear in the epistle of Jeremiah sent to Babylon through Baruch,[57] so much ought the Christian to beware worshiping that which the moderns call accident and the earlier Church called bread and wine, as if they were the true body and blood of Jesus Christ. . . . Even though that sign has a greater efficacy than the signs of the old law and our images (as will become apparent later on), yet it would be too great an infidelity to believe that which is so mean in nature to be God. Such faithless sacrificers, just as other faithless idolaters, become an abomination and an object of contempt to God. This fact ought to be preached to the laity, lest out of stupid piety they be hurled headlong into idolatry. . . .

(15) . . . It is argued about the reason of the accident: Every accident formally inhering in substance does not exist unless it is the truth that a substance is accidentally of a certain sort, as is here supposed. But no such truth can exist without substance, just as no creature can exist without God; therefore,

[57] Baruch 6:1.

there can be no aggregation of such accidents without their subject, which is the consecrated host. . . .

(29) The Church would not be burdened by such unusual novelty unless either faith in Scripture or lively reasoning or effective witness of the saints requires this, but each of these three is lacking in the aforesaid error concerning the sacrament of the altar. Hence the reason why the Church is so burdened. The assumption is clear from the many testimonies of the saints and the truth and sufficiency of the law of Christ. For thus the abomination of desolation would be worshiped, the accident of entity in the slightest degree, as God, or at least an accident would be most falsely worshiped as a sacred sign in lieu of substance, and would impose upon God the responsibility of being the author of falsehood. [58] . . .

4

(1) But it remains to be seen further what efficacy the sacramental words possess, and how the body of Christ has, hidden in those signs, not dimensional but sacramental being.

(2) As for the sacramental words, it seems that Christ in them speaks figuratively or in a trope, just as before it was alleged that the new law often speaks under a figure to the old. For thus Christ says that John is Elijah. [59] . . . "He that sows good seed is the Son of Man. And the field is the world. And the good seed are the children of the Kingdom, and the cockle are the children of the wicked one. And the enemy that sowed them is the devil. But the harvest is the end of the world. And the reapers are the angels." [60] Therefore, just as the Truth speaks in these passages parabolically as the Gospel says, so he seems to speak figuratively in the four Gospels, [61] . . . when he says that bread and wine are his body and blood, just as the apostle teaches. [62] . . . Yet the difference lies in the ways of speaking, since one is tropological or moral and the other is allegorical or sacramental; it has the power to cause the body and blood of Christ to exist *de facto* under the sacramental

---

[58] Wyclif now proceeds to buttress his argument from Scripture, from reason, from the Fathers (especially Augustine). See *De Eucharistia*, 71 ff.
[59] Matt. 11:14.
[60] Matt. 13:37-39.
[61] Matt. 26:26; Mark 14:22; Luke 22:19 f.; I Cor. 11:24.
[62] I Cor. 11:24.

appearances, for which occasion the other figures both of the new law and of the old were imperfect.[63] . . .

(10) And it seems to me now that bread is signified by the pronoun "this," and thus is the proposition true to its own meaning, just as it seems that Augustine concedes, this is Christ, when any creature whatsoever is demonstrated.[64] . . . But in demonstrating this sacrament, there is a certain singular efficacy and significance imposed by Christ. For this reason the theologian ought to note how this ought unconditionally to be conceded. But in case the proposition is understood not figuratively but effectively, then through the pronoun is demonstrated under the appearance of accidents that which in heaven is really the body of Christ. If, moreover, the proposition is understood figuratively, just as it seems that the Gospel history understands it, then by the pronoun "this" the bread ought to be understood and denominated.

(11) But as to the form of the words, Master Armachanus[65] maintains how no form of words as to language and terms is universally required, since authors have written in various languages, as for example Matthew in Hebrew, Mark in Italic, Luke in Syriac, and Paul in Greek. And since even today in these languages and still others men perform the sacrament in accordance with the teaching of the faith of Scripture, the conclusion is obvious.

(12) Thus even though a priest can perform the sacrament in English and in other barbarous languages, yet he would sin thereby out of presumption by disregarding Latin or the language which the Church of his own time, place, and nation commonly uses by mixing language in the act of consecration against the custom of the place. About the limits of this difficulty there is fruitless contention concerning the heaviness of the sin committed in this matter, since man ought, unless for a great, urgent, and reasonable cause, to conform to the praiseworthy custom of the place wherein he dwells.

(13) Furthermore, as to the form of the words in the Latin language in which the Roman Church holds the faith of Scripture, it seems that there is no form of words universally

[63] There now follows a discussion of the Old Testament figures of the sacrament: pascal lamb, water from the rock, manna. See *De Eucharistia*, 86 ff.
[64] Augustine, *In Joannem*, XIII, 3, par. 5, *PL*, 35:1495.
[65] Armachanus. Archbishop Richard FitzRalph, *Summa in quaestionibus Armenorum*, IX (Paris, 1511). For Wyclif's indebtedness to FitzRalph's treatise, see Wyclif, *De ente praedicamentali*, 144, 152, 157; *De potestate pape*, *passim*.

required for the celebration of the Eucharist; for the usage of
our Church differs from all those four, just as all of them vary
among themselves more or less.[66] . . .

(21) No faithful person (I say) doubts that God could give
a layman the power to perform the sacrament, just as a layman,
since he could be a priest (as the logicians say), could perform
the sacrament. Surely it seems according to the testimony of
Augustine, Chrysostom, and other saints that every predestined
layman is a priest, and a much more devoted layman performing the sacrament, since he would give sacred ministry to the
Church, would have the *raison d'être* . . . of a priest.[67] Nevertheless, just as the Church has reasonably varied in the words of
consecration from all these four Evangelists, yet has preserved
the meaning intended, which the faith of Scripture requires,
so has the Church for good reason ordained that only those
priests who possess religiosity and dignity in morals should
perform this sacrament. Of little value, however, is the fact
that Christ gave that office to each one of his apostles individually. Nor does it appear to me an efficacious testimony that the
apostles were wont to act in this as the type of the Universal
Church, but rather of priests individually. Nor is it appropriate
on account of necessity for the ministry of the accidents of this
host to be further extended while it is a fact that the faithful
layman (who has never seen the host) by his toil receives the
body of Christ more efficaciously than the priest, since according to Augustine . . . to believe piously in Christ is to receive
his body. He says: "For what do you prepare your teeth and
belly? Believe and you have eaten."[68] For it is necessary that
there be spiritual eating . . . which consists in the pious and
gracious consideration of how Christ suffered for the human
race. . . .

(38) There is no doubt that error in such matters condemns
the one who falsely adores the host. It is clear that it is necessary
to treat this matter concerning the Eucharist because doubtless
one of these ways is manifestly heretical, . . . [for it] holds
very pertinaciously a sense contrary to the author of Scripture
and dismisses the teaching of Christ in matters very necessary
to salvation. It imposes upon itself implicitly the authorization
of the most wicked abomination, although famous doctors of

---

[66] There follows a comparison of the words of institution as found in the
Gospels and Paul, and as used by the Church.
[67] Wyclif, *De ecclesia*, 457.
[68] Augustine, *In Joannem*, XXV, 6, par. 12, *PL*, 35:1602.

the law of the Church, holding [it] in little esteem, state among other opinions that the bread and wine remain after consecration. On this they argue but do not reject it, as they cannot, although they rather favor the false part. If, therefore, those renowned doctors of the law of the Church do not condemn as heretical the fact that the bread remains, but prove that this follows from the aforesaid law *Ego Berengarius*, it is likely (as before) that the less learned doctors will not attempt to declare this opinion heretical; but so as far as they have tried, I know that they are not able, while they cannot prove this opinion to be false. It is not therefore a matter of concern in what sort of vessel (when his morals are preserved) the priest may consecrate [the Eucharist]. But (as has been said) the custom appropriate to the country should be kept, and—with probity preserved—uprightly to meditate upon Christ. This is infinitely better than to celebrate the sacrament. Nor is it out of keeping that Christ be sacramentally in the wine mixed with water or other liquid, nay, in the midst of the air, but preeminently in the soul, since the end of the sacrament is for Christ to dwell in the soul through virtues. In this way the layman, mindful of the body of Christ in heaven, more efficaciously and in a better manner than this priest who performs the sacrament, yet with equal truth (but in another manner), causes the body of Christ to be with him. . . .

(43) But there is difficulty concerning the equality of the goodness of the host, since it is the sign of Christ and not a part of him; while therefore that host signifies, among other things, the union of Christ with the Church, and the sign of the one bringing about that union more efficaciously signifies it than that sign which hinders the union. Therefore a sacrament of this sort is more efficacious in a good priest than in a bad one. Thus are to be understood many decrees which command that man not hear the Mass of a priest notoriously fornicating; therefore, I say, it ought not to be heard, for it is hateful both to God and man and harmful to the Church.

(44) From this it seems that by no means the Mass but rather the host is better in one priest and less good in another; for it is both an efficacious sign to call to memory the life of Christ and is a good sacrament, but in one priest it is for this a more efficacious sign and in another less efficacious. Therefore, thus is the sacrament proportionally better.

(45) The Catholic distinguishes, I say, between the natural goodness of the host (the same in other, unconsecrated bread)

and the moral goodness thereof, and he will see that he can
understand it more or less according to the merit and holiness
of the priest's life. He cannot through himself take on holiness
from the presence of the humanity of Christ, for thus Judas
eating with Christ and a wicked priest sacramentally receiving
Christ and the host would be holy. For he is capable of greater
holiness than an inanimate object which has holiness ambiguously in itself, as, for example, the water of baptism has in
itself grace as a sign or occasionally produces grace in the person
who communicates through the sacrament; so that the holiness
which he has from the presence of the body of Christ is seen to
be equal in every Eucharist, but the holiness arising out of the
blessing of the priest seems correspondingly to vary as to his
merit. . . .

5

. . . (13) Furthermore, as to the sacramental words, it seems
probable [69] . . . that Christ consecrated . . . this sacrament
with pure intention . . . , before he uttered those words. For
as Matthew and Mark relate: "Jesus took the bread, blessed
and broke and gave it to his disciples and said to them, 'Take
and eat; this is my body.' " [70] Note the order of the words: . . .
the consecration of the bread preceded the words, "This is
my body." Secondly, it seems credible according to the faith
of Scripture that they understood the words of consecration as
referring to the bread and the wine, since all four Evangelists
note that Jesus took the material bread in his hands, broke it,
bade it be eaten, and asserted it to be his body. The same is
true of the wine. What could be plainer than the text of
Mark . . . where it is said, "Having taken the cup and giving
thanks he gave it them, and all of them drank from it, and he
said to them, 'This is my blood' "? [71] Here it is clear that he
calls the wine contained in the cup his "blood." The same is
true in Matthew. [72] . . . That the expression of these verses is
figurative and in some manner (but not essentially) conversive
of wine into blood, seems more in keeping than a literal interpretation of the Master's words. Since the figurative sense is
true, it would be false to hold that this is Christ's body in the
sense of identical predication. If, moreover, the pronoun "this"
refers to bread and wine in the beginning and in the end
conversion takes place, then the proposition would be false

[69] FitzRalph, op. cit., IX, c. 5.   [70] Matt. 26:26; Mark 14:22.
[71] Mark 14:23 f.   [72] Matt. 26:27 f.

in its succession or not pertaining to the conversion, unless it be vainly imagined that God instituted such a proposition in order to have the power of converting in such a manner —a baseless conjecture. If the pronoun refers to Christ's body, then nothing new is constituted (such as the making of Christ's flesh). But if the pronoun connotes that this, under these nonsubjected accidents, is the body of Christ, this idea is groundlessly sought, vainly imagined [as it is] against the order of Scripture. I would like these folk—who fancy from this text that it means conversion without the essence differing —to attend to the [real] meaning of this Scripture. Therefore it seems to me in any event that in the sacramental words there is a figurative expression more efficacious than in these: "But the rock was Christ," while those words occasionally bring it to pass that Christ's humanity is really . . . but sacramentally present in every part of the consecrated host.[73] Thus that host is a sign more efficacious than bread blessed by a layman, and blessed by a priest, according to another form. . . .

7

. . . (57) Here we first state that many means of justifying the false worship of this sacrament have been dreamed up, for example, transubstantiation, conversion, identification and impanation, and the like. In all these the faithful person should beware of heresy; inasmuch as the first heresy of the disciples arose over this sacrament, so has many another heresy arisen therefrom. For this reason one should heed the Catholic sense of Scripture and the precautions of the holy doctors who have spoken on this matter. It will, moreover, serve as a norm for Scripture in every instance to be accepted according to the Catholic faith, and especially according to Christ's words of institution: "This is my body." I have often explained the sense of these words.

(58) Nor does it follow that anyone eliciting such a meaning is quoting Holy Writ, since it is fitting that the Holy Spirit impress the sacred meaning upon Holy Writ. Whence preserving the truth of Holy Writ in its entirety, we Christians are permitted to deny that the bread which we consecrate is identical with the body of Christ, although it is the efficacious sign thereof. For we are allowed some variation in our reasoning so long as we hold to the faith, just as they were wont in the

73 See also Wyclif, *De Eucharistia*, 144; cf. *De apostasia*, 184.

Early Church to baptize in the name of the Lord Jesus Christ
and later (according to a more precise form of the gospel) in
the name of the Trinity. It is just like a wise guard who is permitted to open or close the gates of a castle at his discretion.
For as "many went back," [74] believing Christ's flesh and blood
to be bodily food which they were to eat in a physical
manner . . . , so even today there are many who think that the
bread perceivable by the senses on the altar is identical with
Christ's body. They fail to distinguish between the figure and
the thing figured, and to heed the figurative meaning.

(59) But let us suppose that the whole community of Christians in contravention to the rule [*irregulariter*] recognizes this
meaning, without fabricating a falsehood about accidents
existing of themselves. Let us suppose [further] that they
accept the phrase, "This sign is the body of Christ," in the
Catholic sense, so that *to be* means "to figure sacramentally";
still it does not follow that the bread is identical with the body
of Christ, as is clear to anyone who heeds his sense perception.
Nor does it indeed follow, if the bread thus figures Christ's
body, that it then becomes numerically identical with that very
body; nor is very great authority at hand for the acceptance
of one expression or another. The Fathers of the Church never
truly believed that that bread was numerically identical with
Christ's body; nor do the present-day priests who consecrate
the sacrament so believe. For then would the infirm have
touched the host more devoutly than "the woman who touched
the hem of Christ's garment." [75] Yet they would have treated
the Lord's glorious living body as infinitely more honorable
than they actually treat that bread. And it is obvious that
neither faith in Scripture, nor the holy doctors, nor the laws of
the Church require that all such consecrated bread become
identical with Christ's body.

[74] John 6:67, Vg.; 6:66, E.V.   [75] Luke 8:44.

CONCILIARISTS

Conciliarism as Ecclesiastical Reform

THE FOURTEENTH CENTURY WITNESSED PROFOUND changes in the constitution of the Catholic Church which basically transformed its character and have continued to affect it ever since. The first of these occurred during the fateful period of the Avignonese papacy (1309–1377), when the power over the Church was centralized in the hands of the popes and the administrative structure of the Church was thus essentially altered. As the result of these far-reaching changes, voices of protest and demands for reform gained the support of many prominent leaders. Hence there arose many advocates of reform whose programs, although varied, were at one in their opposition to the abuses of the papacy.

One of these abuses, which called forth determined denunciation, was the pro-French political orientation of the papacy. Ever since the election of the Gascon Clement V(1305), who chose Avignon as his see (1309), most of the popes and cardinals were French. It is no wonder that they were generally regarded as subservient to the French court, although Avignon itself belonged then to the king of Naples. But since during most of this period France and England were at war (the so-called Hundred Years War), it can readily be understood that the English developed a deep-seated and patriotically motivated resentment against the highest ecclesiastical authority which was supporting the interests of their national enemy.

Another cause of the widespread opposition to the papal *curia* was found in its oppressive fiscal policy, which gained for it a reputation for rapaciousness and unscrupulous extortion, for shameless traffic in dispensations and simoniacal practices in general, rarely equaled previously. As the common saying

91

went, "All things are for sale in Avignon." The *curia* increasingly reserved for itself appointments to benefices ranging from local parishes to archiepiscopal sees. A large number of legal cases, formerly within the jurisdiction of diocesan courts, were declared the prerogative of the *curia*. The papacy likewise multiplied its sources of revenue. These and similar changes introduced into the administration of the Church profoundly altered its character: from a body enjoying a considerable degree of local autonomy it was transformed into a highly centralized and absolutistic organization increasingly subject to the will of the pope.

No wonder that throughout the fourteenth century voices were raised against this persistent encroachment upon the ancient rights of the Church! In England, the protest took the form of legal enactments, namely, the statutes of Provisors (1351) and of *Praemunire* (1353). But the most powerful opposition was voiced by John Wyclif. On the Continent the center of the antipapal agitation was the court of the emperor Louis IV, the Bavarian, who, having been excommunicated by Pope John XXII, gave asylum to such prominent and powerful papal antagonists as Marsiglio of Padua, John of Jandun, and William of Ockham.

When at last Pope Gregory XI, yielding to the pressure of Saint Catherine of Siena and of others, returned to Rome (January, 1377), he did not long survive this praiseworthy step he had taken, but died a little over a year later (March, 1378). It was the election of his successor that created the long-drawn-out crisis of the Great Schism, during which there existed at first two rival popes, and after 1409 three. The rival factions of the college of cardinals, unable to agree upon a mutually acceptable partisan candidate, finally compromised on the Neapolitan Bartolomeo Prignano, the Archbishop of Bari, who assumed the name of Urban VI. But if they thought that they could easily dominate him and sway him to their will they soon discovered their mistake. In his zeal for reform, he treated the cardinals, those "princes of the Church," grown accustomed at Avignon to luxury and self-indulgence, with flagrant harshness and discourtesy. Within a few months thirteen cardinals, ten of them French, revolted. Escaping to Anagni, they repudiated Urban, claiming that they had elected him under duress, and anticipating the support of the French king, Charles V, they proceeded to elect a man more to their liking.

They chose, on September 20, 1378, the young Cardinal

Robert of Geneva, who assumed the name of Clement VII;
thus the Great Schism was begun. It was destined to last almost
four decades (1378-1417). Since Clement, after an unsuccessful
attempt to conquer Rome, made Avignon once more the papal
residence, France and the countries within its orbit (some German principalities, Scotland, Savoy, Spain, and Portugal)
pledged their allegiance to him. Those that supported England
remained faithful to Urban. The emperor, Wenceslas IV
(1378-1419), adhered to the policy of his father, the celebrated
Charles IV, who had done much to rescue the Avignonese
papacy from French predominance. But the German princes
were divided between Urban and Clement. In 1381, Wenceslas
sent a delegation to Paris with a view to win the regent, Louis
of Anjou, to the side of the Roman pope. And although the
attempt was unsuccessful, it still resulted in important—in fact,
far-reaching—consequences.

For the University of Paris had among its celebrated masters
many Germans and other nationals whose careers had been
gravely affected by the schism. Since Urban disposed of many
rich and important benefices in Germany, subjects of the Empire teaching at a university under his rival's jurisdiction were
likely to be discriminated against. In fact, the damage was of a
more positive character: Urban frankly used every means in
his power to cause harm to the German masters at the University of Paris.

All this provided a positive motivation toward the demands
that the schism be ended, and led to the emergence of the
conciliar movement.[1] It is, therefore, no wonder that the leaders
of this movement were, first of all, the German masters in Paris,
among whom the learned canonist Conrad of Gelnhausen (d.
1390), and the leading theologian Henry of Langenstein (d.
1397), were the most prominent. But it must not be supposed
that the conciliar principle of representative government in the
Church was originated by them. The idea had been advocated
with varying degrees of radicalism by John of Paris, Marsiglio
of Padua, William of Ockham, and Michael de Cesena. John's
treatise, De potestate regiae et papali (On the Power of the King
and the Pope, 1302), denied the pope the right to define
dogmas and asserted that he could be deposed for a cause.
Marsiglio's Defensor pacis (Defender of Peace, 1324) has proved
a perennial source both of the inspiration and of concrete
proposals of Church reform. He taught that the Church

[1] F. M. Bartoš, Čechy v době Husově (Jan Laichter, Prague, 1947), 26 ff.

is composed of all the faithful. Supreme authority is vested
in a general council, elected by and representative of both
the clergy and the laity of the entire Church. The council
has authority over all matters ecclesiastical and dogmatic,
although its pronouncements must conform to Scripture. The
pope and clergy have no authority in matters secular, although
councils are to be called by secular rulers, not by the pope.
The papacy was not founded by Christ, but was an outgrowth
of the historical process.

Ockham goes even farther in his *Dialogue* (1343), and advocates that women be included as members of general councils.
He asserts not only that the pope can err and fall into heresy,
but that even the Roman Church—general councils, as well
as "the total multitude of the faithful" (he avoids saying "the
Church")—may err. He furthermore makes a distinction between the whole Church as a genus and the Roman Church
as a species, a distinction later used by Dietrich of Niem. When
a pope falls into heresy, it is the duty of the general council
to depose him. In such a case the council may be convoked
by bishops, secular princes, or members of the Church
generally.[2]

The Paris conciliarists, therefore, found these principles
extant and needed only to apply them to the concrete situation
arising out of the schism. The first stage of their program may
be designated as the *via concilii* (the way of the council), for the
essence of the plan rested on the assumption that all that was
needed was to have a general council pronounce on the legality
of the election of one or the other pope.

Conrad of Gelnhausen initiated the movement by the first
formal statement of conciliar principles in his *Epistola brevis*
(A Short Letter, 1379). He advocated the calling of a general
council, and appealed to the French and Roman kings,
Charles V and Wenceslas IV, to bring about its convocation.
The delegates were to be chosen by and from among the whole
Church. But the appeal fell on deaf ears in both Paris and
Prague. Nevertheless, this initial ill success did not discourage
Conrad. In May, 1380, he made public a larger treatise, *Epistola
concordiae* (A Letter of Concord),[3] which represented the first

---

[2] For a fuller, yet succinct, summary, cf. John T. McNeill, *Christian Hope
for World Society* (Willett, Clark & Company, Chicago, 1937), 75 ff.;
also E. J. Jacob, *Essays in the Conciliar Epoch* (Manchester, 1943), particularly 85–105.

[3] F. Bliemetzrieder, *Literarische Polemik zu Beginn des grossen abendländischen
Schismas* (Vienna, 1909), I, 111–140.

full statement of the early conciliar position. The treatise was dedicated to Charles V of France, and a copy of it was sent to King Wenceslas and to his later rival, Elector Ruprecht of the Palatinate. But this appeal was likewise ignored.

Since the principal arguments appeared almost verbatim in Henry of Langenstein's *Epistola concilii pacis* (A Letter on Behalf of a Council of Peace), it is best to defer a discussion of its contents. Suffice it to say that Conrad admitted that his arguments were not "legal" in the sense of not being grounded upon the canon law, but rested upon the necessity of dealing with an extraordinary situation by extralegal means, namely, by the concept of equity (ἐπιείκεια) rather than of positive law. Necessity is above positive law. The papacy exists for the Church, not the Church for the papacy. The good of the whole must be preferred to the good of an individual. All of this is, of course, based on Ockham, John of Paris, and Marsiglio, although Conrad never mentions them by name.

When the French king, Charles V, died in 1380, the direction of affairs passed to Louis, the Duke of Anjou, an ardent supporter of Pope Clement VII. The new king, Charles VI, was only twelve years old. Despite the unpropitious circumstances, the University of Paris unanimously adopted a resolution (May 20, 1381), pledging themselves to work unceasingly for the calling of a general council. They proposed to secure the co-operation of all rulers and hierarchs, provided the French court approved such a measure. This was the work of Conrad of Gelnhausen and Henry of Langenstein, the latter of whom had worked out a detailed program of action in his *Letter on Behalf of a Council of Peace*.[4] Because of the importance of this treatise, large selections of it are included in this volume. The section dealing with the *via concilii* is obviously dependent upon Conrad of Gelnhausen[5]; but the latter's work was similarly used by Peter d'Ailly, who incorporated almost all of Chapters XVI–XIX into his *Tractatus super reformatione ecclesiae* (A Treatise on the Reformation of the Church)[6]; and John Gerson, whose verbatim transcript (save one section) of it was published by the Council of Constance.[7] It was likewise used on the same occasion by Dietrich of Niem.[8]

---

[4] E. du Pin, *Gersoni opera omnia*, II, 809 ff. I have based this analysis on James Kerr Cameron's unpublished thesis, "Conciliarism in Theory and Practice, 1378–1418," in the Hartford Seminary Foundation Library.

[5] A. Kneer, *Die Entstehung der konziliaren Theorie* (Rome, 1893), 84–107.

[6] *Ibid.*, 82.   [7] J. B. Schwab, *Johannes Gerson* (Würzburg, 1858), 12.

[8] Finke, *Acta*, III, 129 ff.

Langenstein cites numerous examples from the history of the Church up to the eleventh century (particularly from the early Spanish councils) to prove that secular princes and bishops were called upon to work zealously for the reformation of the Church. The third division of his work is most important, despite the fact that it was taken almost word for word from Conrad's *Epistola concordiae*. As a theologian, Henry was glad to avail himself of the legal proofs assembled by the canonist, Conrad. He holds, contrary to his friend, that a general council is infallible. As for the mode of papal election, Henry asserts that no method has an exclusive divine authority. The Church has used many different practices down to the time of Nicholas II. The right to elect the pope belongs to the bishops and should revert to them when the cardinals abuse it. In case bishops fail to exercise it, the faithful of the whole Church should then take over the election of the pope. The general council represents the entire Church, not merely the pope and the hierarchy. Henry suggests that national councils be called for the election of delegates to the general council.

This bold program espoused by the University of Paris disquieted the French court, which in the end forbade it as detrimental to the interests of Pope Clement VII. The university had to promise obedience to him. Thus the conciliar idea suffered a setback which greatly delayed the university's efforts to solve the problem of the schism. Moreover, the court's order resulted in the mass emigration of the German masters and students from the university, which thus lost not only its hegemony in the academic life of the time, but about one half of its masters and students as well. These Germans were instrumental in establishing, soon afterward, the University of Vienna, of which Henry of Langenstein became virtually the founder as well as the chief ornament. The University of Heidelberg was likewise organized soon afterward. Henceforth, the leaders of conciliarism at the University of Paris were Frenchmen—John Gerson and Peter d'Ailly.

For some thirteen years the conciliar agitation practically ceased. It was given a new impetus when the Avignonese pope, Clement VII, died (1394). He was succeeded by a Spaniard, Pedro da Luna, who assumed the title of Benedict XIII. But the very fact that he was not French lost him the favor of the French court. Hence the occasion was auspicious for a new attempt at promoting the conciliar aim. The king convened a national council (1395), which voted overwhelmingly for a renewal of the efforts to end the schism. The university now formulated its strategy differently: instead of going back to the original plan of submitting the disputed election to the adjudication of a general council, it now adopted the so-called *via cessionis* (the way of cession). The aim of the new policy was to secure the resignation of both popes and thus to clear the way for the election of a new, generally acknowledged one. Representatives of the university and of the French king were sent to Oxford, Vienna, Buda, and Prague, in an effort to secure support for their plan. King Wenceslas refused to receive the university delegation, although he treated the royal emissaries somewhat more politely. Both popes exerted themselves to the full to thwart the new scheme. Pope Boniface IX, in his determination to bind Wenceslas more firmly to himself, offered to crown him emperor. Shortly after, Wenceslas attended the diet of Frankfort, where the electors advised him against the French proposal. (It is possible that on this occasion the youthful Hus was in the king's entourage and met, for the first time, his future judge at the Council of Constance, Bishop Peter d'Ailly.)[9] Nevertheless, the meeting between the Roman and the French kings did take place at Rheims in March, 1398, but ended without much success for the French plan. All Wenceslas was willing to do was to send a delegation to both Rome and Avignon, but when Benedict refused to consider the plan, Wenceslas did not trouble himself to make a similar inquiry in Rome.[10]

Thereupon, France decided to act alone, and declared its withdrawal of obedience from Benedict (July, 1398). In fact, French troops laid a siege to Avignon, but after some years of fighting, the court concluded peace and again recognized Benedict (1403). Duke Louis of Orléans, the brother of King Charles and the pope's ally, undertook to secure Benedict's abdication on condition that his rival should do likewise; but the crafty Spaniard promised to do so only "if the good of the Church should require it." Of course, in his opinion, the good of the Church never required it. This was a bitter defeat for the University of Paris, for had Benedict consented to abdicate on the conditions proposed, the end of the schism would actually

---

[9] Kamil Krofta, *Listy z náboženských dějin českých* (Historický Klub, Prague, 1936), 146.

[10] Bartoš, *op. cit.*, 151 ff.; Johann Haller, *Papsttum und Kirchenreform* (Berlin, 1903), I, 228 f.; also N. Valois, *La France et le grand schisme* (Paris, 1896), III, 145 ff.

have been in sight. For Boniface was expected to die soon. Actually, he died the next year (October, 1404).

The failure of the *via cessionis* led to the third phase of the conciliarist strategy: to secure the co-operation of the cardinals and the other *curiales* of both obediences, and, by uniting them, to obtain the reunion of the Church. This plan was quite feasible, for it favored the cardinals' interest. The schism had divided the income from papal revenues between the two rival popes and their cardinals. Removal of the schism, therefore, would benefit the cardinals financially. Hence, their co-operation with the newest French plan was confidently expected.

Early in 1405 the university sent out its representatives to Rome. This group was successful in securing the adherence of some cardinals of the new pope, Innocent VII, to the plan. Shortly after, these Roman cardinals won a considerable victory by exacting from Innocent's successor (Innocent had died in November, 1406), Gregory XII, the promise that he would abdicate in the event that his rival, Benedict, would either resign or die. The French ecclesiastical council, which had been called to deal with Benedict, now induced the court to send a delegation to Benedict, requesting his unconditional resignation. Should he refuse to do so within twenty days, the whole kingdom was to refuse him obedience, as the university had already done.

When the delegates arrived in Marseilles, where the pope then resided, they were confronted with a clever *fait accompli*: Benedict had stolen a march on them by having signed an agreement with Gregory, whereby the two popes pledged themselves to meet at Savona for the purpose of terminating the schism. Confronted with such a diplomatic device, the French did not deliver their ultimatum.

Thereupon, there followed a disgraceful, tragicomical performance on the part of the two popes. Gregory secretly sought to free himself from his promise. Benedict, well informed regarding his rival's intentions, went as far as Porto Venere and waited there. Twenty-five days later Gregory, on his part, arrived at Lucca, and nothing his friends or foes could do would move him to take a step farther. He thus rendered Benedict a great service by assuming responsibility for the shameful comedy both were playing.

Despite Benedict's astute diplomacy, his cause in the end failed: in the first place, his powerful supporter, Duke Louis of Orléans, was assassinated in November, 1407. This freed the

French court from the duke's pro-Benedict influence. The obstinate conduct of the two popes now cleared the way for positive action. On January 18, 1408, the French court presented Benedict with an ultimatum to the effect that unless the schism were terminated by March 25, France would withdraw its recognition from him. The pope responded by threatening to place all France under an interdict.

The decisive French action emboldened the Roman cardinals to proceed against Gregory with similar vigor. But when they confronted him with their demands, he replaced them by new cardinals. Nevertheless, the deposed cardinals refused to acknowledge the act as lawful and fled to Florence, an ally of France. They renounced their obedience to Gregory, appealed to a general council, and urged the rulers of the Gregorian party to cease affording him support.

At the same time in France a crisis was reached: Benedict's vindictive bull caused such indignation that in the presence of the king, his court, high officials, and representatives of the university, he was declared a heretic, his bull was torn to pieces, and all subjects were strictly forbidden to render him obedience. The French commander in Italy was ordered to seize Benedict; but the latter escaped by a precipitous flight. Moreover, France reasserted the famous Gallican Liberties, declaring its virtual autonomy in matters ecclesiastical.

Thereupon, some of Benedict's cardinals joined the revolted Roman colleagues in the calling of a general council. They approached King Wenceslas, urging him to abandon Gregory and to join them in calling the council. Since Gregory had refused to restore Wenceslas to his former dignity as the king of the Romans (of which he had been deprived by Boniface IX), and since the cardinals held out a promise of restoring to him the imperial crown, he decided to support their cause. His archbishop, Zbyněk, however, remained faithful to Gregory. Under these circumstances, the united cardinals and the king of Bohemia issued writs calling a general council to Pisa for March 25, 1409.

The theoretical formulation of the conciliar views at this time was best expressed in John Gerson's *De unitate* (On Unity), begun on January 28, 1409. Because of its importance, it is included in this volume. The famed chancellor of the University of Paris also formulated his views in a sermon preached before the English delegates to the Council of Pisa,[11] and in

11 *Propositio facta coram Anglicis* (du Pin, *op. cit.*, II, 123–130; 209–224).

his treatise *De auferibilitate papae* (On Deposing the Pope). Connolly regards the treatise *De unitate* as practically constituting the program of the Council.[12] Gerson declares that the unity of the Church is of such importance that nothing must be allowed to stand in its way. He places his chief reliance on the principle of equity (ἐπιείκεια), which must supersede positive law when the common good of the Church requires it. Indeed, he does not hesitate to declare that when necessary the pope may be imprisoned. There is not the slightest doubt in Gerson's mind that the pope is subject to the general council. But he warns the cardinals to be sure not to elect a new pope unless he be universally acknowledged—the very thing they did not do. The sermon before the English delegation is similar in content, but in it Gerson expresses more clearly his view of the Church. It is a supernatural institution: the papacy is a permanent office, but its holders "fluctuate." "*Papa fluit, papatus stabilis est.*" [13] A general council, therefore, cannot abolish the papacy, but it does have control over the method of electing the pope. Hence, it can remove an unworthy pope and elect another.

The Council of Pisa cited both popes to appear; since they refused to acknowledge its jurisdiction, they were deposed, on June 5, as "notorious schismatics, prompters of schism, and notorious heretics, errant from the faith, and guilty of the notorious and enormous crimes of perjury and violated oaths." Thereupon, on June 26, without heeding Gerson's warning, they proceeded to elect a new pope in the person of the Archbishop of Milan, Peter Filargi, who assumed the name of Alexander V. He was chosen because he was a Greek, and therefore both the French and the Italian cardinals could unite on him. But if the French and English delegates expected fundamental reforms from him, they were quickly disillusioned. Alexander indeed granted minor reforms, but postponed all major ones until the meeting of the next council, which was to be held within three years. Thereupon, the Council of Pisa was closed.

The fiasco consequent upon the action of this Council is well known: for the two obstinate old men, Gregory and Benedict, continued to retain the obedience of a greatly diminished, but still considerable, following. Gregory had supporters in Germany and Italy, while Benedict was acknowledged in Spain and

---

[12] J. L. Connolly, *John Gerson, Reformer and Mystic* (Librairie Universitaire, Louvain, 1928), 170.
[13] *Propositio,* 128. "The pope passes, the papacy remains."

Scotland. Therefore, the election of Alexander V, instead of terminating the schism, aggravated it. Under these disheartening circumstances, the conciliarists had to resume their weary labors in order to bring success out of the failure.

Their purpose was greatly strengthened when John XXIII, Alexander's successor (for the latter had died less than a year after his election), failed to bring about unity of the Church by means of a military campaign against Gregory. Although at first he succeeded in driving his rival from Rome and in occupying the city, in June, 1413, King Ladislas of Naples, Gregory's supporter, drove John out. The latter then took up his residence in Florence. France could not help him, for it was in the throes of a civil war. Hence, John appealed to the Roman king, Sigismund, who happened to be staying in Italy. The latter welcomed the opportunity to advance his personal ambitions. Hence, under the skillful diplomacy of Cardinal Zabarella, who was the leading member of the college of cardinals, an agreement was reached between Sigismund and the college. By its terms, the king undertook to induce the pope to call a general council to Constance (an episcopal city within the boundaries of the Empire, and therefore "neutral"). The negotiating parties agreed (on October 30, 1413) that the council must bring about unity of the Church even if all three popes were to be deposed and a new one elected. Zabarella favored this solution, for he himself aspired after the papal tiara.[14] In December, Pope John sent out the first bulls calling the Council for November 1, 1414.

Among the writings of the conciliarists descriptive of their program at the time, Dietrich of Niem's *Ways of Uniting and Reforming the Church* may be taken as representative.[15] This lively dialogue is conducted by Dietrich with an imaginary high ecclesiastical dignitary. It was written in 1410, but was reworked later, when the author learned of the call for the Council of Constance, for a discussion of the aims of that Council forms an integral part of the work. Moreover, the latest editor, Hermann Heimpel, added the redaction of the text prepared in 1415. Because of its very great importance, a substantial portion of this treatise is included in this volume.

---

[14] Bartoš, *op. cit.*, 373.
[15] Hermann Heimpel, *Dietrich von Niem, Dialog über Union und Reform der Kirche, 1410* (Teubner, Leipzig and Berlin, 1933). This edition prints for the first time a second redaction of the work, dated 1415. There is a delightful essay on Dietrich in Jacob, *op. cit.*, ch. 11.

After an introductory description of the sorry state of the Church, the author defines his concept of what the Church should be. Of all societies, the Church is the highest. But this applies to the Universal Church, which has for its head Christ alone. The Roman Church, with the pope at the head, is only a part of the Church Universal. In this Dietrich follows Ockham. The Roman Church may err, and "may suffer schism and heresy, and may even fail." [16] The concepts of the Universal and the Roman Churches stand to each other in the relation of genus and species.

The chief aim of all reform must be the unity of the Church. In order to gain it, there must be effected, first of all, a reform of the papacy (*unio capitis*). Dietrich discusses three ways in which this reform may be accomplished: the ways of resignation, of deposition, and of forcible expulsion. But what if none of the three rivals should resign? Then "the Council . . . should withdraw from these three as from those who destroy the unity of the Church." [17]

The second task of the Council is to reunite the members into one communion. This will be accomplished if all members pledge their obedience to the one true pope, or withdraw from the obedience of two or three rival popes.

The right to summon the general council belongs not to the pope but "primarily to the bishops, cardinals, patriarchs, secular princes, communities, and the rest of the faithful." [18] Such a council is superior to the pope. "The pope himself is bound to obey such a council in all things. . . . From such a council no one can appeal. Such a council can elect, deprive, and depose the pope." [19]

The treatise then concludes with a detailed discussion of the reforms that the Council should institute. Most of them had been advocated by other reformers, among them John Hus, whom that very Council condemned to death.

The story of the Council of Constance is too well known to need extended description.[20] John XXIII was determined to retain his office at all costs, and so were his two rivals. When John was thwarted in his purpose, and saw the resolute will of the conciliarists to oppose him, he promised to abdicate if his

[16] Cameron's translation, p. 4.   [17] *Ibid.*, p. 14.
[18] *Ibid.*, p. 16.   [19] *Ibid.*, p. 17.
[20] J. H. Wylie, *The Council of Constance to the Death of Hus* (London, New York, 1900); Louise R. Loomis, "The Organization of Nations at Constance," in *Church History* (1932), I, 191–210.

rivals would do likewise. This gesture was greeted with such an outburst of wild enthusiasm that the emperor Sigismund threw himself at the pope's feet and a jubilant *Te Deum* was sung. But all this jubilation proved premature. Less than three weeks later John escaped from Constance in the guise of a common soldier, and almost succeeded in making his way across the Rhine into France. Fortunately, he was seized at Breisbach, and was returned to Radolfzell near Constance. There he learned that he had been deposed by the Council on May 29. Benedict was likewise deposed (July, 1417), but continued to claim the papal dignity until his death (1422). Gregory resigned in July, 1417, but only on condition that he be acknowledged as the legitimate pope—a condition accepted by the Council, whereby it abandoned its own guiding principle. Thereupon, the Council proceeded with the election of the new pope. He was chosen on Saint Martin's Day (November 11, 1417) in the person of Cardinal Odo Colonna, and assumed the title of Martin V. At last the Great Schism was over.

Limits of space prevent the inclusion of some excerpts from the writings of Cardinal Peter d'Ailly, who played a prominent part at the Council of Constance as well as before. Although his services in the cause of conciliarism deserve to be properly acknowledged, many writers (such as Salembier[21] and McGowan) accord him too high an evaluation. In the first place, many of the treatises upon which his fame rests are a verbatim copy of the works of his predecessors, particularly of Langenstein. Thus, for instance, the *Tractatus . . . de ecclesiae reformatione* is regarded by Valois[22] as wholly dependent upon the reform program presented to the University of Paris in 1411. The *Tractatus super reformatione ecclesiae*, read by him at Constance, is d'Ailly's best work, but as has already been pointed out, it is wholly dependent on the last part of Langenstein's *Letter on Behalf of a Council of Peace*. Neither Salembier nor McGowan mentions this fact. Other instances of d'Ailly's borrowing habits are listed by Bartoš.[23] But even though d'Ailly has utilized other people's work in the preparation of his own treatises, he still deserves credit for the courageous stand on behalf of the conciliarist program at the Council of Constance.

The conciliarist theory, which dominated the Councils of Pisa and Constance as well as Basel, was, however, defeated by

---

[21] In *Dictionnaire Catholique*, I, 648.   [22] Valois, *op. cit.*, IV, 204.
[23] F. M. Bartoš, *Co víme o Husovi nového* (Pokrok, Prague, 1946), 85.

the clever manipulations of Pope Eugenius IV (1431–1447). Because of the Hussite Wars, in which the rebellious Czechs were uniformly victorious, he was forced to call the Council of Basel to negotiate with them (1431). This Council, exercising its prerogatives in accordance with the conciliar theory, summoned the pope to appear before its tribunal. He countered by ordering the Council to be transferred to Ferrara, and later to Florence. Nevertheless, a considerable body of the members remained at Basel, and, having deposed Eugenius, elected Amadeus of Savoy as Felix V. But because Eugenius was able to secure the submission of the Eastern Orthodox Church at the Council of Florence (1439), this Council finally gained general recognition. Therewith, conciliarism was to all practical purposes rendered ineffective, although it was not destroyed.

But this does not signify that the cause of reform was dealt a deathblow. Reform efforts, in fact, gained new impetus from the desperately corrupt condition into which the so-called Renaissance papacy had fallen—a state of affairs which could be compared only with the degeneracy of the tenth century papacy. Furthermore, the "political popes" of the last quarter of the fifteenth century added to the moral degradation and personal vice unbridled ambition, which drove them to conduct themselves like secular princes or *condottieri*. This was particularly true during the term of office of Alexander VI (1492–1503), who openly and scandalously supported his son, Caesar Borgia, in the latter's unscrupulous designs for the conquest of Italy. The pontificate of Julius II (1503–1513), characterized by a determined policy of military conquest, strangely contrasted with the claims of his spiritual office. Erasmus openly denounced it.

Under such conditions it is no wonder that agitation for reform was kept alive. Had it not been for those who were consumed with zeal for the Lord's house, there would have been no hope of ending the scandalous condition in the Church. The principal advocate of reform at the time was Desiderius Erasmus, whose story is told elsewhere in this volume. But John Major (1470–1550) also deserves notice. He was professor of philosophy and theology in Paris, and in 1518 returned to his native Scotland, becoming the principal regent of the University of Glasgow. In 1522, Major removed to St. Andrews University, where George Buchanan and probably John Knox were his pupils. Both were deeply indebted to him with respect to political theory. In his Paris period Major had supported

Gallicanism in the spirit of conciliar principles, and had taken a prominent part in the protest of the University of Paris against the abolition of the Pragmatic Sanction of Bourges (1517). Furthermore, the university had advocated the calling of a general council. This action inspired Luther in his struggle with the papacy to make a similar request. Dissatisfied with his appeal *Ad papam melius informandum*, he followed it up, on November 18, 1518, with an appeal to a future general council. This document was drawn up in conformity to that published by the University of Paris the year previously,[24] and reflected phrases from the *Sacrosancta* (1415).

For these reasons, a short *Disputation by John Major on the Authority of a Council*, written after the Reformation had begun, has been included in this volume. It is clear from this example that conciliarism was not exterminated by the anticonciliarist decree *Execrabilis* of Pope Pius II (1460), but had bold advocates within the Church itself, even after the outbreak of the Reformation.

[24] B. J. Kidd, ed., *Documents Illustrative of the Continental Reformation* (Oxford, 1911), No. 20, p. 40.

Henry of Langenstein:
A Letter on Behalf
of a Council of Peace[1] (1381)

THE TEXT

1. THE SINS OF THE PEOPLE ARE THE CAUSE OF THE SCHISM

To all who seek to guide the helm of the bark of Peter amidst the tempests of surging seas, and also to those of orthodox faith who, in working for the reformation of the Church, are in any way bound with me, such as I am, to ponder the things "that belong to the peace of Jerusalem." [1a]

"I have seen iniquity and strife in the city,"[2] said the prophet of God. While the inhabitants of the city of God, the Universal Church of the faithful, have been sitting in dwelling houses of security, comfort, and plenty, they have grown fat, gorged, and gross; their flesh has grown hot, their spirit cold, the world become wise and God foolish [in their eyes]. Thus the devil has raised himself up; virtue has been outlawed, vice has taken its place; the malice of succeeding generations has rendered the straight paths of the fathers crooked; and the decrees of

---

[1] The Latin title of this treatise is *Epistola concilii pacis*. This document was first published by H. von der Hardt in his *Magnum oecumenicum Constantiense concilium de ecclesiae reformatione* (Frankfurt and Leipzig, 1697), II, 1, 3–60, under the title *Consilium pacis de unione ac reformatione ecclesiae*, and reproduced by E. du Pin in his *Gersoni opera omnia* (Antwerp, 1706), II, 809–840. That "*Epistola concilii pacis*" is the correct title was shown by A. Kneer, *Die Entstehung der Konziliaren Theorie* (Rome, 1893), 76. The text of the first chapter and part of the second is lacking in Hardt (*op. cit.*), but was later published by him and then by O. Hartwig, *Henricius de Langenstein dictus de Hassia* (Marburg, 1857), II, 28–31. Much that is contained in these two chapters and practically all of chapters 12, 13, and 15 are taken verbatim from Conrad of Gelnhausen, *Epistola concordiae*, edited by F. Bliemetzrieder, *Literarische Polemik zu Beginn des grossen abendländischen Schismas* (Vienna, 1909), III ff. The arguments against the *via concilii* in chapter 12 had been taken by Conrad from the tractate of Peter Amelius (Cardinal of Embrum) (*ibid.*, 91–110).

[1a] Ps. 121:6, Vg.; 122:6, E.V.   [2] Ps. 54:10, Vg.; 55:10, E.V.

the Church have been violated. It has become the custom for the Church to be built on blood relations and the sanctuary of God maintained as if it were a family possession. Hence the flock of the Lord is today deprived of its shepherd; the patrimony of the Church is consumed in vainglorious ostentation; and the temples for the worship of God lie open and in ruins. The unworthy are raised high with dignities. The ministers of the Church seek after the things of the world, despise the things of the spirit, set their minds on the laws of the world and upon the fomenting of lawsuits, and are not mighty in the Word of God to kindle men's souls.

What more? The regulations of spiritually minded men of former times, most worthy of [our] observation, are by the negligence of their successors overthrown. To them the antiquity of the fathers, out of harmony with the works of darkness, has been displeasing, while the novelty of their own inventions, vying with the law of God, has given them pleasure. For in this way lawsuits are perpetuated and a thousand deceits committed in the city of God. It is simony that sells benefices, that confers bishoprics. It is money that secures indulgences, absolutions, dispensations, and confirmations. It is avarice with its exactions that ruins bishoprics, that impoverishes monasteries. In a word, it is avarice, kindled by its own lust, that does everything, that perverts all.

Finally then, what is the beginning and the end of vice? It is pride, the rival of peace, confounding with discord the entire city of God. Therefore, this is the iniquity that the prophet saw, which, I fear, conceived the distress and brought forth the strife.

2. THE UNHEARD OF CORRUPTION IN THE CHURCH AT THE TIME OF THE SCHISM

But what is this strife? Alas! Alas! The present contentious schism is not merely an opponent of divine and human law. It has tried even to break the inviolable law against contradiction; since positive law seeks to assert that the statements of the cardinals are true, while they themselves make contradictory statements with, as it were, equal testimony of the truth, as will be shown below. What wonder is it, then, if this wretched schism, the progeny of contradiction, the monster of monsters, the begetter of strife, the enemy (by its very hideousness) of all things, when it has destroyed the lawful courses,

confounds everything? This schism is entangled in much equiv-
ocation, is troubled by finely drawn distinctions. It is rending
the seamless robe of Christ, bringing confusion to the ecclesiastical order, dispersing the universities, propagating heresies
and errors, and offending the people of God in a thousand
ways. What is more horrible, it is deforming by its base
grotesqueness the bride of Christ, who, now that her head has
been divided, is become, as it were, headless, or even as a two-
headed monster. . . .

Is anyone amazed at this outcry, when he openly sees impending from this schism a thousand dangers to body and soul,
the corruption of morals, the oppression of the devout and
the humble, the exaltation of the vile and the reprobate, the
seduction of the simple, the introduction of the Antichrist, the
joy of the Saracens, the rejoicing of the Jews, the provocation
of war and battle? The Church's temporal possessions will be
scattered, and with the abandonment of the administration of
its sacred rites and the offering up of its prayers, its worship
diminished. Subjects will rise up against prelates and princes.
The scandalized laity will violently set themselves against the
clergy. Traducers will be multiplied.

[Today] consciences are being disturbed, damnable blas-
phemies are being hurled against the vicar of Christ, since
one of them is commonly believed to be the pope. Nevertheless,
they denounce each other blasphemously as the Antichrist and
a wily serpent, or as Mohammed and an infamous idol, and
with many other names which are and must be utterly abhorrent to Christian ears and lips, because of that fearful word of
the Saviour: "Whoever says to his brother, thou fool, shall be
liable to the fire of Gehenna." [3] . . .

Already,[4] however, by means of this schism, seeds of discord
and ill will are being scattered abroad in the provinces and
among the religious orders, the common people, the princes,
the prelates, and the priests, which are in future times going
to be continually bursting forth. Then the priestly ranks will
become base and degenerate, the devotion of Christians lan-
guish, and fervor for the faith become lukewarm. Liars will be
exalted, honest men outlawed.

Religion is in exile, apostasy rules supreme. The sun of
righteousness is being eclipsed and the moon of earthly filth

---

[3] Matt. 5:22.
[4] Beginning here the text as contained in E. du Pin, *op. cit.*, II, 809, is
followed.

beloved. For there are done, not those things that are of God, that are of justice, but what is agreeable. Because each of those contending for the supreme pontificate wishes to attract many supporters to himself he does not presume to deny anything to any powerful suppliant, and being afraid to offend his adherents, he neglects to do justice and to distribute fairly the dignities of the Church. What more? He pardons all, he absolves everyone indiscriminately. Whom one excommunicates, the other declares loosed; whom one condemns justly, the other, when he appeals to him, wrongfully justifies. . . .

3. These Papal Disagreements Provide an Opportunity for Church Reform

. . . Thus, although the face of flattering fortune is turned away and we are oppressed by adversity and enveloped by the wiles of Satan in the confused intricacies of the present schism, let us not believe that those who are suffering such things are alienated from Christ, but rather hope that we, when we have been reformed through this opportunity, will be restored to him in a better condition. For the prophet Amos said: "You only have I called out from the nations of the earth. Therefore, I shall visit upon you all your iniquities."[5] "Whom the Lord loveth he chastiseth."[6] "He scourgeth every son whom he receiveth."[7] And again, "I rebuke and chastise those whom I love."[8] God sees those who refuse to be corrected of their own desire and pricks them with the goads of adversity. This he is wont to do in a threefold way, as when he drives the reprobate to destruction; the elect, whom he sees to err, to correction; and the just to increase the glory of their merits. . . .

Therefore, let him who suffers trials learn not to complain even if he does not understand why he is being struck by misfortunes. Let him realize that in this way he is suffering justly, because he is being judged by One whose judgments are never unjust. Thus, that he may more easily endure his sufferings, let him drive away his sin for which he is bearing the just retribution. Then indeed is he justified, for he blames himself and praises the justice of God.

5 Amos 3:2.   6 Prov. 3:12.
7 Heb. 12:6.   8 Rev. 3:19.

4. The Solution of These Disagreements Must Be Undertaken by a General Council

. . . Now, of this schismatic iniquity, which is hindering the action of divine grace by its venomous seed, I believe an end can be made by three ways that are open to men. The first is this: that anyone who is conscious of being a party to the above-mentioned crimes take it to heart and through penance reconcile himself to God. The second: that it be arranged throughout the circle of the Universal Church to make continual supplication for divine mercy publicly in fasting, weeping, and prayer. The third: that when these preparations have been carried out for the bestowal of the grace of the Holy Spirit, a general council be called in the name of Jesus Christ to purge his Church from the iniquities and various excesses, all too common at this time, and, after these causes have been removed, to tear up from the very roots the present division in the city of God which this befouling and monstrous schism has brought forth.

Here is a way of peace, a way oft trodden by our fathers before us, a way of salvation. The record of past events, which is the teacher of modern men, ought surely to move Christian kings and princes to undertake with the greatest enthusiasm this way which is pleasing to God and demand its execution without delay. History informs us that formerly, through the devotion, patronage, and encouragement of kings, in past emergencies of the Church provincial and general synods of bishops were in the providence of God frequently called and that they faithfully submitted themselves and their lawsuits, as well as the correction and emendation of their laws, to the holy judgment of their councils. This is evident from a wide consideration of the proceedings of the councils which have been recorded. . . .

5, 6

[The writer seeks to prove his contention by a series of long quotations from the Spanish councils of the sixth and seventh centuries, from which he also draws the following conclusion:]

From these and similar actions of kings, it is evident that not only must secular powers, in proportion to their strength, assist in the summoning of a general council, but that our kings and princes, who are engaged in diverse wars and disputes, must, in accordance with the example and devotion of celebrated kings, faithfully and with obedient humility agree to the summoning of a council for the purpose of bringing about a general treaty of peace. . . .

7. IT IS THE RESPONSIBILITY OF THOSE WHO EXERCISE ROYAL AUTHORITY TO SEEK TO BRING ABOUT A GENERAL REFORMATION WITH THE HELP OF A COUNCIL

Thus may the princes of this age be compelled by every means to sow the seeds of concord and truth among all to the glory of God and for the good of the people, and to banish from the city of God the crime of discord and iniquity. May they be instructed by the examples of their venerable predecessors, who strove with all zeal to accomplish this end.

The emperors Valentinian and Marcian, rejoicing over the peace and tranquillity of the Church brought about by the Council of Chalcedon, spoke as follows: "Now, at last that which we have most earnestly and zealously prayed for has come to pass. The matter of contention has been removed from the orthodox law of Christians. At last remedies have been found for culpable heresy, and the divergent opinions of the peoples have been united in one harmonious agreement. For, from the separate provinces most devout priests have come to Chalcedon and thus an end has been put to the unholy dispute. Now, indeed, that man is truly irreverent and blasphemous who, after the pronouncements of so many priests, is left with something of his belief still to be discussed. It is, indeed, the height of madness to call for a lamp in bright daylight. In fact, whoever, now that this truth has been defined, goes on discussing it still further, is searching after untruth."[9]

8, 9, 10

[The writer addresses the prelates, and by a similar series of quotations from the Spanish councils, illustrating the zeal of former bishops for the reformation of the Church, exhorts them to work together for the uniting and reforming of the Church.]

9 *Decretales pseudo-Isidorianae et capitula Angilramni*, P. Hinschius, ed. (Leipzig, 1863), 288. It is worth noting that Marsiglio of Padua (*Defensor pacis*, II, 21), in defending the right of the emperor to call a general council, used this passage and also referred to the Spanish councils. Langenstein does not, however, draw the same conclusion.

11. An Earnest Exhortation for a New Reformation of the Holy Order in a New General Council and for a Peaceful Settlement

As these matters have been examined, I am now going to interpose a silence on this subject and address all together. I adjure you by the divine name, and by that day, terrible for all, the day of the Judge who is to come, and I exhort you, the patriarchs, cardinals, archbishops, doctors, prelates, and you illustrious kings and princes, and every strong man of the royal court, whom the divine goodness may delegate to take part in the holy council that must be called to remove the schism that has arisen, or render assistance toward that end— you I exhort to carry out a most careful examination of the matters that have forced their attention upon you, without respect of persons, without favor, or hatred, or the least trace of evil intention, or any unfair desire to subvert the truth. . . .

12. Eight Doubts Against the Power of a Council to Settle the Papal Schism

Sufficient advance has, I think, now been made with this kind of exhortation. Therefore, putting aside this florid style of writing, let us now come to the point at issue and again bring forward the truth that has, as it were, been urged advisedly by the indirect method of fine words, and that has now to be discussed in plain and unadorned language with the precise acuteness of a disputation, namely, whether to end the present schism it is expedient and necessary that a general council be held. . . .

[1] In the first place, it is argued that a council does not have such power, because it is abundantly defined and decreed in the law that these pronouncements and letters of the cardinals which pertain to their office, such as actions in conclave and other actions of which nothing can be known or proved by others, must, on account of their importance, dignity, and authority, be believed fearlessly. Therefore, there is no need of a council. For they themselves have asserted unanimously that one of the two elected is pope and that the other was merely elected in pretense owing to fear.

[2] Again it is argued: In the law it is abundantly clear that a forced election of a pope is null. Therefore, since the fact is

well known that at the election of Urban VI terror was aroused
by the rioting of the people, it is not necessary that a costly
general council be held.

[3] Again, it is reasoned: In such a synod, the individual
bishops and prelates merely have power over their own flock
but none of them has power over all the faithful, nor do they
all have power over all the faithful at one time, because, according to the law, the Roman Church alone has power to judge
all the faithful. This matter is, then, prejudicial and injurious
to the rights of the Roman Church, for, according to the
Decretals, none but the pope is able to determine her laws. . . .
Therefore, if all the prelates were to come together without
the authority of the pope, or the apostolic see, their assembly
would not be an authentic council but a conventicle (*conven-
ticulum*) and mock council (*conciliabulum*) which cannot enact
a decree that would be law.

[4] Again, to convoke a council is to call in question the
enactments and provisions of both of those elected, nay, rather,
the rank of both. If this were done, the majority of those who
before considered that they were sure, now that they have been
disturbed would begin to waver and cause an uproar, and the
latter evil would be worse than the former.

[5] Again, since at this time, A.D. 1381, neither of those
elected, Clement VII or Urban VI, is universally obeyed by
Christians as pope, and has not been for the past three years,
neither one is able usefully or validly to call a general council,
nor both together. As it is well known that there cannot be two
popes, it is not clear by which of the two or by whose authority
a council could be assembled. . . .

[6] Again, perhaps it is contrary to the advantage of the
elect that this be done. God changes, according to their necessity, the course of world events from prosperity to adversity. . . .
Surely this would in no way be profitable for the elect, who
must be tested by many inconveniences, trials, and persecutions,
before entering into the Kingdom of Heaven. . . .

[7] Perhaps it is the divine will that each of those elected
should rule and that the papacy be divided for a time, or
forever! . . .
Therefore, since it is not perfectly clear what the divine
will is, even in this matter of papal division, those who are
laboring thus early for the union of the Church in any way
whatever could possibly be fighting against God.

[8] Again, if we consider the condition of the primitive

Church, we shall see that in those days the Church was troubled by the faithlessness of the Jews, oppressed by the arbitrary rule of princes, and attacked on all sides by the uprising of heretics; that the prelates burned with zeal toward God and for the salvation of their neighbors, and were illumined from above by the light of life-giving knowledge and spiritual understanding; and that there was not, as today, an innumerable multitude of bishops and doctors. Then the Church was still young and unadorned by necessary ecclesiastical decrees and rules, and the authority of the pope was not, as today, clearly exhibited and exalted. Hence it was necessary to have various councils, provincial and general, in which wholesome and genuine provision might be made against the matters already mentioned. But now, because sufficient provision has been made by the teaching of the Holy Spirit in former councils and in the papal constitutions for all exigencies in accordance with equity, it is not appropriate that councils again be held. For it is written, "Once has God spoken, and he does not repeat the same matter" [10]; i.e., enough has been said for those who wish to understand.

It is argued that now the world is, as it were, different from what it was in the time of the primitive Church. The practices of the faithful and the zeal and affection of the rulers are all different. Therefore, another way of dealing with the perils that arise seems more fitting today than the way of councils. This way was once expedient, but now it is useless, having been completely neglected and abandoned by the ordering of the Holy Spirit, by whom the Church is governed. For it has been especially reserved for the pope and the college of cardinals to provide for the difficulties that arise.

Indeed, a council does not seem to be particularly expedient in the case of the present schism, because already the princes and prelates have been divided against themselves for a long time, and are, as it were, immovable in their beliefs, refusing, it would seem, to accept further enlightenment. And because the larger party, which adheres to one of the elected on account of their affinity to him, would, without a full discussion having been attempted, immediately decide for him.

Then, as experience teaches, matters are better handled by a deputation consisting of a few strong, experienced men than in the deliberations of a confused multitude which does not command any respect.

10 Job 33:14.

Again, it would be manifestly absurd for the just party or for the party which firmly believes that he is right in everything that was done, because he was himself present, to submit his case, in order that the truth may be known, to a council in which there would be ten times as many from the opposite party. Indeed, if Clement is the true pope, as Saint Peter was, he by exposing himself foolishly to danger and thereby rashly presuming upon the direction of the Holy Spirit would be rejecting and tempting the Lord. For although the Holy Spirit would not permit a council to err in a principal article of faith, nevertheless, this matter is not of such a nature, but is judicial, having to do with the law of election to the papacy in which error may result, as when a woman held the highest pontificate.[11]

Therefore, when these arguments have been taken into consideration, it is to be greatly feared that a new error, far worse than the former, might be raised up by the way of a general council. Thus, it is neither determined nor established to do much for the way of a council or to insist upon it in this instance.

There are many schisms and divisions over the papacy recorded by history; yet not one is ever spoken of as having been terminated by a general council, but by other and more helpful means. Thus, in answer to the proposition, it does not seem fitting that a council be held.

13. FOURTEEN ARGUMENTS BY WHICH THE RIGHT OF A COUNCIL IS DEFENDED

In opposition, it is argued that under both the old and the new dispensation councils of the faithful were often held over minor cases and causes. Therefore, in this case, one must also be held. Here it is permissible to draw a conclusion *a minori*.

The foregoing is obvious from the assembly of the synagogue, Numbers, ch. 27, etc., and also in the New Testament from an examination of the four councils held by the apostles, Acts, chs. 1; 7; 15; 21.

---

11 The legend of Pope Joan arose toward the end of the thirteenth century and was commonly believed until after the Reformation; cf. Döllinger, *Fables About the Popes in the Middle Ages*, Plummer tr. (New York, 1872). Much is made of the story by John of Paris, William of Ockham, Gerson, and Hus; cf. Lenfant, *Histoire de la Papesse Jeanne* (Cologne, 1694).

Likewise, from an examination of the councils of the modern Church it is clear that councils were often held to deal with minor issues. According to Isidore, *Etymologies*, Book VI, c. 16, "Before the time of Constantine Christianity was split up into various heresies, because the faithful had no freedom to come together" [12] (he means in councils, because here he is speaking about councils).

If in the time of the devout primitive Church, when holy popes and prelates, such as Sylvester and others, held office, general councils were assembled, often perhaps in circumstances of less danger or disadvantage than the present, why should not councils be assembled now to correct and cleanse the face of the Church of these stains? . . .

If it is said that then there was more need for councils on account of the heresies and heretics that were scattered abroad during those early times, we reply that in exactly the same way the prolongation of this schism will cause heresies and heretics to arise.

Again, the followers of Clement say that Urban has publicly declared as Christian teaching errors of a heretical nature.

Again, recently, on the fifteenth of June, the following question was put forward for debate in the University of Paris: "Whether or not in the present controversy which exists in the Church over the papacy it is heretical or schismatic to deny that one of the elected is pope." [13] On this subject an assembly was held and the question was keenly debated. Thus, in this case there is no lack of material for heresy. The mere expense, the scandals, and the innumerable dangers past and future of this situation should be sufficient cause for the assembling of a council.

Again, when the emperor Constantine wished to exalt the Church by a grant of temporal privileges, etc., he held a universal assembly of the imperial court. [14] Thus, a fortiori, a universal convocation must be held for the spiritual good of the Church.

Again, the case of this schism is new, complex, scandalous

---

[12] Migne, *PL*, 82:243; cf. *Corpus iuris canonici*, A. Friedberg, ed. (Leipzig, 1889), *Decretum*, pars I, dist. XV, c.1; I, 34.

[13] The Bishop of Paris had, on May 17, declared publicly that all who did not believe Clement VII to be true pope were heretics and schismatics. This statement caused great displeasure and led to the matter's being discussed by the university, which decided against the bishop; N. Valois, *La France et le grand schisme d'Occident* (Paris, 1896), I, 342 f.

[14] *Decretum*, pars I, dist. XCVI, c. 14; Friedberg, I, 342.

and full of danger. In former times the question did not arise and was not considered, except as one that could not be solved. Therefore, a discussion of it demands a general council.

From this it follows that the authority of one or the other of the colleges or of the individuals is not sufficient to settle completely this schism. For, although cardinals have been sent hither and thither throughout the provinces to give instruction about the truth, they have accomplished little. The schism has not ceased nor diminished as a result, but has gone from bad to worse, and the princes are more and more inflamed against one another. . . .

Again, new and perilous cases arising in any diocese are corrected in a particular or provincial council. Therefore, new and difficult cases which concern the whole world must be discussed by a general council. "For what affects all must consistently be dealt with by all or by the representatives of all." [15]

Again, it is evident that in matters of doubt or difficulty, as Augustine says, . . . reference must in the end be made to a council. "Against this heresy" (namely, the Pelagian), he writes, "there was at first much discussion; then, as the ultimate resource, it was referred to the episcopal councils." [16]

Again, in this very dangerous situation, as has been seen, help must undoubtedly be brought to the Church. This can be done in no better way or more efficiently than by a general council.

The conclusion is unavoidable. . . . Help cannot be brought to the Church either by the way of fact, which does not do justice, nor set men's hearts at rest, or by the way of the instruction of the faithful by the legates of the old cardinals, of whom all but two support the second one elected. Indeed, the latter way does not help the one elected second, because the cardinals remained peacefully with the one elected first, namely, Urban VI, for three months, and in deed and in word

---

[15] "Quod enim omnes tangit, ab omnibus vel vice omnium tractari debet et convenit." This Roman-legal maxim, brought into the canon law by Innocent III (*Decretales*, Lib. I, tit. 1, c. 7; Friedberg, II, 152. Cf. G. Post, "A Roman-canonical Maxim, 'Quod Omnes Tangit,'" in Bracton, *Traditio*, IV, 1946, 197 ff.), was appealed to by the earlier advocates of conciliarism, William Durand the Younger, Marsiglio of Padua, and William of Ockham, and then by all conciliarists from the outbreak of the schism.

[16] *De gratia et libero arbitrio*, I, 4: *PL*, 44: 886.

declared that he was pope.[17] They notified the princes by letter that they had elected a holy and upright man to be pope. On account of this and many other acts long since past that were displeasing to the laity, the clerics, and the whole world, the cardinals are no longer believed nor benefited by that way.

Again, what has been said above proves that the Universal Church, of which a general council is representative, is superior to the college of cardinals and to every other particular grouping (congregatio) of the faithful and to every single person of whatever dignity, even to the holder of the highest dignity, or precedence, the lord pope, in matters that are to be described later. Therefore, recourse must be made to such a powerful council, as to the supreme authority, in the present matter affecting the whole Church.

The conclusion is obvious. The foregoing is proved. For the Universal Church, which is not able to err or be exposed to mortal sin, is indeed superior to the college of cardinals and the pope because he does not have this prerogative. It was not said of him, "And the gates of hell will not prevail against her (eam)," [18] but of the Universal Church. Hence, Pope Anastasius II fell into heresy [19] and Pope Marcellinus into idolatry.[20]

It may be added that the college of the pope with the cardinals does not seem to have been more firmly established than the college of Saint Peter and the other apostles, whose constancy Christ, before his Passion, commended when he said, "Ye are those who have remained with me in my trials." [21] Nevertheless Peter denied Christ three times and all the apostles fled from Him and wavered in faith. Who, then, will dare to say that the college of the pope and cardinals is unable to sin, when, as a matter of fact, it is not found that this body was constituted by Christ?

17 Urban VI was elected on April 8, 1378. By July 20 all who had taken part in the election save the four Italian cardinals had fled to Anagni; cf. Valois, op. cit., I, 3 ff., 76 ff.
18 Matt. 16:18.
19 Decretum, pars I, dist. XIX, c. 9; Friedberg, I, 64. Anastasius II (495–498) was accused by many of the clergy at Rome of communicating with Photinus, deacon of Thessalonica, who was of the party of Acacius; Liber pontificalis, Duchesne ed. (Paris, 1886), I, xliii, 258n.
20 Decretum, pars I, dist. XXI, c. 7; Friedberg, I, 71. Marcellinus' (296–304) crime was that of apostasy and idolatry involving the offering of incense at pagan worship. However, he recanted and died a martyr; Liber pontificalis, I, 16.
21 Luke 22:28.

Again, there is no lack of those who say that the pope and the cardinals have often appointed to the principal dignities of the Church men most unworthy in age, knowledge, and morals. Indeed, this college has erred by acting in this way.

Again, Augustine, in the letter to Eleusius, the Felixes, Grammaticus, and the rest of the Donatists, proves that the pope is able to err in passing judgment and that he is subject to a general council. For, in speaking of the college of cardinals and the pope, he says, in words that can still be applied, indeed most justly applied, to them: "Let us suppose, then, that those bishops who pronounced judgment at Rome were not good judges; there still remained a plenary council of the Universal Church, where the matter could be discussed with those very judges, so that, if they were convicted of having judged wrongly, their decisions might be relaxed."[22] Therefore, the authority of a general council is greater than that of the pope and the college of cardinals. Even Saint Jerome, in the letter to Evander, suggests this when he writes, "If it is a question of authority, the world is greater than a city."[23]

Again, Saint Gregory, according to the *Decretum*, says, "I confess that I accept and revere the four general councils, (viz., Nicaea, Constantinople, Ephesus, and Chalcedon), as I do the four holy Gospels."[24] Therefore, the pope and the cardinals are subject to the decision and authority of the Gospel writings.

Again, bishops presiding in council declared Pope Symmachus absolved and freed from the accusations brought against him, as is contained in Dist. XVII.[25]

. . . Again, the archdeacon,[26] approving the gloss already written at the end of Dist. XV, c. *Sicut sancti*, added, "It is exceedingly dangerous to entrust our faith to the will of one

22 *Epistola* XLIII, c. viii, *Corpus scriptorum ecclesiasticorum Latinorum*, A. Goldbacher, ed. (Vienna, 1898), XXXIV, pt. 2:101.
23 *Epistola* CXLVI (LXXXV), *PL*, 22: 1194.
24 *Decretum*, pars I, dist. XV, c. 2; Friedberg, II, 35.
25 *Decretum*, pars I, dist. XVII, c. 6; Friedberg, I, 52. Symmachus (498–514) was accused by a section of the Roman Church of not celebrating Easter at the same time as other Christians, and also of a number of moral crimes. A synod was held at Rome in 501 by the command of Theodoric at which Symmachus was freed of all accusations; *Liber pontificalis*, I, 260; Hefele-Leclerq, *Histoire des conciles* (Paris, 1908), II, 957 ff.
26 Guido de Baysio (d. 1313), Archdeacon of Bologne; his chief work is his commentary on Gratian's *Decretum*, entitled *Rosarium seu in Decretorum Volumen Commentaria*.

man."[27] For this same reason in new and difficult cases the pope is accustomed to have recourse to the deliberations of a council, as the *De Summa Trinitate*[28] throughout makes evident.

Again, popes Sixtus and Leo are said to have cleared themselves publicly at general councils of accusations brought against them.[29] . . .

If it is said that these great popes, whom we have mentioned, acted in this way out of humility, we reply that, as the holy Fathers acted in this way, modern popes ought surely to imitate them in this and the Master of humility, who said, "Learn of me, for I am gentle and lowly of heart." [30] Let them not be puffed up with human pride against one another, but surpassing each other in humility let them strive for the peace of the Church and procure the holding of a general council.

Again, the Archdeacon and Johannes Andreae in the *Novella* hold that: "In a matter of the faith the competent judge of the pope is a council"; and in Dist. XL, c. *Si papa*: "In a matter of faith a council is able to condemn a living pope."

Again, Hostiensis [31] and other modern doctors of canon law hold that "in a case in which the deposition of a cardinal is impending, a general council would have to be convened that this be accomplished." Then, indeed, more so in the case of the present schism. Or is this case different?

Again, even if it were the case that this schism had not arisen, still there has been for a long time a need for a general council to reform the Church Universal in many other excesses and deviations, which are to be enumerated below. Perhaps because previous prelates have been disinclined toward this, God allowed this schism to arise that the ecclesiastics might, so to speak, be aroused, so that in a council, summoned because of this event, the Church might be reformed in this and other matters.

Again, reason dictates, custom makes wont, and nature orders that in every association, community, and social organization, when some particularly difficult situation arises affecting the whole society, recourse be had to a great council of that association or community. The reason is that in a conference

27 This gloss is on dist. XIX, c. 9, *Rosarium seu in Decretorum Volumen Commentaria* (Venice, 1577), Fol. 23, no. 3, col. 2.

28 *Decretales*, Lib. I, tit. 1; Friedberg, II, 5–7.

29 *Decretum*, pars II, C. 2., q. 5, c. 10 and c. 18; Friedberg, I, 458, 461.

30 Matt. 11:29.

31 Henry de Segusia (d. 1271), a renowned Italian canonist of the thirteenth century, became Bishop of Ostia in 1261.

of many, where various people discuss diverse matters, some things come to light which one man alone might never discover. And those matters which are passed by the great council will be received fearlessly and regarded by the people as genuine. Therefore, it follows that the way of ending matters by a council is the safest, the most advantageous, and the most in use. Thus, it has even been said, "Where there are many counsels, there is safety." [32]

Again, from what has been said above we conclude that it is clearer than the light of day that no other human way than that of a council has been found by which this schism can be completely settled and to this recourse must finally be made. Indeed, the party that rejects this way renders his case somewhat suspicious, just as a deceptive person seeks the corners and is afraid to come out into the light. Similarly, the party that takes refuge in a council in this way confirms his case. Thus, the party who is first to humble himself before a council would greatly justify himself, because he would thereby demonstrate that he had zeal toward God.

Again, we conclude that all the princes and the prelates and any others who resist and oppose this most reasonable and suitable way, trodden by and customary among the Fathers, do seriously and damnably sin and err. Such people clearly demonstrate that they are bound and blinded by damnable affections.

Therefore, after every covering and bond of sin, ambition, lust, and fear, etc., have been destroyed, all the faithful, under pain of incurring the divine displeasure, must strive with all their might to bring peace to the Church by this way.

Thus, on account of the above-mentioned reasons an answer to the question must be made in the affirmative.

It ought to add not a little weight to this part of the argument that the University of Paris, solemnly assembled in the Monastery of Saint Bernard of Paris, on the 20th day of May, 1381, unanimously decided through the four faculties, Theology, Canon Law, Medicine, and Arts, to uphold this view and intend, if permitted, to further it as far as possible by sending persuasive and hortatory letters and epistles to the princes, communities, and prelates. [33]

---

[32] Prov. 11:14.

[33] The university's acceptance of the *via concilii* at this assembly was the direct outcome of the work of Conrad of Gelnhausen and Henry of Langenstein. It was to further this decision that Henry, at this time

14. On the Right of the Church to Elect and Judge the Supreme Bishop

In order to explain this matter it must be noted, in the first place, that the pope has not always been appointed by one method. It is maintained on the basis of the Scriptures that Christ appointed one of his apostles to be vicar-general of his Church on earth, namely, Saint Peter, and wished others to succeed him in that governing position right up to the consummation of the age; but that Christ did not pass on a fixed method of appointing the successors of Peter, but entrusted this to the ordering and arranging of the Church. For, firstly, he was appointed by Christ; then, secondly, at another time, the preceding pope appointed his own successor; thirdly, sometimes all the bishops and priests together chose a bishop, who was pope over them. Then, after the building of cathedral churches, whoever was elected by the canons of the cathedral church of Rome was pope. Then, for a time the emperor, when the opportunity arose, took upon himself the power to appoint the pope. Sixthly, the power of electing the pope was made over to the cardinals at a certain council. Hence, Pope Nicholas, in the letter in which he announced what had been decreed at the Roman synod of one hundred and thirteen bishops over which he presided, says: "First of all, in the sight of God it was ordained that the election of the Roman pope is in the hands of the cardinal bishops. Thus, if anyone is enthroned as pope in the apostolic see without their previous consent and canonical election, and without the agreement of the lower religious orders, clerical and lay, he is not to be regarded as pope or the *apostolicus*, but as an apostate."[34]

From these and similar matters which are to be found in the histories of the Church and in the acts of the supreme pontiffs and emperors and without making any unsupported assertions, four conclusions are evident.

The first conclusion: Even if Christ had not appointed any of his disciples to be his vicar-general on earth, the Church still had the power to appoint such a person, and by the teaching

---

vice-chancellor of the university, wrote his *Epistola concilii pacis* addressed to the princes and prelates; cf. Bliemetzrieder, *Das Generalkonzil im grossen abendländischen Schisma* (Paderborn, 1904), 87 ff.; Valois, *op. cit.*, I, 338 ff.

[34] Nicholas II (1058–1061), *Epistola VIII, PL*, 143:1315.

of the Holy Spirit would have made such an appointment. For, according to reason, the best method and most suitable form of government is that in which one supreme pontiff presides. For although Christ did not make mention of the appointment of a vicar-general in temporal affairs, the emperor, nor of particular vicars of himself in spiritual matters, the bishops, these nevertheless are made true vicars of him by being duly elected. Thus, if Christ had not appointed Peter as pope, still through an election made by the Church or part of the Church, he would have been elected vicar-general of Christ on earth.

The second conclusion: The power of appointing the pope resides primarily with the whole company of the bishops of the faithful. Thus, this power should revert to them whenever the cardinals are not able to elect, or do not wish to elect, or have all died, or are obviously abusing the power handed on to them, or have abused it, etc.

Even if all the bishops had also died, would this power of appointing the pope remain with the remnant of the faithful? Indeed, it would, since the priests choose the bishops, as has been done from the beginning of the Church, and the bishops the pope. Perhaps the entire priesthood, with the agreement of the people, would first elect one priest over all the faithful followers of Christ and then entrust him with the appointment of the other bishops, on the same basis.

The third conclusion: As it originally belonged to the whole company of bishops of the faithful to arrange together for the papacy, so it also belongs to them alone to decide whether the appointment or the election of a pope, made by the commissioners of the Church, that is, the cardinals, is valid and legitimate or not.

Therefore, when there is, as today, a difficult and complex dubiety over the election of the pope, indeed, of popes, there is, I say, the greatest need for a general council.

The fourth conclusion: When there is no pope, and when the cardinals are manifestly abusing their power or are erring incorrigibly, the Church is able to deprive them of their power and to elect a pope by herself, or delegate the power of election to a particular archbishop or archbishops, or to others.

In the second place, it should be noted that the present schism could be ended in various ways. This could be done by force of arms, one party destroying the other. However, as long as ecclesiastics are able to proceed by any other reasonable way, they must not rely on this way of blood in the forum of the Church. For David was prevented from building the Temple to the Lord because he was a man of blood. Or, secondly, by the gradual detection of the deceitful person. No violence lasts forever; truth alone is stable and perennial. Falsehood is not really able to lie hid for very long, but will, by breaking out repeatedly, make itself known. "Falsehood," says Seneca, "is weak; if you search diligently, it reveals itself. All fictions, like little flowers, soon fall; nothing feigned can be of long duration." [35] Or, thirdly, by continual, diligent, and persevering instruction of the faithful, in which case the person who has labored more fervently and more effectively will finally prevail. Or, fourthly, by an agreement between the two contestants, one yielding his right to the other for the good of the Church. Or, fifthly, by the assembling of a general council or of some people appointed for this purpose on behalf of the whole Church, according to some method of election or deputation. Or, sixthly, some renowned and experienced men might be appointed by each to come together both at Rome and Avignon at the same time until through correct instruction they arrive at an agreement in fact. Then, when this has been accomplished, it would be communicated to the bishops of the whole of Christendom, so that it might immediately be seen who was in the right. Or, seventhly, ten or twelve of the more learned and experienced men whom it would be possible to secure might be chosen by each to meet in some city assigned to them and there, for half a year or a year, argue with each other in words and writings, even making as many as three or four replies. At the end their arguments would be sent in writing throughout Christendom. Then we would soon see who was in the right or to whom the majority, or the weightier, inclined. [36] Or, eighthly, through the occurrence of some miracle

---

[35] The second part of the quotation is from Cicero, *De officiis*, II, 12, 43.

[36] *Ad quem plures vel valentiores declinarent.* This is not merely a matter of majority but also of quality. In medieval voting the status of the person as well as his vote was taken into account. Perhaps we see here the influence of Marsiglio of Padua (cf. A. Gewirth, *Marsilius of Padua,* New York, 1951, 182 ff.), but more probably that of the voting practices of the University of Paris (cf. Rashdall, *The Universities of Europe in the Middle Ages,* ed. Powicke and Emden, Oxford University Press, London, 1936, I, 412 ff.), or of cathedral chapters in both of which election was determined by the *maior et senior pars* (cf. McIllwain, *The Growth of Political Thought,* The Macmillan Company, New York, 1932, 303). Cf. also

or divine oracle indicative of the will of God. To await this, unless everything that was humanly possible had been attempted with all earnestness, would be to tempt God. The first seven ways are open to men; the fifth seems to be the most reasonable and the most expedient.

In the third place, it should be noted that a general council of the Church may be held in many different ways: First, by an assembly of all the faithful. At the time of the ascension of Christ this was possible; now it is not. Secondly, by an assembly of all the prelates and doctors. Thirdly, of the bishops and provincial abbots only. Fourthly, of the archbishops alone. Fifthly, of all the primates and patriarchs alone. Sixthly, by the bishops of each kingdom of Christendom holding a council among themselves, in which they would appoint one, two, or three to go to a general council on behalf of all, who would provide for their expenses. This method seems the most expedient.

Moreover, the procedure leading up to and during such a council would be as follows: First, before the Church had assembled, it would be announced to the parties concerned, namely, Urban and his cardinals, or at least to those who took part in his election, that they should appear before the Church on a specified day, and in a particular city, with all their witnesses, reasons, defenses, and documents in readiness, without further procrastination. Secondly, when the prelates have come together, the patriarchs would take their places first, because they know their order, then the abbots would be seated; then the minor prelates and doctors of theology and of both Laws, admitted and elected according to the number agreeable to the council. Thirdly, according to the custom of the Fathers, after solemn invocation of the Holy Spirit had been made and prayers reverently poured out toward God that justice and truth might be made known, each party would be heard, before all the Fathers and in the presence of the other, adequately and at length, even to two or three replies. Fourthly, that when everything that each party had said had been written down and handed to each archbishop, and after each had discussed it at length with their clergy, the entire council, or the most capable deputies appointed by the council, would decide which articles, both how many and in what way, had been properly proved or semiproved by each party. Fifthly, that, after

The Rule of St. Benedict, c. 64, where regarding the election of the abbot, we find the phrase, "pars quamvis congregationis saniori consilio eligerit," PL, 66:370.

everything from each party had been properly made known or proved and briefly summed up by the notaries, a definite judgment would be made from the council either in a resolution passed by all, or by certain people unanimously elected by all for this purpose.

It is necessary that one of the two contestants be pronounced pope or neither of them. If this latter were the case, no other means of assistance would remain except for all the former cardinals to assemble again and choose someone according as the Holy Spirit would direct them. The schism would then be ended. Here is a possible way, intelligible and free from danger, and undoubtedly the most reasonable. Therefore a reply must now be made to the reasons stated above that have been advanced against this way.

15. The Doubts Reviewed in Chapter 12, Opposed to the Summoning of a General Council, Are Dispelled, and the Necessity of a Council Confirmed

In answer to the first doubt it is granted that the cardinals must be believed, as assumed, unless in some new and particular case there is sufficient hindrance causing reasonable doubt concerning their assertions, as in the matter proposed.

For, in the first place, they elected one pope and publicly crowned him before all the people and for three months remained with him. They rendered to him everything that is properly owed to a pope, and received from him the sacrament, benefices, and dignities. They secured favors for themselves and their relatives and, as is customary, they announced by letter to the emperor and the other princes throughout the world that they had elected as pope a holy and good man, etc. Afterward, however, all the cardinals who were concerned with the election, with the exception of two or three, publicly asserted, swore with one voice, and preached everywhere that the person previously elected was not pope, that he had only been elected in pretense because of fear, and that everything that was announced concerning him was done on that account.

Here, because of the strong contradictions and plausible statements that have been successively made by them, there is cause for doubt. These statements are so credible that the most learned do not know how to judge which side of the contradiction is of greater weight, or which, in this instance, ought to be considered as having greater weight.

Thus, in order that this may be discussed, there is the greatest need for a general council, which is ruled by the Holy Spirit, according to Matt., ch. 18: "If two or three of you were to come together in my name upon the earth, concerning anything that you shall ask, it will be done, because I am in the midst of you."[37]

Therefore, that party who in this dispute has fewer followers in number but stronger perhaps in wisdom is not to give way to despair, nor is the other to rely on the multitude of his followers, because in a general council, where the Holy Spirit is judge, victory is not achieved by numbers but by truth. And the truth does not fail on account of a small number in such a cause of the Universal Church, in which prayer shall be offered continually by all the faithful, both before and during the council for the grace of the Holy Spirit, so that justice may be made known. Therefore, let a few, nay, let even one person put his trust in this most holy procedure and he will be able to conquer ten thousand. For, "if God be for us, who can be against us?"[38] Let us consider what Moses says: "How could one man have defeated a thousand, and two put to flight ten thousand? Was it not because the Lord had given them up?"[39] Saint Hilary alone overcame the pope with the cardinals, as his *Legenda* records.[40] Many examples of this nature could be found in the histories.

Therefore, it is clear why the way which was dealt with in the ninth argument is useless for terminating the present case; indeed, the case is more simple. Hence, Johannes Teutonicus, the glossator of Dist. LXXIX, says: "If, contrary to what is right, two are chosen, who will be the judge? Not the cardinals, because in that case they would be the judges of their own action; and no superior can be found." And after a few words he adds, "Yes, because a council may be called."

Again, Johannes Andreae, *De electione* of the *Clementine Decretals*, asks, "If an allegation were made concerning the election of the pope, who would have to investigate the cause of

---

[37] Matt. 18:20.   [38] Rom. 8:31.   [39] Deut. 32:30.
[40] The reference is probably to the *Vita* of Saint Hilary, composed by Honoratus (*PL*, 50: 1210), and in particular to c. 3, 22, which tells of Hilary's journey in winter, alone and on foot to Rome, where, presenting himself before Leo I, he requested that the action of the Council of 444 in deposing Chelidonius be confirmed. Hilary did not actually win his case, but was imprisoned by Leo. The *Vita* does not go into details; cf. Smith and Wace, *A Dictionary of Christian Biography* (London, 1882), III, 69 ff.; Hefele-Leclerq, *op. cit.*, II, 477 ff.

this trouble?" In reply he says, "As this matter has not been
decided, nor provided for, they shall be without provision;
and it is certain that this cannot be done except by a general
council."

Again, it is surprising that some people—would that they
were not flatterers—wishing, as it were, to deify the cardinals,
and to represent them as sinless, declare that their words are
always to be believed without exception. Yet the holy doctors,
Augustine and Jerome, and others are sometimes found to have
corrected themselves and to have deviated from the truth, as
is evident from Augustine's *Retractations*. It is even recorded of
Paul that he withstood Peter to his face, because he did not
walk uprightly in accordance with the truth of the gospel.
Does it not often happen in the consistories that one of the
cardinals contradicts another in various matters and cases?
Obviously, if this happens, one of them has erred; or are they
more holy and more firmly established than the above-
mentioned saints? Perhaps by their authority contradictory
statements can be true!

Again, the cardinals are now learning from experience that,
through their mission and preaching with all their ability, the
schism is not being lessened but rather increasing and becoming
established. Therefore they ought to desist from this way,
the sooner the better, as it has not been pleasing to God,
perhaps because of their own or some other's sins, and to yield
to the way of the Holy Spirit, which is a general council, that
peace may be established in the Church. Then it will be seen
that they are not seeking their own good but the good of Jesus
Christ, and that they desire the well-being of all the faithful.

Again, if the two cardinals who have already been sent to
the Germans have in three years not succeeded in winning
over one county to believe that the one elected second is pope,
scarcely in a hundred years by such means will they have won
for him the nine or ten kingdoms which are adhering to the
first elected.

Again, if the instruction and preaching of the cardinals
are valid and effective, and to be received by the faithful in
this dispute, there is no more expedient or suitable way of
doing this than by informing all the prelates of the kingdoms
of Christendom, brought together in a general council, of the
truth of the matter and of the law. If they, assembled in the
name of the Church, believed them, this schism throughout
the whole Church would be settled. Therefore, the way of a

general council is the most expedient and must be especially sought after and demanded by the cardinals.

To the second doubt we reply that, by conceding that it is well known that there was a popular uprising, etc., it does not follow that it is well known that the cardinals were compelled by fear to carry out the election quickly, because from what took place subsequently, the opposite appears, namely, that they truly and freely agreed upon him. This is clear from what has been said in the first explanation.

Whether or not, when all has been taken into consideration, that election is to be considered invalid, on account of the assault and tumult that took place at the election of Urban VI, is at the present time not clear, but a matter of perplexity and doubt.

Again, supposing it is a fact commonly known among the wise that the first elected does not have the law on his side; nevertheless, as a great schism has come into being and has now existed for a long time, it is expedient for the satisfaction and general settlement of the more simple-minded and for the destruction of the malice and impudence of the many that the subject be discussed in a general council. "For often," as Saint Gregory says, "it is expedient that something extra be done for cases that have already been concluded." Thus it follows that at the present time there is need for a general council.

In reply to the third doubt, it is conceded that commonly and regularly, it is true, a council ought not to be held without the authority of the pope. Nevertheless, when a particular need arises, this breaks the law. Indeed, there are many possible cases in which a general council can and must be held without the authority of the pope. First, if the pope, after he had fallen into manifest heresy, were pertinaciously to continue to occupy the apostolic see and did not wish to have a council summoned. Second, if, after the death of the pope, it should happen that all the cardinals were immediately killed, it would be necessary that provision be made for the papacy by a general council. Third, if the pope with the advice of the cardinals brought forward some doubtful decision concerning a matter of faith, and held pertinaciously and incorrigibly to it, and did not wish a council. Fourthly, if, during a papal vacancy, the cardinals owing to disagreement among themselves, or some tyranny, were not able to assemble, or if, on account of malice, or for some other reason, they refused to assemble to elect a pope and did not desire a general council.

In any one of these instances, a general council must be summoned without the authority of the pope, to undertake matters for the common good of the whole company of the faithful. Hence it is now clear that it does not belong to the particular or essential nature of a general council that it be summoned by the pope, but that this is accidental (*per accidens*).

Again, it is known that not only that which is normally permissible becomes obligatory in time of necessity, but even that that which is not permissible except in time of necessity, in time of dire need becomes obligatory and indispensable. For example, in cases of dire necessity, the taking of something belonging to another person without the owner's consent, or the taking of bread in order to live, is not theft. The reason for this is that those things which are of the law of man, namely, the division and appropriation of goods and such like matters, are not able to hinder the natural or the divine law, by which the lower things have been ordained to serve the needs of men. Wherefore, those things which some have in superabundance are, by the natural law, owed to the poor, according to Saint Ambrose.[41]

Therefore, those people abuse ἐπιείκεια[42] who, in the present great and common necessity of the Universal Church, wish all positive laws for the summoning of a general council by the authority of the pope alone to be kept perfectly to the letter. They are thereby hindering the way of peace and salvation, contrary to the intention of those who drew up the canons; as if in no case it were permissible for the people, or for some one, to war against the common statutes without the authority of the prince in defense of their own or their fathers' laws, or to resist, not as king, but as an enemy, a prince who wished to destroy the commonwealth and the entire company of the citizens, for whose preservation he was appointed. Is it the

---

41 Most of this paragraph (also in Gelnhausen's *Epistola concordiae*) is based on Saint Thomas Aquinas, *Summa theologica*, IIª IIᵃᵉ, Qu. 66, art. 7; cf. *Decretum*, pars I, dist. 47, c. 8; Friedberg, I, 171.

42 The doctrine of ἐπιείκεια, taken from Aristotle, *Ethics* V, 10, is the correction of positive law whenever it becomes defective because of its general nature. It was fully discussed by Saint Thomas Aquinas, *op. cit.*, IIª IIᵃᵉ, Qu. 120, and was appealed to by Marsiglio of Padua, Ockham, Gelnhausen, and Langenstein. It received its fullest development during the Conciliar Movement at the hands of Gerson; all are dependent on Aquinas; cf. E. F. Jacob, *Essays in the Conciliar Epoch* (Manchester, 1943), 9 ff.

case that the Maccabees, by fighting on the Sabbath days, became transgressors of the divine law? . . .

Therefore, there is a certain quality, which Aristotle in the fifth book of the *Ethics* [43] calls ἐπιείκεια, which has a controlling power over the legalistic exercise of justice and is better and more noble than it because, through its use, the mind and intention of the legislator are more excellently and more perfectly obeyed.

It is therefore evident that lawmakers very rarely provide for contingent events, because in drawing up laws they normally direct their attention to those things which occur in the majority of cases. Thus it happens that certain people, ignorant of the law and unlearned in theology and moral philosophy, who wish that the common laws and positive decrees be observed in every instance according to the outward appearance or surface of the words, often act contrary to justice and the common good, and against the intention of the legislators. In doing this they are truly transgressing the dictates of reason for the sake of certain traditions of men, whose intention they do not take into account, and are also disdaining to listen to the just interpretation of the laws; seeing that it is indeed permissible for theologians, who are the interpreters of the divine law, to interpret the mind of Christ, and to declare, as is shown in the interpretation of the Great Commandment of the law, that it cannot be fulfilled literally by pilgrims [44] but according to the doctor's understanding of it. [45]

Now to what is said above, that no single person has power over all the faithful, we reply that the Roman Church has such power; but by the "Roman Church" is understood the Church Universal, or a general council.

To the fourth, we say that this need not be feared, nor is it probable, as the way of the Holy Spirit leads to the peace of the Church. The grace of the Holy Spirit which has been and is being devoutly implored throughout all the churches of Christendom, both before and during the council, will not allow this kind of thing to happen.

To the fifth, we reply that it is possible for a council to be summoned by a meeting of the cardinals. Perhaps it would

---

[43] C. 10.

[44] *Viatores*, a technical term of ecclesiastical Latin referring to those in this life journeying on the road to heaven, in contradistinction to those *in patria* (in heaven).

[45] Thomas Aquinas, *op. cit.*, II[a] II[ae], Qu. 184, art. 2.

help to bring about greater security if each of the elected agreed
to the summoning of a council. For there are few who doubt
that one of them is pope and this would seem to satisfy the
canons which seem to stand in the way.

Since it is doubted by whose authority the actions in such a
council would hold good, we reply that in a case of such need
it is by the authority of Christ, the never-failing Head. For it
was by his authority that David ate the showbread, and the
Maccabees fought on the Sabbath, etc.

If, in opposition to what has been said above, it is said,
"The pope is greater than a council," we reply that in our
case the council would ordain nothing until it had assembled
and made clear, either authoritatively or magisterially, before
everything else who is the true pope. Then, when this has been
done, he shall take charge of the council, if he wishes, and
what was done and what still remains to be done will have
validity through him.

Or, we say that by the method stated above the Catholic
Church is, in this instance, superior to the pope, from which
he, as *catholicus*, is not excluded, but rather is its secondary
head. When there is no secondary head, or when there is, yet
without agreement as to his identity, as is the case in the present
situation, Christ, the inseparable and primary Head of the
Church, makes good the deficiency. It is by his grace and merits
that the Church, his mystical body, continually receives
feeling, movement, and vital spirit, and by him it is brought
about that, as the law stands, she cannot err, be wholly defiled,
or suffer death from mortal sin.

To the sixth we reply that, as a good son is bound to strive
by every permissible way to aid and free his earthly mother
when she is in sickness or enduring tribulation (even if God
wills her to die or be afflicted in this way for her own salvation),
so also a fortiori, is he bound to aid his spiritual Mother, which
is the Church, especially when she is being shattered by tribulation, manifestly opposed to the general well-being of the faithful,
as is happening in the present case. If the consideration be
brought forward that, because all things work together for
good for the elect,[46] Christians should not cease from eliminating dissension, disagreement, and such like evils, then by this
same reasoning an end would have to be made of the extermi-
nation of heretics, and of all punishment of evildoers, because,
according to Saint Augustine, the Almighty would not permit

[46] Rom. 8:28.

any good thing to become evil unless he knew and wished thereby to bring forth a greater good. . . .

To the seventh reason we reply that in the first place it is sufficiently well agreed from the sayings of the Scriptures that there ought to be one vicar-general of Christ in his Church until the consummation of the age. And that as a plurality of princes and not of subordinates is prohibited by natural reason, a plurality of supreme pontiffs must be prevented with all diligence of the faithful until either by a miracle or by a special revelation something else with regard to the matter is made known. . . .

To the eighth and last reason, we reply that always in the Church, according to the apostolic assertion, "all who wish to live devoutly in Christ will suffer persecution." [47] Persecution, as Pope Leo said, does not merely consist in what is done by fire and sword or by any other kind of suffering against Christian piety. Now the divergences in customs, the arrogance of the disobedient, and the missiles of evil tongues make up the fury of persecutions, so that it is true of the Church that "in peace is my bitterness most bitter." [48] For carnal peace and comfort have raised up dissension, eclipsed superiors, and deprived the people of their zeal for salvation.

Therefore, since virtue is stronger when united than when spread abroad, it is especially suitable that a council be summoned now, to deal with these difficult matters, for surely among the many some are to be found who still have zeal toward God and pursue it.

To the argument that sufficient provision for all emergencies has been made, etc., we reply by quoting this passage from the seventh Council of Toledo, which reads: "So many constitutions of the canons exist already that they should be sufficient for all correction, if someone would willingly deign to attend to them. Nevertheless, the more carefully and frequently a lamp is cleaned and trimmed, the more brightly it shines. Thus no little benefit is gained for the correction of the many, if, while the canons that have already been drawn up are by means of a brotherly assembly brought back to memory, others that are lacking or are by competent people considered necessary, are added." [49]

For who does not know how many unlawful deeds have been perpetrated up to this time, or how strong the impious pride, avarice, and negligence of the multitudes have become, or

[47] I Tim. 3:12.   [48] Isa. 38:17.   [49] Hinschius, *op. cit.*, 380.

how manifold is the trangression of the law. These new occur-
rences demand the provision of new remedies, just as new
diseases require the discovery of new medicines or, in accordance with the nature and condition of the diseases, the
moderation of former ones.

Again, since particular cases are infinite in number, and an
infinite number of new cases may arise, sufficient provision
cannot be made by a finite number of constitutions, or by
particular laws without it always being necessary to find new
provision in most cases.

Again, as human nature naturally strives toward what is
prohibited and cannot be completely restrained or governed,
it happens that, when the bonds of restraint have been slackened
temporarily, it will revert quickly to its inordinate life; vices
will again spring up, superstitions return, and errors revive.
This is why there is need of continual supervision in the house
of God, for it is composed of men, and of renovation, now in
one part, now in another, after the fashion of a material house.
For unless a house is examined diligently each year, repaired
and renovated when it is necessary, the pillars will take on a
slant, bend outward, recede from the foundations, and be
disjoined from the beams; the pictures and representations
on the walls and pillars will fall from age, and the likenesses
painted on them will be mutilated; the windows (which are the
doctors through whom, as through windows, the house of
God is illuminated) will become filthy because of the adhesion
of dust and will keep out the light.

Thus, unless the Church is by the continual attention of her
master builders examined, repaired, and renovated in due
season before the defects become too great, her pictures will
fall—that is to say, truth and knowledge; the pillars will
totter; and the windows—that is, the doctors—shall not let in
the light; then finally she will suffer irreparable ruin.

16 [50]

[This chapter contains a long catalogue of current abuses by
which the ancient discipline of the Church has been overthrown.]

[50] The contents of this and the following three chapters were published
verbatim by Gerson at the Council of Constance in his tractate *Declaratio
compendiosa defectuum virorum ecclesiasticorum,* du Pin, *op. cit.,* II, 314–318;
cf. J. B. Schwab, *Johannes Gerson* (Würzburg, 1858), 121. Much of these
chapters was also incorporated by Peter d'Ailly in his *Tractatus super
reformatione ecclesiae,* du Pin, *op. cit.,* II, 903–916.

17. On the Most Corrupt Government of the Church of the Present Day

Again, what benefit or what usefulness does the magnificent glory of princes and the superfluous pomp of prelates and cardinals, unmindful of the fact that they are men, confer upon the Church?

Is it not indeed an abomination that one person should hold two hundred, and another three hundred, ecclesiastical benefices? Is it not true that the divine worship is thereby curtailed, that the churches are impoverished and deprived of capable men and doctors, and that evil examples are given to the faithful?

What does the fact that the cardinals were elected from one nation only, or, as it were, from one country, mean? Amongst them there ought to be some from every kingdom and from the noble tongues. Is there with Christ a distinction between Greek and Latin, French and German, Spanish and Hungarian?

Why is it that today one person—would that he were moderately well educated—holds four, five, six, or eight benefices, of not one of which he is worthy, in which eight could be supported who would apply themselves to teaching, prayer, and the offices of divine praise? Consider whether today horses, dogs, birds, and the excessive households of the ecclesiastics rather than the poor of Christ ought to be eating the patrimony of the Church, or whether it should be used as suitable means for increasing the divine worship and for the conversion of the infidels, or pious works of this nature?

Why is it today that the places of divine worship (such as monasteries and churches of the venerable martyrs, at Rome and elsewhere), owing to what has been said above, and to the negligence of the clergy, are deserted and in ruins? Judge if it is even right that the books of the churches, and the like, are sometimes sold, and castles and houses mortgaged to pay to the collectors the exactions imposed by the bishops on the clergy?

Why is it that today all make for the hub of Christendom, which abounds with rich benefices and which is, so to speak, a center of quiet, while the parts of the Church on the circumference, where the ungodly walk, have been neglected and unvisited? Why is it that these places, where faith is feeble and virtue imperfect, where schismatics abound and infidels make their attacks, have been left vacant and unattended by the doctors, who should have been appointed and sent there? Indeed, in these places there is need of prelates, doctors, and masters more experienced in the law of Christ, and in more praiseworthy and fruitful combat.

Why is it that the sword of the Church, excommunication, is now so lightly drawn to its own contempt and thrust so cruelly against the poor for a mean matter such as debt or the like? Why is it that one legal process over an ordinary affair now lasts for many years? Why is the excessive prolongation of the lawsuits—the despoiler of the poor—not done away in a seemly manner?

Why is the means of earning a living from their own property not mercifully given to converted Jews, rather than that they be compelled by extreme poverty to apostatize and accuse Christians of ungodliness? Why is it not ordained that Jews must not remain among Christians unless they earn their livelihood by becoming servants to the Christians or by cultivating the fields or working as mechanics and not by practicing usury, which for themselves is committing sin and for Christians means spoliation?

What is the meaning of the fact that the canons of certain cathedral churches put on boots and short tunics—the clerical habit being put off and the military assumed—and engage with each other in jousting? That even the bishops lay aside their copes, surplices, and books, take up arms and, fully equipped, fight in the fields like secular princes?

Why is it that some prelates place their administrative authority, temporal and spiritual, in the hands of certain powerful and avaricious tyrants for a certain sum of money, to the detriment of the Church, the subversion of justice, and the oppression of the poor? Why is it that today, bishops, abbots, and monks, rather than being ministers of Christ, are fiscal officers, laboring with all their strength for the world in the courts of princes, of secular justice, or of parliaments?

Behold, why are all bishops, prelates, and parish priests now appointed through the pope rather than natives of the countries, who are known and better qualified, so that men who are strange in manners, speech, and customs may not be appointed to the positions of authority in the churches? Why is it that today the sons of powerful men and nobles are appointed to ecclesiastical dignities, while clerics, renowned in life and doctrine, are made subject to them? Why is it that now the government of the Church is being entrusted preferably to men totally ignorant of spiritual matters, who from boyhood have devoted themselves to worldly and argumentative sciences, such as law, the study of which by the priests is prohibited?

Is it not true that the Church is being governed according to the world and not rather contrary to the way of the world, for it is written, "Be not conformed to this world"? [51] There are many other abuses such as these.

18. ON THE EXTREME CORRUPTION OF THE ECCLESIASTICS OF THE PRESENT TIME

Again, open your eyes and see if any nunneries have today become prostitutes' houses? If any monasteries, consecrated to God, have become market places and taverns? If any cathedral churches have become dens of thieves and robbers? Make a careful examination and see if anywhere the priests have committed illicit intercourse, having concubines under the pretext of maidservants?

Judge whether such a variety of images and pictures in the churches is suitable and whether it does not turn many simple people to a kind of idolatry?

See if the large number and variety of religious orders is proper? Consider carefully if the Military Orders are carrying out their duty? Do they uphold the priesthood, guard the practices, the faith, the rules, and the canons of the Fathers? Investigate and see if it is beneficial that there should be such a large number of immunities and such granting of privileges to certain people and such complete exemption from the discipline of the ordinaries?

Is it proper that, notwithstanding the excessive number of the saints, Urban V, and Bridgitta of Sweden, and Charles, Duke of Brittany, should be canonized? Is it seemly that the festivals of certain new saints should be celebrated more solemnly than those of the chief apostles? Is it right that the earlier and more stately churches of the saints should be deserted and in ruins, owing to the taxes exacted by the collectors or the cardinals, and then sometime afterwards new little chapels built to their memory, or, as it were, to their glory?

Again, think whether it is right that the stupid should be in command and the wise in subjection; that the youths should

51 Rom. 12:2.

be the masters and the old men servants; that the ignorant should discuss the difficult questions and the wise not dare to speak; that grooms should be advanced to positions of preferment and students of the Scriptures disregarded?

Inquire if any apocryphal scriptures, hymns, or prayers have been introduced in the passage of time, either through zeal or ignorance, to the detriment of the faith? And correct these. Settle the differences of opinion concerning matters such as the conception of the renowned Virgin and similar subjects. Reform unjust laws and customary practices.

Is it not true that unjust laws are to be met with in Saxony, which elsewhere have been attacked by the theologians? And what practice of Christians could be more worthy of condemnation than this, namely, that the clerics and the laity, prelates and princes, everywhere are so mad as to celebrate the most holy night of the Nativity of Christ in playing dice— not in contemplating the heavenly mysteries?

Is it not true that in Livonia the practice has grown up of not giving the sacrament of the Eucharist to any of the peasants? Is it not true that there one may find that one husband has two wives living, and a matron several husbands?

What need is there to mention more? Inquire of the bishops who come to the general council from any province about all the vicious practices and pernicious rites that have been introduced on some occasion or other into the churches and the conditions of the people of the various provinces.

And, because of these evils now mentioned and similar ones, reform all ranks of the Church in a general council or command that they be reformed in provincial councils, that thus the Church may, with the help of God, be restored and the house of God purged of all impurity, vice, and error.

19. ON THE GREAT NEED FOR PROVINCIAL AND GENERAL COUNCILS TO REFORM THE CHURCH

The holy Fathers of the previous age have ordained that this be done diligently, and those who have come after them have always confirmed their decree in councils, namely, that twice a year in every province a synod be held.[52] . . .

It is argued on the analogy of all these quotations that it is on account of the defect of general councils of the whole

[52] A series of quotations from the Councils recorded in the pseudo-Isidorian Decretals, enforcing the calling of councils, is omitted.

Church, which alone dares to correct all fearlessly, that these evils, which affect the Universal Church, remaining for a long time uncorrected, increase and steadily become worse, until under the disguise of custom they are considered lawful.

20. THE PRAYER OF THE AUTHOR FOR THE HASTENING OF A GENERAL COUNCIL

Now that we have completed this work we have unfolded what we had in mind to do from the beginning.

Invisible Creator, Prince of Peace, I implore the help of thy approval to bestow upon the weak words of my exhortation the strength for accomplishing the desired end, and to enlighten with the bright beams of truth the frailty of men, that no one intending to be devout may show himself obstinate, lest the terrifying severity of the divine punishment attack the opposers; and that abundant mercy, everlasting peace, and eternal glory may sustain those who, with an upright and balanced judgment, embrace the way of a council of peace.

> 'Gainst Urban Clement's gone to law, and so
> My book unto the erring world must go,
>   Called: "Letter for a Council Pledged to Peace."
>   Till Terror, Sloth and devious Error cease
> To mute men's tongues, my Book, run o'er the Earth!
> Crush out the Schism, bring the Council's birth;
>   Shout forth, nor fear to cross the mountain's brows,
>   By woods and waters, vales and wind-tossed boughs,
> Porter of Truth, not wares of vulgar worth.
>   If, speaking Truth, thou make them fume with rage
>   Small loss, though thou be riven page from page. [53]

[53] For some lines of this version I am indebted to Dr. John T. McNeill. A literal prose rendering with notes was kindly furnished by Dr. Edith F. Claflin, Lecturer in Latin, Columbia University.

John Gerson: A Tractate on the Unity of the Church[1] (1409)

THE TEXT

To those who treat of the unity of the Church, one of the zealots of this very cause gladly presents for their consideration a way of peace. Although his body is bound by the chains of affairs, thus preventing him from going in person to the sacred council which is, God favoring us, to be held at Pisa, nevertheless "the word of God," as the apostle says, "is not bound."[2] Therefore, [his] spirit, inclined to and most anxious for peace, has decided to spread abroad in every direction, where the infirm flesh is unable to go, some word of God; not, of course, to determine anything—away with such boldness—but to state and examine in "the tabernacle of God with men"[3] whatever has been entrusted to him out of the fund of knowledge.

The unity of the Church in one undoubted vicar of Christ must not, in the present situation, which now confronts the Church on January 29, 1408,[4] be retarded on account of certain allegations derived from positive law against the holding of a general council or the way of abdication. [Such allegations are:] that a council cannot be held without the authority of the pope; that anyone who has been deprived must before all else be reinstated; and that those who have withdrawn from obedience are to be dealt with as enemies. Righteous fear may also allege that no one is able to say to the pope, "Why do you act in this way?", especially if he is not expressly erring against the articles of faith, since he cannot be judged by anyone, subjected to anyone, or dealt with as a schismatic. [It may be also alleged] that it is dangerous for a shepherd to

---

[1] The text followed is that published by E. du Pin in his *Gersoni opera omnia* (Antwerp, 1706), II, 113–118.
[2] II Tim. 2:9.   [3] Rev. 21:3.   [4] New Series, 1409.

abandon his flock by abdicating; that each has done what has been required of him for the union of the Church, and is not in sin; and, finally, that an inquiry must be made into the justice of the true party, for without this knowledge those who have erred cannot do penance, etc. Therefore, against these allegations, twelve general considerations are set forth, a particular application of which is sufficient for the informed to refute them.

THE FIRST CONSIDERATION

The general unity of the Church has been hampered by divisions among her sons, as putrefying members and sinners against God. "Our sins," according to the words of the prophet, "have separated us from God." [5] Thus through the opposite process, that is, the reconciliation of each to God by the correction of evil practices, by self-humiliation, and by prayer, this unity must once again be secured. If this does not take place, and if the cause of the schism remains, what hope can we have that the schism will end, unless, however, in the pure grace of our Lord Jesus Christ, who is wont to bestow great benefits on the undeserving and the ungrateful? Nevertheless, it behooves us to be his fellow workers, especially now when, as the return of peace seems nearer, the enemy of peace is raging more savagely; and whenever he will introduce, if he is able, in order to continue the schism, the most powerful impediment, namely, division among those who are about to effect a union, by means of pride, lust, or envy.

THE SECOND CONSIDERATION

The essential unity of the Church always remains in Christ, her spouse, for "Christ is the head of the Church," [6] "in whom all are one," [7] according to the apostle. If she does not have a vicar, as when he is dead, corporally or civilly, or because it is not credibly to be expected that obedience will be conferred any longer on him or his successors by Christians, then the Church, by divine as well as by natural law (which no positive law properly understood hinders), is able to assemble in a general council representing her in order to procure for herself one undoubted vicar. This action can be taken not only on the authority of the cardinals, but even with the help and co-operation of any prince or other Christian. For the mystical body of

[5] Isa. 59:2.　　　　[6] Eph. 5:23.　　　　[7] Gal. 3:28.

the Church, perfectly established by Christ, has, no less than
any civil, mystical, or truly natural body, the right and the
power to procure its own union. It is not in accordance with
the absolute and immutable law, divine or natural, that the
Church should be unable to assemble or unite without the
pope, or anyone of a particular rank or association, when
death or error may occur at any time.

The Third Consideration

The unity of the Church in one undoubted vicar of Christ,
who is, to a certain extent [quodammodo] unessential [accidentalis]
and mutable [mutabilis], must in no way be hindered or de-
ferred on account of the contention of two men over the papacy,
or of their supporters, if these seek to maintain their position
on the strength of allegations drawn from positive law, and on
various pleas and complaints, such as: that they have suffered
deprivation, and must, therefore, before all else be reinstated.
On account of the council it is expedient that they should, as
the apostle says, forget what is behind and strain forward to
what lies ahead.[8] For according to Augustine, greater attention
should be given to finding out how the Church is to be delivered
from this exceedingly deep pit of schism than how and through
whom it fell into it.

The Fourth Consideration

The unity of the Church in one undoubted vicar of Christ
must be so greatly beloved that, for the sake of its attainment,
the majority of the evils that have been committed by the
individuals themselves should, according to reason, be dismissed
now, or at some later date, without punishment. Certain rights
[iura], true or pretended, can be put aside, that a voluntary
abdication may be made by them or even forced upon them by
the authority of the Council. The law of nature undoubtedly
prescribes that every part should surrender itself for the sake of
the well-being of the whole. Why, if any of the contestants
strives to justify himself or complain that he has been treated
unjustly, let this be said to him: "You owe yourself and all
that you have to the Church; you, who call yourself a shepherd,
however innocent you may be, must be prepared to offer your
own life for her, that she be saved, united, or not seriously

8 Phil. 3:13.

scandalized. How much more, then, [must you be prepared to surrender] your present dignity, in seeking those things that are Jesus Christ's? This must not be done in accordance with the dictates of personal or carnal interest, but of public and incorrupt spiritual interest, according as the council, which is indeed wise, shall judge. In doing this you will by no means be abandoning the flock, but feeding and uniting it; and you will be called to remain."

The Fifth Consideration

The unity of the Church in one vicar of Christ does not for its attainment at the present time require a literal observance of the outward terms of positive law, or of ordinary processes in summonses, accusations, denunciations, or similar matters. This General Council may proceed summarily, and with the good and important [principle] of equity. It shall have sufficient judicial authority to use ἐπιείκεια, i.e., the power to interpret all positive law, to adapt it for the sake of accomplishing the union more speedily and more advantageously, and, if need be, to abandon it because it was instituted for the peace and well-being of the Church. If it has been instituted properly and not by any tyrannical malignity, it should not militate against the Church, lest the power that has been conferred on human institutions bring about the destruction rather than the edification of the Church. In fact the power of using ἐπιείκεια with regard to a matter of doctrine [doctrinaliter] belongs principally to those learned in theology, which in relation to other [sciences] is fundamental [architectoria], and thereafter with those skilled in the science of canon and civil law, as they have to take their basic ideas from the principles of divine and natural law.

The Sixth Consideration

The unity of the Church in one undoubted vicar of Christ should, it seems, be obtained by the council now to be held, in the following manner. First, security should be granted by the princes and others that the two contestants, if they wish to appear, may proceed to fulfill their oaths and vows. If they refuse to comply, abdication through legitimate proctors should be obtained from them. If they absolutely refuse to do either of these, both contestants should be condemned, then procedure set in motion for the election of one [vicar] with the common consent of the entire council, which would corroborate and approve what two thirds of the college of cardinals, or the greater and wiser part of them, agreed upon or accomplished. If some wish to adhere pertinaciously to one or other of the two contestants, and not follow the decision of the council (this is not to be entered upon lightly), let them look to their own salvation, because this council and its followers shall have in the sight of God and man delivered itself from the accusation of schism.

THE SEVENTH CONSIDERATION

The unity of the Church in one undoubted vicar of Christ is so privileged and holy that those who sincerely seek it must by no means be regarded by the contestants as their adversaries, but as their best friends in Christ. For they ask for their voluntary abdication, or, if they refuse, seek to overthrow them, that their souls may thereby be saved and the Church no longer disturbed. Actually in so acting toward these contestants, they are doing what every Christian must do. Indeed, in this desperate and inveterate disease of our common Mother, they have a command from God. This is the inviolable basis, strengthened by necessity and piety, on which the Most Christian King of the Franks, who is most upright, neither seeking his own interest nor harboring hatred against any, has supported every kind of praiseworthy activity for the restoration of peace, as his open letter *Pax ecclesiastica* demonstrates.[9] Cicero, when he had been accused of having wavered and of having been fickle in his friendship toward Caesar, brought forward in the *Philippics* a famous plea, of which this is only the sense, as I do not have the exact words. "I never loved Caesar," he said, "except in so far as he was seen to love the State. Therefore, when he, by becoming a tyrant, had altered his love toward the State, I completely turned away my friendship from him."[10]

---

[9] Bourgeois du Chastenet, *Nouvelle histoire du Concile de Constance* (Paris, 1718), Preuves, 257–259; *Gersoni opera omnia*, II, 103–105. In this letter, dated January 12, 1408, Charles VI threatened to withdraw obedience once again from Benedict XIII.

[10] For the *sententia*, cf. *Philippics*, II, 45, 116–118; for Cicero's attitude to Caesar, cf. R. Y. Tyrrell, *Cicero in His Letters* (London, 1901), xxxi. For this note I am indebted to Professor G. Johnston, Toronto.

THE EIGHTH CONSIDERATION

The unity of the Church in one undoubted vicar of Christ must not be hindered on the ground that a restoration of obedience must first be made to both contestants, because they have suffered deprivation. [For the argument that] an unjust detainer, or a robber who has been deprived, must be reinstated is derived rather from positive regulation than from the purely natural and divine law. Therefore [positive regulation] holds in stated cases only, and is in no way to be observed to the disadvantage of the natural and divine law and the common good. Thus, for example, no restitution ought to be made to heretics; to those who are obviously schismatics; to the mad and the drunk to their own harm; to those who have been intruded into the papacy; to those who seek to take as a wife one who is not marriageable or a relative within the decrees prohibited by the divine law; to him who seeks to obtain possession of a benefice which he cannot hold, as the legal possessor is still alive; or, finally, to those who seek to use their possessions to the contempt of the Creator, or the enslavement of free men, or against the chastity and life of anyone, etc. Against each contestant it is easy to bring forward many exceptions of this kind.

THE NINTH CONSIDERATION

The unity of the Church in one undoubted vicar of Christ might be more easily accomplished if neither before, during, nor after the council they seek to have put into effect the just or unjust decisions which they have heretofore published. These concern the intrusion of one or other into the papacy; the processes fulminated against each other from the beginning; the violation of oaths and vows; the withdrawal of obedience or neutrality; the restoration of the freedom of particular churches; the accusations of schism or heresy; the approval or condemnation of the allegiance of one or other part of the obedience; and the sentences of excommunication or other forms of punishment. Such activity should in fact cease and procedure be set in motion to bring about the way of abdication in accordance with the conditions [rationes] and the practice demonstrated many times elsewhere, namely, by removing the processes that have been executed; by the justification, ratification, or even toleration of what took place in the past, as the nature of things will allow; or by the replacement without further discussion of most things to the condition in which they were before the outbreak of the present schism; and, finally, by providing both contestants with sufficient security and rank after abdication, if they at this late date wish to do this either in person or through legitimate proctors. Such an abdication carried out by them through the council would be considered as of sufficient worth to free them of all former impositions.

THE TENTH CONSIDERATION

The unity of the Church in one undoubted vicar of Christ has to be sought after with such great earnestness that it can scarcely be the sober and responsible judgment of any Christian that he has sufficiently fulfilled his duty in this. Far less ought anyone to dare to affirm this on oath, especially when most men are of the contrary opinion. What else would this be for such a person but to remain pertinaciously and incorrigibly in his errors? Again, many cases may arise in which, as it would be permissible to resist force by force to obtain public peace or just protection, so it would be permissible to withdraw obedience from one duly elected to be pope; to remain in neutrality; to cast him into prison; to forbid him all public assistance; or to oppose him by appeal or similar remedy, and in this way true obedience rather than opposition and resistance would be offered. [There are many cases] when it is permissible not to fear any of his pretended sentences, or assert that they are to be feared, but to tear them to pieces and turn them against his own head. Again, it would be permissible to accuse him of schism or heresy by instruction [*doctrinaliter*] both in public assemblies by theologians and men of learning as well as privately in brotherly correction, to which he as a sinner is subject in the forum of penance, and lawfully before the whole Church, to which he is subject in the same manner as one who is capable of erring to what can never err [*deviabilis indeviabili*]: It would be permissible to hold a general council against his will; and, finally, to force him to abdicate, or, if he resisted, to deprive him of all honor and rank, and even his life. In a word, all these and similar actions are permissible according to the immutable divine and natural law, because against this truth no law or constitution of a mere man ought to be made without fresh authorization from God, except to be condemned as intolerable error. Whether the above-mentioned instances have arisen in the present schism we have by no means assumed in our discussion, since we are of the opinion that the distinguishing of particular instances ought rather to be omitted.

The Eleventh Consideration

The unity of the Church in one undoubted vicar of Christ does not necessitate that those who are wandering in error, especially those in reasonable doubt about the obedience of the true pope, are not able to do penance, and are not in a state of salvation, unless they absolutely and expressly confess their error, since often in such instances a conditional penance or absolution is sufficient. It is not proper to accuse of schism all who, in this great uncertainty about the papal right which has arisen from various doubtful actions, do not remain in sure and steadfast obedience to the true pope. Indeed, just as a true pope could fall into the sin of schism by remaining pertinacious in rejecting what would be able to bring about a restoration of universal peace, such as a general council, or promptitude of mind for the way of cession to which he had sworn and the fulfillment of his vow, so also the many who have opposed him could be excused, if this were done out of zeal to achieve union, or from some reasonable doubt and ignorance, since they have shown themselves at all times prepared to obey the Church, and the truth that was known to them.

The Twelfth Consideration

The unity of the Church in one undoubted vicar of Christ must be earnestly sought after by means of devout prayer and the correction of morals. And in the reformation of the Church from top to bottom vehement and continued enthusiasm must be restrained by the complete uniting (when this has been accomplished) of its members, important and unimportant alike. This must be done lest anything worse in the just judgment of God befall us; lest, after a wholesome union has, through the mercy of God, been granted, the former situation return. The book of experience, as well as the numerous documents that have been issued on the subject, and the trustworthy reports of the ecclesiastics to the council, can inform us of where reformation is necessary in the government of the Church. Finally, it may happen that the general council will be delayed on account of the divisions among the princes and others in the various countries, or for some other reason, so that many important persons will either be unable or refuse to appear, or to send representatives, preferring to abstain. Further, the cardinals from both sides may discover from trustworthy conjecture that so many of the important members of each side would not adhere to their election. Then it would seem expedient in these instances that the cardinals themselves, being present at the council, at least put forward a method for ending the schism by providing (unless peace has been secured sooner, and because it would be better late than never) that after the death of both contestants peace be secured in accordance with the method agreed upon in the Council of France,[11] namely, that they should seek and obtain through their ambassadors from both contestants and their colleges [an agreement] that there be no election in the event of the death of the one or the other, with other clauses pertaining to this end.

[11] Gerson is probably referring to the fifth French National Council (August to November, 1408), although no other account of this decision is apparently extant; cf. N. Valois, *La France et le grand schisme* (Paris, 1902), IV, 21 ff.).

Dietrich of Niem: Ways of Uniting and Reforming the Church[1] (1410)

THE TEXT

... *Disciple:* Your Paternity, I have often in times past noticed how fervent a love you have shown for the House of God, for the Bride of Christ, for the union of the Catholic Church. Therefore, I your chaplain, an unworthy friend and brother, complain in a voice touched with sorrow of heart, plaintive and mournful: How does the city of the Church that once was filled with people, one in mind and purpose, but now in our time of trouble perilously divided by sin, sit solitary![2] "Now there is not one from all her dear ones to comfort her."[3] Now not one to work for the common good according to the example of Christ and the saints who gave of themselves in toil, hardship, and death for the sheep, who strengthened the simple in the faith and comforted the faithful. "All her friends have spurned her"[4] because she preaches poverty, forbids avarice, and advocates chastity. "They have become her enemies."[5] Alas! now the welfare of the Church is cast down at the feet of tyrants, she is compelled to pay tribute, she depends upon her own resources and under the pretense of peace and union is laid low and sundered into many rival factions.

[1] *De modis uniendi ac reformandi ecclesiae.* The text followed is that edited by H. Heimpel, *Dietrich von Niem Dialog über Union und Reform der Kirche, 1410* (Teubner, Leipzig and Berlin, 1933). In order to facilitate the reading of the dialogue in this abridged form the words *Master* and *Disciple* have been supplied at the appropriate breaks in the discussion. In this abridgment many passages that were taken directly by Dietrich from Marsiglio, *Defensor pacis,* and all five quotations (Heimpel only notes one) taken from Gervasius of Tilbury, *Otia imperialia,* have been omitted. Although strongly influenced by the former and also by William of Ockham, Dietrich tempered what he borrowed by quoting from the much earlier and more orthodox writer; see, for example, n. 26.   [2] Cf. Lam. 1:1.   [3] Lam. 1:2.   [4] *Ibid.*   [5] *Ibid.*

Master: Surely you do not think that a trustworthy remedy for the sole Bride of Christ, our one and only Mother, will be found?

Disciple: I have sought one from my youth, I demand one, I desire one, yet you suspect I shall not see one. Therefore I sadly ask that I may now reply cordially and enthusiastically to your Paternity in what follows; always making it clear that if I, in consequence of possible ignorance, and fortified with the arms of the justice of the House of God, of the Dove of God, of the Bride of God, of the Chosen One of God, if I say anything less than what is just according to the faith of Christ and the rule of the apostles, I shall revoke it, that our devout and praiseworthy desire may be guided aright.

Let us agree, in the first place, upon what Cyprian says: "The Church is one; by fruitful increase she extends far and wide among the people; she has one source; she knows one home, and guards with chaste modesty the sanctity of one couch. [6] . . ."

Master: But, dearest brother, I beg of you an explanation. . . .

Disciple: Father, I wish to do cheerfully what you command. But for the sake of supporting all that must be said, I protect myself with the following statement: The Church of Christ, duly ordained by him, is superior, more honorable, and more worthy of respect than all [other] societies and organizations. This is obvious. These others are the temporal assemblies of the people, but she is the spiritual congregation of the people. These exist for a time, but she even to the end shall never fail. These save the body that perishes, but she the soul that endures forever. . . .

Master: But tell me, I pray, what Church do you mean? St. Athanasius in the Creed spoke of "the one, holy, Catholic, and the Apostolic Church." [7] For if the Catholic [Church] and the Apostolic Church are the same, then it was superfluous to repeat what could have been explained by one word. If, however, they are not the same, wherein do they differ?

Disciple: Indeed, as you well know, the Universal Church is made up of various members of Greeks, Latins, and barbarians who believe in Christ, of men and women, of peasants and nobles, of poor and rich, constituting one body, which is

---

6 *Decretum,* pars II, C. 24, q. 1, c. 18; *Corpus iuris canonici,* A. Friedberg, ed. (Leipzig, 1889), I, 971f.

7 The context requires that the phrase of the Creed *unam sanctam Catholicam et Apostolicam Ecclesiam"* be translated in this way.

called Catholic. The head of this body, the Universal Church, is Christ alone. The others, such as the pope, the cardinals and prelates, the clerics, the kings and princes, and the common people, are the members, occupying their various positions. The pope cannot and ought not to be called the head of this Church, but only the vicar of Christ, his viceregent on earth, yet only while the key does not err.[8] In this Church and in its faith every man can be saved, even if in the whole world a pope cannot be found, the reason being that upon this Church alone has the faith of Christ been grounded, and to this Church alone has the power of binding and loosing been handed down. For suppose there were no pope, but only one faithful person: even then the power of binding and loosing would be available. In this Church are the seven sacraments and our entire salvation. This Church has never been able to err, according to the current law, never been able to fail, has never suffered schism, has never been stained by heresy, has never been able to be deceived or to deceive, and has never sinned.[9] . . . For in this Church all the faithful, in so far as they are faithful, are one in Christ, in whose faith there is no differentiation between Jew and Greek, master and slave.

The other is called the Apostolic particular and private Church. It is included in the Catholic Church, and is made up of the pope, the cardinals, the bishops, the prelates, and the churchmen.[10] It is usually called the Roman Church, whose head is believed to be the pope; the others are, however, included in it as superior and inferior members. This Church may err, and may have erred, may deceive and be deceived, may suffer schism and heresy and may even fail [*deficere*]. This Church is seen to be of far less authority than the Universal Church, as will be pointed out below. It embodies the instrumental and operative functions of the keys of the Universal Church and exercises its power of binding and loosing. It

---

[8] *Dum tamen clavis non erret:* On this matter see further, Gillman, *Archiv für katholisches Kirchenrecht*, CX (1930, Mainz), 451–465.

[9] Cf. *Decretum*, pars II, C. 24, q. 1; Friedberg, I, 965 ff. Cf. Ockham, *Dialogus:* "Ecclesia universalis regitur a Spiritu sancto et ideo ecclesia universalis nunquam deficiet in his quae necessaria sunt ad salutem." Goldast, *Monarchia* (Hanover, 1668), II, 582.

[10] *Viri ecclesiastici:* Those in orders or holding any office as distinct from the laity. Although strongly influenced by Marsiglio of Padua, Dietrich does not, like him, use this expression as referring to all Christians, but rather follows the normal usage.

does not have and, in good conscience, cannot have greater authority or power than that which is granted to it by the Universal Church. These two Churches, therefore, differ as genus and species, since all of the Apostolic Church is Catholic, but not the other way around.[11] . . .

Master: Which Church, then, must we labor to restore and unite?

Disciple: Indeed, laying aside all else, we must labor for the well-being of this Universal Church and for the sake of those of the faithful who have erred and gone astray by reuniting that second Church, the Apostolic, since apart from the Universal Church there is no salvation.[12]

Master: Who will first undertake to lead back the erring members and procure a union?

Disciple: Actually, when the pope is not suspected, and when there is no question over the union of the head, this [task] belongs in the first place to him. At other times it belongs, I believe, to the whole congregation of bishops, prelates, and secular princes, or their greater part. Whatever they shall have done in this situation is to be accepted as if it were a matter of faith.

Master: What have seculars to do with the restoration of the Church and the uniting of its members?

Disciple: Surely if you love the truth and peace, if you have any regard for the common good, if you consider the natural body, how the hand comes to the help of the whole body, and each limb hastens to its defense, then we ought also to attend to the uniting, pacifying, and restoring of the Church, as is evident from Dist. XLI, c. *Parsimoniam.*[13] Not merely the secular princes but the peasants, the husbandmen, indeed every one in so far as he is able, even the least of the faithful, ought to come to her help, and must, if necessary, risk death for the well-being of the whole flock. . . .

Master: But why should we labor for the union of the Universal Church, if that Church is, and always has been, undivided, one, and has never suffered schism?

Disciple: My Father, if it please you to attend, I do not say

---

11 This distinction is a development of views held by Ockham; cf. Heimpel, *Dietrich von Niem* (Regensberg, Münster, 1932), 124ff.; E. F. Jacob, *Essays in the Conciliar Epoch*, 41, 96; and also J. Haller, *Papsttum und Kirchenreform* (Berlin, 1903), I, 207.

12 *Decretum*, pars II, C. 24, q. 1, c. 22; Friedberg, I, 974; Ockham, *Dialogus*, Goldast, *op. cit.*, II, 503.

13 C. 5; Friedberg, I, 150.

that the Universal Church can be reunited since she cannot be divided by schism, because she can even be preserved in one individual;[14] but I say that we must labor for her unity, that is, for the harmony and pacification of her members. For she has been founded in love and called for the common good; and love does not seek its own. Hence in this Church we, the faithful, have been born not for ourselves alone, nor ought our acts of justice and peace to illumine merely ourselves, but also our brothers and other Christians. . . . Furthermore, we must labor for the unity of the Universal Church, as we are wont to say, because the exercise of her power and authority, which is in the Apostolic Church, is greatly impeded by those contending for the papacy and by schisms. . . .

Today the unity of the head is lost, for three dare to call themselves pope. Today there is a division among the members, for obedience and submission is granted to every one of them. Today there is a disappearance, nay, a complete abandonment, of good moral practices, for simony, avarice, the sale of benefices, tyranny, and cruelty hold sway, approved as it were by wont amongst the ecclesiastics. . . .

[*Master:* Tell me, how will it be possible in a future general council? to unite the Church under one head, restore the members to harmony, and reform the Church]

Disciple: Father, I am glad to do what you wish in a brief address.

In the first place I wish to take up the matter of the union of the head, and to delimit the power usurped for so long by that head.

Who could ever have doubted that the laws, decrees—indeed anything that has been justly ordained in any society—have been instituted primarily to conserve the common good and that the well-being of the State redounds to the good of a private individual only secondarily?[15] The intention, therefore, of any legislator is the preservation and protection of the common good. However, "the cause of an attribute's inherence in a subject always itself inheres in the subject more firmly than that attribute."[16] Therefore if laws and rights are made for

14 Ockham, *Dialogus*, Goldast, *op. cit.*, II, 503.

15 Ockham held that the emperor can make laws only for the sake of the common good and not for private advantage; cf. A. J. and R. W. Carlyle, *A History of Political Theory in the West* (Blackwood & Sons, Ltd., Edinburgh, 1936), VI, 48.

16 *Quia ergo propter quod unumquodque tale est illud magis,* the medieval Latin translation of αἰεὶ γὰρ δι᾽ ὃ ὑπάρχει ἕκαστον, ἐκείνῳ μᾶλλον ὑπάρχει.

the sake of the common good, the common good is a law greater than any right. Hence I conclude that where the defense of the common good and the protection of any living private person conflict, laws and rights cease, so that the protection of the common good may be maintained, and do not have for the time being the power of laws, rights, or constitutions. This was carried even to the extent that it was expedient for our Lord to die, as I have said already, lest the whole race perish. Therefore all the apostolic constitutions or laws made in favor of the pope, the cardinals, or the prelates are understood and must be understood so that the common good of the Church, directly or indirectly, publicly or secretly, in whole or in part, does not suffer damage or division. We can say the same about imperial and royal laws.

Master: Are not secular lordship and ecclesiastical primacy quite distinct lordships?

Disciple: Undoubtedly, for the one is temporal and the other spiritual; the one hereditary, the other from God through election; the one for defense, the other for prayer. Thus if for the protection of one kingdom or one province, one king or one secular prince, who was in direct line of succession, is deposed, all the more should one pope or one prelate, who was appointed by the cardinals, be deposed.[17] His father and grandfather could not, perhaps, afford to fill their stomachs with beans. It is hard to think that the son of a Venetian fisherman[18] should occupy the papacy to the detriment of the common good of the whole Church, to the injury of such great kings, princes, and prelates; that he should be the cause of so much discord, and scandal; that they may not undertake anything without great danger to their souls; and that because of one election he should possess hereditarily the sanctuary of God. . . . Hence I hold that in the mystical body of the Universal Church the more harmful a member is, the more quickly must he be cut off and destroyed whenever occasion arises or this can be done to good effect. Therefore an evil pope must be more quickly deposed because he is a more powerful member than any other prelate, since he has complete, but the other prelates only partial, responsibility. This is true also of

---

Aristotle, *Posterior analytics*, I, ii, 72a, 29. I have adopted the translation of the Greek by G. R. G. Moore in *The Works of Aristotle*, ed. W. D. Ross (Oxford University Press, London, 1928), I, *loc. cit.*

[17] *Decretales, Lib. Sext.*, Lib. I, tit. 8, c. 2; Friedberg, II, 972f.

[18] Gregory XII.

other prelates who exercise greater or lesser ministries. . . .
If the pope sins, the whole ecclesiastical company is involved
in sin. . . . But if any of the prelates have sinned, all the others
are not on this account involved in sin. Nevertheless, bishops
and other ecclesiastics, prelates and clerics, ought to abstain
from every appearance of evil.[19] . . .

I would go so far as to say that if Peter, to whom the papacy
was given in the first place before the Passion of Christ, had
persisted in his denial of Christ, by which he sinned mortally,
and had not repented, he certainly after the resurrection of
Christ would not have received the Holy Spirit along with the
others, nor remained the prince of the apostles, nor would the
Lord have said to him, "Feed my sheep."[20] . . .

Here let us consider the pope. He is a man of the earth,
clay from clay, a sinner liable to sin, but two days ago the son
of a poor peasant. It is he who has been created pope. Has he
without any penance for his sins, without confession, without
contrition become an angel, unable to sin? Has he become a
saint? Who made him a saint? Not the Holy Spirit, because the
office is not wont to bestow the Holy Spirit but the grace and
love of God alone; and not the authority, which is communicated to both the good and the evil. Therefore the pope cannot
become an angel. A pope as pope is a man and as pope can
sin even as a man can err. For many of them, as is seen in the
chronicles, were not thoroughly spiritual. "Their civil acts,
like the acts of men, are contentious, carnal, and temporal.
They are able to borrow, lend, buy, sell, strike, kill, fornicate,
be angry, steal, betray, deceive, bear false witness, detract,
defame, fall into heresy, and commit other faults and crimes,
and foment disputes, as are also perpetuated by non-
priests."[21] . . .

Again, the pope is not above the gospel of God. For if he
were, his authority would be greater than the authority of
Christ, and then his power would not be derived from Christ.
But he is subject in all things to the precept and command
of Christ as is any other Christian. Indeed, because he is established in the dignity of a more perfect state, he is much more
bound to serve Christ. Now the precept of Christ says, "If
your brother shall sin against you, reprove him alone by
yourself; if he does not hear you, take two witnesses, but if
not then, tell the Church."[22] Therefore, as the pope is my

---

[19] *Decretales*, Lib. III, tit. 1, c. 10; Friedberg, II, 451.   [20] John 21:17.
[21] Marsiglio of Padua, *Defensor pacis*, II, ii, 7.   [22] Matt. 18:15 ff.

brother, and relation in nature and in faith in Christ, is re-
generated by the same sacraments, and redeemed by the same
Passion, he must be corrected according to the procedure of
the command of Christ.

Therefore, the decree which says that the pope is to be
judged by no one[23] must not be maintained, because voluntary
actions which lead to the inconvenience and injury of another
must be restrained. The measure of such actions is the human
law, for to this end have these laws been promulgated by God
through the mouth of princes.[24] The pope is not greater than
Christ, or Peter, and the other apostles, who, as we read,
"endured in their own persons continually the coercive power
and jurisdiction of the princes of the world, as did those to
whom they preached the law of truth, or instructed by letter
to do, teach, and command the same, under the penalty of
eternal damnation."[25] . . .

However, let us return to the matter in hand. The pope
either received the papacy for his private advantage or for
the common good. If [he received it] for the common good,
then the common good demands his resignation. I say not only
resignation, but that he must be prepared to accept even death
for the protection of the common good, in accordance with
the example of Christ. . . . But if [he received it] for the sake
of his own private advantage, who gave him such authority?
Not his parents, for they, perchance, were merchants and not
the pope! Not his good qualities, neither justice nor holiness.
Such qualities do not seek their own. The papacy is not holiness.
It does not make a man a saint, although it disposes toward
holiness one who is willing, as do the rest of the dignities of the
Church. Not even does that papal chair make a man a saint.
The place does not sanctify the man but the man the place. . . .

It is ridiculous to think that one mortal man should say
that he has the power of binding and loosing from sins in
heaven and on earth, and that at the same time he be a son of
perdition, a simoniac, a miser, a liar, an exactor, a fornicator,
one who is proud, pompous, and worse than the devil. If Peter
had been such a person Christ would never have given the keys
to him. . . . But if he [the pope] by evil acts has shown that

---

23 *Decretum*, pars I, dist. XL, c. 6; Friedberg, I, 146.
24 Cf. Marsiglio of Padua, *op. cit.*, II, ii, 7.
25 *Ibid.*, II, iv, 3. There follows a section in which Dietrich reproduces the
the teaching of Marsiglio (in for the most part his words) that the pope
is subject to the coercive judgment of the secular power.

he is [a sinner], we should consider together what is to be done or will become of him. . . .

[*Master:* How is the union of the Church under one head to be achieved?]

Disciple: The long desired and true union of the Church . . . could be brought about in three ways, especially when two or three are contending for the papacy as they are in fact doing at the present moment, namely, by the way of resignation and renunciation, or by the way of deposition and privation, or by the way of force, violence, and open attack.

In support of the first method, I put forward the following conclusions: Whenever any possible way by which that union may be secured is given, it ought to be accepted immediately by the true vicar of Christ; secondly, that whenever there is a question of the union of the Church, if no more clement way is found, the pope, under pain of committing mortal sin, is bound to accept this way. . . .

Master: Which way will be followed in the future general council?

Disciple: Indeed, above all, advance must be made by the way of justice which is twofold: the way of recognition and reconciliation, and the way of resignation. Now, since everyone knows that the General Council of Pisa was holy and just, it is agreed that the deposition and deprivation of those two who were then and are now contending for the papacy were holy acts and that in this way the subsequent elections to the papacy of Alexander V and John XXIII were also just and honorable. Therefore, let the method that can better be carried out be upheld, namely, that these two, as deprived heretics, recognize their errors and together with their adherents be reconciled to and reincorporated in the Church. If these two cannot be drawn to bring about the unity of the Church by this method, then the way of resignation by all means shall be put into effect by having the true vicar of Christ resign, should this be necessary. . . .

Master: But what will become of the acts of these three up to that time?

Disciple: This will actually be determined by the future council. However, it would seem to me that where anything, such as an official position or a benefice, is held, not by two, but only by one person, this should be tolerated for the sake of avoiding greater scandal. Wherever and however it is possible to give peace and union to the Church, this should be done by the council, proceeding at all times with mercy. Immediately at the end of five or six years, another general council should be held and, with God's help, a more extensive reformation of all things brought about.

Master: But in the event that none of these [rivals] should wish to resign at this general council, or if one should but another did not, what then?

Disciple: In this situation neither the one who is willing should be favored, by having him remain pope, unless the Universal Church should agree to this and withdraw entirely from the other two; nor should the one who refuses be spared. The council and the Universal Church should withdraw from these three, as from those who destroy the unity of the Church. . . .

It would, however, be of little advantage to have one head if the members were not subject to the body. The Church will easily find one to assume the lordship of the papacy, but it will be difficult to reunite under the obedience of [one] head the members of the body of Christ, divided for so long a time. . . .

Those members are placed in different positions, some higher, some lower, in this holy mystical body. These are all to be led back to the unity of the Church in a twofold way: by obedience and by subtraction. By "obedience" I mean obedience to the one true universal and undoubted vicar of Christ; by "subtraction," the general withdrawal of obedience by common consent and unanimous desire from the two, or the three, rivals for the papacy who are scandalizing the whole Church. As I have already said, all Christians under pain of mortal sin are uniformly bound to carry out this withdrawal.

Supposing that the Universal Church, of which Christ is the head, should have no pope, still the believer who dies in love would be saved. For when two or more contend for the papacy, and when the Universal Church does not know which one is the true pope, to accept one or other as pope is neither an article of faith nor a deduction from it, nor is any faithful Christian bound to believe any one of them. For it is plain that such a person is not of the one holy Catholic Church but rather of the divided Apostolic Church.

Hence the apostles, in composing the Creed, did not say, "I believe the holy pope," or "the vicar of Christ." The universal Christian faith is not in the pope. He is an individual person and may fail. But they said, "I believe in the holy Catholic Church." And in order to define what the Church is, for the sake of the many who say and have said that the evil, however much they may be in the Apostolic Church, yet are not in the Catholic Church, [the apostles] said that it is "the communion of the saints." For it is certain that he who is in mortal sin is neither in the Church nor of the Church which is founded in love.

When there are in the Apostolic Church three popes who dispute over the papacy for their own ends and are in mortal sin, it is best to refuse obedience to such litigants and dividers of the body of Christ. For the faithful Christian is saved in the unity of the holy Catholic Church although he does not have the unity of the Apostolic Church. . . .

As a general council represents this Universal Church, I shall express my views on the summoning of such a council.

Elsewhere I have said that, when the reformation of the Universal Church and the case of the pope is discussed, . . . the summoning of a general council in no way belongs to the pope, even though he be the sole universal and undoubted pope. It does not even belong to him to preside as judge or to define anything having to do with the state of the Church. This [prerogative] belongs primarily to the bishops, cardinals, patriarchs, secular princes, communities, and the rest of the faithful. A man of ill report cannot and must not, from the point of view of what is right, be a judge, particularly in his own case, when, for the sake of the common welfare, the resignation and deprivation of a private individual's advantage and honor is the aim. Therefore, according to the example of the ancients, the bishops, the secular princes, the communities, and the ecclesiastics will summon [a council to meet] in some suitable, safe place, having the necessities of life in abundance, and will also summon to this [council] those contending for the papacy. . . . Out of the number [of prelates, cardinals, bishops, and temporal lords] some will be selected who could and ought to preside in this general council. But when there is a question of the reformation of any kingdom or province, of the removal of heresy and the defense of the faith, then it belongs to the pope and his cardinals to summon a council.[26]

Master: Is not such a council in which the pope does not preside above the pope?

---

[26] Marsiglio held that in all circumstances the secular power had the right to summon a general council. Dietrich, however, being in this matter also influenced by the teaching of Gervasius of Tilbury, held that with regard to certain ecclesiastical matters this right belonged to the pope. Cf. *Defensor pacis*, II, xxi; also A. Gewirth, *Marsilius of Padua*, 286 ff.

Disciple: Certainly. It is superior in authority, dignity, and function. The pope himself is bound to obey such a council in all things. Such a council can limit the power of the pope. To such a council, as it represents the Church Universal, the keys of binding and loosing were granted. Such a council can take away the papal rights. From such a council no one can appeal. Such a council can elect, deprive, and depose the pope. Such a council can set up new laws, and destroy old ones. The constitutions, statutes, and regulations of such a council are immutable and cannot be set aside by any person inferior to the council.

The pope is not and has not been at any time able to make dispensations contrary to the canons passed by general councils unless a council has specifically granted this power to him for some important reason. The pope cannot change the acts of a council; indeed he cannot interpret them or make dispensations contrary to them since they are like the Gospels of Christ, which admit of no dispensation and over which no pope has jurisdiction. In this way there will be among the members the unity of the spirit in the bond of peace. . . .

Thus a general council, representing the Universal Church, if it desires to see a thorough union, if it desires to repress schism, if it wishes to bring an end to schism, if it wishes to exalt the Church, should before all else limit and define, according to the example of the holy Fathers who preceded us, the coercive and usurped power of the popes.

The said Lord Alexander V, before his election to the papacy, and while the holding of the said Council of Pisa was being discussed, fully agreed that this be done. He even used to speak to me of this, and with many philosophical, theological, and legal arguments exerted himself to bring about such a limitation. But when he was made pope he did not strive to let it see the light. Indeed, many of the supreme pontiffs, in the course of time, have applied this coercive power contrary to God and justice by depriving lesser bishops of the power and authority bestowed upon them by God and the Church, who in the primitive Church were of equal power with the pope.[27] . . . But now the Roman pope has reserved all ecclesiastical benefices. Now he has summoned all causes to his *curia*. Now he wishes that the granting of penance, the legitimization of clerics, and the holy ordination of anyone without distinction, be carried out at his *curia*. Those who are not able to obtain ordination in their own lands are easily ordained in that very

[27] Marsiglio demonstrates this point at length, *op. cit.*, II, xv, 4.

curia. Now the monasteries of those orders in which monks used to live in religion in large numbers are given to the said cardinals *in commendam.*[28] In each of these monasteries there is scarcely a tenth, or none at all, or only a few, of the monks that used formerly to live in them. Hence you will see some nephews or lay relations of the cardinals passing their time uselessly at that Roman *curia,* cleaving only to luxury and pleasure, and possessing enough pompous and costly clothes to satisfy even a great prince. But the poor religious out of whose income such pomp is produced are continually laboring at that *curia* in great penury, and the poor are not nourished from the patrimony of Jesus Christ, so uselessly squandered by others.

Thus let the holy Universal Council restore and reform the Church Universal according to the ancient laws. Let it limit the misused papal power contained in the *Decretum* and the *Decretals,* and the pretended power in the *Sext* and the *Clementines,* not to mention other papal constitutions. For Christ gave to Peter· no other power than that of binding and loosing— of binding by means of penance and of loosing sins.[29] He did not empower him to bestow benefices, to possess kingdoms, castles, and cities, nor to deprive emperors and kings [of their authority]. If Christ had in such a way conferred power on Peter, then Peter himself or Paul (which it is not right to say) gravely sinned or erred in that they did not deprive the Emperor Nero of his imperial power, whom they knew to be the worst and most savage persecutor of the Christians. . . .

Let the Universal Church put an end to all these and similar [abuses] in a general council and let her restore the former common law. Let not the bishops and clergy be deprived of their authority and the privileges granted to them by God and general councils. . . .

My Father, . . . you seem to infer conclusively that this future council cannot be held because, in the first place, of the actual situation, and, secondly, because of the law.

---

[28] I.e., "in trust" (originally), but later and here it means in practice "with the enjoyment of the revenues but without the exercise of jurisdiction or authority over the internal life of the monastery." The granting of abbeys in this way to secular ecclesiastics and even to laymen began as early as the eighth century. Readily lending itself to abuse, it greatly increased in the fourteenth and fifteenth centuries. During the schism the *commendae* of many abbeys were bestowed by the rival pontiffs on their cardinals in order to maintain their support. Cf. G. G. Coulton, *Five Centuries of Religion* (Cambridge University Press, Cambridge, 1936), III, 425.   [29] Cf. Marsiglio of Padua, *op. cit.,* II, xxix, 25.

Master: Supposing, in the first place, that it does belong to
the cardinals, together with the rest of the prelates, to summon
a council (this follows from the fact that since the cardinals,
being actually rich and powerful men in the Church of God,
and holding first place after the pope, have usurped authority
and power which they did not have before, and which we do
not read was given to them), they would actually write and
say: "For what purpose do we wish to call a council? For the
securing of one sole pope? Surely we have a pope, true, kind,
favorable to us, generous enough in giving us benefices,
commendae of churches and monasteries, a friend and fellow of
ours, quite ready to plead for us, our friends, and others. For
he, as one who experienced such things in his previous rank,
knows our earthly frame and how to satisfy our desires. I
we were to call a council, we should then fear the deposition
of our good pope, and the restriction of our power, and consequently the election of another, who probably would not show
such good favor to us; or he might remain with us a long time
before he would fully recognize us and applaud us as does the
present pope. We do not therefore wish to exchange the certain
for the uncertain, or to throw away our privileges, for [as we
say] the wise man measures the outcome."

Secondly, because of the law, as you argue. Since you
say that it belongs to the cardinals and the rest of the prelates
to convoke this council, perhaps they might disagree over the
convocation. The convocation will either belong principally to
the cardinals or to the prelates. Likewise if this convocation
is issued by one of the three obediences and not by the others,
one would assume a fortiori that it be made by our obedience
which has the larger following. It is then asked: "What would
be the purpose of this convocation? Not to provide one sole
undoubted pope, for we already have one pope according to
the decision of the Council of Pisa. Not to depose these two,
Angelus and Peter, because already they have been deposed
as manifest heretics at the Council of Pisa. Not to settle the
consciences of the faithful, for as long as these two have their
adherents, so long will consciences be troubled. Not to reduce
the number of adherents and obediences, for this is for us a
problem sufficiently well known."

Therefore, as the final purpose of such a coming together
is sufficiently doubtful, it follows that, as the means are also
doubtful, [this proposal] must be set aside. . . .

Again, assuming now that it belongs to the pope alone to

call a council, will not this pope be able to say: "Why is this convocation necessary? Not for the restoration of the universal faith, which as you have said has always been one. Not for a rooting out of those denying the articles of the faith, for all three obediences say that they hold firmly and believe the articles of the Catholic faith and every day with heart and mind repeat and believe the Creed, 'I believe in God,' etc. Not even for me to resign from my papacy, for I am not bound nor obliged to do this; I have neither sworn nor promised to resign, nor do I intend to resign, since I am the true pope, the sole vicar of Christ and the spouse of the Church. Not for the limitation and restriction of my power, because, as the council might then act in this matter contrary to my rights, I refuse to be the cause of my own destruction, especially on account of the ancient rights and constitutions which my predecessors were always seen to have. Again, I do not have a superior on earth who can say to me, 'Why do you do this?' or who can condemn me for any excess. Thus I refuse to call a council for my own destruction, or to the detriment of my power and honor."

Such a convocation does not seem to be necessary. The Council of Pisa either was a holy, just, and true council according to the decrees of the Fathers, or it was not. If it was not, then it was superfluous, and what was done there has no validity and consequently Alexander was not pope; and these two rivals were not deprived and thus there was no withdrawal from their obediences. But if it was a true council, holy and just, then all that was done in it was just and holy, and consequently since these two contendants for the papacy have been condemned as heretics, deprived and ejected, it seems that there cannot be further discussion about their rights and no mention need be made of them, but only that their deprivation be demanded and fully carried out. If, then, the fulfillment of this demand can be effected in the future council, its convocation is of the utmost necessity. . . .

But it is to be feared that the execution of the deprivation of these two rivals for the papacy will be effected with difficulty or not at all by this method, that is to say, by a council. Therefore the convocation of a council will be useless, unfruitful, burdensome, and in no way necessary, if it be made by the pope, his cardinals, and those obedient to them. . . .

Disciple: [Now] . . . as long as there is no just, strong, Catholic emperor or king of the Romans who, by the coercive use of

power with the favorable consent and willing agreement of the
kings and princes and also of the ecclesiastical prelates—not to
mention the common Christian people—will effectively bring
forward a remedy and have it actually carried out against
Angelus and Peter and those adhering to them, it is probable
that these schisms [30] not only will endure for a long time but
it is to be feared that they will [even] gain in strength. Therefore, the Empire must at all costs provide such a prince who
in this matter will really pursue the cause of God and the
faith.

As a matter of fact the ancient histories record that all
schisms formerly arising in the Roman *curia* were ended through
the Roman emperors and kings and with their consent and
support. Many general councils were held or brought about in
various places and at distinct times by their authority to consider these and other difficult matters affecting the Universal
Church. . . . Thus it seems that if the pope is infamously
wicked and incorrigible, the king of the Romans or the Roman
emperor, as the chief prince and patron [*advocatus*] of the
Church, has in this instance to provide a remedy by calling a
general council, as was done by the authority of the Emperor
Otto I in the case of Pope John XII, who was sole pope but
wicked and incorrigible.[31] . . . Therefore, why similar action
cannot be taken by another emperor or king of the Romans, if
indeed he had sufficient power to put into exercise, does not
occur to me. . . .

Now since you ask what is the purpose of the calling of this
council, we reply that there are two main reasons why this
must be done: first, to bring about a union in the head; second,
a union in the practices and statutes of the primitive Church
and in the observance of the worthy decrees and decretals.

If you say that the means are dubious and therefore uncertain, since we already have one pope, we reply that even
though we do have one pope *de iure*, the other two, namely,

---

30 Both the papal schism and the schism within the Empire caused in 1410
by the death of Rupert, King of the Romans. The Imperial Crown was
contested at that time by Wenceslas, former King of the Romans, Sigismund, King of Hungary, and Jobst, Margrave of Moravia.

31 Dietrich gives a detailed account of Otto's activity both here and in his
other conciliarist writings, thus defending his position by an appeal to
the earlier history of the Church. For a very interesting account of this
same incident see the "Liber de Rebus Gestis Ottonis" in *The Works of
Luidprand of Cremona*, F. A. Wright, tr. (E. P. Dutton, London, 1930),
212 ff.

Angelus and Peter, who have been legally deprived, have nevertheless not been deprived *de facto*.

Master: Let the Church, therefore, be assembled to demand that the decrees of the Council of Pisa be fully and really put into effect so as to deprive *de facto* those who have been deposed *de iure*. If this remedy cannot be carried out, . . . [and] if these two, who have been deprived and ejected, seek a general council and promise that they wish to appear there in person and renounce freely and absolutely their own rights which they possess *de facto*, in the event that our Lord Pope John is also willing to renounce his rights, then in this situation what is to be done?

Disciple: I would say without prejudice that if it be not possible to take care of the Church in any other way, and if the union of the head cannot be obtained in any other way, our lord pope will have to renounce and resign freely and voluntarily— were it possible—not once but many times, not one, but many papacies, lest the common good and the whole Church perish because of one man, a sinner, without virtue or good example. For if he be virtuous, he should follow the standards of Christ, who came not to do his own will, but the will of him who sent him; he should obey the will of the whole Church, the Bride of Christ, and he should resign from the papacy when she seeks it. . . .

Master: What if the pope obstinately refuses to obey the command of the council whose orders and decisions are, according to our faith, made by the Holy Spirit?

Disciple: If he does not listen in secret, secondly, when witnesses have been called, thirdly, in public, then, according to the command of Christ, "let him be in the Church as an heathen and publican," [32] and let him be punished as a schismatic and heretic. For whoever provides an opportunity for offense must in accordance with the saying of the Saviour, "Woe to the man by whom scandal comes, it were better for him to have a millstone hung around his neck and to be drowned in the depth of the sea," [33] be seized as soon as possible and ejected from the Church as a base part, or shut up in prison, or cut off by death, as was done in the time of Clement II by the Emperor Henry III. [34]

Master: But if the true pope in the present situation were to refuse to resign and were punished, as has been said, would

---

[32] Matt. 18:15, Vg.; 18:17, E. V.   [33] Matt. 18:6.
[34] The text has falsely Henry II. Cf. Martin of Troppau, *Chronicon, M. G. H., Scriptores,* XXII, 433; Marsiglio of Padua, *op. cit.,* II, xxv, 6.

not those two, who have already been deprived and ejected, or one of them remain pope, or would each of them be bound to renounce his rights and the authority which he has *de facto?* Further, if they say that they are not in any way bound to resign unless the true pope has resigned, but the true pope refuses to do this, what then?

Disciple: I say that the holy council shall renounce the rights of the true pope, shall follow this with a renunciation on behalf of the true pope, and shall promise and bind itself on his behalf. For in certain legal actions the father usually acts for his son, whom in dire need he, according to human law, may even sell. Therefore since the pope is a son and member of the Universal Church, as I have said, the Universal Church can bind him, resign his right to the papacy for him, and promise or do anything else or act in any other way, which may be found or imagined, for the sake of his salvation, as was done in the case of the three papal contestants who were ejected at the instruction or command of the Emperor Henry III.[35]

From all this it is plain that, if such a convocation of the Universal Church is made and if the kings and prelates are girt in the arms of the zeal of God, of the law and of justice, having one purpose and intention, it will not be in vain. . . . Such a convocation will not be unfruitful if there is one holy intention among the kings and princes. For then we shall be bearing one another's burdens; then there will be a holy fellowship in the bond of peace; then we shall live by the Spirit, we shall walk by the Spirit. Then the Universal Church will be reformed by them in these matters that have been alleged, and it will be justly said, "Behold how good and how pleasant it is for brothers to dwell in unity."[36]

But let the Universal Church beware, above all things, never under any pretext to concede to the pope the power of granting dispensations from, or of interpreting or altering the statutes of a general council because of changes in the times and the arising of new situations. These should only be changed by other general councils held from time to time to reform the Church. For it is clearer than the light of day that, as the avarice of the popes, the cardinals, and the priests increased, that which was for the greater part done and ordained in the four principal general councils, and the statutes decreed by other councils

---

[35] The text has falsely Henry II. Cf. Martin of Troppau, *Chronicon, M. G. H., Scriptores* XXII, 433; Marsiglio of Padua, *op. cit.,* II, xxv, 6.
[36] Ps. 132:1,Vg.; 133:1, E. V.

in the course of the years, have been practically altered, reduced to nought, and as it were placed in ridicule and oblivion.
This has been effected by the reservations of the pope as well
as by the unjust constitutions of the apostolic camera, by the
regulations of the chancery and the formulae for hearing the
cases of the *rota*, and by vain dispensations, absolutions, and
indulgences—the *confessionalia* of the confessor's office. . . .

A holy general council which represents the Universal
Church cannot concede to any private individual, by whatever
dignity he may be adorned, even to the pope himself, the
authority and power of granting dispensations from, or changing and interpreting in any other way, the statutes of a holy
council. Although prima facie the rights of the canons may
seem to say the opposite, the proof is, nevertheless, evident.
The Universal Church, as has been said, is a power superior
to the pope. Thus it follows that this great power of the Universal Church cannot be communicated to an inferior by a
council since he is not legally competent to possess it. . . .
Each member of this most holy body has his own functions in
accordance with which he partakes more or less of its power
and government. . . . The power of every limb of the natural
body cannot be communicated to one limb of the whole
body . . . so in the mystical body of the Universal Church of
which, as I have said, the pope is a member, the power and
authority of the Universal Church, or of a council representing
the Church, cannot and must not be communicated either to the
pope or any other private individual. . . . [Further] the rights
of bishops, patriarchs, and prelates, even of minor rectors,
as members, when they are not able to exercise their own
functions, belong to the body of the Universal Church. . . .

Christ did not give to Peter greater power than that which he
gave to any other bishop.[37] How, then, has the pope dared to
take away what Christ alone was able to bestow? As the pope
dare not act contrary to the evangelical statutes, he is neither
able to take to himself nor reserve the power conferred by Christ
upon other bishops. . . .

However, none of the prelates at the time when the reservation and taxation of benefices were made cried out against
them or opposed them because of their own weakness or ignorance or for their own advantage; so now for practically a
hundred years (they have already lasted so long) the pope
and cardinals say that they have transmitted and ordered these

[37] Cf. n. 27.

reservations in virtue of a holy right and canon, and that a general council cannot change them. This [claim] is false.

Let the prelates of the Church arise and offer to God a sacrifice of justice, and let them deign to remove completely all these plunderings, thefts, and robberies of the Roman *curia*. They cannot remain or be enjoined to the detriment and danger of the Universal Church, since they are contrary to the proper nature of the mystical body of the Church, as has been said, and to every just order and harmful to all the spiritual blessings of the Church.

In that very *curia* you will find a thousand officials for the procuring of money from benefices, but probably you will not be able to seek out one for the preservation of virtue. There, every day the conversation is of castles, land, cities, different men of arms, and money. Rarely, if ever, is mention made of chastity, almsgiving, justice, faith, or holy living. Thus what used to be a spiritual court has become worldly, diabolical, tyrannical, worse in morals, even in civil actions, than any secular court. From thence proceed all these and many other evils such as heresies, schisms, and scandals and those all-engulfing reservations and financial constitutions which the pope together with his cardinals have wished to be preserved and maintained. This taxation of churches and monasteries, the payment to the apostolic camera and the college of cardinals of first fruits, of the half of the income of the lesser benefices, and of money for obtaining in that court apostolic letters—even the general and special taxation and reservation of churches, monasteries, and benefices—for the greater part originated in the *curia* while it remained in Avignon. For no cardinal was able to maintain the regal status of that time unless he were daily supported by great sums of money from whatsoever part they came.

Further, if the pope asks: "What will be the purpose of this convocation? Is it not for the defense of the faith? Surely it cannot be for the restriction of my power, or for the bringing about of my resignation?"

O pope, if you fully understand what I have said, if you are a Christian, if you have compassion, if you grieve for the common good of the Universal Church, [you will agree that] a council of Christians is to be called for the accomplishment of all these things. For if you are good, if you are holy as you are called, if you place any value upon holiness, you must fight to the death for the sake of justice. What justice can be greater, what can make your good life better, your holiness and your reputation greater, than that you, realizing that because of your papacy and because of your unfettered power the common good of the Universal Church is perishing and being destroyed, the faith diminishing, the Church being cast under the feet of tyrants, her liberty suppressed, monasteries and churches destroyed, and the consciences of the faithful endangered—[what greater] than that you resign the papacy and allow your usurped power to be diminished? . . .

If, then, you are good, you, as a second Christ, ought to offer yourself in the garden to the Jews, saying: "Whom do you seek? 'Jesus of Nazareth?' Me, the pope? That I resign? 'I am he.' 'If you seek me, seek, return, come.' " [38] But if you are evil, what remains but that you be condemned and cut off from the fellowship of men as a fierce and savage beast, lest because of your own private advantage the common good of the entire Church be destroyed by schism. Therefore, the summoning of a general council is necessary for this reason, namely, for the sake of obtaining your resignation or for any other means by which peace may be given to the Church, the faith of Christ exalted and strengthened, the consciences of the faithful pacified and the flock of Christ reformed. . . .

Master: But how shall this council be assembled, since the several obediences differ in what they desire?

Disciple: I say that at the present time the convocation belongs to the emperor or the king of the Romans under pain of mortal sin and everlasting punishment. In his absence or when there is no emperor, I say that this belongs to the [other] secular kings and princes. [Further] in the present situation it pertains [first] to the emperor (if there is one), who is the defender and patron of the Universal Church, and then, in the second place, to the kings and princes, to be present at the council, to command the execution of its acts, and to force them upon those contending for the papacy, that a new union may be brought about; or to discover other ways by which there can be one shepherd and one flock. . . .

But coming to the other matters, [39] you seem to insinuate that the pope has reserved for his own disposing all cathedral churches and abbatial dignities and even all conventual

[38] John 18:4 ff. and Isa. 21:12.
[39] In the part omitted the master outlined a number of the most recent financial constitutions of Popes Alexander and John and requested the opinion of the disciple as to their legality and validity. It is to these constitutions that reference is now repeatedly made.

priories and the greater episcopal offices in the cathedrals,
even all the principal dignities in the collegiate churches,
whenever they are, or are about to become, vacant, so that the
ordinaries are in no way able to dispose of them. Thus, you
ask whether such reservations may legally be held or defended
according to God and conscience. And whether those who
receive these dignities could legally accept them.

To this difficult question I reply . . . that the pope cannot
ordain or decree anything in the Church beyond what is and
has been granted to him in the first place by Christ himself
and then by the Universal Church. We do not read that
Christ conferred upon him the power to dispense and distribute
benefices, dignities, bishoprics, farms, and lands, nor do we read
that this was even done by Peter. He only handed on to him
the particular power mentioned in Matt., ch. 16, which he
bestowed even on the least bishop in the world, namely,
"Whatsoever you shall bind on earth will be bound also in
heaven,"[40] that is, by penance, and "whatever ye shall loose,"
etc., that is, by absolution and indulgence, but only while the
key does not err.[41]

However, in the course of time, as the devotion of the modern
emperors and kings and the Christian faithful increased,
churches sprang up in various parts of the world which in
diverse ways were in need of government. Therefore certain
powers of dispensing certain benefices and doing other things
were then conferred on the pope by the Universal Church in
various general councils, but the disposing of the remaining
benefices was entrusted to the ordinaries, so that the patriarchs
and cardinals were appointed by the pope, the primates by the
patriarchs, the archbishops by the primates, the bishops by
the archbishops, the abbots and the other dignities by the
ordinaries. . . . Afterwards—this has been touched upon several
times previously—as intolerable pomp, avarice, and ambition
increased among the pope and cardinals, they began little by
little to reserve benefices.

Since, because of the lack of councils, no one opposed their
evil deeds, they have successively by open robbery reserved
every benefice in the world, thus depriving without cause the
bishops and ordinaries of their power, authority, constitutions,
and rights, being unmindful that the occasion for wrongs
ought not to proceed from the very source of rights. If the
rights of each individual bishop are not preserved, what else

[40] Matt. 16:19; cf. n. 29.   [41] Cf. n. 8.

happens than that the ecclesiastical order is confounded? The pope does not publish rights, nor say, "I do not consider that an honor to me in which I recognize that my brothers, the ecclesiastical prelates, lose their honor." Why, therefore, in modern times does the pope so strangely forget the ancient ways and attempt to usurp practically all the rights of his brothers by making a thousand regulations in his chancery for obtaining at all times ready money in abundance? "Indeed when justice has been removed, kingdoms are nothing but great robberies."[42] . . .

Thus I say that according to God and an upright conscience, the pope and his cardinals transgress the limits of reason and justice, which our fathers ordained. They pretend that authority and power of which we never hear anything in the gospel, and which exceed even the limits of general councils, were granted to them by Christ. In usurping such power they do what the popes for a thousand years never dared to do or attempt, who, or at least many of whom, were better, more holy, and more worthy than the pontiffs of this time. Indeed I say that such reservations are manifest robberies, acts of public violence, iniquitous, and misapplied papal rights, diabolical constitutions conducive to all evil. The papal authority itself is not at all legally competent to make such reservations and cannot even exercise its authority unless the Universal Church wished thus to ordain it.

Hence I say that their promotions and provisions do not hold in the sight of God, although perhaps according to the Church Militant they may seem to be valid. Those who accept ecclesiastical benefices or provisions yet without fraud or guile and without simoniac frenzy may legally in the sight of God retain them. For they are excused because of their unconquerable ignorance and pardonable innocence, although I would judge that in the presence of God it is safer and more excellent to forgo them absolutely and not to accept them through reservations. . . .

The pestiferous constitutions [of John and Alexander] count for nothing *de iure*, but [only] *de facto*. Since they have been trumped up through open violence, public simony, wolfish rapacity, and by the dispersion of Christ's flock, they serve no purpose only that their founders, these popes and cardinals, steal, slay, and destroy.[43]

---

[42] Augustine, *The City of God*, IV, iv. For this reference I am indebted to Professor Ford Lewis Battles.   [43] John 10:10.

For this reason I do not see that, "because every spirit should be subject to the higher powers,"[44] a pure conscience compels, or causes them to be compelled, or dares to compel the future Roman king or emperor (the Lord permitting him) and those adhering to the said Angelus and Peter [to obey] as pope such a person [as John XXIII] especially in those matters which do not verge on blasphemy of the Creator or harm the faith and our Redeemer. [For he is] an open thief, a greedy wolf, and a tyrannical robber who does not rule the Church, nor exercise his authority, for the common good but for his own private advantage. His leadership is manifest tyranny. . . .

Judas did, indeed, once sell Christ for thirty pieces of silver, but they [our ecclesiastical superiors] every day sell Christ and his Church a thousand times not merely for thirty pieces of silver but for hundreds and for thousands. And when they have sold [a benefice] to one and received the money, again they take it from him and offer it for sale to another. . . .

Those who receive and procure churches and benefices in this way and make payment for them according to the tenor of these constitutions,[45] knowingly and deliberately commit simony, sin mortally, and are bound wholly to renounce those churches, benefices and positions so obtained and are disqualified from holding other benefices, as the pope is not able to dispense in the Church of God through simony. . . .

[It is] because the prelates of our time are dumb dogs, not able to bark, that these pestiferous constitutions and reservations strive to occupy the place of laws and rights to such an extent that it is horrible to say how many evils arise from them. For those who are of the households of the cardinals, at one time murderers, uneducated, uncanonically ordained cooks, grooms, or muleteers, are through these chancery rules able to hold dignities, and canonries in cathedral churches; but those who are either Masters in Arts or Medicine or Bachelors in Canon or Civil Law, by no means are able to enjoy such grace. From this it is patently evident how, by these reservations, the virtuous and the educated are excluded but the ribald, the unlettered, the froward, the evil-tempered, and the doers of evil are promoted. Now all "that is not of faith" and love "is sin,"[46] wherefore all who receive promotion under cover of these reservations are in a state of damnation and sons of death, unless they wish to do penance and completely relinquish the benefices which

[44] Rom. 13:1.   [45] Cf. n. 38.   [46] Rom. 14:23.

they have received in this way, for "they enter not by the gate but climb in some other way." [47] . . .

Master: Since this general council must by all means be held, must the one who is to be elected pope be taken from this college or from outside it? And in the event of the three resigning, would it be better to choose one of them?

Disciple: It seems to me that none of the three . . . should be made pope. For if this happened, doubt might always remain in the consciences of those who obeyed either one of the others, and perhaps at first they might not believe that he is pope. Likewise, those who obeyed him previously would be able to upbraid the others, and say: "We have always had the true pope. For if he had not been so, in no wise would he have been elected anew." Nor must the pope be taken from the college of cardinals. Firstly, lest those who carry out the election appear to procure the union for their own good, because each would hope that he should be made the vicar of Christ. Then, secondly, lest they be able to set greater errors and offenses for the Church of God in the future. For it is difficult to abandon what is customary. If any one of these men, who individually have experienced and continually practiced simony, the sale of benefices, and the extortion of money, and have held so many benefices and monasteries *in commendam*, were elevated, would such a person be able not to refrain from such practices?

Thus, in order to remove all suspicion, it will be necessary that provision be made by the general council, in so far as it will be possible, that no one from the college of cardinals may ever be elected. Further provision should be made that the pope be always taken from the various kingdoms and provinces in order and in accordance with the ordinance of the kingdoms, notwithstanding the laws made to the contrary, and that he should be the most upright, the most learned, the most serious in life, and the most holy in that province or kingdom. In this coming council the electing of the pope will belong to the most excellent, the most skilled and renowned prelates of that congregation[48] . . . and also to those who are of one mind in regard to the election, and not to those holding divergent

<hr />

[47] John 10:1.

[48] This is none other than an application of the principle of Marsiglio that elections should be carried out by the "weightier part" (*pars valentior*), *op. cit*, I, xii and xiii; also Gewirth, *op. cit.*, 182 ff. Dietrich goes on to refer to Aristotle, *Politics*, III, xi, 1282a 9. See n. 36 in the Langenstein treatise.

opinions, so as to avoid the danger of a new schism elsewhere. Such disagreement must at all costs be guarded against, for then the latter error would be worse than the former. . . .

From all that we have said above, it is clearer than the light of day that the future council must be by all means brought together and ordered by the princes, be they secular princes or ecclesiastical prelates.

Before everything else, let there be a reincorporation and reintegration of the members of the Universal Church.

Secondly let one who is approved and agreed upon by all, of praiseworthy life and honorable conversation, be appointed the one universal and undoubted shepherd in the way I have said.

Then, let there be a certain limiting and moderating of the power of this one shepherd, which is excessive and which has greatly deprived and diminished the rights of the other former prelates.

Fourthly, let there be a reformation and renewal of the ancient laws, decrees, and customary procedure of the primitive Church.

Fifthly, let such statutes and ordinances be made concerning the pope as well as the cardinals that hereafter schisms will no longer be able to arise or continue.

Sixthly, let provision be made for monasteries, churches, and benefices with cure that they in no wise be given *in commendam* to any cardinals or prelates unless they are poor, that they may reside personally in them as rectors with the cure of souls.

Seventhly, let the abuses, indeed the violence, the open robbery, and extortions of the apostolic camera and its pestiferous constitutions, censures, excommunications, and deprivations be abolished.

Eighthly, let the [granting of] *commendae*, the incorporating and uniting of churches, and the other [abuses] that have been committed during this time of schism contrary to God and conscience, and also the erection of monasteries into parish churches and the holding of two or three incompatible benefices under the covering of dispensations, be revoked.

[Ninthly], let provision be made for the universities lest in them doctors and masters be promoted [too] easily.

[Finally], let such diligence be brought to bear on all other matters that God may be glorified, the holy Universal Church pacified, and the entire world and Christendom saved, to His honor and praise who with the Father and the Holy Spirit lives and reigns blessed forever. Amen.

John Major: A Disputation on the Authority of a Council: Is the Pope Subject to Brotherly Correction by a General Council?[1] (1529)

THE TEXT

In dealing with Matt., ch. 18, "If your brother sin against you"[2] and ch. 16, "Whatever you bind on earth, will be bound also in heaven,"[3] the question arises: Is there any brother not subject to correction in this way? On the positive side it is argued that there is one rule [*ratio*] for every brother; and that therefore, if one is subject to correction, every one is subject to correction. On the negative side it is argued that by "the Church" is meant a prelate of the Church; that there is one prelate of the Church who does not have a superior, the Roman pontiff, and that, therefore, if he sins we cannot denounce his sin to the Church. This leads to the question: Is the Roman pontiff above a universal council or the Universal Church which a council represents?

On this subject opposing views are held. One states that the pope is above a general council. Some of the cardinals have professed this view; it is commonly held by Thomists; and at Rome, so it is said, no one has the right to hold the opposite. However, our University of Paris has from the days of the Council of Constance always expressed the other view, so that she is now compelled to bring it again before the public eye. Of course, I could avoid raising this question, yet since it obviously falls to me to discuss it, I can hardly pass it over unnoticed. The examination of certain points, however, I leave to those to whom this belongs. I shall not deal with the matter at length, as this would mean departing from the general pattern of commentaries. I shall present two articles.

1 The text followed is that published by E. du Pin in *Gersoni opera omnia* (Antwerp, 1706), II, 1132–1137.
2 V.15.   3 V.19.

In the first article I shall put forward a definition of a universal council and also one conclusion. *A council is an assembling together of men [congregatio] from every hierarchical rank and summoned, by those on whom this is incumbent, to work together with common intent for the general Christian welfare.*[4] . . .

The one conclusion is this: *A council duly assembled, representing the Universal Church, is above the supreme pontiff.* I mean by "the Church" the Church as distinct from him. It matters little to those of the other opinion whether or not I include him, because they say that he alone has power as great as that of the entire Church, himself included. This conclusion is proved first as follows: when there are two powers, A and B, and an appeal is made from B to A, and not vice versa; and when B is able to depose A and strip him of his authority because of his demerits, and not vice versa, and to enact laws binding upon him, then B is greater than A.

Now this is the case with regard to the council and the Roman pontiff. Therefore the inference agrees with the major premise, and the minor is proved from the words of the chapter with which we are dealing, "If your brother sin against you," etc. For the Roman pontiff is our brother; he has the same Father in heaven as we have; and he says the Lord's Prayer just as we do; and, like other pilgrims, is a man beset with weakness. Every Christian is our brother.[5] Therefore we can reprove him and at times we are bound to do so.

But here you say that we can reprove him in secret, or if he were about to commit the sin again, to bring forward one or two witnesses, but that we are not able to tell the Church, as he has no superior.

Gregory understood this authority [of the Church as we do] when he reprimanded John, patriarch of Constantinople, for signing himself as universal bishop. For in his letters he wrote: "We, against whom a sin has indeed been committed by a piece of bold effrontery, we, I say, are keeping what the truth enjoins when it says, 'If your brother has sinned against you, . . . and if he has not listened to the Church, let him be to you as the heathen and a publican.' I have more than once

---

4 This definition follows that adopted by the majority of conciliarists from the outbreak of the schism. It should be noted that, in contrast to Marsiglio of Padua and William of Ockham, Major does not mention lay representation.

5 *Corpus iuris canonici*, A. Friedberg ed. (Leipzig, 1889), *Decretum*, pars II, C. 11, q. 3, c. 24; I, 650.

through my representatives taken care to reprove in humble
words this sin against the entire Church, and now I myself
write about it. Whatever I should have done with humility,
I have not omitted. But if I am despised in my efforts to correct
you, there remains the Church to which I may have recourse." [6]
Gregory, who was at that time pope, did not intend that he
should have recourse to himself. Pope Nicholas spoke in similar
vein to King Lothair. [7]

Against your view it is argued that the pope is in a poorer
position than other Christians if he cannot be corrected by the
Church. Moreover, by the words, "Tell it to the Church,"
power is given to the whole Church. Here by "the Church"
is meant the greater and lesser clergy, or a general council
representing the entire Church, because there is added in the
plural, "Whatever you [pl.] bind on earth will also be bound
in heaven." [8] No mention is made here of binding and loosing
in the interior forum of penance, because no one reveals the
sin of another to the Church in that forum (even if in the meantime it happens that a man is unable to confess his own sin
without being bound to disclose there the transgression of
another); but, as is known from the contents of the chapter
and the expositions of the doctors, mention is being made of
the denunciation and reproof of a brother in the exterior forum.

The second argument (at all times assuming the validity of
the minor premise): The keys were not given to Peter except in
the name of the Church and for her sake. Therefore they were
given previously to the Church, " because the cause of an attribute's inherence in a subject always itself inheres in the subject
more firmly than that attribute."[9]

This is made evident by Saint Augustine: " 'Whatever you
shall bind on earth shall be bound in heaven,' etc. If this was
said only to Peter, it gives no ground for action to the Church.
But if this is also the case in the Church, then that which is
bound on earth shall also be bound in heaven and that which
is loosed on earth shall be loosed also in heaven. For when the
Church excommunicates on earth, the person excommunicated
is also bound in heaven, and when anyone is reconciled in the

---

6 *Monumenta Germaniae Historica, Epistolarum,* I, 343, reading "*hoc quod in
tota ecclesia peccatur,*" for "*haec . . . peccatores.*"

7 *Decretum,* pars II, C. 11, q. 3, c. 3; Friedberg, I, 642.

8 Matt. 18:19.

9 Aristotle, *Posterior analytics,* I, ii, 72a, 29; cf. Dietrich of Niem, *Ways
of Uniting and Reforming the Church,* n. 16.

Church, he is also reconciled and loosed in heaven. If this is
what is done in the Church, then Peter in receiving the keys
represented the holy Church. If in the person of Peter the good
in the Church were represented, then in the person of Judas
the evil in the Church were represented." [10]

The third argument: An appeal can be made, not merely
from the supreme pontiff, but from the supreme pontiff together with a particular church, to a council or the Universal
Church, and the decision of the supreme pontiff and of a particular council can be relaxed by the universal council. Therefore a universal council is above the Roman pontiff.

This is evident from the letter of Augustine to Glorious,
Eleusius, Felix, and Grammaticus, where he speaks of the deposition of Caecilian, bishop of Carthage, which was carried
out unjustly by the bishops of Africa. Augustine states that these
bishops, seeing that the world remained in communion with
Caecilian, and not with him whom they had appointed, took
their case to Melchiades, bishop of Rome, to have their sentence
confirmed; and that they were condemned by Melchiades.
Then he continues: "As if it may not be said to them, and this
most justly: 'Well, let us suppose that those bishops who have
pronounced judgment at Rome were not good judges, there
still remained a plenary council of the Universal Church where
the issue could be fought out with those very judges, and if
they were convicted of having judged wrongly, their decisions
might be relaxed.' " [11] . . .

The fourth argument: The decisions of a council are issued
in the name of the Church and not in the name of the pope.
This is so only because of the superiority of its authority.

This is evident from The Acts of the Apostles, from which
the Church takes its basis for holding councils. In Acts, ch. 1,
it is written: "And they put forward two, Joseph, called Bar-
sabas, who was surnamed Justus, and Matthias," [12] i.e., the
apostles put them forward, although Peter proposed that this
be done. Similarly in Acts, ch. 6, all the apostles chose Stephen
and his associates. [13] This is seen even more clearly in Acts, ch.
15, where we are told that some brethren had said that it was
necessary to keep the law of the Old Testament, and that after
considerable strife had occurred, Paul, Barnabas, and certain

[10] *Decretum*, pars II, C. 24, q. 1, c. 6; Friedberg, I, 968; Migne, *PL*, 35:1763.
[11] *Epistola* XLIII, c. 7, *Corpus scriptorum ecclesiasticorum Latinorum*, A. Goldbacher, ed. (Vienna, 1898), XXXIV, pt. 2: 101.
[12] V. 23.   [13] Vs. 1–7.

others from both sides went up to Jerusalem to lay the question
before the apostles. There James in the name of the universal
council, although Peter was present, issued the decision and
the entire company of elders who were at Jerusalem sent a
letter to those who were at Antioch. This is evident from the
manner in which they wrote: "The apostles and elder brothers
to those brethren who are of Gentile origin in Antioch, Syria,
and Cilicia, greetings," [14] etc. Then later on in reply to the
matter in question they said, "The Holy Spirit and we have
decided to lay no further burden on you," [15] etc. Thus in this
serious matter Peter did not give the decision, but the assembly
of the apostles and brethren, which represented the Universal
Church. . . . In all these councils of the apostles, the whole
company defined everything in the name of the whole company
and not in the name of Peter. Therefore they wished to make it
known that the whole company was above Peter and of greater
authority than Peter. Therefore this is what must be done in
succeeding councils. If you say that Peter granted this to them
out of humility, I will speak in the same way of James, and say
of many things pertaining to Peter that the Church allowed
him to have them out of humility.

The fifth argument: The pope can be deposed by a general
council for his own wrongdoing. Therefore a council has
authority over him, for an inferior does not depose a superior.
This is clear if he is a heretic. [16]

But you say when he has fallen into heresy he has ceased
to be pope. If this were so when he has fallen into secret heresy,
the papacy would be rendered uncertain; for this very reason
a bishop does not cease to hold office on account of heresy.
Moreover, heresy takes away the papacy from him either by
divine and natural law or merely by human law. . . .

Perhaps you, like others, say: "Although the papacy can
be taken away from the person of this [pope], nevertheless the
papacy in itself is not destroyed"; or this (and it comes to the
same thing): "The council has no power over the pope, but
removes in the manner of a servant [*ministerialiter*] the passive
bond of the papacy from this pope. Indeed, a certain lord
cardinal, [17] making a great deal of this, says that the papacy is
from God, the person of the pope from his father, and the bond
of union of the papacy in the individual person from a man or

[14] V. 23.   [15] V. 28.
[16] *Decretum*, pars I, dist. XL, c. 6; Friedberg, I, 146.
[17] Cajetan (du Pin).

from men, and that now the council has power with regard to this passive bond, but not with regard to the papacy. He adds: "You, who are a professor of philosophy, should not be surprised that someone has power over the conjunction of form with matter who does not have power over the form."

This argument is not valid. The reason is that the two coincide. All who speak sensibly, while holding that the papal dignity is from God, and that the person of the pope is from his parents and universal causes (although the applying of the papacy is carried out by men), also maintain that to take away the papacy from the one who is pope is to deprive him of the papacy, and to exercise authority over the man who is pope; in the same way as separating the intellective form from the matter destroys the man, although it does not destroy the intellective form. And although the person of the pope is the papacy, keep in mind the fact that Leo X (here taking Leo as an example), when he ceases to be Leo, ceases to be pope. Therefore a council is able to depose the pope in a case of heresy, and in every instance in which he pertinaciously scandalizes the Church, is incorrigible and obstinate, as the gloss on the abovementioned canon [18] rightly says when it raises the question why the pope can be accused more speedily of heresy than of any other sin. It says: "Certainly I believe that if the pope is incorrigible and his sin is public knowledge, and the Church is scandalized, he can be called to account, for contumacy is heresy." This is evident in Dist. LXXXI, *Si qui presbyteri*.[19] One who is contumacious is called an unbeliever.[20]

The sixth argument: A king who squanders [his possessions], destroys the welfare of the State, and is incorrigible must be deposed by the community over which he rules. Therefore, if the supreme pontiff proceeds from one error to another, and if this is well known and he remains incorrigible, he must be deposed.

The conclusion holds good; otherwise better provision has been made for secular polity than for the Church.

But, you say, the situations are not the same. The king does not have his power and authority except from the kingdom over which he freely rules, whereas the pope has his authority from God.

I know that they do not exactly correspond, yet I do think

---

[18] *Decretum*, pars I, dist. XL, c. 6; Friedberg, I, 146.
[19] *Ibid.*, pars I, dist. LXXXI, c. 15; Friedberg, I, 284.
[20] *Ibid.*, pars I, dist. XXXVIII, c. 16; Friedberg, I, 144.

that they are in this sense alike, since the Lord gave directly
to the Church the power of correcting brothers,[21] and as no
brother is exempt, the pope must be deposed if he is incorrigible.
This can be done only by his superiors. Therefore to say that it
is necessary for him only to pray to God and that there is no
other remedy is an unwarranted conclusion.

The seventh argument: Christ, the best legislator, bequeathed the best polity to the Church. But the best polity
is monarchy (i.e., one head), because if the monarch works
for his own destruction and that of the entire body, the rest of
the body can put pressure upon him. This may be done by
first humbly warning him, in accordance with the Gospel
order, already often mentioned, and then, if he is incorrigible,
by ejecting him from the papacy. Many eyes see more than
one and they have to correct the delinquent.

The eighth argument: One ought to follow that way which
is most in conformity with natural light, unless the opposite
is taught by the divine law. But as it is most in conformity with
natural light that an incorrigible head be deprived of his
authority that others may take warning and be minded to act
well, and that the arguments of oppressors should be defeated, . . . whatever be the law they hold. Therefore, this is
the most suitable method.

This is confirmed by an example. If the king of France went
to Jerusalem and left the government of his kingdom to some
prince who perverted everything, giving positions to the undeserving and suppressing the worthy, who would judge that
in resisting that prince the queen did not act uprightly? Indeed
that is the presumed intention of the king. This is exactly the
present situation. Christ, whose bride is the Church, ascended
to the Father and left his duties to a vicar. If the vicar, in the
manner of the prince, behaves incorrigibly, who would say that
the Church acts wrongly in depriving the vicar of his authority?

The ninth argument: In this way reformation in head and
members will be carried out, but given the other, reformation
will never take place. Indeed, to the deformity of the head
many more evils will be added, as the old adage says, "When
the head aches, all the limbs ache with it." Inferiors commonly
imitate the wickedness of the head. The lower spheres are
moved in accordance with the movement of the *primum mobile*,
and just as they are affected by their predicates, so are they subject to them.

21 Matt. 18:15.

The tenth argument: The holy and sacred Council of Constance declared that a council has its authority over the supreme pontiff as well as over the rest of the members directly from God.[22] Now a council lawfully assembled cannot err. You say that only those of the obedience of John XXIII passed this decision, and that it was not admitted by the prelates of Gregory XII and Benedict XIII.

That is not in accordance with the truth. The cardinal of Cambray,[23] Nicholas of Cusa, cardinal of San Pietro in Vincoli,[24] the patriarch of Antioch,[25] and John Gerson,[26] famous men who took part in that council, would never have accepted this if it had not been agreed upon by the greater part of the council, and consequently by the whole council categorically. . . . If the fathers of the three or of the two obediences had disagreed with each other, they would again have elected new pontiffs, which they did not do, but they unanimously elected Martin V.[27]

Perhaps you say that the council was referring to that situation in which there were three contenders for the papacy, and consequently none was undoubted pope, and that in this doubtful situation, a council is above the pope.

Against this [I reply] that one of these two or three was the true pope, and that the council is above him and deposes him.

---

[22] The Council of Constance (1414–1418) in the decree *Sacrosancta* passed unanimously at its fifth general session, April 6, 1415; Von der Hardt, *Magnum oecumenicum Constantiense concilium*, IV, 96 f.; cf. Hefele-Leclerq, *Histoire des conciles* (Paris, 1916), VII, 209 f.

[23] Peter d'Ailly (1350–1420), at one time chancellor of the University of Paris, was appointed cardinal by John XXIII and played a leading role at this council.

[24] Major is in error. Having been born c. 1401, Cusa could not have attended the Council of Constance. He did, however, play a significant role at the Council of Basel, writing in 1433 his *De concordantia catholica*, one of the most fully developed works on behalf of the conciliarist cause. Nevertheless, in 1436 he abandoned the Council and his antipapal attitude. He was promoted to the cardinalate in 1449. See further, H. Bett, *Nicholas of Cusa* (Methuen & Co., Ltd., London, 1932).

[25] Jean Mauroux, president of the French nation and one of the most influential members of the French delegation at the Council of Constance. Throughout the entire council he played a significant role in securing the deposition of John XXIII and Benedict XIII; cf. N. Valois, *La France et le grand schisme*, IV, 275–536, *passim.*

[26] B. 1363; d. 1429. Gerson was made chancellor of the University of Paris in 1403. He played a leading part in the Council of Constance from February, 1415, until its close; cf. N. Valois, *op. cit.*, IV, *passim.*

[27] Odo Colonna, elected pope at Constance on November 8, 1417.

Therefore, having in actual fact such superiority, it does depose the pope.

Secondly, [you say] the famous men who took part in the council did not use universally that maxim to which I adhere as a means of proof.

[I reply]: we read of other councils not greatly differing from this one. The Council of Basel made use of this theory.[28]

Indeed, someone says that each council erred in passing the decree mentioned in the tenth argument, and, secondly, in defining that a council was to assemble every ten years, as it belonged to the Roman pontiff alone to impose such laws.

In the third place [I reply]: the Council of Basel refused to remove itself at the instance of Eugenius IV, although it belonged, so he says, to the Roman pontiff alone to change the place.

But such a person cannot reasonably say this of the Council of Constance, which can be compared on an equal plane with the greatest councils. The Council of Constance did not transgress its boundaries, because, when it defined that it had superiority over the pontiff, it was then able to impose binding laws upon him. In the same way it is said that the pontiff is not able to change the seat of a council once it has assembled, if the council dissents, because an inferior does not have power to move superiors against their will.

Someone else says, "The Council of Basel brought forth a basilisk," but he is an imitator of Saint Thomas, wishing thereby to weaken the authority of the council which decreed that the holy Virgin Mary was not conceived in original sin.[29]

The eleventh argument: The plenitude of power remains continually with the Church in accordance with the words of Christ contained in the last chapter of Matthew, "Lo, I am

---

28 This council, summoned by Martin V and confirmed by his successor, Eugenius IV, met in 1431 and lasted for twelve stormy years. The decrees embodying the doctrine of conciliar supremacy passed at Constance were confirmed at the second session, February 15, 1432; Hefele-Leclerq, *op. cit.*, VII, 692 ff.

29 It is true that the Council of Basel did not declare the doctrine of the immaculate conception a dogma, but neither did it declare that the Virgin was conceived in original sin. Actually at its thirty-sixth session the Council declared that this doctrine was a pious opinion, agreeable to the worship of the Church, the Catholic faith, and right reason; cf. *Dictionnaire de théologie Catholique*, VII, 1108 ff. The decree is printed in Mansi, *Amplissima collectio* (Venice, 1788), XXIX, 182 f. Major is in error. Saint Thomas did not hold this doctrine; cf. *Summa theologica*, III, Qu. 27, art. 2.

with you until the end of the world." [30] But if that plenitude of power is in the pope, it would be subject to mortality and corruption at the death of the pope; this would not be so if it belonged to the council and to the Church, in which, when some die, others take their places. "In the place of your fathers, sons are born to you." [31] Therefore a universal council is continuous [*perpetua*] or the Church is continuous, and thus this way of speaking does not refer to the case in question, because the Universal Church never dies; [32] just as Aristotle (speaking of temporal things) says that the government of a city ought to adhere to and agree with the political direction of the weightier part [*valentior pars*] of the city. [33]

You say that the papal dignity is in itself continuous, because men can immediately elect a pontiff.

Against this it is argued that men were for a long time able to prevent an election, and to elect various persons, as was done for forty years before the Council of Constance. Therefore, if a council is assembled, it can exercise all the power which a Roman pontiff can exercise, just as when a king dies without an adult heir, the community can exercise all the powers which the king had in his life; otherwise God would not have well instituted the polity of the Church. It cannot be said that the king has authority from the men over whom he rules, who are capable of receiving all the power of which the king is capable, and also that this is not so in the case of the supreme pontiff as he is from God. This is nonsense. For although the Roman pontiff is from God, yet it is not true to say that God did not leave this power in the Church in the same way as this political power resides among the men of one kingdom.

30 V. 20.   31 Ps. 44:17, Vg.; 45:16, E. V.
32 *Decretum*, pars II, C. 1, q. 4, c. 12; Friedberg, I, 422.
33 *Politics*, IV, x. William of Moerbeke in his translation of the *Politics* used "*valentior pars*" to translate Aristotle's κρεῖττον μέρος; cf. A. Gewirth, *Marsilius of Padua* (Columbia University Press, New York, 1951), I, 184.

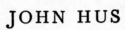

JOHN HUS

John Hus, Advocate of Spiritual Reform

A MONG THE FIRMLY GROUNDED THEORIES REGARD-
ing the significance of John Hus (1371–1415)[1] is that of
Johann Loserth,[2] which represents Hus as hardly more
than an echo of John Wyclif. According to this interpretation,
the thought of Hus "was an exclusive property" of Wyclif.
The majority of German and English scholars have followed
Loserth in this judgment. Thus, for example, Trevelyan, in his
England in the Age of Wyclif, asserts, "The Hussite movement was
Wyclifism pure and simple." [3] The condemnation of Hus by the
fathers of the Council of Constance, based mainly on his alleged
Wyclifism, helped to give substance to this thesis.[4]

But Czech scholarship of the last half century has radically
modified this verdict. The vast literature that has been
produced during that period bears ample testimony to the great
amount of scholarly research lavished on the subject. It
resulted in the generally conceded conclusion that the native
Czech reformation movement, dating back to about the middle

---

1 The date of Hus's birth has most generally been given as 1369. But this
estimate rested on an inference made for the first time in 1590, without
any reliable documentary evidence. It was Dr. F. M. Bartoš, at present
the best authority on Hus, who recently discovered a manuscript which
he recognized as written in Hus's own hand. One of the sermons is dated
"In the second year of my preaching, at the age of 31." This is the first
reliable dating of Hus's birth. Since he was ordained to the priesthood
in 1400 (perhaps in June), the second year of his preaching would be
1401–1402. Hence the year of his birth is 1371. F. M. Bartoš, *Co víme o
Husovi nového* (Pokrok, Prague, 1946), 23–24.

2 Johann Loserth, *Hus und Wiclif* (Munich and Berlin, 1925), 2d ed.

3 G. M. Trevelyan, *England in the Age of Wyclif* (New York, 1906), 262.

4 Cf. my book, *John Hus and the Czech Reform* (University of Chicago Press,
Chicago, 1941), where, in chs. I and II, I discuss Hus's "Wyclifism."

of the fourteenth century, paralleled the English Wyclifite movement, and that in Bohemia the two merged to a large degree after the opening of the fifteenth century. Chief leaders of the native movement, aside from the Austrian Conrad Waldhauser, were Milič of Kroměříz, Matthew of Janov, and Peter of Chelčice. It was Matthew who identified the movement with the Czech university circles. He was a celebrated scholar, a master of the University of Paris, whose own chief work, *Regulae Veteris et Novi Testamenti* (Rules of the Old and New Testaments), was thoroughly imbued with Biblical principles in the spirit of the reform movement. Of this native reform John Hus became a firm adherent, and after 1402, when he was chosen the preacher of the Bethlehem Chapel, the outstanding spokesman. The position which young Hus thus attained bears in itself an eloquent testimony to his qualities of leadership, for the chapel advowson was held by the Czech university masters who would surely have chosen no one of their number but the most zealous, a person thoroughly devoted to the objectives of the movement. At that time, although Hus was an enthusiastic adherent of Wyclif's philosophical realism (as practically all Czech university masters were), he did not know Wyclif's theological works. They were brought into the country a little later.

To be sure, when these books were brought to Bohemia by Hus's close friend, Jerome of Prague, Hus read them eagerly and found in them many ideas that were similar to or identical with those advocated by the native reform. For it must never be forgotten that since the days of Marsiglio of Padua and William of Ockham, educated men all over Europe were acquainted with the revolutionary thought of these outstanding thinkers, and their seminal notions became the common property of practically all subsequent advocates of reform. For all were interdependent. If Hus was dependent upon Wyclif, the latter was dependent upon a host of others such as Grosseteste, John of Paris, as well as Marsiglio and Ockham. But besides this fund of common ideas, the movements also possessed individual traits and differences. The Czech reformers, such as Milič and Matthew, had no faith in State support. Like the representatives of the mystical movement in the Netherlands known as *devotio moderna*, the older Czech reformers placed their chief reliance upon the cultivation of the spiritual life, renunciation of the world, austerities of apostolic poverty, frequent Communion, and the "imitation of Christ." Moreover,

Matthew of Janov had no faith in the role of the clergy. He believed that the needed reform would come from the common people. The younger generation of Czech reformers, and among them Hus, advocated a moderate role of the State in the reform of the Church, although they never placed full reliance on it. In this the influence of Wyclif was clearly apparent. Bartoš has repeatedly called attention to this important result of Wyclifite influence upon the Czech reform.[5]

The struggle against Wyclifism which broke out at the University of Prague in 1403 was at first mainly over its philosophical aspect, although the theological element was not wholly absent, since it was much easier to secure a condemnation of the hated Englishman on the latter rather than the former grounds. But it is significant that the man against whom the opening gun was fired was the senior Czech member of the theological faculty, Stanislav of Znojmo, and not Hus. Later, in 1408, Stanislav was again attacked, but this time along with his colleague, Stephen of Páleč. Both were cited to Rome, and were imprisoned en route at Bologna by Cardinal Balthassare Cossa, the future Pope John XXIII. Having been freed by Pope Alexander V, they were compelled to recant their Wyclifism. Upon their return to Prague, they became the bitterest enemies of the Wyclifite tendency in the Czech reform movement. Incidentally, it was this defection of the two elder leaders, as well as the death of another prominent Wyclifite, Stephen of Kolín, which brought the thirty-seven-year-old Hus to the forefront of the movement.

But even before Hus became the acknowledged leader of the university Wyclifite party, he was involved in the conflict. The first attack centered upon simony. Wyclif's *De simonia* was among the treatises brought by Jerome from Oxford, and was consequently known to Hus. Johann Hübner deliberately provoked the controversy in the *quodlibet* held in January, 1404, by asserting that Wyclif was a heretic and that those who read his books shared in the heresy. Hus replied[6] by charging Hübner with falsifying Wyclif's teaching by biased interpretation of Wyclif's forty-five articles (which had been condemned by the majority of the German masters of the University of Prague the previous May). But he centered his

[5] F. M. Bartoš, *Husitství a cizina* (Čin, Prague, 1931), 37; *Čechy v době Husově* (Jan Laichter, Prague, 1947), 265.
[6] Václav Novotný, ed., *Mistra Jana Husi korespondence a dokumenty* (Prague, 1920), No. 6.

defense upon simony. He quoted Hübner as saying that "the
supreme pontiff should be simply obeyed and we should reprove him in nothing." This Hus positively denied: "You speak
contrary to the canons, and are therefore a heretic if you
assertively and pertinaciously hold to it." [7] Thereupon, he
quoted from Wyclif's *De simonia* regarding the three kinds of
heresy—apostasy, blasphemy, and simony. But even on this
occasion Hus occupied a moderate position in comparison with
that of the acknowledged leader of the Czech university party,
Stanislav of Znojmo, for he based his defense on the ground
of Hübner's falsification of Wyclif's teaching rather than as
Wyclif's own.

For that matter, Hus was not the only person to attack that
all-pervading vice of the contemporaneous Church. It had been
the target of all the advocates of reform throughout the period
of the Avignonese papacy and thereafter. Simultaneously with
Hus, the professor of the University of Heidelberg (but formerly of Prague), Matthew of Cracow, published (c. 1404)
his *Squalores curiae Romanae*, in which he reached the radical
conclusion that since the court of Boniface IX was the very
source of this vice, any contact with it was *ipso facto* morally
reprehensible. Bartoš is of the opinion that the author was aided
by some competent canon lawyer who knew the papal court
intimately, and tentatively identified this person as the future
Cardinal Zabarella, one of the chief opponents of Hus at
Constance.[8] Shortly after Paul Włodkowic, later rector of the
University of Cracow, attacked simony in his celebrated treatise, *Speculum aureum* (The Golden Mirror). This work was
denounced by Albert Engelschalk, professor of theology at the
University of Prague, as heretical.[9]

Hus's fuller acquaintance with the theological views of
Wyclif depended upon the acquisition of further works of the
English reformer. Thus in 1407 two young Czech students,
Nicholas Faulfiš and George of Knĕhnice, brought from England such important works as *De veritate sacrae Scripturae* (On
the Truth of the Holy Scriptures), *De domino divino* (On Divine
Lordship), *De ecclesia* (On the Church), and perhaps *De
potestate papae* (On the Power of the Pope). It was during
this period that Hus informed himself more intimately concerning Wyclif's teaching and found his own views, formed on the
basis of the native reform movement, fundamentally consonant,
but not quite identical, with those of the English reformer.

[7] *Ibid.*, 13.   [8] Bartoš, *Husitství*, 39.   [9] Bartoš, *Čechy v době Husově*, 271.

It is not the aim of this introductory study to trace in detail the events that led Hus to the stake outside the city of Constance. All that can be done here is to remind the reader of the main points of the controversy which ended in such fatal consequences. The first of these was the controversy with Archbishop Zbyněk, which led to the denunciation of Hus at the papal *curia*; and the second was the abandonment of Hus by King Wenceslas. The controversy with the archbishop—a young noble, trained originally for the career of arms, but as archbishop at first a decided adherent of the reform party—broke out over the question of papal obedience. When the Council of Pisa deposed and excommunicated as heretics the two quarreling popes, Gregory XII and Benedict XIII (June 5, 1409), the German element at the University of Prague, and unfortunately Archbishop Zbyněk as well, remained faithful to Gregory. The Czech masters, who had enthusiastically supported King Wenceslas' Pisan policy, pledged their obedience to the Pisan pope, Alexander V. It was this event that brought about a rupture between Hus and Zbyněk. For the latter now used his authority against the reform movement by reason of its alleged or real connection with the already condemned Wyclifite heresy. For even prior to Alexander's election, the archbishop had ordered that all copies of Wyclif's writings, whether philosophical or theological, be surrendered to him "for examination." Hus obeyed under protest, while others refused. Five students actually appealed to the cardinals at Pisa against the archbishop's order. The latter, after a short but sharp resistance, and after he had been cited by Alexander, abandoned Gregory's obedience for that of the new pope.

This happy result of the struggle could have led to a reconciliation between Zbyněk and Hus. Unfortunately, it did not. The archbishop, who smarted under the humiliation caused him by the forced submission to Alexander, continued his enmity toward the reform movement and Hus. Moreover, the latter had now definitely reached the position of leadership when he was elected, in October, 1409, rector of the University. This was the result of the changed constitution of the university (ordered by the king in the decree of Kutná Hora), whereby the Czech element secured ascendancy. The result of the conflicts between Zbyněk and Hus was fateful to both men, although more tragic to the latter. Having made his submission to Alexander, Zbyněk sent a delegation to the former's court, which secured for him papal support in his struggle against Hus.

For the pope, in order to gain the archbishop more completely to his obedience, not only quashed the proceedings consequent upon the appeal of the five students against Zbyněk's order, but even empowered the archbishop to proceed against Wyclifism in Bohemia and Moravia by forbidding preaching in all but the parochial and monastic churches; in other words, by forbidding preaching in the Bethlehem Chapel. For Hus's enemies knew well that this measure would hurt him the most. Moreover, they confidently expected that Hus would not obey the order, and thus would place himself squarely in opposition to his archbishop's and the pope's authority. In this calculation they were not mistaken. When the archbishop published his condemnation of fifteen works of Wyclif, forbade all defense of Wyclif's teaching, and prohibited preaching in chapels, Hus decided that to obey the order would be tantamount to a betrayal of his deepest convictions. He had to obey God rather than man.[10] Hence, he appealed to the successor of Alexander (who had died on May 5), Pope John XXIII. The archbishop thereupon promptly excommunicated Hus, although his action was generally ignored.

Nevertheless, the process thus begun at the papal court culminated in an interdict by which all religious ministration was stopped throughout Prague and its environs (June, 1411). But King Wenceslas was so incensed by this act that he ordered the interdict to be ignored, and as a punishment for it sequestered all ecclesiastical property. Zbyněk was thereupon forced to sue for peace. He was obliged to come to terms with the party of Hus, but refused to abide by the conditions he had accepted. Instead, he fled the country, intending to take refuge at the court of Wenceslas' brother, the Hungarian king Sigismund. But death overtook him at Bratislava (September 28, 1411) at the age of thirty-six.

Zbyněk's demise put an end to the three-year-old struggle with Hus. Although the archiepiscopal party continued to hate the Czech reformer, they dared not attack him so long as the king lent him support. Moreover, they needed Wenceslas' consent to the sale of indulgences which Pope John XXIII had just proclaimed in order to secure resources for his war against King Ladislas of Naples and his protégé, the deposed Pope Gregory, who continued to offer John formidable opposition. Thus Hus, who had escaped the danger that had threatened him from Zbyněk, was now confronted with a far greater danger.

---

10 *Ibid.*, 329 ff.; also my *John Hus*, 36.

His friends urgently counseled him against any opposition to the sale of indulgences, for they felt that such an action would cost Hus the king's support. But all in vain. Hus had to stand against what he regarded as trafficking in holy things. When in June, 1412, he actually denounced the papal bull at a university meeting and called the pope Antichrist, he not only lost the support of such valued and honored friends as Stanislav of Znojmo and Stephen of Páleč, but of King Wenceslas himself.

Thus was inaugurated the final phase of Hus's reform activity, which terminated at the stake outside of Constance. His opponents at the papal court not only secured the closing of the Bethlehem Chapel, but intended to have it razed to the ground. The Prague Germans actually made an attack upon it, but were repulsed by its Czech defenders. In order to spare Prague the horrors of an interdict, newly imposed on the city or any other place of Hus's residence by Cardinal Peter degli Stephaneschi, he left the city in October, 1412, and found refuge in the castles of his numerous noble friends. By this time the original occasion of all this commotion—Hus's opposition to the sale of indulgences—ceased to exist, for at that very time the pope concluded peace with King Ladislas.

During this period of exile, which lasted about a year and a half, Hus engaged in a most fruitful literary activity, during which most of his Czech treatises were written. Since he could no longer preach from the pulpit of his beloved Bethlehem Chapel, he sought to provide his ever-growing numbers of adherents with literature written in the vernacular which would strengthen them in the faith. Among these Czech treatises the most important is *An Exposition of the Faith* (along with *An Exposition of the Decalogue* and *An Exposition of the Lord's Prayer*), intended to teach the common people what to believe, what to do, and how to pray; further, he prepared for popular reading a selection of his sermons, the *Postil*; and included among this class of his writings a sharply polemical work, *On Simony*.[11] The last-named book, along with his Latin treatise *De ecclesia*, is regarded as his best and most effective work. Its last editor, Václav Novotný, characterized it as "the most daring and sharpest" of Hus's writings.[12]

Since *De ecclesia* is available both in the Latin original and

---

[11] All these works are found in K. J. Erben, ed., *M. Jana Husi Sebrané spisy české* (Prague, 1865), I.

[12] Václav Novotný, ed., *M. Jana Husi O svatokupectví* (Prague, 1907), preface.

in an English translation,[13] it was thought most advantageous to include in this volume the hitherto untranslated treatise *On Simony*. The Czech texts used for the purpose were: (1) that of K. J. Erben,[14] which is based on the only extant MS. from the end of the fifteenth century, kept in the Gersdorf Library in Bautzen (Saxony); (2) the edition of F. Žilka,[15] actually a reprint of the Erben edition; (3) and particularly the slightly modernized text of Václav Novotný,[16] who, however, was not permitted to collate the text with the Gersdorf MS.

There is no doubt of the date of its composition, since Hus himself informs us that it was finished on February 2, 1413. He began the work shortly after leaving Prague.

The purpose of the work was thoroughly practical: since he could not reach the masses to whom he customarily preached in the Bethlehem Chapel (although he preached wherever he happened to reside), he substituted the written word. Hence, he preferred a popular treatment of the subject, rather than a scholastic work suitable for the learned. The contents fully conform to this aim.

After an introductory definition of the theme (Chapters 1–3), the author applies the concept of simony to the pope, bishops, monks, priests, and chaplains, as well as to the lay people. Thereupon he discusses the responsibility of masters and canon lawyers. The last chapter is devoted to the means of eliminating simony: since Hus has but little hope that the ecclesiastical authorities would effect such a reform; and since secular authorities were likewise not likely to clean up the ecclesiastical house, Hus places his chief hope in the local congregations, the people.

Although the work was intended for popular use, it was nevertheless grounded upon Biblical and scholastic proofs. Hus was a forerunner of Biblical theologians, for he subordinated scholastic reasoning to the Scriptures. In this he belongs to the Reformation rather than to the Middle Ages. To be sure, he likewise made copious use of Gratian's *Decretal*, Lombard's *Sentences*, as well as the writings of Wyclif and many others of his predecessors in the reform movement. There is no doubt of his verbal and ideological dependence on Wyclif's *De simonia*. Jan Sedlák estimated that something like one ninth of Hus's treatise was excerpted from Wyclif's work.[17] I have indicated

[13] David Schaff, tr., *John Hus's De ecclesia* (New York, 1915).
[14] *Op. cit.*   [15] F. Žilka, *Vybrané spisy M. Jana Husi* (Jilemnice, n. d.).
[16] *Op. cit.*   [17] Jan Sedlák, *Studie a texty* (Olomouc, 1914–1915), I, 179.

such dependence in the footnotes. But to single out Hus as if he were the only medieval writer indulging in such a practice would be wholly erroneous. Opposition to simony was too common among the reforming movements, including the conciliar, to be fathered upon any one person in particular. And unacknowledged verbal copying by a medieval writer from any convenient source which came his way was a common practice. All the great writers—Thomas Aquinas, Alexander Hales, John Gerson, Peter d'Ailly, as well as Wyclif and Hus, were "guilty" of it.

The really important consideration is wherein the treatise of Hus differs from that of Wyclif. First of all, a comparison of the two quickly reveals that Wyclif's work is technical, while Hus's treatise is couched in pungent, popular language. Hus minces no words either in describing the contemporary evils or in laying the blame for them upon particular persons or groups. Furthermore, Wyclif's argument is restricted largely to the papal, episcopal, and monastic practices of simony, while Hus enlarges the argument considerably by including in its scope the parish clergy, academic circles, and laymen. As for the means of reform, Hus's emphasis on the parochial and lay measures (by nonpayment of revenues) has already been alluded to.

It may be pointed out that in his *De sex erroribus* (On the Six Errors), which Hus inscribed on the walls of the Bethlehem Chapel, and which he later expanded in the Czech translation, he included many of the Patristic quotations which are found in his work *On Simony*.[18]

Finally, it may be pointed out that Hus's influence on the Reformation was greater (except in England) than that of Wyclif. Luther's testimony in this regard is well known. Moreover, Luther instigated the publication of two large folio volumes of Hus's chief works (under the editorship of Matthias Flacius Illyricus[19]), while Wyclif's works remained practically unknown until the nineteenth century. Further, the influence of Hus was concretely perpetuated in the two ecclesiastical bodies organized in Bohemia: one of these, characterized by the restitution of communion in both kinds, was the separatist Utraquist Church; while the other body, the Unity of Czech Brethren, was an independent organization whose real spiritual father was Peter of Chelčice. Hence, the Czech reform preceded the Lutheran by well nigh a century.

[18] Bohuslav Ryba, *Betlemské texty* (Orbis, Prague, 1951), *passim*.
[19] *Joannis Hus, et Hieronymi Pragensis . . . historia et monumenta* (Nüremberg, 1558).

On Simony (1413)

THE TEXT

I

Because simony has been on the increase, I wish, with God's help, to write books concerning it, that it may be condemned and guarded against by the faithful, and that some simoniacs may repent. For since simony is a heresy, and since evil men regard good men as heretics, I wish to explain, for the warning and strengthening of good men and for the improvement of evil men, first of all what heresy is, in order that men may learn whether those whom they call heretics are such, or whether they themselves have fallen into it.

Know, then, that heresy (to use Saint Augustine's definition [1]) is a stubbornly defended erroneous doctrine contrary to the Holy Scriptures. . . . But, since a simple man may find it difficult to adhere to the definition if someone should affirm that no one is a heretic while he sleeps or keeps silence, or when he speaks truth; or, that a mute who holds a heretical tenet, or one who holds it but is not teaching it, is not a heretic; for the sake of an easier comprehension I affirm that heresy is a stubborn adherence to an error contrary to the Holy Scriptures. I say "adherence to an error," for without that one could not be a heretic. And since there can be no adherence without consent, no man can hold a heresy without consenting to the error. Hence heresy, equally with every mortal sin, has its nest and basis in the heart, that is, in the hearty will. As the Saviour said, it is out of the heart that evil thoughts, murders, adulteries, fornications, robbery, false witness, and blasphemy proceed.[2] Thus, no man, not even God, can make anyone a

---

[1] Hus is quoting from his own exposition of the *Sentences*. Václav Flajšhans, *Super IV sententiarum* (*Spisy M. Jana Husi*, Prague, 1904–1906), III, 586–587. The quotation is from Augustine's *De utilitate credendi* (Migne, *PL*, 42:64 ff.).

[2] Matt. 15:19. Hus used a Czech version of Scripture which is adhered to throughout this translation.

heretic without his consent. Secondly, you perceive that heresy can exist in none but a rational spirit which willfully opposes the truth of the Holy Scriptures. For as every mortal sin is found only in a rational spirit, and every heresy is a mortal sin, hence all heresy exists only in a rational spirit.

Furthermore, it is stated that heresy implies a stubborn adherence [to the error], such as a man refuses, temporarily or permanently, to give up. For when a man, holding an error as truth, recognizes that what he has held for truth is an error, and immediately acknowledges it to be such, he is not a heretic. Therefore, Saint Augustine says that no matter how much some might have gone astray, if they have diligently sought the truth, and, having found it, immediately have forsaken the error, such should not be regarded as heretics. Why? Because they did not persist in the error, but were willing to forsake it and gladly to accept the truth. Accordingly, every faithful Christian should be so minded as not to hold anything contrary to the Holy Scriptures. But if from ignorance he should happen to fall [into error], he should be willing immediately and gladly to relinquish it. Likewise the masters in schools, when they dispute with other masters or engage in writing, declare that they do not intend to hold anything erroneous. For this same consideration also are the simple folk held clear of heresy when some of them imagine as if the Holy Trinity were a woman, or as if God the Father were an older person than God the Son. Therefore, it is the stubborn persistence in error which constitutes heresy.

Furthermore, since some adhere to an error against the Holy Scriptures in deed, while others in word, not only is he a heretic who holds the error in word, but likewise he who holds it in deed. For example: If Peter were to say that fornication is not a sin but would not commit it; and if John were to say that fornication is a sin but would stubbornly persist in committing it; then John would be a heretic in deed and Peter in word. But if a third person were to say that fornication is no sin and stubbornly persisted in committing it, he would be a twofold heretic. And as he who, teaching others errors contrary to the Holy Scriptures, leads them into heresy and is a heretic himself, so likewise is he a heretic who by his evil deed seduces many from following Christ. For deeds teach more and with greater effect than mere words. The heretic in deed contradicts the article of faith of the Holy Scripture which affirms, "I believe in God." Accordingly, Saint Paul says that "they

profess that they know God, but by evil deeds deny him." [3]
Therefore, Judas was a worse heretic when, while betraying
the Lord Jesus, he said to him, "Hail, Master!" than Peter,
who had sworn and forsworn himself saying that he did not
know the man they had pointed out to him. [4]

From this discussion you perceive that he who stubbornly
persists in committing mortal sin is a heretic, because he stubbornly holds an error contrary to the Holy Scriptures. First,
against the tenet, "I believe in God"; and if he be a fornicator,
against the Scriptural Commandment, "Thou shalt not commit
adultery"; or if he commits some other mortal sin, he trans-
gresses some other pertinent Scriptural commandment. O Lord!
thou knowest that there are many heretics in deed who esteem
themselves good Christians and who call others—good people—
heretics!

Learn, furthermore, from this discourse that were there no
Holy Scriptures there would likewise be no heresy; as there
would be no night had not day preceded it. Moreover, as no
man can detect heresy unless he knows the Holy Scriptures
which the heresy contradicts, so no one should call his neighbor
a heretic unless he knows the [passage of the] Holy Scriptures
which the latter stubbornly contradicts in word or deed. And,
since he does not know his neighbor's intention, he should not
recklessly and rashly call him a heretic.

. . . But perhaps you say: hence every Jew and every pagan,
since they do not believe in Christ here on earth, is a heretic.
And this does not seem to be true. For only a Christian
who has gone astray in respect of some precept of the Holy
Scriptures is called a heretic. But to this I reply that every pagan
and every Jew who stubbornly holds an error contrary to the
Holy Scriptures is a heretic; but whether or not he die in heresy,
I leave to God. Hence when it is asserted that only he is a
heretic who had first been a Christian, it is not true. Furthermore, I affirm that everyone excommunicated by God and
hence accursed of God, if he stubbornly persist in such an excommunication and curse, is a heretic. For he is cut off from
God and his holy Church even though he shine before men
as a saint; and, on the contrary, many a one cursed and
condemned before men is a great saint in the sight of God.
Accordingly, let us beware of errors, nor let us recklessly and
maliciously revile our neighbors as heretics, if we desire to be
blessed in the end!

[3] Titus 1:16.   [4] Cf. Matt. 26:49, 69, 70.

2

. . . There are three kinds of heresy, namely, apostasy, blasphemy, and simony. Apostasy consists in turning away from the law of God. Blasphemy consists in defaming the power of God, which is done in a threefold manner: first, when a man thrusts upon God what is unbecoming, as for instance that God may lie or commit sin. The second form of blasphemy consists in a stubborn mental detracting from the power of God, as when he affirms or teaches that God is unable to feed anyone at any time or any place. The third form of blasphemy consists in ascribing to human power or to another creature that which is proper solely to God himself.[5]

Those priests who affirm that they are the creators of God, that they create the body of Christ whenever they wish, and that they forgive sins whenever and whosesoever they wish, and send to hell whomever they desire, are guilty of such blasphemy.[6] For such [priests] understand the Scriptures even less than the Jews. For the latter, supposing that to forgive sins belongs to God alone, and presuming (although erroneously) that Christ was not God when he said to the man sick of the palsy whom he had healed, "Son, be of good hope; thy sins are forgiven," replied, "This man blasphemes; for who can forgive sins save only God?"[7] They also blaspheme who say that the pope cannot err and that men should obey him in all things, for he can send whomever he wishes to heaven or hell. For such power belongs to God alone. It is likewise a blasphemy when they affirm that the pope is an earthly god who can do on earth as he pleases, ruling over all mankind as he wishes; likewise, those who say that he may establish a law contrary to God's law, or that he may rightfully order something against the holy apostles. They also assert that no one on earth should speak against him, let him do what he may. But blessed be the mighty God forever that he permitted Peter, for our instruction, to fall into a great sin, so that we may know that even that first vicar whom he himself had elected, appointed, established, and confirmed, had grossly sinned. Furthermore, after the descent of the Holy Spirit, he [Peter] again went astray and was therefore rebuked by Saint Paul, as the latter says: "Before

---

5 This paragraph follows verbally Wyclif's *De simonia* (ed. Herzberg-Fränkel and M. H. Dziewicki, London, 1898), 1.

6 Cf. Hus's *Super IV sententiarum*, 587 and 639.   7 Matt. 9:2, 3.

all, I resisted Peter, who was worthy of condemnation." [8] For which of the popes is so much above Saint Peter that he could not sin? Or above Saint John, the beloved of God, who says, "If we say that we sin not, we deceive ourselves, and the truth is not in us"? [9] In truth, by this blasphemous flattery the messengers of the Antichrist deceive both the pope and the people, so that they suppose it to be as they say.

This blasphemy constitutes the self-assertion of the Antichrist whereby he lifts himself above all which is called God; that is, even above Christ's divinity as well as Christ's humanity, grasping God's power but rejecting humility, poverty, and the other virtues and work of Christ. Thus, as Christ, when he lived on earth, had been in all things obedient unto the Father, he [the Antichrist] is in all things contrary to Christ; hence he is called the Antichrist, which means the adversary of Christ; of whom, God willing, I shall write more later. [10]

It was on account of the heresy of blasphemy that the Lord Jesus was put to death, for they accused him of blaspheming. For when they were about to stone him as a blasphemer, he said to them, "Many good works have I shown you from the Father; for which of those works do ye stone me?" The Jews answered him: "For a good work we stone thee not, but for blasphemy; that thou being a man, makest thyself God." [11] And again when Bishop Caiaphas inquired of him, saying, "I adjure thee by the living God, that thou tell us whether thou art the Christ, the Son of God," Jesus replied, "Thou hast said; nevertheless, I say unto you, henceforth ye shall see the Son of Man sitting at the right hand of the power of God, and coming on the clouds of heaven." Then the high priest rent his garments, saying: "He has spoken blasphemy: what further need have we of witnesses? Behold, now ye have heard the blasphemy. What think ye?" They answered and said, "He is worthy of death." Then did they spit in his face and buffeted him; and some boxed him on the ear, and smote his face with palms or fists of their hands, saying, "Prophesy unto us, thou Christ, who is he that struck thee?" [12] This passage makes it

---

[8] Gal. 2:11.   [9] I John 1:8.

[10] Hus mentions his intention to write about the Antichrist in a letter written to Prague in November, 1412 (F. Palacký, ed., *Documenta magistri Joannis Hus*, Prague, 1869, 40). In his *Postil* (completed in October, 1413) he writes as if the book were already written (K. J. Erben, ed., *M. Jana Husi Sebrané spisy české*, Prague, 1865, II, 11). It is perhaps his treatise entitled *On the Six Errors*, completed on June 21, 1413.

[11] John 10:32, 33.   [12] Matt. 26:63–68.

evident that the evil blasphemers condemned to death the innocent Christ on account of blasphemy.

They also accused him before Pilate of rejecting the law of God, saying, "We found this fellow perverting our people." And further they said, "He stirs up the people, teaching throughout all Jewish lands, beginning from Galilee even unto this place." [13] By that charge they accused him of heresy, which is turning away from the law of God. But they did not accuse him of simony, for they could find no sign of avarice in him.

The third heresy is simony, which is an evil consent to an exchange of spiritual goods for nonspiritual, about which more will be said. But know that these three heresies are not entirely independent of each other, but are connected with each other. Nevertheless, they are differentiated from each other so that apostasy is the rejection of the law of God; blasphemy is the defamation of the divine faith; and simony is the heresy of overthrowing the divine order. Thus with these three heresies the entire Holy Trinity is contemned: God the Father is contemned by apostasy, for he rules mightily by a pure and immaculate law; he also has provided a bride of Christ which is the congregation of all the elect; God the Son, who is the Wisdom of God, is contemned by the second heresy—blasphemy; and God the Holy Spirit, who in his supreme goodness wisely and humbly governs God's house, is contemned by the accursed simony which is contrary to his order. For the simoniac opposes the Holy Spirit, intending to derange his good order, and thus also peace. And since in accordance with the testimony of Christ the sin against the Holy Spirit is unforgivable both in this world and the next, [14] I will write about this sin. For simony is a spiritual leprosy which is difficult to be driven out from the soul save by God's special miracle. Moreover, since this leprosy spreads from one to another, so that one simoniac infects many others, faithful Christians should diligently guard against it. But because a man cannot easily guard against an evil he does not know, simony must therefore be made known.

Simony, as the word signifies, [15] is trafficking in holy things. And since both he who buys and he who sells is a merchant, a simoniac is both he who buys and he who sells holy things. *Consequently, simony comprises both buying and selling of holy things.* But since there can be blameless buying and selling of a holy thing, for a man may buy himself the Kingdom of Heaven, not

[13] Luke 23:2, 5.   [14] Matt. 12:31.
[15] In Czech, *"svatokupectví"* means "trafficking in holy things."

every buying or selling is simony. For, as has been said above, simony is an evil consent to an exchange of a spiritual for a nonspiritual thing. For that a man may worthily buy the Kingdom of Heaven, which is blessedness, the Lord affirms through the prophet Isaiah, "Come and buy without silver." [16] And the Saviour affirms that the Kingdom of Heaven is like unto a merchant seeking goodly pearls, who, having found one pearl of great price, went and sold all that he had and bought it. [17] Thus it behooves a man to buy the holy thing, for unless he purchase it he shall not attain to heavenly joy. Likewise a preacher or a teacher may properly exchange his learning for temporal necessities. As Saint Paul says, "For if we give you spiritual things, is it a great matter if we receive of you carnal things?" [18] Therefore, in order that you may know that simony has its source and nest in the evil will, it is defined as an evil consent to such an exchange. Accordingly, you perceive that one commits simony not only when the transaction is completed or when a tacit exchange of the spiritual for the material thing takes place, but even when one's corrupt will consents to such an exchange. For fornication is first a mortal sin in the soul, and afterward in deed.

Nevertheless, a difficulty presents itself in regard to what a spiritual thing is. For every man who commits a mortal sin is a simoniac, since he sells his soul and his human dignity— which are spiritual things—to the devil. Therefore, understand that simony in a particular sense designates an improper exchange among men dealing with the spiritual offices of the house of God.

The simple-minded imagine that there is no simony except that a priest haggle about the body of God, saying: "What will you give me for the body of God?"; or, "How much will you take for that altar, or that church, or other benefice?" But the saints who know the Scriptures regard [as simony] the evil will whereby a man demands for a spiritual thing a material recompense, favor, or praise. Accordingly, Saint Gregory says: "There are many who do not take money payments for ordination, but yet grant the ordination for human favor, and from this human praise seek their sole reward. Thus the gift which they had freely received they do not freely give, because they expect in exchange for the granting of the holy office the payment of favor. Thus the prophet has well said in describing a righteous man, 'Blessed is he who withdraws his hand from

16 Isa. 55:1.   17 Matt. 13:45, 46.   18 I Cor. 9:11.

every gift.' Excellently he says 'from every gift'; for some gifts
consist of service, others are transmitted by hand, others by
the tongue. The gift consisting of service is the appointment of
an unworthy candidate; the gift transmitted by the hand,
that is, anything which may be purchased, is money; the gift
conveyed by the tongue is praise or improper promise. Hence
in conferring consecration, he withdraws his hand from every
recompense when in exchange for the sacred things he not
only asks no money but likewise no human praise." [19] . . .

Thereby Saint Gregory means that whenever anyone confers
a spiritual gift improperly either himself or through another,
either openly or covertly, either in consideration of service, of
material gift, or human favor, he thereby commits simony,
contrary to the Scriptures and Christ's command, "Freely
have ye received, freely give." [20] The apostles received freely,
without bribery, without unworthy subservience, or material
favor; therefore, they likewise gave freely, without such bribery.
But since now clergy do not receive freely, they likewise do not
give freely, neither absolution, nor ordination, nor extreme
unction, nor other spiritual things.

From this exposition, as well as from the customs which we
plainly observe among clerics, we may learn that there are
but few priests who have secured their ordination or their
benefices without simony, so they on the one hand and their
bishops on the other have fallen into simony. And since simony
is heresy, if anyone observe carefully he must perceive that
many are heretics. Nor is there any difference among them,
except that among those who occupy higher ecclesiastical
offices they are more numerous, more persistent, and fatter
simoniacs, and accordingly heretics. . . . Pope Paschal says
that "manifest simoniacs should be rejected by the faithful as
the first and pre-eminent heretics; and if after admonition they
refuse to desist, they should be suppressed by the secular power.
For all other sins in comparison with the heresy of simony
are as if of no account." [21] . . .

Furthermore, Saint Gregory writes: "To you, priests, I say
this with weeping, that we have found that many of you ordain
for money, selling spiritual gifts, and from these sinful evils
you heap up material profit. Why do you not call to mind

19 Sancti Gregorii papae, *Opera omnia* (Migne, *PL*, 76, cols. 1091–1092).
20 Matt. 10:8.
21 Paschal I (817–824). Aemilius Friedberg, ed., *Decretum Magistri Gratiani*
(Leipzig, 1889), Vol. I, pars II, C. I, q. VII, c. 27.

what the voice of God says: 'Freely have ye received, freely
give'? Why do ye not bring before your eyes how the Saviour,
having entered the Temple, had overthrown the tables of the
sellers of doves and had scattered the money of the money-
changers? And who are the sellers of doves in God's temple
today but those in Christendom who accept money for laying
on of hands? For the Holy Spirit from heaven is given by
laying on of hands. Accordingly, a dove is sold when the gift
of the Holy Spirit is sold for money. But our Redeemer over-
turns the tables of the dove sellers, for he destroys the priesthood of such traffickers. Therefore the holy canons condemn
the heresy of simony and order the degradation of such from
priesthood."[22] . . . And, knowing that priests employ much
cunning in excusing themselves, he immediately adds: "The
day will surely come and is not far off, when the Pastor of
pastors shall appear and shall make public the deeds of every
man; and he who now punishes the sins of the inferiors through
their superiors shall then condemn the sins of the superiors
themselves. For that reason having entered the Temple, he
made a whip of cords and expelled from the house of God the
wicked traffickers and overturned the tables of the dove sellers.
For he chastises the transgressions of the subjects through the
pastors, but the wickedness of the pastors he himself shall
punish. This judge shall surely come, and before him no one
shall hide in silence, nor shall anyone deceive him by
denials."[23] . . .

Saint Remigius,[24] commenting on the same passage as Saint
Gregory, writes as follows: "Hear and apprehend this, priests
of the holy Church, that is, of the Christian communion, and
beware lest ye convert the house of God into a den of robbers.
For he is a robber who seeks [material] reward from the law
and is diligent in the sacramental service for sake of gain.
Hence they should fear that they be not cast out of the spiritual
temple, as the others [the dove sellers] were cast out of the
temporal temple; for the Lord visits his Father's house (i.e., the
holy Church) every day and casts out those who busy themselves with unrighteous gain, accounting as guilty of the same

22 The original passage is found in Migne, *PL*, 76, col. 1145. The final
   clause is omitted in the Czech text.
23 Migne *ibid.*, cols. 1145–1146.
24 Remigius of Auxerre (c. 910) in *Quadragesimale*, a copy of which is found
   in the Prague University Library. But no such passage is to be found
   in his writings published in Migne, *PL*, v. 131.

sin both the buyers and the sellers. For the sellers are those who bestow ordination for remuneration; and buyers those who pay money for the truth [i.e., the holy office], and, having paid money to the sellers, buy sin for themselves.

Let us notice that the passage says, "He overturned the tables of the money-changers, as well as of the sellers of doves." What else can be understood by the tables of the money-changers but the altars which are converted by the covetousness of the priests into the tables of money-changers? And what else can be meant by the tables of the dove sellers but the dignity of masters in the holy Church, which dignity, if it be used for gain, shall be emptied? And what can be signified by doves but the Holy Spirit, who appeared above the Lord in the likeness of a dove? And who are the dove sellers but those who, by the laying on of hands, sell the Holy Spirit for a consideration? . . . For whenever a bishop sells the gift of the Holy Spirit, even though he dazzles men by his episcopal robes, in the eyes of God he is already deprived of his priesthood. Accordingly, the holy canons condemn the heresy of simony, and ordain that those who demand money for the gift of the Holy Spirit be deprived of priesthood. . . .

3

For the better understanding of simony it is fitting to explain whence it originated. We have Scripture that this heresy existed both in the Old and the New Testaments. There are two fathers of that sin—one in the Old Testament, called Gehazi; the other in the New, called Simon. The first took gifts from Naaman for the cure of leprosy;[25] the second offered money to the apostles for the power of granting to men the Holy Spirit by laying on of hands. But I wish to describe the simoniacs still more clearly, for they are like sons who, having the example of their evil fathers before them, put on their fathers' shoes.

Know, then, that as after Simon they are called simoniacs or Simonites, likewise after Gehazi they are known as Gehazites; after Balaam, Balaamites; after Jeroboam, Jeroboamites; after Judas, Judasites. If you wish to designate them properly, call them the heirs of Gehazi, of Simon, of Balaam, and of Judas. They are the heirs of Balaam because he prophesied for

25 II Kings 5:20–23.

hire to a pagan king,[26] for they preach on account of and for money, as those deceivers who sell indulgences for money, of whom the Saviour prophesied, "There shall arise false prophets and shall lead many astray."[27] And Saint Peter likewise says, "There arose false prophets among the people, as among you also there shall be false teachers who shall bring multitudes into destruction."[28] And he adds that they deny him who redeemed them, bringing upon themselves swift destruction: "And many shall follow their fornications, by reason of whom the way of the truth shall be blasphemed. And in covetousness shall they with feigned words make merchandise of you; whose sentence lingereth not, and whose destruction slumbereth not."[29] And further he says, "Having a heart exercised in covetousness; children of cursing; forsaking the right way, they went astray, having followed the way of Balaam who loved the hire of wrong-doing."[30]

Thus does Saint Peter describe the sons of Balaam, of whom there are many. . . . Such were those lying, fornicating, covetous men who this year by their evil deed denied Christ, ridiculing the right way of Christ, robbing men by their lying indulgences, having invented fantastic notions and absolutions. They granted indulgences for all sins and torments. Furthermore, the masters[31] have confirmed their practice, defending them by writing that the pope has the right to go to war and to grant indulgences for sins and torments. Thus having the aid of the masters, they all the more boldly deceived the people with their lying speeches. . . . But the good Lord gave to faithful priests his Holy Spirit so that they preached courageously against those liars, and likewise to faithful laymen, that they boldly risked their lives. Three of them, Martin, John, and Stašek, sacrificed their lives for God, for they were beheaded in Prague for opposing the lying sermons.[32] Others were torn,

---

[26] Num., chs. 22; 24. Also cf. Hus, *Super IV sententiarum*, III, 641, where he quotes Peter Damiani as condemning Balaam. But the story really represents Balaam as blessing Israel, not cursing it.   [27] Matt. 24:11.

[28] II Peter 2:1.   [29] *Ibid.*, vs. 2, 3.   [30] *Ibid.*, vs. 14, 15.

[31] Masters of the university. The passage refers to the sale of indulgences ordered in 1412 by Pope John XXIII, who needed money for his war with King Ladislas of Naples. The indulgence sellers were led by Wenceslas Tiem. Hus protested to the university, but was opposed by the theological faculty, particularly Stanislav of Znojmo and Dean Stephen of Páleč.

[32] Because of popular riots against the selling of indulgences, King Wenceslas forbade any overt opposition to them. But three young men,

A.O.R.—14

scourged, and beaten by the choirboys in a Prague church; still others were condemned, dishonored, and imprisoned. Glory be to thee, O dear Christ, that thou still grantest thy faithful such gifts to confess thy truth!

In order to ascertain who the heirs of Gehazi are, it must be understood that Gehazi was a servant of the holy prophet Elisha who had cured the leprosy of Naaman, a pagan prince, but had declined to take any reward for it.[33] But when Naaman departed cured, Gehazi said: "My master hath spared this Naaman the Syrian, in not receiving at his hands that which he brought; as Jehovah liveth, I will run after him and take somewhat of him. So Gehazi ran after Naaman. And when Naaman saw him running after him, he alighted from the chariot to meet him and said, Is all well? And Gehazi said, All is well. My master hath sent me, saying, There came to me from the hill country of Ephraim two young men of the sons of the prophets; give them, I pray thee, a talent of silver and two changes of raiment. And Naaman said, Be pleased to take two talents. And he urged him, and bound two talents of silver in two bags, with two changes of raiment, and laid them upon two of his servants; and they carried them before him. . . . And Elisha said unto him, Whence came Gehazi? And he said, Thy servant went nowhere. And he said unto him, Was not my heart present when the man turned from the chariot to meet thee? Now you have accepted silver and raiments to buy the gardens of Olivet, vineyards, sheep and oxen, menservants and maidservants. But the leprosy of Naaman also shall cleave unto thee and unto thy posterity forever! And he went out from him a leper [white] as snow."[34]

Behold, thus the Scriptures describe Gehazi, whose posterity are all who demand reward in exchange for spiritual gifts. Accordingly, Cardinal Peter Damiani says: "There are many who before [performing an] ordination or before deciding a cause have not contracted for, or have not in so many words demanded, a payment; but afterwards they demand it as a debt. These have fallen into the sin of Gehazi who, after Naaman had been healed and was already returning home, dared

Martin, John, and Stašek, boldly protested against the practice in the churches of Týn, St. James, and St. Vitus. They were arrested, and although the magistrates promised Hus that they would not be cruelly dealt with, they were beheaded on July 11.

[33] II Kings, ch. 5.

[34] II Kings 5:20–27. It may be noticed that the version thus cited differs from the presently current text.

to demand money for the gift of the Holy Spirit. But as he was stricken with no less a disease than leprosy, on account of which men were expelled from cities, so likewise he who misuses the sacred things of the holy Church is committing not a light, but a grievous, sin." [35] . . .

From this you may perceive that all who receive payment after confession, baptism, extreme unction, the celebration of the Mass, burial, consecration of a church or of an altar or a chalice or a cope, or after the appointment to a benefice, or after preaching, all such commit a sin similar to Gehazi's. Alas! how many such sins are committed by the pope, the bishops, and the parish priests, who do not, like Elisha, punish their servants for this sin, but share with them their material gains as well as their sins! And even if perchance some of them never accept a payment, as Elisha, yet some Gehazi of theirs lies on their account, and running out, insists that his master asks for it. And there are so many of these Gehazis that at the pope's [court] there is here a cardinal, there a scribe, there a chancellor, or a doorkeeper, or a bull scribe, or a keeper of the seal, or a lobbyist. And who can count those at bishops' [courts] and elsewhere!

Next the Jeroboamites are called so after Jeroboam. It is written about King Jeroboam that whoever would fill his palm would be appointed priest of the idols. [36] And afterwards the Scriptures say that his house, i.e., the kingdom, was overthrown and razed from the earth on that account. Accordingly, those who in like manner accept money for making bishops or priests or for granting other benefices are followers of Jeroboam. May God grant that they be not ruined as he was!

The heirs of Judas are those who sell God's spiritual gift, saying either in so many words or by some sign: What will you give me for consecrating your church, or for celebrating a Mass, or for granting you absolution, or for baptism or confirmation, or for the body of God, or for the appointment to a parish or a bishopric? It is about such that it is written: "The vendors who sell the Holy Spirit as if he were a lackey are like Judas the traitor who sold Christ!" [37] Alas! how many there are of that

[35] Peter Damiani, "*Contra philargyriam et munerum cupidatem*" (Migne, *PL*, 145, cs. 535–536). Hus quoted this text previously in his *Super IV sententiarum*, IV, dist. xxv, 4.

[36] I Kings 13:33, 34. But this passage does not affirm that Jeroboam made the appointments for money.

[37] *Decretum Magistri Gratiani*, pars II, C. I, q. I, c. 21. Hus alludes to, rather than translates, this passage.

race! One sells himself to sing a Mass, another to preach, and
another to sell some other sacred thing, as has already been
mentioned. Such in some respects are worse than Judas the
traitor; for, as *Parisiensis*[38] says, Judas secretly sold the Truth
in mortal body to the leaders, while the simoniacs, on the
contrary, openly sell the now immortal Christ to all sorts of
people.

In particular, the simoniacs or heirs of Simon are those who
sell spiritual power or the gift of the Holy Spirit for money or
other valuables, or for improper services—sometimes openly,
at other times secretly—or express willingness to pay for what
they desire. They are like their father, Simon the magician who,
having been baptized and having become an adherent of Saint
Philip, offered the apostles money that he might receive power
from them. Saint Luke writes about him: "Now when Simon
saw that through the laying on of the apostles' hands the Holy
Spirit was given, he offered them money, saying, Give me also
this power that on whomsoever I lay my hands, he may receive
the Holy Spirit."[39] Therefore, all those who buy or sell the
gifts of God, either for money or for some other consideration,
or knowingly aid in such traffic, are called simoniacs, or in
Czech *svatokupci*. Therefore the Master of Deep Understanding[40]
says: "Although simoniacs, that is, Simonites, are in particular
those who, like Simon the magician, wish to procure an un-
vendable gift for money; and those who accept money for
sacred services are called, after Gehazi, Gehazites; yet both
those who give and those who receive are simoniacs, that is,
traffickers in sacred things, and are both condemned by the
same judgment.[41] . . .

Accordingly, now you can discern who are the heirs of
Balaam: namely, those who preach on account of pay and
condemn men unrighteously, or give false advice, as Balaam
gave to Balak, in order to lead men astray by fornication from
keeping God's commands. O how many priests there are in
that road! For are there not many fornicators [among them]

---

[38] *Parisiensis* is most probably William of Pérault, referred to frequently
by Wyclif. But the latter also refers by that appellation to William of
Auverne, bishop of Paris (1228–1248) (cf. R. L. Poole, ed., *De civili
dominio*, I, 301, n. 28). The passage itself is found in Wyclif's *De simonia*,
11.
[39] Acts 8:18, 19.
[40] Peter Lombard (c. 1100–c. 1160), bishop of Paris and author of the
celebrated textbook of theology, *Quatuor libri sententiarum*.
[41] *Ibid.*, IV, 25, c. 4; cf. Hus, *Super IV sententiarum*, IV, dist. xxv, 1.

who spend the alms upon the seduction of maidens, widows, and wives, and who feed and clothe prostitutes more sumptuously than husbands their wives? However, the Scriptures declare what has befallen Balaam: "Balaam also, the son of Beor, they slew with the sword." [42] But that were nothing, were he not damned besides; for he is worse off in hell! The same fate shall overtake his heirs, unless they sincerely repent. For Saint John was commanded to write: "And to the angel (understand, the bishop) of Pergamum write: These things saith he that hath the sharp, two-edged sword: I know where thou dwellest, even where Satan's throne is; and thou holdest fast my name, and didst not deny my faith." Furthermore he says: "But I have a few things against thee, because thou hast there some that hold the teaching of Balaam who taught Balak to cast a stumbling block before the children of Israel, that is to eat and to commit fornication." "Repent, therefore; or else I come to thee quickly and will make war against them with the sword of my mouth." [43]

Wilt thou, O Lord, make war against those Balaamites with a two-edged sword, the sword of thy mouth? They fear not the sword of thy Word, for they boldly and falsely preach and fornicate! And there is no bishop—an angel of thine—who does not tolerate them, for the bishops themselves commit fornication! But thou knowest when thou shalt make war against them . . . saying, "Depart from me, ye cursed, into the eternal fire!" [44] Thou didst pronounce, through thy servant Elisha, a curse upon Gehazi and his posterity, so that leprosy might be his portion forever. . . .

Likewise, Saint Peter gave his "blessing" to Simon, who had requested power for money, having said to him and his posterity: "Thy money perish with thee, because thou hast thought to obtain the gift of God with money. Thou hast neither part nor lot in this word; for thy heart is not right before God. Repent therefore of this thy wickedness, and pray God, if perchance the thought of thy heart shall be forgiven thee. For I see that thou art in the gall of bitterness and in the bond of iniquity." [45]

Thus did Saint Peter bless Simon and his simoniacal sons. But not so the vicars of Peter; for the more money one offers them, the more likely he is to receive a bishopric or some other spiritual office. But not so the holy Pope Leo, who says that

[42] Num. 31:8.   [43] Rev. 2:12–14, 16. A clause is omitted.
[44] Matt. 25:41.   [45] Acts 8:20–23.

simoniacs give and receive only a lying spirit.[46] Likewise
Saint Gregory, who says that simoniacs are heretics and lose
their priesthood;[47] and Saint Ambrose, who says that they are
damned and cut off from communion of the body of Christ;[48]
and Pope Paschal, who says that simoniacs are the greatest
heretics;[49] and Pope Gelasius, who says that they are included
in Simon's condemnation;[50] and Gregory of Nazianzus, who
says that they cannot remain in their priestly office, but are made
lepers by the prophet Elisha and are sent into perdition by
Peter, and have been driven out from the temple by Christ.
Thus it is stated in the books of *Decretals*.[51]

Unfortunately, they pay no attention to all this. Nevertheless, the time shall come when they shall attend when they
perceive their condemnation. But since this heresy has greatly
increased, it is well to open the eyes of the simple, that they may
know the simoniacs and beware of them. Furthermore, it is
proper to begin at the head and to examine whether it be defiled
with that leprosy, and then to pass on to the other members.
Perhaps it will be found that the whole body from head to
foot is afflicted with leprosy.

4

Let us now inquire whether a pope may be a simoniac.
It would appear that he cannot, since he is the lord of all the
world, who by right takes whatever he wishes and does as he
pleases; moreover, that he is the most holy father who cannot
sin. But know that many popes were heretics or otherwise evil,
and were deposed from the papacy. It would be a long story
to write about such. Accordingly, have no doubt whether a
pope can be a simoniac. If someone would defend him by saying that he cannot commit simony or other mortal sin, he would
exalt him above Peter and the other apostles. As for the argument that he is the lord of all the world, who by right takes
whatever he wishes and does as he pleases, the answer is that
there is only one Lord of all the world who cannot sin and who
has the right to rule the world and to do as he pleases, and that
Lord is God the mighty One. Furthermore, as for the argument that the pope is the most holy father who cannot sin, I

[46] *Decretum Magistri Gratiani*, pars II, dist. I, q. I, c. 1.
[47] *Ibid.*, pars II, dist. I, q. I, c. 5.   [48] *Ibid.*, pars II, dist. I, q. I, c. 7.
[49] *Ibid.*, pars II, dist. I, q. I, c. 12. This is Paschal I (817–824).
[50] *Ibid.*, pars II, dist. I, q. I, c. 6.   [51] *Ibid.*, pars II, dist. I, q. I, c. 11.

deny it; for it is our Father most holy, the Lord God, who alone cannot sin.

But perhaps you say, "In this world the pope is the most holy father." I answer that if you prove that he lives the most holy life, following Christ in His poverty, humility, meekness, and work, then I shall admit that he is most holy. But his manifest covetousness, pride, and other sins predispose men to believe that he is not the most holy father! But you retort: "The whole world calls him the most holy father except yourself! Why should you be more worthy of belief?" Thereupon I answer that you exaggerate when you speak of "the whole world," since hardly perhaps one in a hundred acknowledges him as the bishop of Rome.[52] But even though all men were to call him holy and the most holy, if his acts be contrary to Christ he is not holy, whether or not he is called so. For thus says the Lord, "O my people, they that call thee blessed deceive thee."[53] For what else are they but flatterers who call people holy in order to get pay, and promise people holiness when they pay them! Likewise priests and clerics, desiring papal favor, call him the most holy. And he thinks it is as they say and approves that they address him so to his face and in writing! Woe to him that allows himself to be so deceived!

Furthermore, they put forth the excuse that he is most holy on account of his office. But the saints reply that office does not make a man holy, as is proved by the apostle Judas and by the bishops and priests who murdered Christ. Moreover, the saints affirm that the worthier the office the greater the damnation of the incumbent if he be sinful. Accordingly, the saints acknowledge that priesthood and episcopacy are the worthiest offices on earth; but woe to him who should befoul them by a mortal sin! I know that the apostles, after Christ, were the most holy fathers on earth, and that they could in truth be so called; but they would not permit it. Moreover, if a pope lived in an apostolic manner, he likewise would be a holy father. But men should beware of flattering him, and he of pride, so that both would avoid sinning. For what avails it that a man be called holy when in the sight of God he is damned? What avails it to the Antichrist that he exalts himself above God when Christ shall hurl him into hell? And on the other hand, what

---

[52] I.e., only those who are subject to the diocese of Rome. But in that case Hus himself exaggerates the extent of the non-Roman Christendom.

[53] Isa. 3:12. The verse in the A.S. version reads, "O my people, they that lead thee cause thee to err."

harm if a man be reviled by the world, provided God praise him?

Asserting, therefore, that the pope may be a simoniac, let us see in what manner that may be. In the first place, he is such when he desires the papal dignity on account of emoluments and worldly esteem. For there is no estate in Christendom more liable to fall [than the papal]. For if he does not follow Christ and Peter in his manner of life more than others, he should be called the apostolic adversary rather than the apostolic successor. Therefore, everyone who runs after and strives for that dignity on account of material gain or worldly eminence is guilty of simony. But such a desire may be hid from men; therefore, if he neglects to perform his task properly, for the sake of the Christian communion, as Christ and Saint Peter have done, and if he seeks worldly goods and carnal life, he manifests to the people that he fell into the way of simony.[54]

The second form of that kind of simony consists in the various regulations contrary to the law of God which the pope promulgates in order to secure material gain, even though not openly, but in such a manner that it could be interpreted as against the law of God. For is it not against God's order that he commands that his cooks, doormen, grooms, and couriers be accorded the first claim upon benefices of great dignity in lands the language of which they do not know?[55] Or that the announcement of an appointment be withheld until the appointee first place the money on the board? And how many other such regulations there are!

The third form of papal simony is the appointment of bishops and priests for money. A proof of this is at present plainly to be seen in the payment of many thousand gulden for the archbishopric of Prague.[56]

---

54 The whole paragraph is strongly reminiscent of Wyclif's treatment in *De simonia*, 28, 40.

55 Many high ecclesiastical offices in Bohemia were held by papal appointees: there were six archdeacons during the second half of the fourteenth century who were complete foreigners and absentee holders. Likewise among the canons of St. Vitus Cathedral and of the Vyšehrady Church there were foreigners in large numbers.

56 When Nicholas Puchník was appointed archbishop of Prague (1402), he promised to pay the pope not only for his own appointment (3,300 gulden), but to pay the arrears of his two predecessors (1,480 gulden). But when he died before he was confirmed, this whole "debt" passed on to his successor, Zbyněk Zajíc of Hasenburg, who promised to pay the accumulated arrears as well as his own payment of 2,800 gulden. But he actually paid only the latter sum.

In these three forms the pope then may become a simoniac. But if any pope avoids simony and follows the Saviour in his manner of life, he has the right to make use of all things in the world, just as the apostles. For if anyone should prove holier than the pope, he has a better right, before God, [to the use of all things] than the pope, since he is a more beloved and worthier son of God, who is the King of all the world.[57] Besides this right to the use of the world, he has likewise the right to serve the holy Church, and to order, teach, and direct it in accordance with the Word of God. But that is a different matter from the worldly rule in which men, particularly clerics, easily go astray. For the papal office, as well as the apostolic, consists in preaching the Word of God, in administering the sacraments, and in praying diligently to God on behalf of the people. To administer temporal possessions belongs to the lower estate, the secular. Consequently, the pope should observe that Christ and Peter did not meddle with ruling over worldly possessions. For to one who had said to him: "Master! bid my brother to divide the inheritance with me," Christ said, "Man, who made me a judge or a divider over you?"[58] And again when another said to him, "I will follow whithersoever thou goest." And Jesus said unto him, "The foxes have holes and the birds of heaven have nests; but the Son of Man hath not where to lay his head."[59] Furthermore, when Pilate told him, "Thine own nation and bishops delivered thee unto me; what hast thou done?" Jesus answered: "My kingdom is not of this world; if my kingdom were of this world, then would my servants fight that I should not be delivered to the Jews. But now is my kingdom not hence."[60]

Here the pope has an example whether he should judge the world for money, or rule a kingdom, to subject the whole world to himself and to rule over vast treasures; or should say with Saint Peter: "Silver and gold have I none; but what I have that I give thee. In the name of Jesus Christ, arise and walk!"[61] For thus may a faithful Christian well reason that the pope and every other bishop should follow Christ, administer spiritual goods for the glory of God, but should not meddle with the

---

[57] In this assertion, Hus's dependence upon the familiar Wyclifite doctrine that the right of clergy to temporalities depended upon their worthy conduct, is plainly discernible.

[58] Luke 12:13, 14. In the passage beginning with, "For the papal office" and ending with the Lucan quotation, Hus follows the text of Wyclif's *De simonia*, 30.   [59] Luke 9:57, 58.   [60] John 18:35, 36.   [61] Acts 3:6.

administration of secular affairs. The same is true regarding the
appointments to bishoprics, to priestly benefices, and to other
prelacies. For even a simpleton can understand that a pope
does not know whether a man whom he has never seen, and
who may live a hundred or two hundred miles away, is of good
character; nor does he know whether he is acceptable to the
people over whom he is to be appointed bishop or priest; nor
does he know whether the good people who are to be his
spiritual flock will receive him with favor. Why, then, does he
meddle with it? But the pope may assert that he merely issued
his letters [for the appointment], and the first who seizes [the
vacancy] has the right on his side. Then, as we commonly
observe, some avaricious Judas who sleeps not hastens to the
bishops . . . first, thus outdistancing his rival who likewise has
a [papal] letter. Nevertheless, even if there were a hundred
appointees, since they themselves strove to secure a bishopric
or some other dignity, they all have acted against the proper
order and should be driven away! For Saint Paul says, "Let
no man seek the honor unto himself, but when he is called of
God, even as was Aaron." [62] And Saint Gregory says that "as
he who runs away from the dignities which he had not sought
should be constrained to accept them, so he who seeks them
assiduously and brazenly pushes himself forward, should without fail be driven away." [63] When will the words of these saints
be fulfilled? . . .

But someone will make a further objection: after a bishop's
death the pope may keep the bishopric vacant as long as he
pleases, and may retain the income and all other revenues to
boot; why, then, should he not with propriety take the annates
from him who desires to become a bishop or some other prelate? Furthermore, since he may do so is a proof that he is the
supreme lord of the world. Secondly, [it may be objected]
that he grants dignities only to the worthy and without a
[preliminary financial] agreement and thus does not commit
simony, because he receives what is really only his own; and,
thirdly, that since the pope has arranged it so, no one should
oppose it—as the pope's heralds, priests, and canonists of his
laws affirm.

The answer is easy: When they say that "after a bishop's
death the pope may keep the bishopric vacant as long as he
pleases, and may retain the income," I reply that the pope
cannot do so rightfully, in accordance with God's law, nor

[62] Heb. 5:4.   [63] In Migne, *PL*, 77, col. 1029.

should the holy Christian Church allow him to do so. For there may be a pope so avaricious that he may retain the incomes of all deceased bishops and other priests, and leave the people shepherdless. Thus he himself would not labor, nor would he appoint others to labor, unless it were such as would seek gain for their own purses but not the salvation of souls and the glory of our Saviour Jesus Christ.[64] . . .

Although Saint Paul has demonstrated to the Corinthians as well as to other good Christians that the whole world is theirs,[65] nevertheless, he did not exalt himself above them on account of his greater dignity, in order that he might rule over their property. For he did not wish to accept their support, but while preaching to them he worked with his own hands so that no reproach could be brought against him or his preaching, as he himself has testified.[66] As for his saying that all the world is theirs, notice the expression: "Let no one glory in men. For all things are yours; whether Paul, or Apollos, or Peter, or the world, or life, or death, or things present or things to come; surely all things are yours, and you are Christ's, and Christ is God's."[67]

Here you observe that the whole world belongs to a just man and, accordingly, likewise to a pope if he be just. But he should not on that account be called the supreme lord of all the world but, having done all that God has commanded him, he should confess himself an unprofitable servant, as Christ has commanded His disciples to do, saying, "When ye have done all the things which are commanded you, say, We are unprofitable servants."[68] Moreover, he should be moved by the example of Christ, who reproved his disciples because they had quarreled among themselves as to who was the greatest among them. Having called them to himself, he said to them: "Ye know that the rulers of the Gentiles lord it over one another, and those that are greater exercise authority over the rest. Not so shall it be among you: but whosoever would become great among you, let him be your minister; and whosoever would be first among you, let him be your servant. For the Son of Man came not to be ministered unto, but to minister, and he gave his soul a ransom for many."[69]

O loving Servant, dear Master of all the world! We, thy priests, have fallen away from following thee; we neglect thy

---

[64] This argument is reminiscent of a similar one in Wyclif, *De simonia*, 57f.
[65] I Cor. 3:21, 22.   [66] I Cor. 9:12–15.   [67] I Cor. 3:21–23.
[68] Luke 17:10.   [69] Matt. 20:25–28.

service; we strive excessively for power even more than the Gentiles and, transgressing thy commands, we yet boast of being the lords of the world, and of having the highest dignity in thy holy Church! Not so the apostles, nor Saint Gregory the pope, who, living in holiness, always called himself unprofitable, and was the first to call and write himself "the servant of the servants of God." [70] He ordained that no one should so write himself unless he indeed proved himself in the service of God. Thus I know not whether any pope is right in designating himself "the servant of the servants of God." If he follows Christ in virtues, then he designates himself so rightly; but if he lives contrary to Christ, then he writes himself so falsely.

Furthermore, it is said that the pope grants benefices or dignities only to the worthy and without a [financial] agreement; but such talk may be answered by a plain proof which is known even to simpletons, that many bishops are unworthy and are not fit even to herd swine properly! Moreover, who has ever been granted a bishopric without an agreement unless he first pays for the pallium? In the days of Puchník, those who stood guarantee for the archbishopric of Prague, even after his death, were Kbel and Malešic and others, and they had to pay even though he had died and had not profited from the bishopric, not having been installed into the office at all. [71] And as for the assertions that the pope does not personally set the price, nor is it done through a Gehazi, it had long ago been decreed by Pope John XXII what each bishop must pay. He was the first pope to decree and order that he must be paid the annates from all benefices, that is, the amount which each [appointee] expects to receive the first year. Consequently, this miserly pope collected into his coffers immense treasures! [72]

As for the third assertion that "whatsoever the pope decrees no one should contradict," that would every faithful Christian admit if the pope decreed nothing wrong. But when he decrees something wrong, what faithful man can approve it? Even the pope's own heralds must admit—for they teach it even in their own schools—that what one pope has decreed, another annuls, while later ones subvert the annulment. And what faithful man would approve as good the papal decree that the Word of

70 *Servus servorum Dei.*

71 See n. 56 above, which explains the circumstances.

72 Pope John XXII (1316–1334) greatly extended the financial exactions for which the Avignonese papacy was sadly notorious. The bull imposing the annates is mentioned in Wyclif, *De simonia*, 58.

God be not preached in chapels nor in any other places save in parish churches and in monasteries? [73] Indeed that decree is directly contrary to Christ's command. Such a bull was issued by Pope Alexander V, who, having issued it, died almost immediately thereafter. I opposed that bull and appealed from it, so that the Word of God should not be dishonored. [74] From this example, even without any other proof, it is evident that whenever a pope decrees anything unworthy and the Christian community detects it . . . it should hold it as unworthy and should not obey the pope therein; for otherwise by following a blind man they would both fall into the pit of eternal damnation.

But perhaps a sprite shall suddenly appear and say that no one should judge papal acts nor say to him, "Why do you do thus?" Such a sprite is to be told to stop blaspheming and ascribing to a sinful man what belongs to God alone. For Him alone may no one reprove, nor judge his acts as if they were evil, nor say to him, " Why doest thou thus?" But how can the sprite rightfully prove that one should not regard in his mind plainly evil acts as evil, whether they be the pope's or another man's? For almost all rational Christendom judges that Peter, the first vicar of Christ, sinned mortally in having forsworn his Saviour. Thus we should judge that all, including the pope, have gone astray and have been corrupted, except the One who, having committed no wrong, redeemed us from eternal death. For Saint John, the beloved of God, whose holiness the present-day popes can never attain, testifies, "If we say that we have no sin, we deceive ourselves and the truth is not in us." [75]

Finally, be it known to you that papal power is limited by God's law, the law of nature, and the pronouncements of saints which are grounded in God's Word. The law of God constrains the pope to do nothing contrary to it; consequently, he should give spiritual gifts freely as the apostles have done. The law of nature, which is an intelligent being's reason, by which he should regulate his life, asserts that the pope should do nothing unworthy. Likewise, the pronouncements of saints who, having an understanding of the Word of God, have

[73] Hus refers here to the prohibition of preaching in chapels, which Pope Alexander V decreed. It was prompted by the archbishop Zbyněk, who took this step to silence Hus, since the Bethlehem Chapel was not a parish church but only a preaching place.
[74] Hus appealed "ad papam melius informandum" on June 25, 1410. But Alexander was already dead, having died on May 3.   [75] I John 1:8.

grounded them upon it. . . . May the Lord grant that the present pope and his successors, instead of meddling in wars, bestow no benefice upon unworthy men for money but rather follow Christ! But it seems to me that but few of them will be willing to enter upon the way of Christ, the way of humility, poverty, and of work, until the word of Christ be fulfilled; for the miserable worldly possessions have blocked the way of Christ and have given birth to confusion among the priesthood, so that it is full of simony, avarice, and quarrels. Consequently, simony will not be expelled from the holy Church as long as priests do not surrender wealth and rule. . . .

For the devil puts forth still another excuse: when applicants come to the pope seeking the episcopal or other dignities, he does not set the price nor does he talk about money by demanding any stated amount, but merely inquires how much he who seeks the dignity is willing to give; consequently, the pope has not committed simony, nor has he incurred any guilt. Such argument is answered by the act of Saint Peter who, refusing to accept money from Simon in order not to participate in his trafficking, told him, "Thy money perish with thee, because thou hast thought to obtain the gift of God with money!" [76] . . .

But perhaps Old Nick [77] will say: "Simon said, 'Take the money and give me the power'; while the pope says nothing, but in silence grants [the benefice] before or after he has received the payment. Consequently, there is no trafficking." But Hodek, the baker, or Hůda, the vegetable woman, [78] would answer Old Nick that when he [Hodek] has bread for sale and when someone comes and in silence lays the money on the counter, either before or after taking the bread, Hodek or Hůda concludes that the customer has bought the bread. . . .

But Old Nick replies, "The pope had no intention to take the money." O Nick! if it were so, then he would have said, like Peter, "Thy money perish with thee!" Under such circumstances no one would try to offer the pope any money, as no one did to Peter after Simon had tried it. But how can we believe such a thing when we always dispatch a great sum of money to Rome for the archbishopric of Prague whenever a new archbishop is to be appointed? [79]

[76] Acts 8:20.
[77] Hus used the term "Lucek," a colloquial diminutive of contempt, as standing for "Lucifer."
[78] Equivalent to the colloquial "Tom, Dick, and Harry."
[79] Cf. n. 56 above.

But perhaps someone will argue still further: "A pope must have a great deal of money in order to impose obedience upon those who are disobedient and rebellious; therefore, he must secure money the best he can, and there is no better way than to accept payment for benefices, since it is offered voluntarily. Likewise, he grants indulgences in order that men may buy for themselves the Kingdom of Heaven . . . and at the same time help the pope to put down evil men. But this argument is answered by the life of poverty led by Christ and the holy apostles, for they did not possess much money, nor did they desire to force the disobedient and rebellious to obedience. Behold, the Saviour with one word could have overthrown the disobedient and the rebellious, and could have converted them to himself when they came upon him with swords and clubs and other weapons; yet he humbly spoke to them: "Are ye come out against me as against a robber with swords and clubs? I sat daily with you, teaching in the temple, and yet ye took me not." [80] "And again he said to them, Whom seek ye? And they answered, Jesus of Nazareth! He said unto them, I am he: if therefore ye seek me, let these go their way." [81] Peter also when he was in Rome did not force the disobedient to accept the faith, but [sought to win them] by the preaching of the Word of God. . . . And even if it were right for the pope to force the disobedient to obedience, he is not justified thereby to secure money by such methods. For no one should do wrong that right may follow, as Saint Paul said, speaking to those who thought, "Let us do evil that good may come." [82]

Moreover, anyone who wishes may observe that the use of force, or secular means, avails the popes nothing. Read the chronicle[83] and observe that whenever popes have waged wars, their temporal power steadily decreased. As Saint Hildegarde prophesied that the pope's rule shall so dwindle that hardly his episcopal biretta shall be left on his head. Whether or not that shall come to pass, thou, O Lord Christ, well knowest! [84]

In regard to the granting of indulgences for money, Saint Peter well shows, by his refusal to sell to Simon the power of laying on of hands on men that they might thus receive the

---

[80] Matt. 26:55.   [81] John 18:7, 8.   [82] Rom. 3:8.
[83] It is not possible to ascertain which "chronicle" Hus means; but he often refers to *Flores temporum*.
[84] Saint Hildegarde (1098–1179), abbess of Rupertsberg, famous for her prophecies.

gift of the Holy Spirit, that such indulgences are improper. . . .
But now the priests, because of their avarice, vie with one
another in a race to buy indulgences, and the people, wishing
to rid themselves of their sins by a payment of money, do not
repent rightly. Thus both sides are deceived: the priests in selling and the people in buying. For the priests sell a lie, as Saint
Leo the pope says: "When the gift [of the Holy Spirit] is not
freely given or received, it is not a gift. But since simoniacs
do not receive freely, hence they do not receive the gift which
greatly benefits the priestly office. And since they do not receive
it, they do not possess it. Accordingly, since they do not possess
it, they cannot give it to anyone else, either freely or for a payment. What, then, do they give? Certainly only what they have.
But what do they have? Surely a lying spirit. How shall we
prove it? Because, if the spirit of truth—as is attested by the
Truth from which it springs—is received freely, it is proved
beyond all doubt that the spirit which is not received freely
is the lying spirit." [85] . . .

But what excuse can they give who farm indulgences for the
purpose of selling them at a profit, or who rent confessional
stalls for a stated sum? There are confessors in Rome, secular
priests as well as monks, ignorant and rascally vagabonds, who
sit in confessionals which they have rented for a certain amount
of gold, and absolve people from whatever place and with whatever sins they come, instead of directing them to the right path!
O merciful Lord! how little care is taken about the souls which
thou hast redeemed with thy precious blood and thy cruel
death! They have, alas! greater care to fill their purses than to
restore unto thee a soul from damnation. Accordingly, Saint
Bernard wrote to Pope Eugenius, "If a she-ass stumbles, there
is someone to lift her; but a soul perishes and there is none to
care about her." [86] . . . They are like the Jewish priests of whom
the Saviour said that when their ass fell into a pit on a holy day
they immediately hoisted it out without calling it a sin; but
when the merciful Saviour healed a sick man on a holy day,
they accounted it a sin. [87] . . . O how many there are who take
more care for cows, bulls, swine, money, and horses than for
their own souls, to say nothing about other people's! May
God grant that all may be soundly converted, to the salvation

[85] *Decretum Magistri Gratiani*, pars II, C. I, q. I, c. I.
[86] Saint Bernard, *De consideratione libri quinque ad Eugenium Tertium*, in
Migne, *PL*, 182, col. 786 B.
[87] Luke 14:1–5.

of their souls as well as to diligence for the salvation of the souls of others!

5

It is fitting now to examine how a bishop may fall into simony. . . . In the first place, he may become a simoniac upon entering his office if he accept the episcopacy either entirely, or for the greater part, on account of temporal benefits, or for worldly esteem, or for carnal pleasure, rather than for earning himself blessedness, or for God's glory, or for the salvation of his as well as his fellows' souls, that he may lead them to God by his own good example and by the Word of God. But if he enters [the office] by means of bribery, or by rendering service, or by worldly favor, then he has already succumbed to simony. For his perverse will has already inclined him to such an exchange.[88] . . . Accordingly, in order to be a worthy bishop of God, one must have previously led a holy life, and must have been called of God through men without bribery; and having been thus called, he must consider himself unworthy; and having been strenuously urged [to accept the office], he must do so humbly, for the sake of God's glory and his salvation as well as that of other men. But he must pay no money for the confirmation [to the office]. He who accepts the episcopacy in the above-described manner . . . enters upon the office worthily. . . . But the Prague bridge is more likely to fall down than that a candidate for the Prague bishopric should secure it by such a holy course![89]

. . . That a bishop should conduct himself in this manner, Saint Paul points out that every bishop "being taken from among men is appointed for men in things pertaining to God, that he may offer both gifts and sacrifices for sins; who can bear gently with the ignorant and erring, for that he himself also is compassed with infirmity. And by reason thereof he ought, as for the people, so also for himself, to offer for sins. And no man should take this honor unto himself, but he that is called, as was Aaron."[90] Furthermore, he writes to Titus saying that a bishop "must be free from mortal sin as a good steward of God,

---

[88] The text to this point follows almost verbally the text of Wyclif's *De simonia*, 70.

[89] That these strictures were based on facts may be seen from the circumstance that between 1376 and 1412 the five archbishops of Prague who had held office during that time had been appointed by the papacy, and not elected by the chapter. The same applies to the appointments of the bishops of Olomouc and Litomyšl.   [90] Heb. 5:1–4.

not proud, not irascible, no drunkard, no fighter, not greedy of filthy lucre; but given to hospitality, a lover of good, temperate, just, holy, chaste; holding to the faithful word in teaching, that he may be both able to exhort in the sound doctrine, and to punish the opposer."[91] In writing to Timothy, he adds that "he must have good testimony of them that are without (that is, from strangers); lest he fall into derision or into hate, and the snare of the devil."[92]

Here, then, is Saint Paul's description of what a bishop should be. . . . In addition, as the Saviour says, he should risk his life for his sheep.[93] But he who enters otherwise than through Christ, and thus by any other path than that which has been pointed out, is a thief and a robber.[94]

In the second place, a bishop may be a simoniac during his term of office, and that in three ways: first, if after he entered by simony he neglects the episcopal duties and does not live in accordance with Saint Paul's injunctions in respect of every bishop.[95] He thus aggravates the simony by adding to it other sins. . . . Secondly, he sins grievously by committing simony when he squanders, either upon himself or upon his retinue, the revenue intended for the poor, or endows with it his friends; for thus he misuses his episcopal office. Accordingly, Saint Gregory says: "An evil rumor has reached us that some bishops do not distribute the tithes and Christian offerings to the priests of their diocese, but rather to laymen, knights, and servants, and even (what is worse) to their relatives. Thus whenever a bishop is found to have transgressed this commandment of God, he shall be held not the least among the greatest heretics and Antichrists. For the Council of Nicaea has ruled regarding simoniacs that the bishop who grants and laymen who accept it from him, either for service or as a gift, shall be condemned to eternal burning with fire."[96] . . .

If bishops rightly examined their conscience and this holy ordinance, they would find, each grasping his head, whether or not they belonged among the heretics and Antichrists. Likewise, if priests wished to preserve themselves from simony, not many of them would strive after episcopacy; for this dignity

---

[91] Titus 1:7–9, freely rendered.   [92] I Tim. 3:7.
[93] John 10:11.   [94] John 10:1.
[95] This passage is based on Wyclif, De simonia, 71.
[96] Decretum Magistri Gratiani, pars II, C. I, q. III, c. 13; but it is there ascribed to Gregory VII, not to Gregory I. The whole paragraph is based on Wyclif, De simonia, 72.

is so entwined with miserable lucre that for its sake many enter it unrighteously and live in it unrighteously. Therefore, many are stricken with spiritual leprosy or die as if of poison. This was intimated when Emperor Constantine first enriched the Roman bishop, having given him estates; for a voice was heard from heaven, saying, "Today poison has been poured into the Christian communion!"[97] O how many souls have already died of that poison! How many have been stricken with the leprosy of simony! And how many have been murdered on its account!

In the third place, a bishop may become a simoniac when he accepts money or material gifts contrary to rules. That is done in very many ways, in accordance with the cunning of Lucifer, who has long been taking lessons in that art.[98] For there is no doubt that a bishop is a simoniac when he accepts money, contrary to rules, for the consecration of churches, altars, deacons, and others, particularly if he makes a [previous] agreement in respect of it, or stipulates it, or demands it. And that the consecration of churches, chapels, or altars for money constitutes simony, Saint Gregory testifies: "A church which is consecrated on an agreement [to pay] should rather be said to be desecrated than consecrated."[99] Furthermore, Pope Innocent says: "Whoever should secure a prebend, or priory, deanery, or any other ecclesiastical dignity or sacrament, such as chrism or holy oil, or consecration of altars or churches, through accursed avarice by means of money, let him be deprived of his wrongly acquired dignity. And both the purchaser and the seller, the contractor and the intermediary, shall be branded with the mark of infamy. For nothing should be charged or paid either prior to or after the act for the food or for any other reason. For it is simony."[1]

Behold . . . such is the holy provision of the canon law. . . . But alas! that holy provision has died out among the bishops. For they have now made a law for themselves to charge for [the consecration of] an altar at least two *kopy*,[2] and for a church as much more than two *kopy* as they can get. And they

---

[97] Hus shares with his age the belief in the authenticity of the legendary Donation of Constantine.

[98] Based almost verbally on Wyclif, *De simonia*, 73.

[99] *Decretum Magistri Gratiani*, pars II, C. I, q. III, c. 11.

[1] *Ibid.*, pars II, C. I, q. III, c. 15. The pope referred to is Innocent II.

[2] A *kopa* amounts to 60 groschens; one groschen contains from 1·88 to 3·62 grams of silver. It represents a day's pay of an unskilled laborer. Cf. F. Graus, *Městská chudina v době předhusitské* (Orbis, Prague, 1949), 180.

keep this law more faithfully than the command of Christ. . . .
And if they are not paid what they ask, they refuse to consecrate; and if they consecrate but are not paid, they revenge
themselves by lawsuits and excommunications. . . .

Furthermore, they hide behind Simon's excuse, commonly
affirming that they sell no benediction or consecration, but
physical labor; also, that they receive money for food, but
not for consecration. This excuse is like that of an avaricious
innkeeper who, having served food, demands payment only
for the beer; but this payment exceeds the cost of both food and
drink. Or it is like the incident someone has told of an avaricious master who attended an annual fair. He was told by a
servant that in that city the innkeepers charge nothing at the
table for very fat geese, but a great deal for beef, veal, and other
meats. Thereupon, the master ordered his servants to eat goose
(which was free), but he himself ate the food to which he was
accustomed. When the dinner was over and the bill was
rendered, he was charged for the veal at such a high rate that
even the geese were too expensive at that price. Similarly, the
simoniacs aim to deceive God's people by saying that they sell
labor, but give freely the benedictions, consecrations, and
confirmations. Against such cunning the holy regulations
decree: those who buy material things, but do not buy spiritual,
are not simoniacs. But it is added immediately: "Nevertheless,
the answer is given that not only those who buy spiritual gifts
for money, but also those who buy material things annexed
to the spiritual, are called simoniacs." [3]

The regulation decrees that preaching, celebrating the Mass,
consecrating, confirming, baptizing, hearing confessions, administering the sacrament of the Lord's Supper—all these
labors—are connected with the clerical office . . . and hence
should not, indeed cannot, be rightfully sold for money.
Although lay people should indeed support the priests in this
work, the latter should not sell or demand additional payment
for such services. For all simony could thus be justified on the
score that "I sell work!" Accordingly, the Lord says through
the prophet Malachi: "Who is among you who would shut the
doors and kindle the fire on mine altar without pay? I have no
pleasure in you, saith the Lord of hosts, neither will I accept
an offering at your hand." [4] Gratian, author of the *Decretal*,
remarks that "to close the doors is not the office of the holy

[3] *Decretum Magistri Gratiani*, pars II, C. I, q. III, the heading.
[4] Mal. 1:10.

offering; nevertheless it belongs to the spiritual office." [5]
Accordingly, the excuse with which they defend themselves
who say that they sell work is not justified.

There is still another argument against this excuse. Since
the bishop sells work, all bishops should charge the same
amount. But because a parish could secure someone who
could perform the duties of the episcopal office for less pay, the
bishop ill uses his children by charging them so highly for his
services. [6]

Or again: Although the layman who carved and set up the
altar performed much harder work than the bishop who
consecrated and anointed it, yet the former receives perhaps
less pay for his work. Why does the bishop, being their father,
take more from his sons? Nor is it an excuse to say that the work
of the bishop is worthier than that of the lay carver or mason.
For the bishop's work is worthier only by reason of its connection with his spiritual office. But because his work is more
valuable on account of this connection, it proves that the bishop
receives pay for spiritual things. [7] Otherwise it ought to be a
great shame for the bishop, a man very talented and of great
dignity, to hire out to peasants!

Or again: The bishop is endowed with land in order that,
possessing resources for his own support, he may observe the
spiritual rule in all things pertaining to his spiritual office.
Therefore, he acts unworthily when he accepts pay from his
people for his work. As if a workman, having received wages
for his work, demanded to be paid the second time.

Again I should like to inquire at what rate the bishop's work
of consecrating an altar ought to be estimated? Formerly, the
rate was lower. Also, a poorer bishop charges less for the work
than a rich one, and a suffragan . . . is given smaller pay than
the bishop himself. Hence, the richer the bishop, the higher he
charges for his work! . . .

As has already been stated, a bishop may be a simoniac not
only on account of selling . . . the priestly consecration to
candidates, but also on account of conferring it from favoritism,
or for his own glory, as Saint Gregory and Saint Remigius
assert. Saint Ambrose similarly declares that "when one was
ordained for money, what he gave was gold and what he lost

[5] *Decretum Magistri Gratiani*, pars II, C. I, q. III, the heading of the *questio*.
It is quoted in Wyclif, *De simonia*, 74.

[6] Based on Wyclif, *De simonia*, 74.

[7] Based on Wyclif, *De simonia*, 74–75.

was his soul. And he who administered such an ordination, what he received was gold, and what he gave was leprosy." [8]

. . . Furthermore, Saint Ambrose sorrowfully wrote: "I speak truly that I am pained that the archbishop—i.e., the pope—consecrated the bishop carnally [i.e., from a carnal incentive], for he consecrated a spiritual leper for money. May the money perish with thee because thou hast bought the gift of the Holy Spirit for money, and hast made this strange purchase for the damning of souls!" And elsewhere he says: "Even if to human sight he appears a great bishop, in God's sight he is a leper. For he secured an unworthy priestly ordination with much money, but before God he lost his soul. His body received the dignity, but his soul lost honesty." . . . And again he says: "There are many who desire to buy the gift of the Holy Spirit by bribery, paying money for the episcopal dignity, forgetting the words of Peter spoken to Simon: 'Thy money perish with thee, because thou hast thought to obtain the gift of God with money.'" [9]

Here, then, you may perceive that a bishop should not consecrate for money either churches, chapels, altars, or clergy. In regard to both of these cases, the decree affirms: "We decree that as no charge should be made for consecrating altars, churches, nor for priestly ordination, so likewise nothing should be charged for the balsam for the consecration, nor for the candles, so that the priests who receive the oil, i.e., are being ordained, should pay nothing for it. Let the bishops pay for the balsam and the candles from their ecclesiastical endowments each in his own church." [10] When will they who charge for the holy oil fulfill this rule, and those who, having received it, sell it then at a higher price and thus fall into heresy? This huckstering was condemned by the Council of Tribur in its decree as follows: "It is asserted that it has become customary in some localities to make payment for chrism or oil, as well as for baptism and the Communion of the Lord's body. The holy council pronounces this practice simony and condemns it. It decrees that hereafter no payment is to be demanded for ordination, chrism, the holy oil, nor for a funeral or the adminis-

---

[8] *Decretum Magistri Gratiani*, pars II, C. I, q. I, c. 14.

[9] *Ibid.*, pars II, C. I, q. I, c. 7. It appears probable that Hus copied these two quotations from Thomas Hybernicus, *Flores doctorum* (Vienna, 1751), 691 f.

[10] *Ibid.*, pars II, C. I, q. I, c. 106. This decree was passed by the Council of Cabillon in the reign of Charlemagne.

tration of the Lord's body. Let Christ's gifts be freely and voluntarily distributed."[11] . . .

Furthermore, because confirmation takes so little time and is a public act, bishops are ashamed to charge for it.[12] But some of them have young Gehazis who make the demand of those who are being confirmed that each offer a coin; or the [local] priest at the bishop's bidding makes a suggestion to that effect. When a church or an altar is to be consecrated, the priest suggests that an offering be made in honor of the saints to whom it is dedicated, and announces other offerings and indulgences. . . .

In connection with the ordination of clergy, it is the clerks who profit, for they take a groschen and a coin for the certificate of the first ordination, and two groschens and two coins for the second; while for the third and fourth they charge three groschens.[13] The only reason for this difference in the charge for the certificate is that the later ordinations are to a higher dignity. In some localities even a gulden is given, at other places more or less. Elsewhere they must pay even the barber and the gatekeeper along with the clerk. And all this sinning is laid at the door of the bishop! For he has trained these servants of his in chasing after money, for otherwise he does not admit anyone to ordination. And if he admits, he does not grant the first papers[14] until the payment is made. Or the bishop calls for the payment for the certificate under pain of excommunication. So when this scattered simony is collected all together, it annually makes quite a heap! Nor is simony excused on the ground that once in a while the bishop charges but little. For as the Saviour bears witness to the poor widow who, having given two copper mites out of her great willingness, contributed more than all the others,[15] so likewise a priest or a notary who out of great desire receives one or two coins only is still guilty of great simony. Accordingly, the great pope Saint Gregory says, "As it is not proper for a bishop to sell the laying on of hands, so a clerk or a notary should not sell his voice or pen at ordinations."[16] . . .

[11] *Ibid.*, pars II, C. I, q. I, c. 105. The Council was held in 895.
[12] Cf. Wyclif, *De simonia*, 78.
[13] A groschen was equal to 7 denarii, and one denarius to 2 heller. It is not clear from the text which of these is meant under the term "coin."
[14] Every candidate received a certificate of ordination which he had to present when he sought the next higher grade.
[15] Mark 12:42.
[16] *Decretum Magistri Gratiani*, pars II, C. I, q. II, c. 4.

But someone will say: "Should the notary write for nothing?
How is he to provide for his needs?" To this there is an easy
answer: The bishop should provide for his needs, for he is endowed with goods just for this purpose that he may derive therefrom his own support and support such of his clerks as are
necessary to his spiritual rule. Thus he is to serve the holy
Church faithfully, distributing spiritual gifts freely.

But some may defend the bishop with the excuse that such
practices are indulged in without his knowledge.[17] Or, in the
second place . . . the clerk forces no one to give, but accepts
only what is offered him voluntarily. This, then, is no sin, for
even Saint Gregory says: "If the one who is being ordained
offers a present for the certificate or the pallium without a
[previous] stipulation, of his own will, and without having
been asked for it, but out of good pleasure, we do not forbid
acceptance of such a gift. For it causes no stain of sin, since it
does not come from a greedy request." [18] This excuse may be
answered by saying that the bishop who is diligent in overseeing
his clerks, so that none of them indulges in simony, is free from
blame. But if he is cognizant of such a practice, or if when he
should be cognizant he neglects this duty . . . then he shares
in the sin.

The second excuse is answered by the act of the bishop's
clerks. For they and the notaries sometimes make excuses,
sometimes exhort, or take a deposit; but those [candidates] who
have nothing, or refuse to give, they drive away. Therefore,
they are very far from the exception allowed by Saint Gregory,
who permitted the acceptance of a gift for the certificate or the
pallium only when it was granted without a previous contract,
not from compulsion or a demand. But alas! the bull or the
certificate granting the episcopacy and the pallium . . . are
sold nowadays at such a high price that one could buy a Bible
for the cost of the bull. And for the cost of the pallium one could
buy the twelve apostles a robe apiece, if they still held the
episcopal office!

The titular bishops, furthermore, excuse themselves on the
ground that they would have nothing to wear and to eat if
they did not charge for ordinations. To that, in the first place,
may be answered that since they are the bishop's substitutes or
assistants, they should be given the necessary means by the

---

[17] Cf. Wyclif, De simonia, 78.
[18] This is a continuation of the previous quotation from Gratian (pars II,
C. I, q. II, c. 4).

bishop, for the latter feeds his pages and many others who do not possess the episcopal rank. In the second place, let the titular bishops live in poverty, like Peter or the apostle Paul, and let them preach the Word of God. In the third place, let them preach to the people of the dioceses of which they bear the episcopal title. But alas! they bear the title, but do no good to the people over whom they hold episcopacy. Accordingly, the Czechs have given them the name of "barren bishops," possibly because they are of so little profit to the people, particularly of their own diocese. In the fourth place, one may ask why such a bishop sought the consecration, knowing that he intended not to work among his people, especially if he does not know their language. Perhaps if he were to tell the truth, he would confess that he secured the episcopacy on account of worldly esteem, or for material profit and freedom. It is for that reason that such "barren bishops" and patriarchs are usually monks . . . for in such a manner they free themselves from obedience to the superiors of their Order.

But someone may still object: If there were no such bishops, who would ordain the clergy and consecrate churches, altars, and such? [19] I answer that it should be done by the archbishop or the diocesan bishop, for they were appointed for that purpose. But you reply: Not every bishop is capable of performing the functions, and some are not even in priestly orders, while others refuse to do it. Thereby you correctly show their unworthiness for the episcopal office, and that unless they repent they shall dearly rue it! It is a strange state of affairs. Formerly, the higher a dignity one held, the more he labored in his office for the benefit of the holy Church. Today just the opposite is the case: They themselves do not touch the work, but entrust it to others, while they themselves feast. Thus one bishop secures another to perform ordinations, a canon to carry on the administration, and a parish priest to preach and to minister in his stead. When a monk becomes abbot, even though formerly he often participated in the services, he then does so but rarely, and appoints a chaplain in his stead. This has now become established as a law. They excuse the practice by saying that a blacksmith has pincers in order not to burn himself. To that a simple man may reply that the devil, leaving the pincers alone, will grab the blacksmith.

They also defend themselves with another excuse furnished them by the canon lawyers, namely, that whatever is done by

[19] The suffragan bishops commonly performed such functions.

a substitute is as if done by oneself. It is true that a priest who has not left his office from vanity or carelessness, but in all diligence lives worthily in accordance with his position . . . yet is not able to do all the work himself, and therefore appoints a substitute, may rightly secure an assistant. The same applies to a wrong deed: Whoever causes another to sin, either by direct aid or by a command, or by failure to oppose him, is as guilty as if he himself committed it. Hence, the Scriptures say that the Jews crucified Jesus, that Pilate whipped him, and that Herod murdered the infants. In accordance with that example, it is clear that they who do not do the work of their office but have others do it for them, should receive nothing for the others' work. Thus Saint Bernard says: "Whoever has a substitute for work shall have a substitute for reward." . . . Therefore, the Saviour well says that the lord of the vineyard has commanded that the workers be called and each be paid in accordance with the work he has done in the vineyard.[20] And elsewhere he says that the Son of Man will come and will reward each man according to his, and not according to someone else's, deeds.[21] For truly, if it were possible for one man to do the work of another as well as he could do his own work, then a cobbler or any other person whatsoever could be a bishop or a parish priest, and could properly hold many benefices. For by securing a substitute for each of his benefices, he could do enough to satisfy men—according to this argument.

But faithful Christians know that every bishop and every parish priest and other prelates must render an account for the sheep whose shepherds they are. And since they must do so if they are to be saved and justified, they must themselves feed the sheep. Therefore, those who do not do so, have a greeting from God: "Woe unto the shepherds who feed themselves, but my sheep they do not feed!"[22] And how can he be a good shepherd whom the sheep neither hear nor see, and who neither knows them nor feeds them? For the Shepherd of shepherds says that "a good shepherd knows his sheep, and the sheep hear his voice, and he goes before them and leads them to pasture and they follow him."[23] He also said to Peter three times: "If thou lovest me, feed my sheep, feed my sheep, feed my sheep."[24] . . . How, then, do they feed the sheep who, being evil livers, do not teach and of course do not feed their sheep with material food, but rather shear them? Even a peasant can understand

[20] Matt. 20:8. But the point of the parable is just the opposite.
[21] Matt. 16:27.   [22] Ezek. 34:2.   [23] John 10:3, 4.   [24] John 21:15-17.

that he who has never fed sheep is not to be called a shepherd.
And when he accepts responsibility for a flock, even if he has
ten hirelings, in case one sheep dies, he must pay for it to the
owner. Thus each must himself give an account of every sheep
he neglects, even if he had a thousand substitutes. . . . This is
his burden which he assumes when he becomes a priest, as
his office implies; sometimes he even takes an oath to that
effect. Woe unto him who does not bear the burden, particularly to him who lives unworthily and who, having abandoned Christ's sheep, takes no care of them; or if he appoints in
his place a plainly vicious and unworthy rascal; or if, abandoning his own office, he takes up a secular one. . . . Woe unto him
who feeds himself but not the sheep; who seeks money but not
souls! . . . Saint Bernard . . . wrote to Pope Eugenius that his
office is to feed souls rather than to rule, for he must render
an account of all souls.

    . . . But perhaps you reply: "Do you want bishops to beg?"
I answer that I do not, but do want them, having sufficient
food and raiment, to be content therewith, as Saint Paul
says.[25] And if they possess endowments, they should give
them to the poor, themselves living more frugally. But you say
that it is proper for a bishop to wear handsome robes and to
have many pages and rich food. I answer that the dignity of
Christ as bishop and of his apostles shone forth in poverty,
without retinue, without selfish pleasures, but in holy life.
Therefore, Christ's poverty, labor, and humility would afford
a better adornment [to the bishop] than all the resplendent
robes, as Saint Gregory says. For I know that the sons of Antichrist ridicule Christ's work, humility, and poverty, and regard
anyone who desires to follow Christ and his apostles as a fool.
For so their father, the Antichrist, wishes to have it. Look and
observe if you can find a bishop nowadays who would follow
Christ! . . .

    But someone else objects further: "You said that, according
to Saint Gregory's statement, bishops are simoniacs when they
endow their pages and friends.[26] But it is only natural that a
man should help his father and mother, as well as his friends.
Why, then, should a bishop be ranked with the greatest heretics
and antichrists if he endow his friends?" Saint Gregory would
answer that if the bishop's friend were in as great a need—

25 I Tim. 6:8.
26 The word "friends" also has the significance of "relatives." It is not
clear which meaning Hus had in mind.

or even greater—than another man (not the bishop's relative), then if out of pity he would make him a gift of church alms for the sake of God (but not for the sake of elevating him or rendering him mighty in the world, or enabling him to live a life of ease and comfort, or because he is a relative), then by such a gift the bishop should not be ranked among the greatest heretics and antichrists. But in the opposite case, he becomes one of the Antichrist's order.

Here, then, is your explanation how a bishop may become a simoniac, both in entering upon his episcopal office and in exercising it. But there may be even a third way, of leaving the office, and that in two modes: first, that he transfer it to a friend or another person for money, and thus having irregularly entered upon it, he leaves it irregularly; second, that having entered the office wrongly, and not repenting of it, he should die while in the office. . . . Saint Gregory writes as follows: "If a man does not possess a saintly character and has not been called [to his office] either by the clergy or the people, nor has been constrained to accept it by urgent request, and yet notwithstanding he shamelessly accepts the episcopal or the priestly dignity; and if, despite his being stained with sin (his heart being filled with a sinful desire), he yet accepts the priesthood of Christ on account of the request of someone's unclean lips, or on account of clamor, or for worldly service, or because of a deceitful bribe; not for the benefit of souls, but because he is filled with the vain desire of praise; and if he does not voluntarily surrender [the office] during his lifetime, but is overtaken by death before he had bitterly repented [of his deed], without doubt he shall perish everlastingly.[27]

. . . Consequently, those who have entered upon their dignity wrongly and retain it although they could leave it are thieves and robbers who hold their office wrongly. . . . May the Lord grant that they who are smeared with simony may truly repent!

6

Let us now observe how monks may become simoniacs. . . . In the first place, both he who receives one into the Order and he who is received may at the time of entrance become simoniacs. He who receives them for money or for some material benefit, or for any other nonspiritual reason, has become a simoniac because he has thus already exhibited an

[27] *Decretum Magistri Gratiani*, pars II, C. I, q. I, c. 115.

evil intention by selling the [monastic] vow which ought to be a spiritual matter. The same applies to the reception [of the monk] into an Order on the basis of a contract involving payment, or from custom, or for provisions, or robes, or a ring, or a silver cup, or a bolt of cloth. In order that monks may guard against such practices, Pope Urban orders that no abbot be permitted either to demand or to accept any money from those wishing to enter their Order. For he says, "Following an ancient rule, I decree that no one may accept anything whatever for ordination."[28] There are many enactments and reasons supporting this declaration, but I shall pass over them because of their length. Nevertheless, let the monks be aware that if they ambitiously hasten to secure higher dignities in their Order by means of gifts, or through worldly favor, or by intrigue, or by any other unworthy method, in order that they may be raised above others, they are stricken with simony. Likewise he who wishes to enter a monastery in order to enjoy physical comfort, to be sure of his loaf of bread, to live idly, or to be held in greater esteem by the world than he would have been outside the monastery (as, for instance, in order to become an abbot, or provost, or some other officeholder)—if he enters the Order for such reasons, he is a simoniac because he assumes a spiritual dignity or a monastic rule irregularly for nonspiritual profit.

It is necessary, therefore, that he who wishes to enter a monastery take counsel with the Holy Spirit, so that he may become conscious of the motive for his desire to enter the Order. . . . Also he should consider what he wishes to do in the monastery in order to be of benefit to the holy Church. And should he conclude that he could be of greater benefit as a priest, leading people in apostolic virtues and living humbly, he ought not to enter the monastery. This is particularly true if he should be apt in preaching the Word of God to people, so that he would not put the light of the sacred Scriptures under a bushel.

The monks already living in monasteries fall into various kinds of simony when they importune from the pope or nobles attachment of parishes to their monastery by offering money or other gifts. That they do it from avarice is evident from the fact that they seek only such parishes as yield great revenue,

---

28 *Decretum Magistri Gratiani*, pars II, C. I, q. II, c. 3. The pope referred to is Urban II. The text from the beginning of the chapter is reminiscent of Wyclif, *De simonia*, 84.

but the poor ones they do not want. I had an occasion once to say to certain monks, "Why do you desire the possession of such and such a parish?" for they had paid the priest thirty *kopy* and a lifelong pension in order that he might cede the parish to them so that it would henceforth remain in their possession. They answered me by saying that it lay adjacent to their own properties and bordered them. I said to them, "If that is the whole reason, why do you not secure the one still nearer?" They kept silent. Then I said, "Is it not rather that the latter yields less revenue and has less endowments?" And I said further: "Now you desire this particular parish because it lies adjacent to your property; but when you secure it, then some other parish will be adjacent to that, and you will desire to possess that as well; and so forth and so on, until you will desire to possess the whole world." They felt ashamed.[29]

And can anyone tell us what good comes of this owning of parishes? For we plainly see that monks are getting worse and worse: for when formerly they kept within the monastery, they did not commit adultery; but now that they have rushed out into the world they have become adulterers. . . . And when the parish decays and its endowments are exhausted, they abandon it, and thus God's people are left without care. What reasonable man doubts that such conduct is contrary to God's will? . . .

How much money they expend for indulgences, in order to secure for their Order (and especially for their own monastery) fillets resembling episcopal miters, so that their abbot or provost or prior may be crowned therewith! What profit is in it for holy Church save their own pride and boasting? Moreover, their huckstering is thereby increased, for they have to pay their bishop for the consecration or coronation. And how much miserable toil and avarice must they expend so that they may procure for their Order a costly crozier and a miter!

Furthermore, what lies they must employ before the pope and other persons, whose recommendations to the pope they need! They pretend that they are very poor, that they are not able to subsist because of the poverty of their monastery and are unable to bear the labor! Hence, they beg that a parish be allotted to them. In reality, if one should count the persons, the plows, fields, fishponds, and other revenue of the monastery, he would find that the share of each monk would be between

---

[29] This incident cannot be documented, nor is it known which particular monastery is meant.

twenty or thirty *kopy* of revenue, with a plow and a fishpond to spare! Yet this I know, that Christ and his disciples, as well as the founding fathers of their own Order, had been satisfied with much less.

Secondly, they argue before the pope that if they were granted the parish, they would greatly benefit the holy Church thereby. For otherwise he might not grant it to them. . . .

In the third place, they promise, as is proper, to protect and increase the rights of the parish and thus benefit the holy Church. . . . Thus their first reason why the parish should be granted them is that they are poor; the second, that they are poorer than others; and the third, that benefit would thereby accrue to the holy Church.[30] If these three reasons were true, they would provide ground for expecting that the request be granted. But who knows whether or not the facts justify their claims and whether the grant would benefit the holy Church? For they resort to the common methods of simony in order to gain their ends by offering bribes: so much to the pope, so much to the noble patron, so much to the person who recommends the cause, so much to the clerks, the advocates, and all others who might aid in this business. And when they secure the parish, they commonly rent it according to the municipal law, thus securing for themselves perpetual revenue. Hence, simony persists for a long time on both sides: for they receive revenue without labor; or, if he who has rented the parish should at some time redeem it from them,[31] he must then recoup himself for his expense by hounding the people in order to recover the money he had paid the monastery, and to gain a profit besides.

The seizure of dignities or parishes and revenues came about in the following manner: at first the people who were to be governed in accordance with the divine law themselves elected their bishop or other prelate, pastor, or spiritual leader. In such a manner have the saintly bishops and priests been elected whose holidays the Christian community still observes. Later, secular princes and lords, as patrons, regarded it as a means toward worldly esteem to elect their own bishops and priests to the bishoprics and parishes which they themselves had endowed. Thirdly, when their consciences troubled them by reason of bad appointments which they sometimes made, they placed the parishes (to which they held the right of advowson)

[30] The text of these three arguments is reminiscent of Wyclif, *De simonia*, 89.

[31] The meaning of the sentence is obscure.

under the supervision of monasteries, and thus subjected them to financial charges. The lords thought that they had thus avoided bad appointments, and that the monasteries would make better appointments. But later neither the lords nor the monasteries retained their rights of advowson: for they were taken over by the pope.[32] And he appoints men he does not know and who push their way into Church preferments, seeking not the salvation of the parishioners but only the revenue, so that they might live luxuriously according to the flesh.

Thus the devil spreads simony among the people and will continue to do so in an ever increasing measure to the end of the world. . . . When monks used to appoint unworthy [priests] to parishes because of the intercession of secular lords or friends, they acted in accordance with Lucifer's will. . . . Also in accordance with carnal promptings they favored their own relatives who were unfit to minister to God's people. Likewise in conformity with the standard of the world they used to grant [parishes] to their servants—even though unworthy in many ways—only if the latter lived in accordance with their will or paid them larger annual pensions or revenue. Thus instead of serving God the Father, the Son, and the Holy Spirit through their appointments, they served the devil, the flesh, and the world.

You can now perceive how simony proceeds in securing and granting parishes among monks, and likewise in squandering revenue. For Saint Gregory says that bishops who squander their goods on a multitude of servants, on knights and friends, are of the number of the greatest heretics and therefore are simoniacs,[33] and that statement equally includes abbots, provosts, priors, and other monks. How, then, can they who act thus be justified of the charge of simony? For they are less justifiable than bishops, since by their vows they have cut themselves off from the world, and are more bound by them to poverty. They signify their profession of poverty and the repudiation of the world by the hood, the tonsure, and other symbols. Thus by wasteful squandering of their possessions, which had been given for the sake of God to the poor, they are even more involved in simony than the bishops. . . . For they, by living in luxury and other evil ways, have dishonored the

---

[32] The whole paragraph is based substantially on Wyclif's *De simonia,* 92–93.

[33] *Decretum Magistri Gratiani,* pars II, C. XVI, q. VII, c. 3. But the author is Pope Gregory VII, not Saint Gregory.

vows which they have taken to live in poverty, suffering, and repudiation of the world. Thus they do not observe what they had promised God and their patron, and despite their vow they are unfaithful to God and holy Church, [and their patron].[34] . . .

They also waste alms profligately in banqueting and drinking bouts with their friends and other people who acquiesce with them. And what some of them squander on dogs and bitches! Who can describe, furthermore, the different foreign drinks they guzzle! The monk Saint Bernard writes that they drink wine flavored with wormwood, rosemary, juniper, sage, muscat,[35] or ginger; some sweet, some fragrant, pouring it from one drinking cup into another.[36] And although you, O Saint Bernard, had not lived in Bohemia, I tell you that here they have new and old beer, as well as thick and thin. When casual strangers visit them, the monks give them the thin drink, in order to make them think that they themselves drink such potions, so that they [the strangers] would drink less of it. But when they sense that their visitor may desire to be buried in their monastery, or that there is a chance to receive something from him, then they draw the good potion from their supplies so that one potation calls for another. For the word "potation" signifies to them abundant drinking and plentiful eating.[37] Hence, the poor dears, who have abandoned the world's carnal delights, have no equals in the world in enjoying the most delightful livelihood! Kings, lords, and princes do not always have drink and food so wholesome and so certain. The cellars of lay people are sometimes exhausted; but theirs never! The king and the lords sometimes lack in baked and cooked food, or in bread; but for them bread of the finest and whitest flour is never lacking. Cold does not bite them, for they have boots and greatcoats; heat does not scorch them, for they have cool cells and cloisters, that is, courts of paradise. Therefore

"Whoever wishes to live well
Let him enter the monks' cell."[38]

[34] The last clause is omitted in the text edited by F. Žilka.
[35] Hus uses the term "Oman," which I take to be a geographical term (for SE Arabia) applied to the wine known in modern times as "muscat."
[36] A free quotation from Saint Bernard's *Apologia* (Migne, *PL*, 182:910 f.).
[37] The word Hus employs ("*pitancie*," here translated "potation") is apparently of his own coining, for he uses it in jest.
[38] Perhaps a free rendering of the Latin couplet added in the MS.: *Felices claustra; miseri, qui castra sequuntur*. I have translated the Czech version somewhat freely for the rhyme's sake.

But not only I myself say so, for Saint Bernard and they themselves say it as well, particularly when they wish to lure someone into joining their monastery, as children, both boys and girls, who do not yet possess discretion. O that they would remember what the pope called Boniface said! "We have never read that Christ's disciples, or those who had been converted to the faith by their preaching, had enticed anyone to faith in God by a gift; except perhaps when someone gave a poor man food. For no one whatsoever was ever denied food for the body." [39]

. . . I confess to have entertained an evil desire when I was a young student, for I had thought to become a priest quickly in order to secure a good livelihood and dress and to be held in esteem by men. But I recognized this as an evil desire when I comprehended the Scriptures.

Another lesson from the statement of Pope Boniface is this: that in the days of the apostles and of other converted Christians all material goods were held in common for the use of every needy member. As Saint Luke writes . . . , "they had all things in common." [40] That order does not exist among the conventual monks: for not only are their possessions not shared in common with the poor, but sometimes even among themselves only the church door and a few other things are in common, but the cup, the purse, the groschens, money, the pouch, and the hood are all private. Furthermore, if one wishes to investigate the matter in greater detail, he will find that monks and nuns possess private incomes. It appears that monks keep the vow regarding private possessions about as well as a prostitute does chastity! They are constantly confessing other sins, but pay no attention to their disregard of the vow. Would that they kept the vows they had taken—that is, chastity, obedience, and poverty without private possessions—and in addition avoid and confess other sins!

But they say that they cannot live without private property. To that I reply: If that is true, why did they bind themselves so foolishly? But because what they say is not true, their excuses are not justified. For it were better not to enter the monastic Order than, having entered, not to keep the vow. If we wish to lead a life according to a monastic rule, let us retire to a

---

[39] *Decretum Magistri Gratiani*, pars II, C. I, q. II, c. 2, where the quotation is ascribed to Pope Urban II. Hus follows Wyclif in referring it to Boniface (cf. *De simonia*, 85).

[40] Acts 4:32.

desert, and let us deny ourselves in eating and drinking, in
sleeping and toil, as the first monks did, and let us not place our
monasteries and houses in the midst of the richest cities and
in the most delightful locations. . . .

Still another excuse which they use in justifying their wasting
of goods is that if they did not spend it upon men, the latter
would not contribute in return. And, secondly, that they fear
injury to their property from such people. Accordingly [they
say], we must share and deal generously with them. But surely
this excuse will not clear them of sin, for by this assertion they
show themselves to be of that company who say, as Saint Paul
wrote, "Let us do evil that good may come." [41] They should
know that no man ought to consent to any wickedness in order
to bring about a good result. Saint Anselm, the great teacher,
and others also warn that no one should sin willingly, even if
he were to save the whole world thereby. For he cannot be
pleasing to God by sinning, for God cannot sin, nor can he
command anyone to sin. That being so, what excuse have they
who say that they must live in that fashion for the sake of preserving their property? Nay, they should rather rejoice if they
are deprived of it because they refused to live unrighteously.
And all other faithful Christians ought to do likewise. . . .

There remains still another hole [42] through which monks
commit simony: for they issue letters of participation in their
good deeds, such as fasts, prayers, Masses, austerities, and
other good works. [43] But they are mistaken when they write,
declaring, "We make thee a participant. . . ." For to make
anyone a participant in good works which would benefit his
soul to salvation belongs to God alone. The great and holy
prophet David knew this. Hence he did not say, "I make other
people participants in my acts." But he prayed God, saying,
"Make me a partaker, O Lord, with them that fear thee, and
of them that observe thy law." [44] In the second place, they err
in extolling their own deeds above those of others, contrary
to the Saviour's word, "When ye shall have fulfilled all the
commandments that are commanded you, say, We are unprofitable servants." [45] For thus did the apostles do. Saint Paul

[41] Rom. 3:8. The same argument is found in Wyclif, *De simonia*, 96.
[42] Czech, *skúla*.
[43] This is technically known as the *participatio bonum operum*.
[44] Ps. 119:63, which in the Czech Bible of Kralice reads, "I participate
with all who . . . ," and in the American Standard Version, "I am a
companion of all . . . that observe thy precepts."
[45] Luke 17:10, freely rendered.

did not issue letters of participation, but in the [epistles to the] Romans and the Corinthians, and in all his other epistles save those written to the Hebrews, Timothy, and Titus, always requested prayers from all faithful Christians for himself. But the monks, as if they had an overabundance of good works, grant some to others. Moreover, it is strange that they offer them to the rich, from whom they expect to receive something, while with the poor they do not share. They also accept the rich into their brotherhood. . . .

Since all faithful Christians have such a good Brother and gracious Father [as Christ], they love each other according to his commandment, and have the same spiritual food, his holy body, and the same drink, his holy blood. They all are clad in the same robe—love—and live in the same house—holy Church. They all share in common good works, so that each participates in them in accordance with his Father's pleasure. That is called the communion of saints. . . . This communion is so ordered by God that should a son of God desire to exclude another from the communion, he himself is immediately deprived of it. Consequently, a faithful Christian is diligent in fulfilling God's commands in order to be in communion with the entire Christian brotherhood. Nor is it necessary to pay for letters from anyone for that purpose, for each has certainty of it from Christ. And the more he loves Christ, his Father and Brother, and the more he keeps his commandments, the more he participates in the communion of saints.

But this holy communion is not made known to the people, for but few preach about it, because on account of avarice man-invented brotherhoods are extolled instead. For this latter kind of "brotherhood" has increased so greatly they wish to create as many of them as there are trades in towns. I have heard of one such "brotherhood" [46] composed of priests and pages—the latter having been dragged in by the former; they meet with one of their number one day and with another another day, and so forth continually. They eat, drink, and guzzle to surfeit, but do not remember the poor and fail to attend Masses at home; and returning from the fraternal revels, these "brethren" take several days to grow sober! Hence with their revels they transgress the law and brotherhood of Christ principally by acting contrary to the word of Paul, who says: "Let us cast off the works of darkness, and let us put on the armor of light. Let us walk becomingly, as in

[46] I.e., a guild.

the day; not in revelling and drunkenness."[47] . . . How strange!
Do they wish to earn for themselves forgiveness of sins and
delivery from hell by these frequent indulgences? On the contrary, as the Saviour testifies, the rich man who had fared
sumptuously and bountifully every day was buried in hell.
And what other sins they commit in those "brotherhoods"
when, sitting at the tables, they indulge in loose, slanderous,
vain, and lying talk, we shall know only when men shall receive
their reward for their deeds in the day of judgment.

. . . But perhaps some God-fearing monk shall ask, "What
shall I do to avoid sharing in the sin of simony, since I am bound
to obey my superior?" I reply that he should refuse to obey
and stand up against it. But if he replies, "I shall be put in
prison," I respond that he will be blessed if he suffer for truth's
sake and will not yield to wrong even if he should die in prison
for his stand. What better thing than holy martyrdom can
happen to him in this world? But I know for certain that if he
should decide to live in poverty, in complete surrender of
property, purity, chastity, and Christ's love, he would instantly
be set upon by the rest. And should he exhort them not to pile
up possessions and to avoid other sins as has been said before,
then without any doubt he would be declared a heretic. For
they are so accustomed to their practices and so alienated from
the holy rule that a life such as saints have lived is abhorrent to
them.

7

That priests or chaplains may likewise sin by simony may
be observed from the above discussion and from their deeds.
For a priest may become a simoniac when he enters the priesthood . . . on account of worldly dignity or income or carnal
pleasures, or when he is unfit by reason of other sins or is incapable of ministering to the people. Likewise, if he pays money
or a gift [for the office], or if he ministers for the purpose of
getting money; or if he obtains the office by force, or in order
to secure worldly favor; by any of these means he has fallen into
simony. For he has the evil intention, which constitutes simony,
of exchanging an unspiritual for a spiritual thing. If he gives
money to the pope, the bishop, or anybody else, that is a perfectly clear case of simony: for he paid money—like Simon—
for the power of laying on of hands, the power exercised in
confession, baptism, or in the administration of sacraments as

[47] Rom. 13:12, 13.

is proper for a priest. . . . This is such patent simony that men regard it exclusively as such, disregarding any other mode. . . . Concerning this obvious kind of simony by purchase, Saint Gregory says, "If a priest secures a parish by a money purchase, he shall not only be deprived of it, but of the priesthood itself as well." [48] O Saint Gregory! if you should now deprive them of their parishes and depose them from priesthood, very few priests would be left. For although some of them did not pay money to the pope or the patrons . . . yet they did pay the bishops or their officials for confirmation; for the latter refuse to grant them the cure of souls . . . unless they [the applicants] pay them for it. Is that not a sale of spiritual goods, that the priest has no right to baptize, to hear confessions, to preach, and to lead men out of their sins unless he pays them money for it? What a strange thing! The [proprietary] lord grants the priest the right to enjoy the material revenue without pay in order that, by securing his livelihood therefrom, the priest could lead men to salvation; but the spiritual [lords] refuse to grant him the spiritual right by which he could benefit the souls of his fellows.

Once I advised a certain priest, in the presence of his lord, who had granted him a parish for God's sake [i.e., freely], not to pay anything for confirmation. Thereupon a master of the sacred Scriptures who was present said: "What are you talking about? Should they render him service without pay? Why shouldn't he pay?" Thereupon I answered him: "The certificate is unnecessary. They should examine the priest only as to whether he be of good life and of virtuous morals, whether he is given good testimony by the people, and whether no one knows anything against his life; and whether he knows how to minister to the people in regard to the Word; thereafter, they should entrust him, in God's name, with the care of souls, saying, 'Go, preach the Word of God to the people, and first of all lead a good life yourself.' For thus did Christ send his apostles, and the apostles in turn sent other holy men. And if a written certificate must be issued him, then I say let it be done free of charge, for God's sake." The master answered, "But what are the notaries to live on?" I replied: "Let the archbishop provide for their needs. For that is why he draws a revenue of several thousand, so that he could provide the needed officials for the administration and the service of the people. For the archiepiscopal office is not endowed for the

[48] *Decretum Magistri Gratiani*, pars II, C. I, q. I, c. 3.

purpose of proud display of retinue, nor is it right that the endowments given for God's service be squandered and wasted upon a multitude of retainers unfit for the office." Thereupon the master became angry with me and said, "You always want things according to your will." But I answered, "Not according to my will, but according to Christ's will . . . and according to the apostolic will, as well as that of other saints." He then left me in anger.

Nevertheless, if the notary asks no payment, but the recipient of the spiritual right makes him a present of his own free good will, the notary may accept it, as Saint Gregory has declared. But when he regularly demands payment for his services, then I say that the charge for the certificate should be limited to two coins; why, then, should one person give two *kopy*, another five, and another four? [49] No one can truthfully assert that the paper, the wax, or the labor of writing costs that much. And nothing besides these is granted save the spiritual right. How can they truthfully say that they do not sell the spiritual right for money? . . .

But the priest says: "The benefice is granted me [freely], but they will not grant me the spiritual right without a payment. What shall I do?" I answer as I have answered many, that he should go to the archbishop and tell him: "Priest! I have been called to a certain parish to serve God's people there. I beg you in God's name for your blessing so that I may lead these people in God's way." If he gives the blessing, accept it and thank God; if he does not but sends you to the notaries, tell him: "Priest! the proprietary lord or the community has called me without payment: you too should grant me the spiritual right without payment. But since you refuse, I am going to those that called me and resign to them the office." And presenting yourself before the proprietary lord, tell him or them: "You gave me the right to the benefice and the parish that I might serve the people. But the bishop refuses to grant me the spiritual right without payment. Hence, I return it to you, for I do not wish to enter the office by simony."

But immediately you counter, "If . . . no one should make payment and the officials refuse [the spiritual right]; then if every priest should act in that fashion, no one would become possessed of a parish." To that I answer that if every priest should act thus, the officials would be obliged to admit them freely. But again you reply, "If I do not pay, another will."

[49] One *kopa* equals sixty groschens.

My answer is that if you wish thus to excuse yourself, then the executioner, the catchpole, or the prostitute could likewise be excused. For each could say: "If I should refuse to be an executioner, or a catchpole, another would. If I should not be a prostitute, another would." Or you perhaps add, "Others openly make the payment." To that I answer that if others sin openly, you should not sin on that account. You say to that, "It is an ancient custom." To which I answer that the longer an evil custom lasts, the greater punishment it receives from God. . . . I marvel why we rather do not keep the still more ancient good custom of the holy apostles, which they received from Christ. . . .

A priest may become a simoniac, in the second place, by demanding payment for baptism, confession, a funeral, the sacred host, holy oil, the marriage rite, thirty Masses, purification,[50] and when he refuses to receive confession unless the sick person first leave a legacy to the parish. Likewise when a chaplain follows this path, he also commits simony, particularly when, having received episcopal permission thereto, he demands that he be paid a groschen for each confession, saying, "I had to pay for the letter of permission, therefore you must also pay." But behold the enormity of this trafficking: he paid a groschen for the letter, but if ten men pay him a groschen each, he has gained nine groschens from his one. And if he charges more—richer men paying two or three groschens each —then his gain is correspondingly higher in accordance with his ability to make gains. Hence, he sells doves in God's temple, making it a den of thieves. . . . Moreover, his excuse . . . convicts him more than it excuses him; for he accuses himself of being guilty of Simon's sin, having requested the right—by the payment of money—of laying on of hands on people's heads in absolution so that they may receive forgiveness of sins and consequently the Holy Spirit. I know not what other purpose the letter serves save that both parties to the transaction make money. But a priest of holy purpose ought to tell the bishop: "Priest! I serve people who have fallen into great sins. Give me your blessing that I may absolve them." And the bishop, examining the priest or the chaplain whether they be reasonable men, ought to say: "May God give you his blessing. Freely you have received, freely give. But know, priest, that if you should demand money for confession, I will punish you in accordance with the holy ordinance."

[50] The ritual purification after childbirth (i.e., churching).

They also sell more dearly the consecrated oil than the ordinary oil, and that for no other reason than that it is consecrated: in some places they charge two groschens, elsewhere twelve coins, elsewhere a groschen. For thirty Masses they commonly charge thirty groschens. This is perhaps in remembrance of Judas, who sold the Saviour for thirty pieces of silver! Some priests accept orders for so many Masses that if they celebrated five, six, or ten a day they would not get through in fifty years! And they say, "What am I to do when a man comes and begs me to accept an order for celebrating thirty Masses?" I respond that he should say: "My dear brother, all the Masses in the world are yours, if you are in God's grace. I was ordained for the purpose that I might, with God's grace, celebrate the Mass whenever I can; so that I should celebrate no more for payment than what I would have celebrated freely. Hence, I cannot enter into an obligation with you, nor is it right that I should. Go your way and may the good God be with you." But I am aware that an avaricious heart will find it difficult to refuse any offer of money. Therefore, the avaricious ask whether they may include concurrently in the thirty Masses two or three people, or if by inserting a collect . . . into the Mass, they may look upon it as if the whole Mass had been said. Thus they squirm right and left. But a priest of free spirit, by not accepting such payments, is certain of not committing simony and hence has no such weight on his conscience. Accordingly, when some such good priests came and asked me how they should conduct themselves in similar matters, I advised them to act in the above-described manner. If someone should beg the service, saying, "I beg of you for God's sake, take this money and celebrate thirty Masses," or whatever number he should name, the priest should tell him that he does not wish to celebrate Masses for money, nor to break the established order. "Hence, I do not want your money." But if the suppliant should say, "Nevertheless, take the money for God's grace," then, if the priest is needy, he may take it, in accordance with Saint Jerome's opinion, but without an obligation; if he is not needy, let him say, "I have no need, but give it to the miserably poor, as God has commanded."

However, how difficult it is for some sons of Mammon to receive this instruction! For they have fallen away from Christ's command . . . and from the statement of Saint Paul, who says: "Having food and raiment, let us be content therewith. For those who desire to grow rich fall into temptation and a snare of the devil, and into many foolish and hurtful lusts, which drown men in perdition and damnation. For the root of all evil is covetousness, which some having fallen into, have been led astray from the faith and have entangled themselves in many sorrows. But thou, O man, beware of these things." [51] . . .

But a poor priest [i.e., a chaplain] says, "I am serving a parish priest and am earning nothing but my food: how shall I clothe myself and buy books to help me in preaching?" To that the prophet David replies, "I have not seen the righteous forsaken nor his seed begging bread." [52] And the Saviour replies to him, saying, "Seek ye first the Kingdom of God and all these things"—that is, food and clothing—"shall be added unto you." [53] Therefore, my dear priest, man of God, if you observe that you are benefiting the people, trust in his holy mercy that he will not leave you naked.

But it is truly a great shame that parochial priests allow their brethren [i.e., chaplains] who toil for them to suffer want; for they should share in the chaplains' material needs whatever they themselves possess. In real truth he who, in working with the people, brings forth good and gracious results, and is himself of good life, is worthy of the revenues contributed by the people. Hence, there are perhaps many chaplains who are worthier of the parish revenues than their [beneficed] priests. As the Saviour testifies, "Provide neither gold nor silver, nor money, for the laborer is worthy of his food." [54] Accordingly, a faithful and industrious chaplain is worthy of clothing and food, while the priest who does not work is unworthy of support. . . . Thus Saint Paul says to the citizens of Thessalonica, "For ye yourselves know how ye ought to imitate us: for we have not burdened you, nor have we eaten any man's bread for nothing." Then he continues: "For when we were with you, we commanded you, If any would not work, neither should he eat." [55] O woe unto the canons, priests, bishops, and other clergy and prelates who eat, gorge themselves, guzzle, and feast abundantly, but in spiritual matters amount to nothing! O Saint Paul! If those who do not work should not eat, surely many would starve, unless they consider it work to drink heavily and to feed grossly and to indulge in other carnal pleasures, as I have heard that some of them

[51] I Tim. 6:8–11 (altered).   [52] Ps. 37:22.
[53] Matt. 6:33.   [54] Matt. 10:9, 10.
[55] II Thess. 3:7, 8, 10.

complained while dining: How much we suffer for God's
holy Church!

But as they excuse their simony by saying that it is a venerable custom to pay for the confession, funeral, sacrament,
baptism, and the other already referred to sacred rites, my
reply thereto is that the custom of charging for those ministrations is . . . a simoniacal custom. As Pope Innocent says,
neither before nor after the ministration should the customary
payment be demanded, for it is simony.[56] Another decree
likewise affirms that the custom of paying for such services
is the heresy of simony and is damned. Another ruling forbids
anyone to demand or force a payment for a funeral or [holy]
oil, or to excuse his sin on account of whatever custom may
exist; for its antiquity does not diminish, but rather increases,
the sin. . . . Therefore, whoever excuses a sin on the ground of
custom could by that same argument excuse any sin. For if the
argument were valid, one could excuse even fornication, saying,
"It is an ancient custom to fornicate." As the Sodomites replied
to the holy man when he exhorted them not to commit sodomy,
saying, "You came to live among us, not to give us law." [57]
And alas! they now excuse fornication by affirming that it is
natural. But they lie. For no sin, nor any vice contrary to virtue,
is natural, although man is by nature more inclined to one sin
than to another. Thus commonly one man is more inclined to
fornication, or to anger, than another.

Hence, mark well that neither custom nor natural temperament nor inclination can serve as an excuse that sin be not sin,
although natural or temperamental inclination makes sinning
easier or harder for different men. Accordingly, when both he
who has a quick temper and he who does not possess such a
temperament become angry, the former man's sin is lighter.
The same holds for fornication. . . . And since anger and fornication cannot be excused on the ground of antiquity, how can
simony be so excused? Therefore, it is a great evil for laymen
and clergy to excuse their sins on the ground of custom: as the
Czechs say, "It has been done from ancient times"; and the
Germans, introducing a bad custom, refuse to abandon it,
saying, "*Ist unze Recht*," that is, "It is our right." And people

---

[56] This is a decree of Pope Innocent III, in *Decretum Magistri Gratiani*,
pars II, C. I, q. III, c. 15; the decrees which follow are *ibid.*, pars II,
C. I, q. I, cs. 102–105. But the text paraphrases, rather than cites, the
decrees.

[57] Gen. 19:9; a free rendering.

have so relied on these customs that they refuse to abandon them, but rather defend them to the death. . . .

. . . Hence, Saint Augustine says: "It is in vain that some, vanquished by a reasonable argument, press upon us a custom, as if a custom were greater than truth, or as if in spiritual matters what is better revealed by the Holy Spirit were not to be followed by preference." [58] The holy man asserts that men in vain defend themselves by an evil custom as if it were worthier than truth. For reason convinces us that truth should conquer custom. And further, when a good practice is followed in spiritual things and the Holy Spirit shows us something better, we should immediately accept it. As again Saint Augustine says, "We should follow truth rather than custom, for reason and truth ever drive out custom." [59] Likewise the great martyr and bishop, Saint Cyprian, whom Saint Augustine praises highly, says, "Custom without truth is an old error; accordingly, abandoning the error, let us follow the truth." And again he says, "We are to follow not human error but God's truth." [60] And Saint Ambrose writes, "All novelties which Christ did not teach we contemn." Likewise Saint Isidore writes, " Let an evil custom be vanquished by God's love and reason." [61] And Saint Gregory says, "When Paul says, Another foundation can no one lay except that which had been laid, which is Jesus Christ, it proves that where there is no foundation laid by Christ, good works cannot be built thereon." [62] . . .

. . . The priest-canons or parish priests abuse the alms given for God's sake in so far as they make presents of it to relatives in order that men may think them well-born. Sometimes they give even to nonrelatives in order to be regarded as belonging to the recipient's family. In this fashion those who are regarded in the world as utterly base-born are thus elevated, and often repudiate their fathers and their poor relations, or are ashamed of them. Those who aid their relatives excuse themselves by saying that both naturally and by God's command a man should love his father and his mother as well as his relatives more than others. This argument prompts many to pile up benefices. But this seeking of worldly esteem dishonors

---

[58] *Decretum Magistri Gratiani*, pars I, dist. VIII, c. 7. The phrase "reasonable argument" appears by mistake in the text of Hus as "an unreasonable argument."

[59] *Ibid.*, c. 6.

[60] Both passages are in *ibid.*, cs. 8–9.

[61] *Ibid.*, pars I, dist. XI, c. 1.

[62] *Ibid.*, pars II, C. I, q. I, c. 26.

the doctrine of our Lord Jesus Christ. For although Christ was
a man of the highest dignity, he was pleased to be born of a
poor race. . . .

What profits it a man, particularly a priest, that he boast
of his descent, or that when he is not well-born according to the
world's opinion, he desire to be held as if well-born? Does he
not know that he sins gravely if he is ashamed of his descent
and desires to boast falsely of one not his own? Behold, Christ
says, "He who loves father and mother (and of course the more
distant relatives as well) more than me, is not worthy of me." [63]
Hence, those who in pride prefer to love their relatives more
than Christ are not true followers of Christ. And because under
great penalty we all should follow Christ, and he, being the
supreme and almighty bishop, did not enrich his own mother
with material possessions here on earth, nor his particular
relatives, but allowed them for a time to live in considerable
poverty, how, then, does that priest follow Christ who enriches
his relatives? . . . As for the argument which they advance,
that it is natural and in accordance with God's command that
a man should love his father and his mother and other relatives
more than others, one may answer that if his father or mother
or other relatives are needy and lovers of God's law, then the
priest may, by the grace of God, help them so that they will not
suffer want. But that is far from the enrichment and from the
haughtiness of pride [which he would thus manifest]; for he
would then do it in accordance with God's commandment.

Furthermore, priests sin in yet other ways. The first of these
is that they feed many flatterers in order to be praised by them,
and that they are generous toward the rich and invite them
[to feasts] against Christ's admonition, "When thou preparest
a dinner or a supper, call not thy friends and the rich." [64]
Another custom they have is that they employ servants not
needful to the priestly office, such as bowmen, chamberlains,
and a multitude of pages. The third . . . that they buy much
unnecessary household furnishing such as silver plate, cups,
spoons, pillows, magnificent beds, and many other things. The
fourth . . . that they build excessively expensive houses: they
pull down good dwellings in which they could live comfortably
and build new ones. And as soon as they dislike these latter,
they promptly again pull them down and erect others. But when
something in the church falls into disrepair, they refuse to put
it in order but urge the poor parishioners to provide for the

[63] Matt. 10:37.   [64] Luke 14:12.

repairs. The fifth custom they have is that they keep beautiful horses equipped with splendid harness; also they own many hunting dogs on which they waste the alms of the poor.

Even a very stupid man will realize that these five vain customs have not been bequeathed to the priests by the Saviour, and that they contribute nothing essential to the priestly office. On the contrary, they are Satan's bonds, wherewith he binds them and incites them to pride and leads them, like the blind, to perdition. And these servants of the devil are so stricken with spiritual blindness that when one asks them, "Why do you act like that?" they answer that the work or worldly honor demands it. But because the devil much excels worldly honor, it were a more handsome and a truer answer to say that the devil demands it. . . . Therefore, as no man can excuse fornication by saying that the flesh desires it, likewise he cannot excuse it by saying that the world desires it. For it would be similar to an excuse of a knight who had allowed himself to be captured by his enemy without resisting; when his king asked him, "Why have you allowed yourself to be captured?" he would reply that the enemy wanted it so! I marvel greatly that men are so blind that they do the will of their enemies by serving the devil, the world, and their flesh for a very vain reward, that is, the world's praise; for this brings in its train another reward, namely, exclusion from everlasting joy and the damnation in fire with the devils, in darkness, in anguish, and in everlasting pain. . . .

And how shall priests excuse themselves who shamefully spuander pay for requiem Masses in fornication, in adorning their concubines, priestesses, or prostitutes more sumptuously than the church altars and pictures, purchasing for them skirts, capes, and fur coats from the tithes and offerings of the poor? Their fornication has become so customary that they keep their women openly and without shame, some hypocritically calling them sisters. . . . Above all, there is no one who is genuinely concerned with this sorry state of affairs. Superiors are not, for they themselves would have to be among the first to give up such a practice; the lords ignore it, for sometimes they themselves live in a like fashion, and some on account of worldly favor. Others do not regard it as their duty to improve the situation. Others make a start at it, but give it up—although regretfully—for they fear, on the one hand, that they may be brought before a court, and on the other, that prelates would promptly free the culprits. And the parishioners either do not care or are not allowed to interfere, or are not able to stand courageously against such an open wrong. But they should follow Christ's commands and should, either they or the patron, first admonish the priest; if he disregards them, they should all gather and tell him to cast off the offense; if he refuses, they should then . . . shun him as an overt sinner and as one hell-bent.[65] Furthermore, they should request the bishop to apply proper correction; should the latter ignore the request, they should then withhold the tithes from him and no one should attend the Mass celebrated by him. For there is a regulation that no one should hear the Mass read by a priest concerning whom he has certain knowledge that he keeps a mistress or a prostitute; and this regulation is issued under pain of an interdict;[66] not that the Mass would not be valid, but that the priest should not administer it unworthily, and the people should not share in his sin. If all this should prove of no avail, or he should refrain from [the duties of] his office, having enough private means to support himself without the contributions of the parish, then he should be dealt with in accordance with what Saint Paul has ordered about the fornicator. . . . What did Paul command? "Cast out the old leaven!", meaning thereby the fornicator. For he said prior to that, "When ye are gathered together in the name of our Lord Jesus Christ, and with the power of our Lord Jesus Christ, deliver such an one unto Satan to the destruction of the flesh, that his spirit may be saved in the day of the Lord Jesus Christ."[67]

. . . But men say: "We can easily get along without such an action; it is none of our concern. It does us no harm!" Saint Paul promptly replies: "Your joy is not good. Know ye not that a little leaven, that is, a small portion of the yeast, leavens the whole lump? Cast out the old leaven."[68] Here it is shown that they do not rejoice rightly who suffer such a vice. For they themselves are leavened thereby, that is, are infected by this same sin, which is communicated to them because of their neglect to eradicate it. Therefore, Saint Paul says to them, "Ye are puffed up,"[69] that is, by having neglected to cast out from among you the person who was guilty of the vice. . . .

---

[65] Matt. 18:15–17, freely rendered.
[66] Hus refers to Decretum Magistri Gratiani, pars I, dist. XXXII, c. 6, where Pope Alexander II forbids attendance upon Mass read by a priest living with a concubine.
[67] I Cor. 5:7, 3–5.   [68] I Cor. 5:6, 7.   [69] I Cor. 5:2.

The apostles of Christ decreed that anyone who committed fornication after baptism could not become a priest; and that if a priest committed fornication, he was to be deprived of priesthood. But the vicars of the apostles—the bishops—themselves commit fornication, and do not forbid it to others! Like father, like son. The son gives, and the father receives, money so that the son can have a mistress. The latter sells sin; the former buys it—one *kopa* a year for a mistress. I have been told of a priest in Moravia who paid a *kopa* a year as a cradle payment: [70] therefore, it was dubbed *cunabulales*—in Czech, a cradle tax. And in Hungary a priest pays a stated sum for each child he has: the more he has, the more he pays to his bishop. I was told this by those who had lived in Hungary. Should those be called shepherds who rob Christ's sheep and spend it on the devil's prostitutes?; accepting the goods of the people, alms and tithes, they offer them to the devil?; and having the duty of going ahead and leading the people after Christ, they lead them by their evil example into the devil's throat? . . . Woe, woe to such shepherds, in truth thieves, robbers, and ravening wolves! I know not how the holy Church can rid herself of them unless the community follow the order which Christ and Saint Paul have established. May the gracious Saviour grant that we all may guard against sins, and the priests leave their mistresses and follow Christ in his virtues, abandoning the evil practice of accumulating benefices and possessions as well as wasting their substance profligately, but rather instructing the people by good works and in the Word of God!

I shall further mention that they commit simony by the exchange and renting of parishes—for in this practice much chicanery obtains. [71] Since they continually exchange the cure of souls in connection with each parish, who can excuse them from sin? Such a priest rents the parish to another and he himself lives in idleness in town. In the meantime the renter diligently shears and milks the sheep: at one time he forbids thirty Masses; at another, he requests ten Masses; or he orders that the worshipers pay five groschens at the cross on Good Friday in commemoration of the five wounds of Christ; or he demands three pounds of wax to be offered to God, but he himself appropriates and sells it; or else he orders that beautiful

---

[70] I.e., he had a child a year.
[71] This was a common practice. In Prague itself at the time out of 350 parish changes, 186 were held in exchange; even so the records are not complete.

candles be offered so that he could sell them. He will not
stop until he has reimbursed himself for the money he had paid
as rental. Notice what Christ says: "The thief cometh but to
steal." [72] And who is the thief? Christ says: "Whoever enters
otherwise than through the door is a thief and a robber." [73] . . .
Hence, whoever is a renter, not for his own and other men's
salvation, but on account of avarice, is a thief and a robber.
He cares not for the sheep, for they do not belong to him.
One robber has rented the sheep to another robber: the latter
keeps and milks them and transmits a portion to the other,
who feeds himself by robbery and without labor. . . .

But someone will say, "I must rent the parish, for it does
not yield enough to support me." You fool! How then can
the renter provide enough for himself and you? Will
additional robbery fill both bellies? Again some say, "I cannot
stay by the parish; I must look after another benefice." O you
miser! You cannot adequately minister to one, how then dare
you hold two parishes? Again you say, "I must serve the
[royal] court." But I say that you thus intend to serve the devil;
for if you are a pastor, feed the sheep and leave serving the
court alone! Again you say, "I have a difficult patron." To
which I reply: "Perhaps the patron is good, but you are bad;
stop your complaints and get along with your patron and your
sheep. And if the patron is indeed hard, let your goodness
overcome his badness. And if you cannot overcome him, seek
help from God and from good people. If nothing avails,
because perhaps the people are not worthy of you or you of
them, resign and go elsewhere." . . .

Furthermore, I know not whether renting a parish can ever
be arranged properly as far as both parties are concerned. If
the parish priest cannot remain with his parish, he should
entrust it to a good priest. But since he entrusts the other with
souls of which he himself must give an account to the supreme
Pastor, why does not he entrust him with the droppings of the
sheep as well? Consequently, I do not know how he can rightfully rent his parish. On the other hand, I do not know how a
renter can rightfully rent the parish except with the purpose
that—seeing the lack of instruction of the people in the Word of
God, and seeing the lack of qualification in the parish priest—
he assume the task because he is conscious of his own ability
to remedy the lack. But he must strictly beware lest he be moved
by avarice or lest he be overcome by it later, so that in no way

[72] John 10:10.   [73] John 10:1.

he become a stumbling block to the people. In such a case perhaps he would not be called a hireling before Christ, but a true shepherd. . . .

8

After proving the simony of priests, it is proper to touch upon the simony of the laity. For they too are besmirched with many kinds of simoniacal practices. These comprise, in the first place and the coarsest fashion, those in granting bishoprics, priorships, canonries, or benefices for gifts either of money, cups, horses, or other valuables, or for written guarantees of payments or services. All who practice them have the King Jeroboam for their dear father, about whom the Scriptures testify, "Whoever filled his hand was appointed a priest of the high places." And immediately after it adds that "for that reason the house of Jeroboam sinned and was cut off and razed from the earth." [74] . . . Hence, if it was not proper that such priesthood be sold, how, then, is it proper to sell for money the priesthood of Christ? . . .

The second simoniacal custom is the granting of episcopacy or other dignities for service. For that reason many serve at courts; others, desiring larger revenues, leave their parishes and serve at courts also.

The third custom is that of granting the dignities because of kinship. Many a noble grants such an office to incapable relatives who are not fit to keep swine!

The fourth custom consists of granting offices because of request or for other worldly favor; as some appoint a priest for the sake of companionship, since he can go hunting with the patron, or can play chess or other games with him. Others use a deceitful dodge: they bet a wager, "What do you wager, O lord, that you will not give my son a benefice?" And the lord answers: "I wager fifty *kopy* that I will give it." Then the challenger replies: "The wager is taken." The lord exclaims: "Very well, I give your son the benefice; hand over fifty *kopy*."

The devil has many other clever devices by which he deceives both the lay people and the clerics, leading them into simony. Thus when a father or mother wishes to open a way to a spiritual dignity for their son, they give presents, serve princes and lords, and buy papal bulls. It appears to me that the reason so many people send their children to school is that they may

[74] I Kings 13:33, 34. The passage is freely rendered.

become rich, receive honor in the world, and become able to help their relatives. It is for these reasons also that the sons give themselves to study. Hence we see that afterwards they commonly live bad lives, because they have entered the priesthood unworthily. Also because the priestly possessions are constantly increasing, the number of students and priests likewise increases. For everyone desires to live well and to become rich. For that reason serfs are expensive, fields lie fallow, servants are lacking, since every peasant wishes to have his son become a prelate. If priests were to live as the saints of old used to live, there would be precious few of them! And it were better if there were but a few good ones of us than, as it is now, every nook full of rascals. . . . And because both sides sin, the clergy and the lay people—fathers and mothers by the evil intent with which they send sons to school, and the sons by the evil intent in pursuing their studies—hence from both sides we benefit the holy Church but little. Accordingly, father and mother! if you wish that your child become a good priest, pray God that he may endow him with gifts to his glory and your son's salvation, as well as your and holy Church's benefit. And you, pupil, study with the same goal in view: for if you study in order to become rich, it leads you into avarice; if for worldly fame, it leads you to pride; if for carnal well-being, it leads you to concupiscence. . . .

But perhaps you reply that since the clerical office is so hemmed in on every side, it is not wise to seek priesthood or episcopacy. But that is contrary to reason, which shows the pre-eminent worth of that estate which no one can rightfully occupy or enjoy unless he deliberately seeks after it. For Saint Paul says, "He who seeks episcopacy, desires a good work." [75] . . . Saint Gregory, therefore, comments on the word of Saint Paul that the latter's admonition is observed whenever he who aspires to episcopacy is ready at any hour to undergo martyrdom. [76] For in the beginning of the Christian faith bishops were the first to suffer martyrdom. The proof is to be seen in Christ, his apostles, and many other holy bishops. But because bishops nowadays have undertaken the management of property, they seek property, and episcopacy on account of property. Furthermore, since bishops no longer fear martyrdom, they eagerly run after episcopacy. Formerly, it was hardly possible to find a man willing to be bishop; for it involved being poor and ready for martyrdom. But now, when a bishop dies,

[75] I Tim. 3:1.   [76] The source of the quotation could not be traced.

anyone who has a chance to get it strives after episcopacy!
So it was after the death of the priest Zbyněk,[77] of happy
memory, when twenty-four of them strove for the archbishopric,
whose names we have recorded.

Take care, therefore, if you wish to seek priesthood or
episcopacy, that first of all you examine your conscience. If
you are of a holy life in hope, not stained with a mortal sin;
if you are prepared to teach people the Scriptures and ready to
lay down your life; if you are drawn by the love of God and the
salvation of yourself as well as of the people, leave it to God if
he is pleased to have you. Then if you enter the office, beware
that simony, pride, self-indulgence, and avarice, and above all
hypocrisy, do not gain sway over you. Nor deem yourself
worthier of the office than others. Even if you are thus prepared
in entering upon episcopacy, you will nevertheless soon stain
it. . . . Perceiving that, many saints ran away from election to
that office, as did Saint Gregory. Saint Mark the Evangelist
cut off his thumb in order to avoid being a bishop; Saint Leo
cut off his hand because he had felt a carnal desire when he
had touched the lips of a woman during the administration of
the body of God; for he regarded himself as no longer worthy
to celebrate the Mass and to distribute the body of God.[78]
How seldom nowadays do men hide from episcopacy, or cut
off their thumbs to escape it! Likewise, it is rare nowadays
that a dove indicates the papal candidate.[79] For sordid wealth
darkens now the window.

From these examples we may perceive how uncertain and
terrible it is for a layman, prince, lord, or any other layman,
as well as for a clergyman, to possess the advowson of a
bishopric, a parish, an altar, or of another kind of benefice.
For if he does not grant it to a worthy person who is available,
or if he does not intend to give it to such a person with the right
purpose, he shall have committed a grave sin and shall not
before God be counted as worthy to hold the advowson unless
he contritely repent. And should he knowingly grant the office.
to a less competent person because of money, gifts, material
service, worldly favor, kinship or relationship, flattery, or

[77] Archbishop Zbyněk Zajíc of Hasenburg: note that although Zbyněk
was really responsible for Hus's prosecution and condemnation, the latter
speaks of him as of "happy memory." The record of the names of the
twenty-four candidates does not appear in any of his extant writings.
[78] These two examples are, of course, legendary.
[79] This is founded on a legend that Pope Fabian was elected because a dove
alighted on his head.

A.O.R.—17

someone's request, woe unto the man who holds the advowson! . . .

But notice that patronage is not a church, an altar, or another material thing; it is a spiritual power which the patron holds, and he has the responsibility for a proper disposition of the original endowment given to the glory of God. Accordingly, the person holding the advowson is called in Latin *patronus*, that is, a father or a defender. For as a faithful father he should be diligent that the parish, the altar, the chapel, or the contributed alms be properly dispensed.

A person became a patron on account of three things: the ground, the building, and the endowment. On account of the ground because he donated it so that a church could be built thereon; on account of the building because he erected the church; and on account of the endowment from which the priest could be supported. But these three things entail for the patron three other things: honor, responsibility, and profit. Honor from the people and the priest, for they should hold him in esteem; responsibility, because he must exercise care in granting the benefice to a good priest, so that the spiritual ministration would be well cared for, and also that he would not become proud; and profit, which consists of the eternal reward, unless he lose it. He also is entitled to material profit, so that if he should become so impoverished as to have no fitting means wherewith to feed himself or his children, it would then be proper that he receive aid from the church endowment, particularly if he himself had donated the ground, or built the church, or gave the endowment. Likewise, if a child of his had been rendered indigent by such a building of the church or its endowment, it is right to draw upon it; for the established laws so provide. Hence, those monks, parish priests, and other beneficed clergy act shamefully when, possessing the endowment, and living in comfort, they allow the patrons or their children to suffer want.

Furthermore, since the advowson is a spiritual power, it is not proper to sell it. It is called spiritual also for the reason that it is related to the spiritual office established for the salvation of souls, and hence is not itself material. But coarse-minded people regard the church, the altar, or the chapel as material, and therefore buy and sell it in the same gross way as if it were an ox or a cow, for material profit, or for glory, or that they might appoint their relatives or servants to it. Take note, then, when you say, "I have the advowson of a church," that you possess the power to grant the church to a good priest and that you dispose of it to the glory of God so that it would stand well with the priest and the people. . . .

As for the alms which were left in trust to be distributed among the poor, patrons sin gravely when they do not so distribute them. Some donors have specified by will that cloth be distributed among the poor, or certain food, or some other alms, but patrons keep it to themselves, or distribute it among their relatives or servants, or to others for favor's sake, as if they were giving of their own, desiring thus to gain praise; and to the very needy unfortunates they give nothing. This sin is particularly common among monks, priests, and burghers: for monks, collecting bequests enjoining them to distribute money, cloth, or food among the poor, do not do so; the priests, that they might feed the poor in lean days or at other times, do not feed them; and likewise the burghers. Hence they pull the devil's carriage like three horses whom he spurs on by whips of avarice, dragging them into his barn. Conciliar canons provide concerning them: "Priests or lay people who desire to appropriate or alienate the estates of their father, mother, or other people, which estates were bequeathed to the poor, are condemned as thieves and sacrilegious, and are excluded from churches, until they return what they have appropriated." [80]

Hence, learn to know yourselves, ye robbers of the poor, murderers, thieves, and sacrilegious! . . . It is certain that they are robbers; for they dispossess the poor of their property. Likewise it is evident that they are thieves, for they steal what belongs to others. They are also simoniacs and sacrilegious, because they steal holy alms, which are called holy because they were dedicated to the Lord, who is holy above all that are holy, and because man gives to the poor in order to be holy. A reasonable man will perceive therefrom how gravely men sin in respect of alms, those that give them, those that manage them, as well as those that receive them: the first by giving out of ill-gotten wealth; the second by keeping it for themselves or by an improper distribution; and the third by receiving it unworthily. For the last named are guilty of receiving alms unworthily if they have no need of it; or if they take too much; or if they waste it profligately; and all of them by generally wrangling about the alms.

It is best, therefore, that a man give alms while still alive, without aspiring to leave behind him a perpetual charity

[80] *Decretum Magistri Gratiani*, pars II, C. XIII, q. II, c. 11.

trust. For nowhere in the Scriptures is it stated that men should establish perpetual charity endowments, but it is stated that while living men ought to give alms to the poor, so that after they die they may immediately enjoy the reward of eternal bliss. Hence, those people, particularly the priests, are foolish who pile up money in all kinds of ways only to set up a perpetual charity trust. They are likewise fools who save well-earned money in order to establish similar trusts, and seeing those in need, do not aid them; for thereby they sin gravely, mortally. As Saint John the apostle says, "If one has this world's goods, and sees his brother in need, and shuts the bowels of compassion from him"—that is, does not help him—"how does the love of God abide in him?" [81] . . . The many quarrels, litigations, and murders as well as other sins which result from those perpetual charity trusts who can describe? For one assumes a great responsibility—the management of the trust—and retains it for his use till his death, and then wills it to another, with the intention that his successor perform the stipulation of the trust. But the latter likewise retains it for his own use till his death; and so it goes on until nothing remains of the endowment. Miserable people! How lacking in sense they are, desiring that others should do for them what they themselves, although able to do it, fail to do. But a faithful lover of God gives the poor, while he is alive, whatever he can, in accordance with His command; for thus he lays up a treasure for himself which he can enjoy promptly after death. For he dispatches it on ahead, that it may be ready for him after he leaves the world. For the Lord Jesus, his apostles, and other saints, have not established perpetual charity trusts.

9

In order that men may beware of all participation in simony, all ought to know that everyone who has consented to simony committed by another person sins, and is an accomplice of the simoniac. Such consent takes six forms: abetting, defense, counsel, approval, neglect of duty, and noncorrection.

He is guilty of abetting simony who recommends, acts as an intermediary among simoniacs, or in another way affords pretext for it—as by letters, messages, loans of money, legal aid in courts, and by other means. In the second place, he is guilty of it by defending . . . simony. In this class are included

[81] I John 3:17.

very many laymen and clerics, particularly masters and papal canon lawyers, who defend simony in the schools, justifying it in various ways, as, for instance by arguing that the pope cannot be a simoniac; or that no one is a simoniac unless he be convicted of it and sentenced in their very presence and in accordance with their rules; likewise they hold that simoniacs pay for the work performed. But they justify these practices because they themselves follow the path and desire to accumulate many benefices. They excuse themselves by saying that they are masters of the Holy Scriptures, and especially that they are doctors, i.e., teachers of the papal laws; and they suppose that the Lord does not regard their sins on account of their master's degree! Accordingly, possessing many benefices, they live in pride and enjoyment, held in honor in churches, schools, and streets. Accordingly, they wear voluminous broad and long robes lined with white fur, ermine, mink, and silk—all to make a show before the people! Believe the truth of Christ, who says: "The masters and the lawyers have seated themselves on Moses' seat: all things, therefore, whatsoever they bid you, do and observe; but do not ye after their works. For they say and do not. They bind heavy and unbearable burdens" (i.e., such as they themselves cannot bear) "and lay them upon men's shoulders; but they themselves will not touch them with their fingers. And they do all their deeds to be seen of men: for they make broad their phylacteries and enlarge the borders of their robes, and love the first seats at suppers and chief seats in the churches, and salutations in the market places, and to be called masters!" [82] Behold, here you have an apt description of the sins of the masters! Understand that when the Saviour says, "The masters have seated themselves on Moses' seat," and emphasizes the phrase, "have seated themselves," he does not refer to those who went before him, but to those who were after him. . . . Nor are we to understand by the term "seat" a wooden or stone seat of Moses, for that does not exist. But in accordance with the comment of Saint Augustine and of other saints, by that word we are to understand ecclesiastical dignities such as are held by popes, bishops, and other priests, especially masters. The Saviour commands that they be obeyed. . . . Saint Augustine comments . . . : "What they bid you in accordance with my words, that do; but if they bid you something of their own, that do not do." . . . For their works are against the commands and counsels of God. Hence,

[82] Matt. 23:2–7, rendered freely.

men should diligently distinguish when the masters follow God's commands and counsels—when they bid them what is not against God's will, in order to observe and do it. But when the masters command what is against God's will, people should not obey. To confirm that this is Christ's meaning, Saint Mark remarks: "The multitude heard him gladly. And in teaching them, he said, Beware of the masters who desire to walk in white robes and to be saluted in the market places, and to occupy chief seats in schools, and the first seats at feasts." [83]

Observe carefully the Saviour's warning, "Beware diligently of the masters!" And what are they to beware of? In the first place, that people follow not the masters in evil works and obey them not in evil. . . . I myself have intently listened to their lectures in schools when they discoursed concerning humility, patience, poverty, courage, and other virtues which they celebrated so persuasively and eloquently that no one could do it better, as if they themselves had practiced all of them. But later I found none of these virtues actually among them, for they were full of pride, avarice, impatience, and cowardice. As the dear Christ has described it, they lay heavy burdens on men, issuing their regulations, striving with each other over the chief ecclesiastical dignities; and when men do not bow before them as before gods, they grow angry; and how many disputes they carry on among themselves concerning the first places in schools! In fact, I know a certain master, the monk Maurice,[84] who secured a papal bull to the effect that he be granted a place above all other masters. In this bull the pope ordered, on pain of the loss of benefices, priesthood, and all dignities, and even on pain of excommunication, that he—Maurice—be given the specified position. But still the masters refused their consent. They did wrong in refusing to consent from pride, and he did wrong in demanding it. Thus pride was on both sides. For the Saviour says that they love the first seats in churches and broaden the hems of their robes, capes, gowns, and hoods.

Alas! I too had gowns, robes with wings, and hoods with white fur; for they so hemmed in the master's grade with their regulations that no one is able to obtain the degree unless he possess such an outfit. In order that men beware of such pride,

---

[83] Mark 12:37–39, freely rendered.
[84] Maurice Rvačka, formerly the inquisitor for Bohemia, later professor of theology, was a most determined opponent of Hus. The latter wrote a treatise against him entitled *Contra occultum adversarium.*

the Saviour said to his disciples and to the multitudes, "But be ye not called masters: for one is your master—the Christ."[85] . . . In truth I cannot conceive how otherwise a man could be a master worthily than with the intention of obtaining a steadier opportunity for the teaching of God's truth and thus profess and defend that truth more zealously. But I have found that ordinary poor priests and poor laymen— even women—defend the truth more zealously than the doctors of the Holy Scriptures, who out of fear run away from the truth and have not courage to defend it. I myself—alas—had been one of them, for I did not dare to preach the truth plainly and openly. And why are we like that? Solely because some of us are timid, fearing to lose worldly favor and praise, and others of us fear to lose benefices; for we fear to be held in contempt by the people for the truth's sake, and to suffer bodily pain. We are like the Jewish rulers of whom Saint John says in his Gospel that "many rulers believed on him; but because of the lawyers did not confess it, lest they should be cast out of the congregation. For they loved the praise of men more than the praise of God."[86] . . . O how many there are—princes, masters, priests, and others—who, being afraid of excommunication, have not courage to confess the truth of Christ, and thus also Christ himself; and how many there are who fear to confess the truth lest they lose their miserable goods, or, above all, who, lacking the courage to risk their earthly life, abandon the truth!

Those three fears—of losing the praise and favor of men, of losing goods, and of losing earthly life—cause timid men to abandon the truth of confessing the Saviour Jesus Christ, who promised honor, goods, and life. Honor, in saying: "Whosoever shall confess me and my words before this adulterous and sinful generation, the Son of Man also shall confess when he comes in the glory of his Father with his angels."[87] The goods he promised under an oath, saying, "Verily, I say unto you, that no one has left house, or brethren, or sisters, or mother, or father, or children, or lands, for my sake and the gospel's, but shall receive hundredfold."[88] And he promises life, saying, "And in the age to come eternal life."[89] And elsewhere he says, "Whosoever shall lose his life for my sake and the gospel's, shall save it."[90] . . . O woe unto us, miserable men, that we

85 Matt. 23:10. 86 John 12:42, 43.
87 Mark 8:38; the wording is somewhat changed. 88 Mark 10:29, 30.
89 Mark 10:30. 90 Mark 8:35.

do not value the everlasting glory more than the temporal, lean, and transient, and that we do not esteem the eternal goods more than the temporal! For concerning this the Saviour says, "What does it profit a man to gain the whole world, and harm his soul?" [91] Woe unto us that we dare not risk this miserable, sorrowful, and painful life, which is ever dying, for the eternal life—glorious, joyous, and free from pain! . . .

Furthermore, he participates in simony by counsel who gives advice either to the would-be purchaser or the would-be seller. Of such there is a great multitude in the pope's entourage who devise strange contrivances for his benefit or for the sake of those who wish to secure benefices for the purpose of getting more money for the pope, and of extorting from the buyers more. It may happen that the same benefice is sold several times. Nevertheless, even to describe those dodges which have come to my personal attention would require too much time. But this I used to tell those who had met with disappointment, that if I were to ask the pope for a benefice, I would insist that he specify in the bull that he desires that no one contrive anything whereby his grant would be nullified. It is in these undertakings that the canon lawyers are chiefly involved; and the rest who could count? For father advises his son, brother his brother, friend his friend, that they apply for a benefice; and parish priests put pressure upon their chaplains to overcharge for thirty Masses, or confessions and the sacraments, and the chaplains in turn urge the parish priests to like machinations. But I trust God that there be many among them who are not guilty of such practices.

Moreover, all such participate in simony who approve or confirm it by giving consent, saying, "It is well!" Of such participation are guilty particularly mighty kings, princes, and lords, bishops and other high officials, whose duty it is to destroy simony, but who approve it instead, or are indifferent to it, as if it were no concern of theirs. What excuse can they give to God, who gave them the power and the exalted position above others for the purpose of ruling them and not allowing them, as far as is possible, to commit such vices? Nor can they excuse themselves . . . by saying that it is no concern of theirs what the clergy do. For I know that if a priest were to defame a secular prince, or steal from him, or lie with his wife, the prince would not tolerate it, but would immediately revenge himself, if he could. How, then, is it no concern of his when a

[91] Mark 8:36.

cleric commits a greater sin? For is not simony a greater sin than theft, fornication, or defamation of a secular prince? By simony men specifically defame the Holy Spirit whose gifts they buy or sell, and thus they regard the Holy Spirit as a servant. Hence it is written that simony is a graver heresy than that of Macedonius, who taught that the Holy Spirit is a servant of the Father and the Son; and simoniacs make the Holy Spirit a servant of creatures! . . . Such a tenet contradicts the Scriptures: "The Father is equal, the Son is equal, the Holy Spirit is equal, that is, in dignity."[92] The simoniac, by giving or receiving material goods for the gift of the Holy Spirit . . . assumes that the grace of the Holy Spirit may be bought with money, and thus the Holy Spirit is lower than a creature! . . .

In the fifth place, some may participate in simony by neglect of duty, as while possessing power from God they do not use it against sin. . . . For seeing his neighbor drowning in a damning sin, and possessing the God-given power to help him (as a member of the same body), how can such a man be justified if he does not use the power? For if he sees a man drowning in a river, and does not help him, although he is able to do so, he is guilty of his death. So much more in spiritual matters, if he does not help his neighbor so that his soul would not drown.

In the sixth place, some participate in simony by non-correction or silence; thus whenever one in a high position or another who could turn a man from such a sin by loud remonstrances, preaching, or instruction and does not do so; or even if he could not dissuade him, yet does not do everything in his power to do so. Such participation in simony is particularly common among princes, prelates, and masters. This argument has its ground in the Scriptures, for Saint Paul says: "Those who do such things deserve to die. And not only they who do them, but likewise those who approve those who practice them."[93] Accordingly Saint Isidore writes, "Whoever approves those who sin, and defends them, shall be accursed before God and men, and shall be punished by the cruelest punishment."[94] And furthermore he writes that there is no doubt of the guilt of him who, being able to punish a sinner, neglects to reprove him. For it is written that "not only those

---

[92] Hus cites, in reality, the Athanasian Creed as if it were Scripture.
[93] Rom. 1:32. The text greatly alters the Biblical version.
[94] *Decretum Magistri Gratiani*, pars II, C. XI, q. III, c. 100.

who commit [sin] but likewise those who consent to it participate in it."[95] For whoever consents to vice allows the sinner a
broad approach to it; consequently, both deserve the same
punishment. But those who defend the evildoers so that good
men cannot interfere with them in their sin have the heaviest
share in the sin. Hence it is written that "whoever defends the
errors of others is worthy of greater condemnation than he
who errs."[96] For not only does he err, but enables and confirms
others in their erroneous offenses. Accordingly, he is not only a
heretic but a master of errors as well, and should be called the
prince of heretics.

From this discourse a spiritually discerning person may
perceive that he who himself commits simony and defends
others committing simony along with him is a heretic above
heretics and a prince of heretics. Next to him are his underlings,
who in turn defend him; and of such there are very many.
For a better recognition of this type, let me cite an example:
Suppose that a king owns a town which he himself had built;
and when he had lost it, he won it back from his enemies at
the risk of his own life. If then someone should, without the
king's consent, turn over that city to another for money, he
who bought it would be guilty equally with the intermediary
who arranged the sale; likewise the scribes of both the seller
and the buyer; also the messengers of both parties and the
hostages; also the negotiators; equally guilty would be the person who did not oppose it when he could, and he who would
defend one or both although he could reprove them; likewise
he who would counsel one or both of them, or who would
loan money for the transaction; he also who would furnish
paper for the documents as well as he who would compose
the text; also the citizens of the town who would submit
voluntarily, along with the town crier who would not oppose
it, and anyone else who would voluntarily aid in the surrender
of the town against the king's will. Similarly in simony, as
when a bishop desires to be and is installed in a simoniacal
manner in a town. . . . Those who alienate the city from the
king receive very severe punishment; but they care not about
Christ's city when thieves and robbers scale it in order to
plunder not only the goods but the souls as well! . . .

That we should beware of such participation, Saint John
writes in his Revelation, saying: "I saw an angel coming down

[95] *Ibid.*
[96] *Ibid.*

from heaven, having great power; and the earth was illuminated with his glory. And he cried out mightily, saying: Babylon the great is fallen and has become the dwelling place of devils, the haunt of every foul spirit, and the guard of every foul and ugly bird. For the wine of the wrath of her fornications has been drunk by all nations, and the kings of the earth have committed fornication with her, and the merchants of the earth have grown rich with the multitude of her delights."[97] Babylon, the great city, is the congregation of the wicked; for "Babylon" is interpreted to mean reproach and transportation. For all those evildoers are reproached and transported from God's grace into his wrath, and from a holy life into damnation. For the great angel who descended from heaven with great power illuminating the earth is our gracious Christ. He cries mightily that Babylon has fallen away from his grace. As he has said in the Gospel of Luke, "I beheld Satan as lightning fall from heaven."[98] And Babylon has become the dwelling place of devils—as the Saviour says—because of "the evil spirit joining with himself seven other spirits worse than himself, and they dwell in the man."[99] Likewise, in the congregation of the wicked there dwell all manner of unclean spirits, who guard it that it escape not their power. Such a congregation is full of uncleanness, of unclean fowl such as horned owls, that is, of men who love not the light of Christ, as bats who fly in the darkness of sin but not in the light of Christ. . . .

Further, Saint John says that the wine of that Babylon's wrath and of fornication was drunk by all the nations, that is, by all conditions of people, such as virgins, widows, wives, unmarried young people, widowers, and married men. Some of them have consented to that fornication, that is, to the forsaking of Christ. For the Scriptures call every mortal sin fornication, since by its means the soul forsakes her spouse, Christ, for the devil. Furthermore he says, "the kings of the earth," that is, those who rule the earth, also fornicate along with the congregation. And the merchants of the earth, that is, the misers, who have grown rich by means of that congregation. For the congregation of the wicked elevates the avaricious, particularly the simoniacs. The faithful should beware of any participation with them; for Saint John immediately proceeds to say: "And I heard another voice, saying, Come out of her" (i.e., from Babylon), "that ye be not partakers of her sins, lest

[97] Rev. 18:1-3. [98] Luke 10:18.
[99] An allusion to Luke 11:26.

ye receive of her wounds. For her sins have reached unto heaven, and the Lord hath remembered her iniquities." [1]

Behold, here you have a voice from heaven to God's faithful people, that they come out, not only by walking, but by a holy life, from that wicked congregation, so that God's people be not partakers in its sins as well as in its punishment: partakers by aid, counsel, defense, confirmation, or neglect of duty, i.e., by nonparticipation in the destruction of simony and by silence; as it has been explained at the beginning of this chapter.

10

There remains yet an explanation how best to avoid this sin [of simony]. With that in view there is no likelier way than that of conducting episcopal and parochial elections in accordance with the will of God. For thus have the apostles conducted the episcopal election of the one who was to take Judas' place, even though they did not have a special revelation concerning it. . . .

In the same spirit Saint Peter appointed Saint Clement.[2] For the apostles have commonly appointed bishops and priests in such manner; since they had no revelation [concerning the procedure], they nominated two men—Matthias and Joseph—and then cast lots in order that the Lord might show which of the two he chose. And the Lord indicated Matthias.[3] Hence, if the church people should receive no revelation as to whom the Lord is pleased to choose, they should make a nomination of a bishop, with pure intention and without undue favoritism, of several good men; thereupon, they should pray the Lord earnestly that he may indicate if any of them is worthy; or if none is, that he may be pleased to indicate another. But alas! nowadays they strive with one another [for the office], and the people favor their acquaintances, or relatives, or the proud. . . .

Furthermore, that the church should elect [its priests], Saint Jerome confirms as follows: "The Lord has commanded that when the priest is appointed, the congregation also be called [for the purpose]. Hence, the appointment of a priest must be made in the presence of the people—so that they all

---

[1] Rev. 18:4, 5.

[2] Hus believed, with all the Middle Ages, that Clement of Rome was appointed a bishop of Rome by the apostle Peter, who, of course, was regarded as the first pope of Rome.

[3] Cf. Acts 1:23–26.

might see and be certain that only the most outstanding, the most learned, the most holy, and the most proficient in all virtues of all the people be chosen for the priesthood; and [that the choice be made] with the approbation of the people, so that afterwards there would be no retraction or gnawing of conscience." [4]

... From this pious exposition one may understand how perverse are the practices in regard to the appointment of bishops of our day and our times. For formerly the custom prevailed that either our loving Lord appointed the bishop by means of a revelation or the people . . . elected him. But nowadays the power of the people to request or elect a worthy priest is denied them; and a way is thus opened for avaricious or otherwise dishonorable men to buy people from the pope as if they were cattle, for the material profit of the buyers. The proof of it is afforded by such as have secretly procured papal letters, whereupon they immediately call upon their clergy to contribute toward the expense for the pallium. [5] Some of them have not even received the letters yet and already ask for contributions. This is what has happened this year in our own archiepiscopal diocese; some contributed with the purpose of driving out those who preach the Word of God and denounce their sins; others contributed out of fear, that they might suffer no harm, for they had been forbidden to enter their churches until they had paid the money to Simon; [6] and still others, moved by the Holy Spirit, but nevertheless afraid that they might likewise be punished afterwards because they were unwilling to make the contribution, appealed to the pope. But it would have been better had they courageously appealed to God and refused their consent to participate in simony; also, that they appealed to the lords and the city for their aid in not allowing them to be forced into that sin and material loss. [7]

The second perverse practice in episcopal elections is the usurpation of the right of election by the canons, as well as

---

[4] *Decretum Magistri Gratiani*, pars II, C. VIII, q. I, c. 15.

[5] This is confirmed by the bull of Pope Boniface IX (Oct. 23, 1402), by which it is ordered that whenever an archbishop is elected, the clergy of the Prague diocese must "voluntarily" contribute toward the cost of his pallium.

[6] This probably means "to commit simony."

[7] This perhaps refers to the contributions demanded of the clergy at the time of the appointment of Conrad of Vechta as archbishop (end of 1412 and the beginning of 1413). But there is no other documentary evidence regarding it.

its restriction to a member of their own chapter.[8] . . . In both
these practices they bar the way of the Holy Spirit, as if they
were to say, "We alone are worthy of the choice; the Holy
Spirit has not been given to others!" Or as if they were to say,
"Only among us is the one worthy of episcopacy; the Holy
Spirit has granted that distinction to no one else!" And when
they elect someone, they do not choose the most proficient in
virtues, but rather one who is best fitted to defend their
property and from whom they expect to derive the greatest
material profit, as well as who would acquiesce in their vicious
customs. Thus, electing an unworthy person, they are the
source of all the evil and all the neglect which the elected will
commit. . . . They disobey the Scriptures referred to above
which specify the election procedure, as well as Saint Jerome
who says, "Only such should be chosen prelates—i.e., placed
above others—in comparison with whom all others may be called
a flock." And Saint Augustine says, "To the episcopal dignity
no one should be elected who has not learned to administer a
lower office; for the command of a boat should not be entrusted
to a man who cannot wield an oar."[9] . . . O thou dear Saviour!
Thou seest that they elect not the best of all, but the poorest!

But someone may say: "You assert that no one should
push himself into an office; but on the other hand, you also
assert that only the best should be chosen. How, then, shall the
bishop or the parish priest be chosen if no one offers himself,
and the lord possessing the advowson or the electors do not
know the best?" To this I answer that although no one, short
of God's command or revelation, should push himself into an
office, nevertheless he may accept it when he is called. But he
must possess a pure mind and intention: mind, that being lifted
up to God he may lead Christ's sheep in His way according to
God's law; and intention, in order to cast out every sin which
would interfere with his office—especially pride, avarice, and
carnality. In the third place, he must have a great longing to
fulfill God's will in that office and to advance in it as much as
he can. But where can one find such a person? . . .

The second kind of election obtains when a man inclines
to choose the better part [of two alternatives]. This kind
of election is also twofold: the first is called prudent, as when
a man of good intentions chooses the part which appears to

---

[8] This was, of course, an ancient custom; but Hus opposed it just the same.
[9] Jerome, Ep. LXIX, par. 8, *P.L.*, 22:662; Augustine, Ep. XXI, par. 2,
P.L., 33:88. I owe these references to Professor Ford Lewis Battles.

him more in accord with God, or more conducive to salvation. The elect sons of God are thus led in their choices by the Holy Spirit, although the Scriptures do not specifically indicate how they should act. . . . And in such cases . . . there is so great a need for the direction of the Holy Spirit that even saints may sometimes err. For it has occurred between Saint Paul and Saint Barnabas that Paul thought one way and Barnabas another; for although both were great saints, they nevertheless quarreled and separated from each other, one departing for one country, and the other for another. [The cause of this quarrel] was that Saint Barnabas wished to take along a deacon named Mark, while Saint Paul besought Barnabas not to take him, since he [Mark] had left them on a former occasion.[10] . . . The same has likewise occurred to me, that when our brethren were overtaken by persecution, for interdicts and stopping of divine services had been imposed, some advised me to continue preaching, while others counseled against the continuance. I felt that both parties counseled me with good intention; but because of the two kinds of advice, I was uncertain which was according to the will of God.[11] In such cases it is necessary for a man to pray to God earnestly and often that He may be pleased to guide him. . . .

The second kind of election is called careless; as when one chooses according to human regulations, disregarding God's law. By such an election the popes, bishops, and other prelates are commonly chosen. Such practices, which have no basis in God's law, always lead to unsatisfactory results. Accordingly, the electors should, following God's law, choose one who is, in common estimation, the most eminent in holy living, in competent learning, and in spiritual labors; [they should elect him] solely for the glory of God and the benefit of the holy Church, disregarding all material favor. . . . But at present the pope appoints someone for money without any knowledge as to what and how worthy he is; another is appointed by a king or a prince, although he is known to be unworthy; another is chosen by canons on account of gifts or for other reasons and not solely for the glory of God; others are elected by lords, pages, and burghers neither in accordance with the Scriptural

10 Acts 15:37-40.
11 Hus refers here to the events of 1412, when Prague was placed under an interdict. He at first continued to preach despite the prohibition, but later, because of the remonstrances of his friends and the wish of King Wenceslas, he left Prague in October.

instructions nor with a sincere intention. Consequently, there
exist disorders in Christendom, and many criminals are to be
found among the clergy, while Christendom abounds in all
manner of unrighteousness. The Antichrist has so firmly established his will in such simoniacal elections, grants, and traffick-
ings that it exceeds human power to punish and prevent such
evils.

But I know three persons who could help in preventing this
evil, if the Lord were to manifest his grace in them: The first
of them is the pope, if the Lord granted one who would destroy
all simony according to the Scriptures and the enactments of
holy bishops. But when will such a pope come forth? It would
indeed be a great miracle if he should now make his appearance. Moreover, I know that his apostles would not let him
remain alive for long!

The second and more likely help would come if secular
princes and lords, having been divinely instructed, would
forbid the trafficking and the irregular appointments of unworthy prelates over the people. They could best accomplish
it if they would not allow the waste of their fathers' endowments by taking them into their own hands and custody, so
that in the future they would not be misapplied. For as fire
keeps on burning and scorching as long as it has something to
feed on, so likewise the devil's fire which blazes throughout
the world into which it has been cast burns as long as it is
fed. . . . And that fire cannot be quenched except it be deprived
of that which it desires. An example is afforded by the desire
of a man for a beautiful woman, or a woman for a man. . . .
Such a desire would be quickly extinguished if the woman were
taken away from the man, or the man were by death taken
away from the woman. . . . Likewise, if the priests' excessive
revenues were taken away and they were given only sufficient
for their modest needs, then the evil desire of simony would be
destroyed. But as long as the lay people increase the endowments, so long will they incite the clergy in that desire—they
by increasing [the fuel], and the devil by his fanning [the
flames] as a smith does with his bellows. But secular princes
and lords are prevented from abolishing simony because of
hypocritical blindness, for priests have blinded them by their
hypocritical saying, "You have no business meddling with
spiritual matters!" And they, hearing that, abandon all concern
for it. In the second place, they are drawn together by a common
bond: for they are bound together in the joys and favor of this

world which they both enjoy and in which they flatter each other. Thirdly, laymen are so busy with their secular affairs that they cannot aid in the good spiritual work; they are more concerned with growing rich, or with the desire to be held in esteem by men, and with playing, jousting, and merrymaking, than with rendering the Lord faithful service.

Consequently, the third solution is the most likely, namely, that the church community withhold revenues from open simoniacs so that they could not traffick in them. But then the church would have to risk the clergy's lawsuits and condemnations wherewith they would defend their evil practices for a time. Let us beseech the gracious Lord that he would enable Christendom, by his might, to destroy simony by such or any other means he pleases! [12]

But immediately there rushes out of the forest a wild boar, digging up Christ's vineyard and uprooting it, saying, "The kings, lords, or any other seculars have no right to rule over the spirituals!" I answer, in the first place, that throughout the Old Testament [period] kings ruled the priests and bishops. For King Solomon deposed the highest bishop Abiathar from the priesthood and sent him back to his fields, and appointed Zadok in his place. And he did this in accordance with God's will, as the Scriptures testify. [13] . . .

Secondly, I say that because every king receives the power over his kingdom from God so that he may rule it in truth and justice, and since priests constitute a part of that kingdom, he should rule over them in truth and justice. He does not rule over them in truth and justice if he allows them to live in plain opposition to the supreme King, but, like a careless servant, he thus proves himself unworthy of his royal office.

The proof of this assertion is in the bull of Saint Peter, [14] in which he enjoins that all be subjected to the king as supreme. . . . Therefore Saint Peter says, "Be subject to every man for God's sake: to the king as supreme; to leaders, i.e., princes, as sent by him (that is, by God) for vengeance upon evildoers and for the praise of the good." [15] . . . The same is proved by Saint Paul, that the prince "beareth not the sword in vain, but as the minister of God for vengeance upon evildoers." [16]

---

[12] The above-mentioned three "remedies" are also advocated by Wyclif in *De simonia*, 93, 94.   [13] I Kings 2:26, 27, 35.
[14] Hus actually calls it a "bull," perhaps in considering Peter as the first pope.   [15] I Peter 2:13, 14.   [16] Rom. 13:4.
A.O.R.—18

But perhaps the ravening wild boar, gnashing his tusks, would reply that the prince does indeed wield his sword, but not over the priests. To that Saint Paul retorts, "Let every soul . . . be subject to the higher powers; for there is no power but of God." And the things which are from God are right. "Therefore whoever opposes the power, opposes God's order. And such as oppose it earn damnation for themselves. For the princes are not a terror to good works but to the evil. And if thou wishest not to fear the power, do good and thou shalt have praise for it. For the minister of God is to thee for good. But if thou do evil, be afraid, for he beareth the sword not in vain; but as the minister of God punishes in wrath those who do evil." [17]

There you have a second apostle who shows that every man, hence also the priest and the bishop, should be subject to secular princes and should fear them when they [the clerics] do evil. . . . How is it that we priests wish to exempt ourselves from this double command of the holy apostles when we commit something plainly wrong? . . . O Christ! it will take a long time before the proud priests will become so humble as to subject themselves to the Church for sin, as thou, being innocent, hast subjected thyself!

That kings should banish simony in particular from the holy Church is shown by the example of our gracious Saviour when the inhabitants of Jerusalem greeted him as king, crying out, "Blessed art thou, the king eternal, the son of David!" [18] and casting garments before him as he rode on the ass. For when he entered the Temple, he forced the traders out of it by whipping them, although they sinned less and more circumspectly by their trafficking than is done by the simoniacs today. By that deed he gave the kings an example that they might drive out the simoniacs and unworthy priests, for these do more harm to the Kingdom than foreign enemies or thieves. Nor can the Kingdom prosper in peace as long as simony prevails in it. [19] Hence, Saint Gregory wrote to the Frankish queen: "Because it is written, Righteousness exalts the nation, but sin makes men miserable; accordingly, the kingdom shall be established when known sin is promptly punished. Therefore, because the cause of men's fall is to be found in wicked priests— for who shall deal with the sins of the people when the priest who should pray for them commits even heavier sins? as in

17 Rom. 13:1–4.   18 Luke 19:38, paraphrase.
19 Wyclif expresses the same opinion in *De simonia*, 103.

our territories priests conduct themselves shamelessly and dishonorably—we ought fervently to oppose such evil deeds and avenge them, so that the sin of the few should not lead to the damnation of the many."[20] . . .

But because the simoniacs nowadays shamelessly commit simony, how should a king or a prince oppose them and banish them from their lands? For they deserve it, as a pope, Paschal by name, writes: "It is clear that the simoniacs, as the first and the most particular heretics, should be rejected by all the faithful. And if they do not desist after having been admonished, they should be suppressed by external powers."[21] . . .

. . . Hence, because wicked priests blaspheme God, the king ought, by his power, to avenge God's glory by his order, and restrain them from sinning. Likewise the princes and lords are in duty bound to do the same, for they possess power from God that they may avenge the wrongs which men do against God. For otherwise they shall be unfaithful servants of the supreme King. . . .

There exist many other proofs, but I shall cut them short by saying that if kings, princes, and lords, having been instructed in God's law, were to forbid priests to practice simony and themselves refrain from it, the Lord would grant them peace in their realm, praise, and prosperity, and afterwards the Kingdom of Heaven. O faithful kings, princes, lords, and knights! awake from the fell dream into which the priests have lulled you, and drive out the simoniacal heresy from your territories. Remember that God has entrusted you with the rule of the people in conformity with his law. Hence, restrain [the priests] from simony and other sins. Do not allow the people to be despoiled by demonic guile, nor permit harm to your possessions by which you shall suffer loss. When you oppose those who steal cows, you should much more oppose those who, having guilefully extorted money from the poor, destroy their souls and their own as well. . . .

Now, lords! listen to your reward, if you should be faithful and careful servants: it consists in the blessedness of a complete enjoyment of eternal joy and the possession of all good. For he is blessed in heaven who possesses whatever he desires, and desires no evil. For because all in heaven have God, who is the supreme good (above which the will cannot reach to anything

---

[20] To Queen Brunhilda, in Migne, *PL*, 77:1209.
[21] *Decretum Magistri Gratiani*, pars II, C. I, q. VIII, c. 27. The pope referred to is Paschal I.

higher), hence that good which is granted to the blessed beings brings with it all the rest which the will may desire. . . . O faithful Christian, do not lose that eternal wealth by exchanging the supreme for the temporal and the short-lived, and the joyous for the insignificant and sorrowful! Seek ye first the heavenly Kingdom, desiring it first and endeavoring with all your might to secure it. Then, as the Saviour promises, all needful things shall be given you.[22]

But some may raise the question: "Because there are so many simoniacs . . . and the priests have enjoined that no one should be called a simoniac unless he were proved to be such by their own judgment, how, then, shall anyone punish simony when they themselves act as judges and have the power to judge whom they wish? Furthermore, they bring false witnesses and jail, condemn, torture, and burn. . . . In answering that question, I shall say first to all generally, as Saint Paul wrote to Titus, "A man that is a heretic, after the first and second admonition, cast out."[23] And our Lord Jesus says, "Let him be unto thee as an heathen and a manifest sinner."[24] Had we kept that divine command, who would practice simony or otherwise sin openly and mortally? In the second place, I affirm that princes and lords and ecclesiastical communities, provided they themselves are free from simony, should not allow simoniacs to assume office. Thirdly, as has been said before, if they refuse to desist from their sin, let them be deprived of their revenues. But I do not counsel that any of them be put to death lest perhaps an innocent man may on occasion lose his life.[25] Hence, a judge who wishes to do no violence to truth should possess his power in such a manner as to do no wrong to anyone, as God the Father in his power [does no wrong to anyone]. Secondly, he should have a good conscience, fearing God filially, in imitation of Christ's humanity. Thirdly, he should have an understanding of truth in the likeness of the wisdom of God the Son. Fourthly, he should have a genuine good will like the will of the Holy Spirit. When he possesses these four qualities, he will then be able to render right judgment.[26] . . .

But many among the priests will strike out with an objection that they, as elders whose office it is to judge, and those who

---

[22] Matt. 6:33, 34.   [23] Titus 3:10.   [24] Matt. 18:17.
[25] The same opinion is expressed by Wyclif in *De simonia*, 104.
[26] These qualifications of a righteous judge are given in Wyclif, *De simonia*, 100, 101.

know the Scriptures, should rather be given credence; for since they are entrusted with the rule of the people, should they not be believed rather than the poor, despised priests?

The answer is given by the malefactor, unlearned in the Scriptures, who bore the true witness against all bishops, masters, knights, and others who had heaped dishonor upon and had blasphemed against, the innocent Christ. For he said that Christ "had done nothing wrong."[27] This malefactor is to be believed rather than all those who shouted that Jesus was worthy of death. Similarly, the holy Church joyfully sings, "It is better to believe the righteous Mary than the false Jewish hordes." For the merciful Lord grants unto the simple, who humbly keep his commandments, the knowledge of the truth, while he hides it from the wise men of this world. Therefore has Christ praised his Father for it and has confirmed the truth that the humble should be believed, saying, "I praise thee, O Father, Lord of heaven and earth, that thou hast hid these things from the wise and prudent, and hast revealed them unto babes" (i.e., to the humble and the despised of the world).[28] For should not men have believed the twelve apostles, poor, humble, and despised by the world, rather than all the bishops, masters, priests, and lawyers both pagan and Jewish, since the apostles followed the way of Christ? For men ought to adhere to those who live in conformity with the law and life of Christ, rather than to a thousand others whose lives do not so conform. For example, when men bowl, they first set up the target and then they throw the ball; and whoever comes closest to the target, wins. And when they cannot discern who is the closest, they take a ruler and measure the distance from the ball to the target, and thus determine which ball is closer. Similarly, Christ and his truth: Christ is placed before us as our example, and we should come near him by good practice and thus attain the heavenly Kingdom. If one wishes to judge among those who quarrel among themselves who is the closest to Christ and to his truth, let him take the measure from our target, Christ, and measure by his command, humility, meekness, purity, poverty, and his Word; and whoever . . . is closer by the measure (as by straws) should be declared the winner over the others. And even if thousands of thousands were to adhere to one who does not keep God's commands, nor exhibits humility, meekness, purity, and love, they all are in the wrong.

. . . Accordingly, let us follow him, obey him, and place

[27] Luke 23:41.   [28] Matt. 11:25.

our faith, hope, love, and all good works on him, look upon him as our mirror, and strive after him with all our might. For he says, "I am the way, the truth, and the life."[29] He is the way in example, which if anyone follow, he will not go astray; he is the truth in promise, for what he promised he shall fulfill; and he is the life in reward, for he will give himself to be enjoyed eternally. He is also the way, because he leads to salvation; he is the truth, because he enlightens the reason of the faithful; and he is the eternal life, in which all the elect shall live in joy forever. That life, and that way and truth, I myself desire to follow, and to it I wish to draw others!

I have written these books, knowing well that I shall receive for it neither praise, favor, nor material profit from the avaricious priests and worldly people. For I do not desire these things from them, but a reward from God and their salvation. If I receive denunciation and persecution, I have decided that it is better to suffer death for the truth than to receive material reward for flattery. For Saint Paul likewise affirms that "if I pleased men, I should not be the servant of God."[30] Understand thereby that if I pleased men by flattery, I should not be the servant of God. Therefore, I guard myself against flattery that I may not fail them as well as myself, and may not befoul myself thereby. I have spoken plainly and simply that I may in some way destroy and uproot simony. May the merciful Saviour aid me therein! These books have been completed in the year one thousand four hundred and thirteen, on the day of his being offered in the Temple by the Virgin Mary, and the day when Simeon took him in his arms (the day which the Czechs designate as *hromnice* [February 2]).

Whoever should read these books, let him observe that my intention is not that good men be defamed and harmed, but that they should guard themselves against evil, and that evil men should repent. Amen.

[29] John 14:6.   [30] Gal. 1:10.

DESIDERIUS ERASMUS

Desiderius Erasmus, A Humanistic Reformer

THERE ARE TWO ERASMI: ONE AN ARDENT, ERUDITE, classical scholar and enthusiast for "good letters," the "prince of the humanists," whose sharp wit and satire evoked dread and consternation in the camp of the "barbarians"; and the other a sincere and devoted believer in "the philosophy of Christ," a zealous, if moderate, reformer of the Church. Although Erasmus is not a schizophrenic, and neither side of his personality may safely be ignored, it is the latter side of him with which we shall be chiefly concerned.

The primary influence that contributed to the development of Erasmus' religious nature was the training he received at St. Lebwin's school at Deventer. This institution was greatly affected by the spirit of the Brethren of the Common Life. Moreover, many of its students, including Erasmus, lived in the dormitories of the Brethren, where they came under their direct influence. The ideals of the Brethren were semimonastic, and many of the boys who lived in their dormitories or were trained in their schools either joined them or entered the related monastic Orders either of Augustinian canons or of the Franciscans. But the piety of the Brethren was inward, mystical, modeled on the pattern of *The Imitation of Christ*, rather than upon the prevailing ritualistic or scholastic types. It belonged to the *"devotio moderna"* movement, which was consciously in opposition to the aridly intellectual *"devotio antiqua"* of the scholastic period. Not that it was doctrinally unorthodox; but it stressed spiritual communion with God, subjection of the autonomous human will—the "I," the "mine"—to the will of God, rather than high intellectuality. Consequently, it was not so much hostile to, as fearful of, learning, of high cultural

attainments, which often resulted in pride, or at least usurped
the chief place which belonged to true spirituality. As the
Imitation expressed it: "What availeth it to reason high secret
mysteries of the Trinity if a man lacks meekness, whereby
he displeaseth the Trinity?"[1] The Brethren were mildly
ascetic, otherworldly, world-renouncing. As Albert Hyma
characterizes them: "For wealth, fame, and honor they cared
not; the world, the devil, and the flesh were their enemies.
The interest displayed by most of them was not the interest of
educators in our sense of the word. They had no desire to make
the schoolboys learned in worldly ways, but to draw them to
God, that is, to make them pray much, read the Bible and
other devotional books, meditate in their rooms—in short, to
practice the Christian religion in imitation of the apostles."[2]
In these features the Brethren were, as humanistic Erasmus
wrote, "barbarous." Nevertheless, he himself was basically
formed under these influences, and in his own religious life
he stressed undogmatic, nonritualistic, inward, ethical piety.
He stoutly attacked ritualism, sacramentarianism, and scholasticism of his day; he fought the corruption of the clergy and
the monks; he was a stanch foe of all superstition and pagan-
ism of popular religion.

Erasmus' own mature religious views, which were shaped
by his close intercourse with such men as John Colet, Thomas
More, and Jean Vitrier, he liked to characterize as "the
philosophy of Christ." His pointed disregard of the more usual
designation, or the technical distinction between philosophy
and theology, could hardly have been unintentional. But, on
the other hand, this "philosophy" included a great deal more
than a reasoned or humanistic approach to religion: it comprised also a way of life, an ethic which, although certainly
not ascetic, was at least Stoic. It exhibited a close connection
between religion and humanistic culture. And it likewise
stressed a return to the Biblical and early Patristic sources of
Christianity in conscious repudiation of Scholastic systems.
This cultural Christianity of which he is the most notable
exponent is characterized by a "back to early Christianity"
emphasis, and among the Church Fathers Erasmus quite
understandably prefers Jerome, the most literary and the least

---

[1] Edward J. Klein, ed., *The Imitation of Christ* (Harper & Brothers, New
York, 1941), 3.
[2] Albert Hyma, *The Youth of Erasmus* (University of Michigan Press,
Ann Arbor, 1930), 104. For a fuller description, cf. Ch. X *passim*.

dogmatic of them all. Reforms which Erasmus strenuously advocates are of this nature. Furthermore, he is absolutely opposed to any violent break with the existing Church and strives rather to transform the Church from within. Hence, his break with Luther over the latter's "schism."

The works which best illustrate these characteristics of his thought are *Enchiridion militis Christiani* (The Enchiridion of the Christian Soldier), *The Praise of Folly*, the Greek New Testament, and *De libero arbitrio* (On the Free Will). The last-named work is mentioned as an example of his polemic against Luther's "scholasticism," rather than as a basic and integral part of Erasmus' own interest, since he wrote it unwillingly and under pressure.

The *Enchiridion* was chosen for inclusion in this volume because it represents more of the characteristic traits of Erasmus' conception of Christianity than any other of his works. The excellent translation made by Ford Lewis Battles is entirely new, for all the previous so-called translations were found to be mere paraphrases, which contained not only omissions (unfortunately, the present translation for lack of space comprises only a little over two thirds of the whole treatise) but also in some instances the translator's additions as well.[3] Nor is either of these facts stated by them explicitly or implicitly. The edition of the original used for this purpose is the one published in 1515, and is the second reprint of the first edition.

The *Enchiridion*—a word which signifies both a handbook and a dagger—was written, according to the author's own account, while he was staying in the great abbey at St. Omer. Under these circumstances, it plainly bears evidences of the influence exerted upon Erasmus by Jean Vitrier, warden of the Franciscan monastery at St. Omer, and a devoted reformer of monastic life after the pattern of spiritual, rather than ritualist, piety. It was published in 1503 at Antwerp in a volume entitled *Lucubratiunculae*, along with other treatises. Erasmus tells us that he wrote the work at the request of a local noble whom he addresses as John the German. In the Froben edition of 1518 he gives additional information about the noble by characterizing him as a hot-tempered and profligate soldier who was "almost illiterate." His wife was a woman of character and piety. In another connection Erasmus refers to this John as having been recently ennobled. Allen suggests that this

[3] This is particularly true of the "translation" of Philip W. Crowther (London, 1816).

may point to a certain John of Trazegnies who received the
Order of the Golden Fleece in November, 1516.[4] In the opening sentence of the work, Erasmus asserts that the noble
entreated him with no ordinary zeal that he prescribe for him
"a sort of compendious guide for living." . . . Since the noble
was "almost illiterate," and the original treatise was written
"in very few days" (a phrase which Erasmus allows to stand
even in the published edition), it is obvious that it must have
been very much shorter and simpler than the present text.
Therefore, the original must have been greatly elaborated and
expanded for publication. In its present form it does not fit
the thesis that it was written for a simple, rough soldier. Moreover, the references which Erasmus makes to this supposed
noble in the "Conclusion" are mystifying. For he speaks of
him as if the noble were contemplating entering a monastic
Order and writes, "Certainly just as I do not urge you to it,
so I do not urge you against it." He furthermore advises his
friend to separate himself as much as he can from human intercourse and urges him "to commit to memory" the words of
Paul. The plethora of classical references with which the
work abounds points to a very considerable elaboration of
the original version. One therefore concludes that, although
there is no positive proof against Erasmus' assertion that the
treatise was written for an "almost illiterate" soldier, neither
is there a positive proof for it. It is possible that it was written
for no particular individual at all. For with his exquisite literary
taste and skill, Erasmus was quite capable of inventing such a
plot and investing it with every mark of verisimilitude, if he
felt that it would enhance the charm of his book. That is exactly
what the story of the noble soldier-rake does. Although it
might have actually happened the way Erasmus asserts, it
could just as well amount to no more than a realistic, and somewhat romantic, background for an extended commentary on
the text that the Christian life is a warfare.

The first chapter reminds the soldier of the words of Job
that "the life of mortals is nothing else than a sort of perpetual
warfare." Every sort of vice attacks us, the devil, the world, and
our own flesh. It behooves us to take up arms against these
vile enemies and to urge an incessant warfare against them.
Erasmus concludes by saying, "Wherefore we ought to steer a
middle course between Scylla and Charybdis, so that we neither

[4] P. S. Allen, *Opus epistolarum Des. Erasmi Roterodami* (London, 1906), I,
373.

act too securely because we rely on divine grace, nor cast away our mind with our arms, because we are dispirited by the difficulties of war." It was this semi-Pelagian sentiment which was to bring its author into conflict with Luther.

The second chapter deals with the weapons of which the Christian knight must avail himself: the chief of these are prayer and knowledge, i.e., study of the Scriptures. "For all Holy Scripture was divinely inspired and perfected by God its Author." For its study the classical literature is the best preparation, particularly the Platonic writers—a strange advice if addressed to an almost illiterate soldier. But even so, the Scriptures alone are pre-eminently the book of instruction for the Christian. Erasmus furthermore chooses as the most reliable interpreters of the true spiritual sense of the Scriptures —for "the letter killeth"—Paul, Origen, Ambrose, Jerome, and Augustine. He deliberately turns to the ancients as against the moderns (e.g., Duns Scotus) because the latter counseled that it was not necessary to study the Scriptures, regarding themselves as the "absolute theologians."

The subsequent six chapters provide "the dagger" with which the brave soldier is to arm himself. They comprise the ancient Socratic art of "knowing oneself"; of the philosophical distinction between the outer and the inner man; of affections; of the Scriptural concept of the outward and inner man; of man as consisting of body, soul, and spirit; and of twenty-two general rules of life. This chapter comprises more than a third of the whole treatise. The remaining chapters are devoted to particular rules for the eradication of lust, avarice, and other specific sins.

First of all, then, Erasmus compares the concept of the *philosophia Christi* with the Johannine concept of the *Logos*, the principle of reason which "enlightens every man coming into the world." It was the Logos of the Stoics as well as of Philo, who wedded the Greek concept with the Hebrew Wisdom. The writer of the Fourth Gospel adapted this seminal idea to convey to his Hellenic readers the thought that the Christ who manifested himself in the flesh was the same Logos by whose agency the world was created. He likewise manifested himself in the prophets as well as in the Greek sages. For whatever reason men possess, its ultimate source is the divine Reason, the Logos. In this way Erasmus found the Greek wisdom of such philosophers as Socrates and Plato as truly derived from the divine wisdom as that of the Hebrew prophets and the Christian fathers, and its supreme manifestation in Christ himself. Hence, he could speak of the *philosophia Christi* and likewise write, *"Sancte Socrates, ora pro nobis."* [5] To be sure, he was in danger of limiting the revelation of Christ to the measure of truth apprehended by the sages of Greece and Rome—a pitfall which he by no means avoided at all times. But the partial truth which he comprehended better than his contemporaries is the principle that all reason, all truth, all wisdom, is ultimately derived from the divine Wisdom, which is Christ. This apprehension links Erasmus with such Christian thinkers as Clement of Alexandria and, above all, with Origen and Augustine, as against Tertullian, for whom all Greek and Roman wisdom was demonic and who repudiated all culture: "What truck has Athens with Jerusalem?" It also helps to explain Erasmus' hostility to Duns Scotus and Martin Luther, for both of whom Christian revelation contradicted philosophical truth.

This understanding of Erasmus' *philosophia Christi* explains the application he made of it in striving to reform the prevailing religious life. In the *Enchiridion*, he earnestly calls Christians away from the sacerdotal, ritualistic, institutional, and dogmatic religion to the practice of the fundamentals of Christian faith which alone are required for belief and life. He reduces these practical duties of religion to certain ethical requirements, the first of which he defines, in Platonic fashion, as that of knowing oneself. Since man consists of body, soul, and spirit and these war against each other, the noblest warfare anyone may wage is the conflict for the mastery of himself —the spirit dominating the unruly team of the body and the soul. Man need not yield to vice; he can control his passions by reason. This is very good Platonism or Stoicism; but Luther had difficulty in recognizing Paulinism in it. One can hardly blame him!

Erasmus then proceeds to identify "reason" and "passions" of the philosophers with what Paul calls "spirit" and "flesh." Thus in Christian terms our fight is between the spirit and the flesh, or, in Origen's terms, between the spirit and the soul-body entity. This conquest is to be achieved by following the general and specific rules wherein Erasmus elaborates the technique of self-mastery. First of all, ignorance has to be overcome by the study of the Scriptures, which are more to be trusted than any other guide.

[5] *Colloquia,* 683 DE.

Furthermore, the Christian must seize the way of salvation without delay. Christ must be his goal in life. Erasmus assails those who trust in saints instead. It would be better, Erasmus suggests, if such petitioners imitated the virtues of the saints, and prayed for an increase in virtue.

But more commonly Erasmus makes excellent use of his exquisite and mordant wit, pungent sarcasm, delicious satire, good-natured ridicule, and clever innuendo as weapons against the corrupt morals of the clergy and the monks; the overweening pretensions of the papacy; the worship of saints, the Virgin, the relics, and the wonder-working images; and the foibles of humankind generally. These he employs, as a skillful fencer does a slender rapier, in defense of "rational" (and sometimes rationalistic) Christianity. All his works abound with such sallies, many of which are anything but the work of a gentle, if not unaggressive and timorous, scholar, as Erasmus is often pictured. To mention only a few and at random, one may remind the reader of the description of Erasmus and Colet's pilgrimage to Canterbury, or of the many volumes of his *Colloquies*, written during a period of thirty-six years, with the primary purpose of teaching boys sound and elegant Latin, but also with the equally prominent aim of instilling in them the principles of rational Christianity. Among the many sly thrusts at the current superstitions, the purported letter from the Virgin Mary (of Basle) to Ulrich Zwingli is particularly daring; in it she thanks Zwingli for ridding her of the mob of petitioners who requested her aid in their silly, criminal, or selfish exploits.[6] Another daring pasquinade, entitled *Julius Excluded from Heaven*, satirizes Pope Julius II. But the best-known and ever-popular (although not intrinsically the weightiest) of his satirical works with a serious purpose is his *Praise of Folly* (1511), which exhibits to perfection his method of serious jesting as well as the delicacy of his touch. It aims at reforming the current Christian world by shaming men into a life of reason and true inward piety. His Folly is not stupid but playful, delightful in her apparent naïveté; and then before the victim is aware of his danger, she stabs him like a wasp. Or, to change the figure, the seemingly playful lady conceals a stiletto up her sleeve with which she stabs the victim. That is what hurt the most: there is so little to get hold of in the disarming, witty sallies of the charming mistress of the world, for she laughs at herself as well as her victims. The audaciousness

6 Quoted in Preserved Smith, *Erasmus* (New York, 1923), 294.

of her attacks leaves her victims gasping. Among them
Erasmus' contemporaries are easily recognizable: he includes
his former fellow student at the College of Montagu, John
Major, who is ridiculed for Duns Scotus' theological asininities,
and Pope Julius II for his utter worldliness.

But the great humanist, whose classical scholarship evoked
the admiration of his age, utilized this knowledge for the
advancement of the scholarly study of Patristic, and particularly of Biblical, literature as well. When, in 1499, Erasmus met
John Colet at Oxford for the first time—the latter was then
lecturing on Saint Paul—he made a decision that affected his
entire life. Colet urged him to remain at Oxford and to lecture
on the Old Testament. Instead, Erasmus resolved first of all
to learn Greek, "without which," as Colet later said, "we are
nothing." For five years Erasmus pursued his aims,[7] and then
came back to England equipped for his life work, which was
to serve the cause of Christianity by restoring to it the immense
riches of intellectual and religious wisdom produced by the
Greek and Latin fathers. For the next thirty years he labored
to lay the foundations of critical scholarship in sacred learning.
During that long and most laborious period he produced some
thirty folio volumes of critically edited Patristic texts: the works
of Jerome, edited in nine folio volumes, and re-edited later;
Cyprian; Augustine (ten stout folio volumes); Arnobius;
Chrysostom; Irenaeus; Ambrose; Hilary; Basil; Haymo; and
finally Origen—the work interrupted only by the editor's
death. Thus he not only laid the foundations of critical Patristic
studies, but directed theological interest away from the
medieval schoolmen, particularly from the hated Duns Scotus,
and toward the Fathers of the Early Church.

But perhaps the most important of his scholarly contributions
to the modern approach to religion were his Biblical studies.
The greatest of these was his Greek New Testament. But
even prior to the appearance of this great work, Erasmus
produced, during his second visit to England (1505–1506),
a new Latin translation from two Greek MSS. of the New
Testament furnished him by his friend, Dean Colet. In 1512
he began to work on the most notable of his Biblical labors,
the Greek New Testament. It was completed in 1514, although
not published until 1516. Thus it was the first Greek New Testa-

---

[7] Already in 1501, in the *Enchiridion*, he claimed to have acquired, "not
without many vigils . . . a fair knowledge both of Greek and Latin."
But this may represent a later insertion.

ment to appear in print, although the Complutensian edition
of Cardinal Ximenes had been printed two years earlier, but
was not licensed for publication until 1520. Erasmus' edition was
a bulky volume of about one thousand pages, containing, along
with the Greek text, Erasmus' own Latin translation and notes.
Later he edited the work four times more, incorporating whatever improvements he secured from additional Greek codices.
The influence of this work on the Reformation was incal-
culable. But even this great contribution did not exhaust his
interest in this kind of work, for he produced, in the course
of many years, *Paraphrases*, a commentary on the entire New
Testament save the book of Revelation. Its success was
truly immense. Queen Catherine Parr arranged for the translation of the entire series into English—an undertaking in
which several scholars participated. It was completed in 1549.
Under King Edward VI a copy of it was placed in every
parish church throughout England and Wales, in order to
counteract the influence of more advanced Evangelicals.

Finally, Erasmus' attitude toward the Reformation, and
particularly toward Luther, must be examined. By temperament and lifelong training, he was loath to engage in open and
raucous controversies, although he was almost morbidly
sensitive to criticism and avid for praise. For this reason, when
Luther became the champion of the reform movement, Erasmus
found himself in warm agreement with most of his positions,
although he personally did not wish to become involved in the
struggle. On the other hand, he himself continued to carry on
his accustomed attacks upon the abuses within the Church,
and was particularly incensed against the "Pharisees"—those
who stubbornly defended the superstitions and the evils, and
persistently charged him with having laid the egg which Luther
hatched. Erasmus' position was exceedingly difficult, for he
could not wholeheartedly join either camp, nor could he remain
neutral without exposing himself to severe censure from both
parties for either lukewarmness and indifference or for moral
cowardice or preference for security. However, there was much
in Luther's reform which Erasmus enthusiastically supported,
for he knew that "should Luther go under, neither God nor
man could longer endure the monks; nor can Luther perish
without jeopardizing a great part of the pure truth." [8] Yet as

---

[8] Erasmus to Spalatin, March 12, 1523, in Preserved Smith, tr. and
ed., *Luther's Correspondence and Other Contemporary Letters* (Philadelphia,
1913), I, 581.

time went on both men realized the basic differences in their temperament and character. Erasmus, with his instinctive prudence, could not but marvel at the rashness of the German, who did not seem to care whether he lived or died. Erasmus, for all his biting criticisms of the clergy and the monks, and of the whole hierarchical regime, was not inclined to become a martyr or a schismatic. To divide "the seamless robe of Christ" appeared to him the greatest of crimes or follies. Moreover, Luther's violent language and robust, perhaps insolent, defiance of the Church authorities disgusted the fastidious and prudent scholar. He fought with a rapier, not a two-handed battle-ax. Despite all that, however, he did not approve the way in which Pope Leo X handled, or rather mishandled, the Lutheran case, and wrote publicly in defense of some of Luther's reforms. No wonder that his role of peacemaker, or perhaps of two-faced Janus, brought him into disfavor with both parties! The papal party, particularly his colleagues at the University of Louvain, demanded that he declare himself a Lutheran, or positively dissociate himself from the movement by attacking Luther. Erasmus saw with increasing clarity that he could never join either the Lutherans or the "Pharisees." He heartily wished that a plague should take both the houses! But for a long time he fought a delaying action, and refused to be drawn into the fray on the plea that he had never read even a single page of Luther's writings!

When at last, at the urgent and repeated proddings of his old friend and fellow Hollander, Pope Adrian VI, as well as of King Henry VIII, Duke George of Saxony, and a host of lesser lights, Erasmus consented to write against Luther, he at the same time published his *Inquisitio de fide* (1524) [9] which in effect asserted that Luther was orthodox in the fundamental articles of the Christian faith, namely, in all the articles of the Apostles' Creed, and that the Church had no right to demand from him more than this. Erasmus thereby declared that all doctrines and usages which went beyond the Apostles' Creed were nonessential. When one realizes that this transparent defense of Luther (who was impersonated as Barbatius, while Aulus was Erasmus himself) was published in the same year as the attack upon Luther himself, it is indeed a cause for astonishment!

---

[9] Craig R. Thompson, ed., *Inquisitio de fide* (Yale University Press, New Haven, 1950). The fact that Erasmus was just then recuperating from a serious illness from which he did not expect to recover adds significance to the treatise.

In the *Inquisitio*, then, Barbatius positively and even fervently affirms his belief in all the articles of the Apostles' Creed. He believes in God in the historic Christian sense, and in Jesus Christ as the God-man. Jesus died in order "that by this sacrifice he might reconcile to himself us who were guilty, we putting our confidence and hope in his name." Nothing is said for or against the doctrine of salvation by faith alone; authentic Luther could hardly have spoken thus. And so it goes on without a hitch, even though some may detect a slight hedging about the descent into hell, until the article about the holy Church is reached. To that, Barbatius answers, "No!" Then he proceeds to explain that he believes in "a holy Church which is the body of Christ, that is to say, a certain congregation of all men throughout the whole world who agree in the faith of the gospel, who worship one God the Father, who put their whole confidence in his Son, who are guided by the same Spirit of him; from whose fellowship to be cut off is to commit mortal sin." [10] Aulus then, in conclusion, fires a point-blank question at Barbatius: "Do you believe these things from your very heart and unfeignedly?" To which the latter replies, "I believe them so certainly, I tell you, that I am not so sure that you talk with me." Whereupon Aulus remarks, "When I was at Rome, I did not find all so sound in the faith." [11]

Nevertheless, in the end Erasmus yielded to the pressure and took up theological cudgels against Luther. He went unerringly to the heart of the matter—the doctrine of free will. Western theology has ever oscillated between the two extremes —either God is all in all, and man is nothing, or man is at the center, and God plays a secondary role. The two antagonists, Luther and Erasmus, represented to varying degrees these two historic antitheses: for Luther, the work of salvation was all grace: man had no part in it; for Erasmus, on the other hand, the humanistic position was asserted, although with moderation. In his *De libero arbitrio* (1524) [12] Erasmus was very polite and considerate of Luther; nevertheless, he firmly asserted his contrary view. He defined free will in the usual way as man's moral ability to accept or reject the proffered grace of God. Augustine's or Luther's refinements of the doctrine of grace in the form of distinction between the ability to choose freely,

---

10 *Ibid.*, 68, 69. I made a slight change in the translation.
11 *Ibid.*, 57–73.
12 This work will be published as Vol. XVII of THE LIBRARY OF CHRISTIAN CLASSICS.

and the selfish desire which dictates the choice and makes it always selfish, moved him not. He surrounded himself with a cloud of witnesses among the Fathers in behalf of free will, including even Augustine. But like the reasonable man that he was, he concentrated his argument on Scriptural proofs, the alleged ground of Luther's opposing system. He candidly admitted that the problem of free will was quite susceptible of being argued pro and con on the basis of the Scriptures, and hence there was a need for an authoritative interpreter. This function, Erasmus affirmed, was rightly exercised by the Church. This admission placed Erasmus firmly in the papal camp, and all his criticism of its abuses could not change this fundamental fact. On the affirmative side, Erasmus cited numerous passages corroborating the Patristic doctrine of free will, but frankly conceded that there were other Scriptural passages contradicting it. The most important of these was in Saint Paul, where he treats of the hardening of Pharaoh's heart by means of God's direct action. Erasmus wrote: "Since it seems absurd that God, who is not only just but good, is said to harden the heart of man so that by the latter's malice he might illustrate his power, Origen in his third book, Περὶ ἀρχῶν, thus explains the difficulty: that while he admits the occasion of the hardening of Pharaoh's heart is due to God, yet he charges the blame thereof on Pharaoh, who by his malice is made the more obstinate by those very things by which he ought to be led to repent, just as from the same showers of rain the cultivated field produces delectable fruit, while the uncultivated field produces thorns and thistles."

And Erasmus concluded: "I am pleased with the opinion of those who contribute something to free will, but very much more to grace. You must not avoid the Scylla of arrogance in such a way that you may be cast on the Charybdis of despair and inaction. . . . 'Why,' you may ask, 'should anything be granted to free will?' That there may be something which may deservedly be charged to the wicked who have willingly failed to respond to the grace of God; that the calumnious charge of cruelty and injustice on the part of God may be removed; that despair on our part may be avoided; that excessive security may be shunned; and that we may be stimulated to endeavor. For these causes free will has been laid down as a dogma by almost all men, but of no avail without the grace of God, lest we might arrogate anything to ourselves. But someone may say, 'Of what avail is free will if it works nothing?' I reply, 'Of what avail is man at all, if God works in him just as the potter in his clay, or just as he would in a stone?' "[13]

In 1533, when Erasmus again thought he was about to die, he penned an irenic treatise on Church unity, *Liber de sarcienda ecclesiae concordia*, in which he once more expressed his moderate and considerate judgment about the doctrine of free will. It is "a thorny question which it profits little to debate; let us leave it to professed theologians. But we can agree that man of his own power can do nothing and is wholly dependent on the mercy of God: that faith is of great value, a gift of the Holy Spirit, though we may have differences of opinion as to the precise mode of its operation."[14] Would that Luther and the theologians since his time had taken to heart Erasmus' moderate advice!

To express a judgment upon the position which Erasmus took regarding Luther and the Reformation may amount to no more than revealing one's own preferences or prejudices. At the risk of such a judgment, let it be said that in the light of both the treatment which Luther and the whole Reform endeavor (including Erasmus' own share in it) received at the hands of the Church authorities, Luther's resolute stand (although not all his individual deeds or temper) is amply justified. What was needed to break the rock of offense was a sledge hammer, not the jeweler's tool. Erasmus' own essentially conservative stand, which regarded the main fabric of the Church as good, although certain details (particularly the accretions of the ages since the times of the early Fathers) could well be abandoned or reformed, was insufficient to effect the very reformation which he himself throughout his life ardently desired. This is proved by the intransigent attitude of the reformed papacy which was expressed in the decrees of the Council of Trent. There are times when compromise is wrong. The results of the Reformation justify Luther's adamant reform aims, although not all the measures he adopted to carry them out.

But all this is not said to detract from the undoubted and immensely valuable contributions which Erasmus made to the cause of true Christian religion. If his genius fitted him for work which was mainly intellectual, the cause of the Kingdom has need of such services. He labored unremittingly, and despite

[13] J. J. Mangan, *Life, Character, and Influence of Desiderius Erasmus* (New York, 1927), II, 248, 249.
[14] Quoted in P. S. Allen, *Erasmus*, 90, where the translation of the treatise is given.

the sufferings which his frail bodily frame and consequent ill-health caused him, the results of his labors were as astonishing in their mere bulk as in the excellence of their performance. For has not our Lord himself bid us, in summing up all law and prophets, to love the Lord God not only with all our heart and soul, but with all our mind as well? Erasmus loved with his mind; that too is the true service of God and his Church.

The Enchiridion
(Handbook of the Christian Soldier)

THE TEXT

Erasmus of Rotterdam to John the German His Courtier Friend,[1] Greeting: You have entreated with no ordinary zeal, best beloved brother in the Lord, that I prescribe for you a sort of compendious guide for living, that having been instructed by it, you can arrive at a state of mind worthy of Christ. Indeed you say that while for a long time you have been pushing forward in court life, you have been concerned how you can flee from Egypt with its vices and delights, and with Moses as leader be happily set upon the road to virtue.[2] You are so dear to me that I rejoice exceedingly in our salutary proposal, which I hope (at least with regard to our need) He who has deigned to arouse you to it will make prosperous

---

[1] "To John the German, his courtier friend." Latin, *Ioanni Germano amico aulico*. This letter, including the concluding sentences of the *Enchiridion*, is printed as No. 164 in Allen, Vol. I, 373–375. Allen suggests that John may possibly be John de Trazegnies, who might have met Erasmus at Tournehem in 1501. It is to be noted that Allen's text, taken from the *Lucubratiunculae* (1503), does not mention the name John in the superscription: " . . . *Aulico Cuidam Amico*. . . ." On the circumstances of the writing of the *Enchiridion* see also Erasmus' Letters to John Botzheim (Allen, I, 1), to John Colet (Allen, I, 181), and to Adolphus of Veere (Allen, I, 93); as well as the preface to the edition of 1518 of the *Enchiridion*, addressed to Paul Volz, Abbot of Hugshofen, near Schlettstadt.

The text of the *Enchiridion* used for the present translation was that published at Strassburg by Matthias Schürer, 1515. This was collated subsequently with the text as printed in the edition of the complete works of J. Clericus (1703–1706), and with the recent edition of Holborn, *Desiderius Erasmus Roterdamus ausgewählte Werke*, Munich, 1933. Holborn's edition and Marcel Bataillon's edition of the Spanish translation, *El Enquiridion o Manual del Caballero Cristiano*, Anejo XVI, *Revista de Filologia Española*, have been especially helpful in the work of annotation.

[2] See, for example, Origen, *De principiis*, 4.3.12; tr. Butterworth, 307.

and carry forward. Yet I have with too much willingness yielded to you as a man and friend, or as one yearning for pious sentiments. But you strive not to appear to have begged our assistance without cause, else might I seem fruitlessly to have gratified your wish. Indeed with common prayers let us implore that kindly spirit of Jesus, that it may suggest to me as I write words which bear salvation, and render them efficacious for you.

1. In Life Man Must Be Watchful

First of all, as you too must remember, Job [3] (that veteran, undefeated soldier) testifies that the life of mortals is nothing else than a sort of perpetual warfare,[4] and that the generality of mankind is too often deceived, whose minds that schemer, the world, holds in the grips of the most seductive wantonness. These folk, as if the war were already brought to an end, celebrate unseasonable holidays, when nothing could be so unlike *real* peace. It is wonderful in how much security they live, and in what a leisurely manner they go to sleep in both ears, while we are endlessly attacked by so many iron-clad troops of vices, are laid hold of by so many artifices, and are fallen upon by so many stratagems. Behold, in your last going forth they keep watch upon you with the highest vigilance, these most worthless demons, armed against us with a thousand deceits, a thousand noxious arts, who strive with fiery darts and poison arrows to pierce our minds from above; no javelin of Hercules or Cephalus was ever more certain than these weapons, unless they be fended off by the impenetrable shield of faith. Time and again the world attacks us here, from right and left, from front and rear, the world of which John [5] speaks as entirely constituted in vices, and to Christ himself sometimes unsafe, sometimes unseen. Nor, indeed, is the reason for attack a simple one. For at one time in adverse circumstances, raging like Mars undisguised, the world shakes the walls of the mind with a heavy battering ram; at another time, by large but exceedingly vain promises, it incites the mind to betrayal; at still another time, by secretly contrived pitfalls, unexpectedly it snatches the mind,

[3] Job 7:1.

[4] For a study of the military metaphor in early Christian literature, see A. Harnack, *Militia Christi* (1905). Paul's contribution is discussed on pp. 12–18. The application of the Pauline metaphor to the Bible as a whole, and particularly to the Old Testament, was largely the work of Origen. With Augustine, Gregory the Great, and later writers, the metaphor became a commonplace.   [5] I John 5:19.

so that between the negligent and the secure it oppresses us all. Finally, that slimy snake, first betrayer of our peace, now hidden by its green hue in the grass, now concealing its hundred coils in dark grottoes,[6] desists not from lying in wait for the heels of our woman once she has been corrupted. Understand "woman" as the carnal part of man. For this is our Eve, through whom the most crafty serpent lures our mind to death-bearing pleasures. As if it were not enough for him so to threaten at the door, we at last bear the enemy within the inner recesses of our mind, more than we would a close friend, more than a servant, than whom, as nothing is deeper within, so nothing can be more dangerous. Here, indeed, is that old earthly Adam, in habit more than a citizen, in zeal more than an enemy, whom it is not permitted to enclose with an entrenchment, nor possible to drive out with an army. Him we ought to watch with a hundred eyes, lest perchance he may lay open God's fortress to demons.

Therefore since all of us are engaged in such a formidable and difficult war, and with such numerous enemies, so sworn and devoted to our destruction, so watchful, so armed, so treacherous, so experienced, are we not insane not to take up arms against them, not to stand our watch, not to hold all things suspect? Accordingly, then, just as in quite peaceful times, we snore stretched out, we leave off work, we indulge in pleasure, and (as they say) at leisure take care of our own little skin.[7] One would think that our life were a Greek drinking bout, not a war, so do we wrap ourselves in bedclothes rather than armor and skins, we are girded with the rosy delights of Adonis rather than with hard arms, we indulge ourselves with luxury and ease in place of military efforts, we practice upon the peaceful harp rather than the javelins of Mars. As if not this sort of peace, but war, were the most loathsome of all things!

Indeed he who enters into peace with vices violates the agreement struck with God in baptism. And you insanely cry, "Peace, peace," when you hold God as an enemy, who alone is peace and the author of peace![8] And clearly he proclaims through the mouth of the prophet, saying, "There is no peace to the wicked."[9] Nor is there any other condition of peace with him, unless, while we fight in the garrison of the body, with great hatred and the highest force, we wage war upon vices.

6 Gen. 3:15. Virgil, *Aeneid*, 5:84; *Eclogues*, 3:93.
7 Horace, *Satires*, 2:5:38.   8 Cf. Jer. 4:10; 6:14; 8:11.
9 Isa. 57:21.

Otherwise if we consort with them, we shall doubly make our foe Him who alone can as a friend bless us, as an enemy damn us. First, we stand by those vices with which God can in no wise agree (for what has light to do with darkness?).[10] Second, we, most ungrateful, do not stand by our pledge to him, and with the most sacred ceremonies we impiously fend off the fell blow. Or perhaps you do not know, O Christian soldier, when you were already being initiated into the mysteries of the life-giving bath,[11] that you gave yourself by name to Christ as your leader, to whom you doubly owed life, at one and the same time given and restored, and hence you owe more to him than to yourself? If you should too little stand by your covenant, does it not occur to you that you pledged yourself to such a kindly leader, that you dedicated your head, bound by his sacraments as if by a votive offering, to his fateful purposes?

To what purpose was he delaying to impress the sign of the cross on your brow, unless, while yet alive, you might fight under his banner? To what end was he putting off anointing you with his sacred ointment, unless that you might undertake an eternal struggle with vices? What great shame, what almost public execration of humankind, for a man to cut himself off from his princely leader! Why do you hold Christ your leader in derision, neither compelled by fear of him, since he is God, nor forbidden by love of him, since for your sake he is man? Bearing his word before you, you ought to have been warned what you promised to him. Why treacherously do you desert to the enemy, when once he redeemed you by the price of his blood?[12] Why as a double deserter do you serve in the army of the enemy? With what impudence do you dare to raise the hostile battle standards against your King (who expended his life for your sake)? For he who does not stand for Him, as he has said, stands against Him, and he who does not gather with Him, He scatters.[13]

Moreover, you deserve not only a loathsome title but also a most wretched pay. You wish to hear what your pay is, whoever you are who fight for the world? Paul, that standard-bearer of the Christian warfare, replies, "The wages of sin is death."[14] Who, then, would undertake this splendid warfare, if the death of the body were proposed to him? Will you indeed

10 II Cor. 6:14.
11 Life-giving bath. Latin, "*vivifici lavacri*," i.e., baptism.
12 I Peter 1:19.   13 Luke 11:23.
14 Rom. 6:23.

bear such a loathsome death of the soul, obtaining it in place of a reward? In these insane wars, which men wage with men either in beastly madness or out of miserable necessity, do you not see, if at any time either the magnitude of promised booty or the dreaded cruelty of the victor, or the disgrace of reproached cowardice, or, finally, the desire for praise, has goaded the minds of the soldiers, by what eager effort they accomplish whatever toil there is, what an empty life they lead, with how great ardor they are taken prisoner into the enemy camp? And what a paltry pay, I ask you, is sought with so much attention, so much zeal, by these miserable folk? Surely it is that by this mere human leader they may be honored with the noisy ovation of soldiers and camp and with elegant little odes, that they may be wreathed about with a grassy crown or with oaken leaves, that they may bring home a little more pay. We, on the contrary, are aroused neither by shame nor by reward, since we now have the same one as spectator of our struggle as we are one day going to have as giver of our reward. What rewards has our Agonothetes[15] proposed for the victor? Surely not mules, such as Homer pictures Achilles as receiving,[16] or tripods Virgil Aeneas,[17] but that which "neither eye has seen, nor ear heard, nor has ascended into the heart of man,"[18] and this indeed imparts meanwhile a sort of solace of labors for those who are still struggling. What then? Happy immortality. But in those absurd struggles glory is the chief part of the prize, and the resources of the conquered are distributed by lot. As far as we are concerned, the affair is carried on under a great and double danger, nor is the struggle concerned with praise, but rather with the head. And as the highest pay proposed ought to go to him who has stuck to his task, so the highest punishment ought to be meted out to him who deserts it. Heaven is promised to him who fights strenuously, and does not the widowed virtue of a generous mind glow with the hope of such a happy prize? Especially if it is promised by that Author who can no more deceive than be unable to be. . . .

It is the body's nature to perish, because even if no one kills it yet it can not remain alive. But for the soul to die is a matter of extreme misfortune. With what caution do we remove the wounds of our mere body; with what solicitude do we doctor them? And yet we neglect the wounds of the soul?

---

15 Agonothetes: Greek ἀγωνοθέτης, judge of the contests, president or director of the games, judge.   16 Homer, *Iliad*, 23:259 ff.; 24:277 f.
17 Virgil, *Aeneid*, 5:110.   18 Isa. 64:4; I Cor. 2:9.

How we hold in horror the frightful death of the body, because it is seen with bodily eyes! To be sure, since no one sees the soul dying, few believe, and very few are frightened, although this death is as much more awful than that one as the soul is greater than the body, as God is greater than the soul.

Do you wish for yourself signs, such as I might point out, by which you may discover either disease or death of the soul? The stomach has indigestion; it cannot retain food. From this you recognize a disease of the body. Bread is not as much the food of the body as the Word of God is the food of the soul.[19] If it is bitter to you, if it tastes nauseous, what doubt is there that the palate of your soul is infected with disease? If it does not retain victuals, if it does not pass them into your intestines, you evidently have proof that your soul is sick. When your knees totter, and your sick limbs can scarcely be dragged about, do you not recognize that you have a bad body; and have you not contracted a disease of the mind, when it languishes, is nauseated toward all duties of piety, when strength does not suffice for bearing light abuse, when by the expenditure of a mere pittance it is broken? After the sight leaves the eyes, when the ears fail to hear, and after the whole body has been overwhelmed, no one doubts that the soul has departed. When you have the eyes of the heart obscured[20] so that you do not see the brightest light (that is, truth), when you do not perceive with your inner ears the divine voice, when you lack every sense, do you believe the soul to be alive? You see your brother suffering indignities, yet your mind is not in the least moved. . . . Why at this point does your soul feel nothing? Surely because it is dead. Wherefore dead? Because God, its life, is not present. Where God is, there is love. For "God is love."[21] Otherwise if you are a living member, why is any part of your body in pain when you are not only not in pain, but also not feeling anything?[22] Here is another sign which is even more certain. You have defrauded a friend, you have committed adultery, your soul has received a major wound, and yet up to now it is not in pain, so that you even as it were rejoice over gain, and boast that you have committed wickedness. Surely you must consider that your soul lies dead. . . .

On the other hand in the words of the Gospel the disciples say to Christ: "O Lord, whither shall we go? You have the words of life."[23] Why "words of life"? Surely because they

---

[19] Luke 4:4.   [20] Cf. Rom. 1:21.   [21] Cf. I John 4:7, 8, 11.
[22] I Cor. 12:26.   [23] John 6:69.

flowed forth from that soul from which never even for a moment did divinity depart, which likewise restores us to everlasting life. But when Paul was ill in body, the Physician took care of him. Not rarely have pious men recalled a lifeless body to life. But God does not revive a dead soul except by a singular and gratuitous power, and certainly does not resuscitate it if dead it leaves the body. Then the sense of bodily death is either nothing or at least certainly very brief, while the sense of the soul's death is everlasting. And besides, the soul is more than dead, yet, in some fashion or other, to the sense of death it is somehow immortal. Then since we ought to struggle against such a new danger, what is that stupor, that false sense of security, that supineness in our minds, which not even the fear of a very great misfortune rouses up?

Yet, on the contrary, it is nothing for either greatness of danger or the enemies' resources, power, and artifices to perplex your mind. He helps him whom you hold to be a serious adversary; he will straightway help him whom you hold as your present succorer. There are innumerable ones against you, but He who stands for you is one more able to stand for all. "If God is for us, who is against us?"[24] If he sustains us, what is lacking? Take upon yourself the vow of victory with your whole heart. Your encounter is not with an unbroken enemy, but with one already once broken, melted, stripped, yet till now triumphant over us. Think upon Christ our Head, by whom the devil will without doubt in turn be conquered. Think also upon ourselves. Take care that you are in the Body, and you will be able to do all things in the Head. In yourself you are indeed exceedingly foolish; in him you avail something.

Hence, therefore, the outcome of our Mars is not at all doubtful, for the reason that victory in no wise depends upon fortune, but all this lies in the hand of God, and, through him, also in our hands. Here no one has failed to conquer unless he did not want to conquer. The Helper's kindness has never been lacking to anyone; if you took care not to lack his kindness, you were victorious. He will fight for you, and will impute his liberality to you for merit. You must understand every victory as received of him, who, first and alone immune from sin, oppressed the tyranny of sin, yet bestows these blessings upon you not without your own effort.[25] For he who said, "Trust in me, for I have conquered the world,"[26] wishes you to be of a great, not a secure, mind. Thus at last we will conquer

[24] Rom. 8:31.   [25] Cf. I Peter 2:22 ff.; I John 3:5.   [26] John 16:33.

through him, if we fight according to his example. Wherefore we ought to steer a middle course between Scylla and Charybdis, so that we neither act too securely because we rely on divine grace nor cast away our mind with our arms because we are dispirited by the difficulties of war.

2. Of the Weapons of the Christian Warfare

I think that principle which among the first pertains to the discipline of this military service is that you give especial thought and consideration to what kind of arms is most powerful for the sort of enemies you must encounter, then that you have them always in readiness lest at any time that wiliest of schemers may crush you unarmed and unaware. In your earthly wars it is quite common for you to pause either while the enemy is in winter quarters or when there is a period of truce. For us while as yet we fight in this body it is not permitted to be separated even a finger's breadth (as they say) from our arms. Never should we fail to stand in the battle line, never should we cease to keep watch, because our enemy never ceases in his attacks. Verily, when he is peaceful, when he pretends flight or a truce, then he is most of all preparing traps; nor ought we ever more cautiously to stand watch than when he shows the appearance of peace; never ought we to be less frightened by him than when he rises against us in open war. Therefore let the first care be that the mind be not unarmed. . . .

But we will speak about Christian armor in detail in its proper place. Meanwhile, to speak summarily, two weapons should especially be prepared for him who must fight those seven nations, the Canaanites, the Hittites, the Amorites, the Perizzites, the Girgashites, the Hivites, the Jebusites,[27] that is, against the whole troop of vices, of which the seven capital sins are numbered most powerful. These two weapons are prayer and knowledge. Paul always expresses the desire that men be so armed, for he commands them to pray without ceasing.[28] Pure prayer directed to heaven subdues passion, for it is a citadel inaccessible to the enemy. Knowledge furnishes the intellect with salutary opinions so that nothing else may be lacking.

"So truly does each claim the other's aid,"
and make with it a friendly league."[29]

[27] Deut. 7:1.   [28] I Thess. 5:17.   [29] Horace, *Ars poetica*, 410 f.

The former implores, but the latter suggests what should be prayed for, that you should pray eagerly, and, according to James, "nothing wavering." [30] Faith and hope prove that you should seek the things of salvation in Jesus' name; knowledge shows you how to do this. The sons of Zebedee heard from Christ these words: "You do not know what you seek." [31] But prayer is indeed more powerful, making it possible to converse with God, yet knowledge is no less necessary. . . .

But hear what Christ teaches us in Matthew's Gospel: "When you pray, do not talk much as the heathen do, for they think they shall be heard for their much speaking. Be not therefore like them, for your Father knows what your need is before you ask him." [32] And Paul contemns ten thousand words spoken in the spirit, that is, with the lips, in favor of five put forth in the understanding. . . .[33] Then, therefore, you should familiarize yourself with this fact: when the enemy attacks and the remaining vices molest you, you should immediately with sure faith arouse your mind toward heaven, whence comes your help.[34] But also raise your hands to heaven. It is safest to be occupied with the duties of piety, that your works may be concerned, not with earthly studies, but with Christ.

But lest you contemn the support of knowledge, consider this. . . . Believe me, dearest beloved brother, there is no attack of the enemy so violent, that is, no temptation so formidable, that an eager study of the Scriptures will not easily beat it off; there is no adversity so sad that it does not render it bearable. . . . For all Holy Scripture was divinely inspired and perfected by God its Author.[35] What is small is the lowliness of the Word, hiding under almost sordid words the greatest mysteries. What is dazzling is no doctrine of mortals, for it is not blemished by any blot of error; the doctrine of Christ alone is wholly snow-white, wholly dazzling, wholly pure. What is inflexible and rough expresses the mystery clothed in the letter. If anyone touches the surface, the pod, what is harder and harsher? They did not taste the manna without the husk who spoke, "This is a hard saying, and who can hear it?" [36] Pluck out the spiritual sense: now nothing is sweeter, nothing more succulent. The word *manna* sounds to the Hebrews like, "What is this?" This agrees beautifully in divine Scripture, which contains nothing idle, nor one tittle . . . not worthy of these

30 James 1:6.   31 Matt. 20:22.   32 Matt. 6:7f.
33 I Cor. 14:19.   34 Ps. 120:1, Vg.; 121:1, E.V.   35 II Tim. 3:16.
36 John 6:61, Vg.; 6:60, E.V.

words, "What is this?". . . For what is the water concealed in the veins of the earth but the mystical meaning imprisoned in the letter? What is this same water when it is made to gush forth but the mystical meaning drawn out and explained? Because it is spread far and wide for the edification of the hearers, what prevents its being called a river? [37]

Therefore if you will dedicate yourself wholly to the study of the Scriptures, if you will meditate on the law of the Lord day and night,[38] you will not be afraid of the terror of the night or of the day,[39] but you will be fortified and trained against every onslaught of enemies. Nor would I, for my part, disapprove your taking your preliminary training for military service in the writings of the pagan poets and philosophers, but gradually, at the proper age, . . .and cursorily—not tarrying, as it were, to perish on the sirens' rocks. Saint Basil also calls the young to these studies to establish them in Christian morals and recall them to the muses.[40] Our Augustine was his pupil.[41] Nor is Jerome displeased by the well-beloved captive.[42] Cyprian is praised because he adorned the temple of the Lord with the spoils of Egypt,[43] but I do not want you to imbibe the morals of the Gentiles along with their letters. And yet you will find out very many things there conducing to right living. Nor ought you to despise pagan authors, for they too are often good moral teachers. Moses did not despise the advice of his father-in-law Jethro.[44] Those letters shape and nourish the child's nature and wonderfully prepare one for the understanding of divine Scriptures, to break in upon which with unwashed feet and hands is almost a sacrilege. Jerome belabors the impudence of those who, advanced in secular studies, dare to treat the divine Scriptures,[45] yet how much more shamelessly do they act who not even having tasted Scripture dare so to do!

But as divine Scripture does not bear much fruit if you persist in and cling to the letter, so is the poetry of Homer or Virgil quite useful if you remember the whole of it to be allegorical. That is something no one will deny who finds the learning of the ancients supremely to his taste. I will not at all insist that you undertake the study of obscene poets—certainly not to look into them more deeply—unless perhaps you learn rather to

[37] Ex. 17:5f.   [38] Josh. 1:8; Ps. 1:2.   [39] Ps. 90:5f.
[40] Basil, *Ad adulescentes: Sermo de legendis libris Gentilium, PG*, 31:563–590.
[41] Augustine, Epistle 26, *PL*, 33:103; *De ordine*, 1:8:23f., *PL*, 32:988.
[42] Jerome, Epistle 70:2, *PL*, 22:664–668.
[43] Cf. Augustine, *De doctrina Christiana*, 2:40, 61, *PL*, 34:64.
[44] Ex. 18:13–24.   [45] Jerome, Epistle 53:7, *PL*, 22:544.

abhor the vices described and by the contention of wicked things more strongly to love honest ones. Among the philosophers I would prefer you to follow the Platonists, for the reason that in very many of their opinions and in their way of speaking they approach as closely as possible the prophetic and Gospel pattern.[46] . . . Therefore as soon as you feel nausea, you ought to hasten as fast as possible to the manna of heavenly wisdom, which will abundantly nourish and revive you, until as victor you reach those palms of promised reward which will never be lacking. . . .

The first requirement is that you feel worthy sentiments concerning Scripture. Consider these oracles as genuine and sprung from the presence of divine mind. You will feel yourself breathed upon by divine will, affected, seized, transfigured in an ineffable manner, if you approach Scripture religiously, with veneration, humbly. You will see the delights of the blessed Bridegroom; you will see the riches of the richest man, Solomon; you will see the hidden treasures of eternal wisdom. But beware lest you wickedly break into the chamber. The doorway is low. Watch out lest you dash your head against it and be thrown back. Hence believe none of those things which you see with your own eyes and handle with your own hands to be as true as what you read there. It is certain from the divine words that heaven and earth will pass away, but not one jot or tittle of the law is going to pass away before all things are fulfilled.[47] Although men lie and err, the truth of God neither deceives nor is deceived.

From the interpreters of Holy Scripture choose those especially who depart as much as possible from the literal sense. Of this sort, after Paul,[48] among the first are Origen, Ambrose, Jerome, Augustine. For I see the modern theologians too freely and with a certain captious subtlety drinking in the letter, rather than plucking out the mysteries and giving their attention (as if Paul had not spoken the truth) to the fact that our law is spiritual.[49] I have heard some who are to such an extent pleased with these little human comments that they contemn the interpretations of the ancients almost as if they were dreams. To such an extent has Duns Scotus brought confidence to them that, without ever having read the Holy Scriptures, they nevertheless think themselves to be absolute theologians. Even if they say the acutest things, it is for others

46 Cf. Introduction, 285 f.   47 Matt. 5:18; cf. 24:35.
48 Cf. Rom. 7:6.   49 Rom. 7:14.

to judge whether their words are worthy of the Holy Spirit. If you prefer to be more animated in spirit than trained in contention, if you seek the feasting of the soul rather than the itching of natural inclination, read especially the ancients, whose piety is more tried and tested, whose learning richer, and whose prayer is neither poor nor sordid, and whose interpretation of the sacred mysteries more appropriate. Nor will I say that I contemn the moderns, but that I prefer teachings more useful and more conducive to what you have proposed.

Moreover, that divine Spirit has its own sort of language and its own sort of figures, which you ought at the outset to learn by diligent observation. The divine wisdom babbles to us and, like a sort of attentive mother, adjusts her language to our infancy. She provides milk for the tiny infants in Christ, herbs for the sick; but you must hasten to grow up to avail yourself of solid food.[50] She lowers herself to your humility, yet you on the other hand are to rise up to her sublimity. Always to be an infant is indeed a misfortune; chronic illness is much too reprehensible. Meditation upon a single verse brings more wisdom, more nourishment (if you pluck out the marrow from the broken pod), than an oft-repeated universal psalm in the letter.

I warn you of this the more diligently because I have knowledge that this error has occupied, not the minds of the crowd alone, but also the minds of those who in garb and name profess perfect religion. These persons think that the highest piety resides in this one thing: counting over as many psalms as possible every day although they can scarcely understand them even in a literal sense. I believe that monastic piety grows cold, languishes, disappears on every side for no other reason than that the monks grow old and gray in the letter, and do not escape to the spiritual understanding of the Scriptures. Nor do they hear Christ in the Gospel proclaiming, "The flesh profits nothing; it is the spirit that makes alive."[51] Nor do they hear Paul adding to the Master's words, "The letter kills, but the spirit makes alive."[52] And we know since the law is spiritual it is not carnal.[53] And spiritual things should be compared to spiritual.[54] Once in the mountain, now in spirit, does the Father of spirits desire to be worshiped.[55]

Yet I by no means despise the weakness of those who from

---

[50] Heb. 5:12f.; cf. I Cor. 3:1f.; Rom. 14:2.
[51] John 6:64, Vg.; 6:63, E.V.   [52] II Cor. 3:6.   [53] Rom. 7:14.
[54] I Cor. 2:13.   [55] John 4:20ff.

feebleness of mind do the single thing they are able to do, pro-
nouncing mystic psalms with simple and pure faith.[56] Indeed
just as in magic rites certain words not understood by those
who pronounce them yet are believed to be efficacious, so
divine words, although little understood, yet ought to be
believed to be beneficial for those by whom they are either
spoken or heard in sincere faith and pure affection. And they
know that the angels who are present are summoned to bring
assistance. Nor indeed does Paul contemn those who sing in
the spirit, or those who speak in tongues, but he urges the better
dividing of graces.[57] To this end if it does not fall to anyone's
lot to strive forward because of vice, not of mind, but of nature,
certainly it will not prove an obstacle to those who strive
toward better things. And according to Paul's word, "Let not
him who eats despise him who does not eat; and let not him
who does not eat judge him who eats."[58]

Surely I do not at all want you, who are endowed with such
a fortunate nature, to tarry in the barren letter, but to hasten
to the more recondite mysteries, and to aid by frequent prayers
the enormous effort of toil, until He who has the key of David,
who closes and no one opens,[59] will open unto you the book
sealed with the seven seals,[60] the secrets of the Father, which
no one knows except the Son,[61] and him to whom the Son
wishes to reveal them.

But to whom shall our prayer incline? It was proposed
that we should prescribe for you the form of life, not of study.
. . . Now if it pleases you to go to the storehouse of Paul, that
not inactive leader, you will surely find "that the weapons of
our warfare are not of the flesh, but mighty before God for the
destruction of fortifications, destroying imaginations and every
height rearing itself against the knowledge of God." [62] You will
find the arms of God by which you can withstand in the evil
day;[63] you will find the arms of justice on your right, and
at your left you will find truth as side armor,[64] and the breast-
plate of justice, the shield of faith, upon which you can extin-
guish all the fiery darts of the evil one. You will find also the
helmet of salvation and the sword of the Spirit which is the
Word of God.[65] If one is carefully covered and fortified by all
these arms, he will at last be able fearlessly to utter the courageous word of Paul: "Who shall separate us from the love of

[56] Origen, *Contra Celsum*, 1.24, *PG*, 11:703–706.　　[57] I Cor. 14:2ff.
[58] Rom. 14:3.　　[59] Rev. 3:7.　　[60] Rev. 5:1.　　[61] Matt. 11:27.
[62] II Cor. 10:4f.　　[63] Eph. 6:13 f.　　[64] II Cor. 6:7.　　[65] Eph. 6:14ff.

Christ? Tribulation, or distress, or famine, or nakedness, or peril, or persecution, or sword?" [66] See how many enemies the devil leads, and how frightened they are at everything ! But hear something even stronger. There follows: "But in all these things we overcome, because of him who has loved us. For I am sure that neither death, nor life, nor angels, nor principalities, nor powers, nor things present, nor things to come, nor might, nor height, nor depth, nor any other creature shall be able to separate us from the love of God which is in Christ Jesus." [67] O happy confidence which the arms of light have furnished to Paul, that is, to an insignificant man who calls himself a castoff of this world! [68] Sacred letters supply you abundantly with the power of such great armor if you with whole heart will turn your attention to them so that there will be no future need for our warnings.

But as you so desire (lest we seem not to have complied with your wishes) an *enchiridion*, a dagger which we are to forge, one that you are never to lay down from your hand, even when you are eating or sleeping. Even if you are forced to travel in the business of this world and become wearied at bearing around this righteous armor, yet you should not leave yourself even for a moment totally unarmed, lest that wily foe should oppress you. Be not ashamed, then, to have this little sword with you, neither a burden to carry nor useless for defending yourself. It is indeed very small, but skillfully use it, together with the shield of faith, and you will easily sustain the enemy's tumultuous assault and avert a deadly wound. But now is the time for us to teach ourselves a sort of "manual of arms." And I promise you, if you exercise yourself diligently in it, our sovereign Christ will transfer you, rejoicing and victorious, from this garrison to the city of Jerusalem, where there is no tumult of war at all, but everlasting peace and perfect tranquillity. [69] Meanwhile all hope of safety rests in iron.

3. THE CROWN OF WISDOM IS THAT YOU KNOW YOURSELF; AND OF THE TWO SORTS OF WISDOM, FALSE AND TRUE

Peace therefore is that highest good to which also the lovers of the world turn all their efforts, but theirs is a false peace,

[66] Rom. 8:35.   [67] Rom. 8:37–39.
[68] I Cor. 4:13. For *purgamenta* (Vulgate) Erasmus has *projectamenta*. Cf. *Novum instrumentum* (ed. 1543), *rejectamentum*.
[69] Jerusalem is interpreted as ὄρασις εἰρήνης or *visio pacis* from Philo Judaeus onward. See Philo, *Somn.*, 2:250; Vol. v, 554f., Loeb.

as has been said. It is this same sort of peace that the philosophers falsely promised to those who adhered to their teachings. But Christ alone grants that peace which the world cannot give.[70] There is but one way to attain this, if we wage war with ourselves, if we fiercely contend with our vices. For God, our peace, is separated from these enemies by an implacable hatred; his nature is virtue itself, and he is the parent and author of all virtues. And the dregs drawn from every kind of vice are called folly by the Stoics, the strongest defenders of virtue; in Scripture, malice. Among all of these writers absolute probity is called wisdom. Does not the oracle of the wise man say that "wisdom conquers malice"?[71] The father and prince of malice is that governor of darkness, Belial; anyone who follows his leadership, walking in the night, hastens to eternal night. On the contrary, the Author of wisdom, and himself Wisdom,[72] Christ Jesus, who is the true light,[73] alone shattering the night of earthly folly, the Splendor of paternal glory, who as he was made the redemption and justification for us reborn in him,[74] so also was made Wisdom (as Paul testifies): "We preach Christ crucified, to the Jews a stumbling block, and to the Gentiles foolishness; but to them that are called, both Jews and Greeks, Christ is the power of God and the wisdom of God."[75] Through this Wisdom, by his example, we also are able to triumph over the malice of the enemy, for if we are wise in him, in him also we shall conquer. This you will embrace with a wisdom contemptuous of the world. . . .

I doubt not but that these wise fools now hatefully molest you; that these blind leaders of the blind[76] shout that you are raving mad, insane because you are preparing to go over to Christ's side. These are merely Christians in name; in other respects they are, first, mockers, then attackers of Christ's teaching. Watch out lest their babblings move you at all, whose blindness ought to be pitied, deplored, rather than imitated. For what is this preposterous kind of wisdom that is so cautious and skillful in worthless things and nothingness, nay, for wicked ends, but in those things which alone pertain to our salvation is no wiser than a dumb beast? Paul wishes us to be wise, but in good; simple in evil.[77] These are wise that they may act evilly; they know not how to do good.

When that eloquent Greek poet judges him as useless who

---

[70] John 14:27.   [71] Wisdom 7:30.   [72] I Cor. 1:30.   [73] John 1:9.
[74] I John 2:8; Heb. 1:3; I Cor. 1:30.   [75] I Cor. 1:23–25.
[76] Matt. 15:14.   [77] Rom. 16:19.

neither is wise through himself nor listens to a good counselor,[78] in what class will these be placed who, when they are most wickedly foolish, do not cease to disturb, to mock, to hinder those who have already recovered their senses? . . . But of the wisdom of Christ, which the world considers foolishness, you read: "Now all good things came to me together with her, and innumerable honors through her hands. And I rejoiced in all these, for this wisdom went before me, and I knew not that she was the mother of them all."[79] For she leads as her companions modesty and gentleness. Gentleness renders us able to receive the divine Spirit. For upon a humble and gentle person the Spirit rejoices to rest,[80] at the same time imbuing our minds with that sevenfold grace. Finally that happy crop of all virtues will sprout forth, with those blessed fruits—especially inner joy, secret joy, joy known only to those whom it has touched, which at last neither vanishes nor is removed with the joys of the world, but is gathered up into eternal joy. My brother, you ought in accordance with James's[81] admonition to seek this of God with the most ardent intentions, and (according to a certain wise man) to "dig it out" from the veins of divine Scripture "like treasures."[82]

The crown of this wisdom is, believe me, to know yourself, a saying which antiquity believed sent from heaven,[83] and one in which the great authors took delight, holding it to epitomize the fullness of wisdom. But let this teaching be of little weight among us unless it agrees with Scripture. That mystical lover in the Canticles threatens his bride, ordering her to go out of doors, unless she at the same time know herself: "If you know not yourself, O beautiful among women, go forth and follow after the sheep of your flock."[84] Then let no one arrogate to himself the fantastic opinion that he knows himself well enough. Might I also question whether anybody knows his body completely, or that anyone will recognize a· habit of mind? Paul, to whom it befell to learn the mysteries of the third heaven,[85] yet dared not judge himself, would undoubtedly have dared to do so if he had known himself well enough.[86] If a man were clearly spiritual to such an extent that he could judge all things, without being judged by anyone, yet knew

---

[78] Hesiod, *Works and Days*, 293–295. [79] Wisdom 7:11f.
[80] Judith 9:16, Vg.; 9:11, E.V. [81] James 1:5. [82] Prov. 2:4b.
[83] Cf. Juvenal, *Satires*, 11:27. [84] S. of Sol. 1:7. [85] II Cor. 12:2.
[86] I Cor. 4:3.

himself so little, what are we carnal folk to put our faith in?
Surely a soldier who knew neither his own forces nor the
troops of the enemy would seem quite useless. Yet the war is
not between man and man but within the self: from our inward
parts the hostile battle line springs forth in opposition to us,
just as the poets relate of the earthborn brothers.[87] One's
friend is distinguished from one's enemy by such a fine line
that it would be an enormous danger for us incautiously to
protect an enemy as a friend or to attack a friend thinking
him to be an enemy. That notorious leader ever takes on the
appearance of an angel of light.[88] "Are you one of ours, or one
of our adversaries?"[89] Therefore, since you have undertaken
war with yourself, and the first hope of victory lies in this,
whether you know yourself as much as possible, I shall put
before you a sort of likeness of yourself, as in a picture, that you
may plainly know what is within and what is skin-deep.

4. Of the Outer and Inner Man

Man therefore is a certain prodigious animal composed
of two or three widely divergent parts, a soul like a sort of
divine will, and a body comparable to a dumb beast. As far as
the body is concerned, we do not surpass the remainder of
animal kind; hence, we are inferior to them in every bodily
endowment. But in regard to the soul we are capable of divinity,
so that it is granted us to climb in flight above the minds of the
very angels themselves, and to become one with God. If you
did not have a body added to you, you would be a spirit;[90]
if you were not endowed with a mind, you would be a beast.
That greatest craftsman of all has joined together in happy
concord these two natures, so different from one another;
but the serpent, hating peace, again has split them in unhappy
discord, so that now they can neither be separated without the
greatest suffering nor live conjointly without constant war.
And plainly (as is proverbially said), "Each one holds a wolf
by the ears in the other."[91] That most elegant little verse could
appropriately be applied to either one:

"I cannot live either with you or without you."[92]

[87] Ovid, *Metamorphoses*, 3:101–130.   [88] II Cor. 11:14.
[89] Josh. 5:13.   [90] Spirit. Latin, *numen.*
[91] *Adagia*, (ed. 1559), 1:5:25; cf. A. Otto, *Sprichwörter der Römer*, 199 [Holborn, 41n.].
[92] Martial, *Epigrams*, 12:47; Ovid, *Amores*, 3:11:39.

To such a degree are they stirred up by perplexed sedition, one would think they were diverse, but they are really one. For inasmuch as the body is itself visible, it delights in things visible; as it is mortal, it follows things temporal; as it is heavy, it sinks downward. On the contrary, the soul, mindful of its ethereal nature, presses upward with exceedingly great force, and struggles with its earthly weight. It distrusts things seen. Because it knows such things to be transient, it seeks those things which truly and everlastingly are. The immortal loves things immortal, the heavenly things heavenly, like takes to like, unless it be deeply immersed in the sordid things of the body, and contagion causes it to degenerate from its natural-born generosity. Even the fabulous Prometheus did not implant this discord; nor did its primitive condition impart these mixtures to our mind from any particular living thing. But sin evilly corrupted what had been well founded, sowing the poison of dissension among ones before at peace. For previously the mind used to command the body without trouble, and the body obeyed the mind freely and willingly; but now on the contrary, with the order of things disturbed, the passions of the body strive to get control of the reason; and in the opinion of the body the reason is thought to forsake the feet.

Therefore it is not absurd to compare man's breast to an unruly state. For a state is composed of various sorts of men, whose dissensions make it necessary to contend with frequent disturbances and factions. The highest power is concentrated under one supreme authority of such a sort that he commands nothing except for the state's welfare. Wherefore it is necessary that he who is wiser ought to prevail in these matters, while he who is less wise ought to obey. Nothing is more senseless than the lowest classes, and for this reason they ought to obey the magistrates and not hold office. But those who are the aristocracy, or greater by birth, the king ought to listen to in his consultations, yet in such a way that the final decision remains in the hands of the king alone, who ought indeed sometimes to be warned, but never allow himself to be forced or to be led. . . .

But in man reason discharges the office of king. And you may understand his nobles to be certain affections—indeed, bodily ones, but yet not brute ones. In this class are included: true piety toward parents, charity toward brothers, benevolence toward friends, mercy toward those who are afflicted, fear of dishonor, desire for an honest reputation, and like qualities. Consider to be, as it were, the last dregs of the lower classes those disturbances of minds which dissent as much as possible from the decrees of the reason, and are least humbled to lowliness of heart. Of this sort are lust, lechery, envy, and passions of the diseased mind like these, which we ought to resist, one and all, as overseers restrain dirty, vile slaves, so that if they are able they may carry out the day's task assigned by the master. But if less, let them not give occasion for loss. All these matters Plato, divinely intelligent, wrote about in the *Timaeus*.[93] . . .

Now these are the proper endowments of kings: first that they be as wise as possible, that they may not sin through error; then that they devise only those things which are good, that they may not commit anything against the judgment of the mind, falsely and corruptly. Judge him who lacks any one of these qualities not to be a king but a criminal.

5. OF THE DIVERSITY OF PASSIONS

According to eternal law, divinely engraven upon him, our king can indeed be oppressed, but cannot be corrupted, without protesting, without recovering. If the rest of the common people are subject to him, he will commit nothing either punishable or pernicious, but all will be treated with the greatest moderation and the greatest calmness. On the subject of the affections the Stoics and Peripatetics disagree, although both schools are agreed that one must live by the reason, not by the passions. But it is the view of the Stoics that when by those passions which are most closely excited by the senses you have been educated to the point of judgment and have arrived at a true sense of discrimination between what is to be sought and what shunned, then those passions are to be abandoned. For they are not only useless for wisdom, but even pernicious. And for that reason the Stoics wish to free that perfect wise man from all passions of this sort, as diseases of the mind. They scarcely concede to the wise man those first more human impulses which precede the reason, calling them fantasies. But the Peripatetics teach that the passions are not to be extirpated but subdued, as of some use; for they believe them to have been added from nature as certain incentives, urgings to virtue. For example, anger is the incentive to fortitude, envy to industry, and so forth. . . .

93 The text of this passage is a patchwork taken from *Timaeus*, 69c–d, 42b, 44d, 45b, 70a, 90a, 73c, 74e, 75c, 69d sq, 70a, 70d–e.

It is fitting therefore, first, for all to recognize the motions of the mind, then to know none of them to be so violent but that they can either be restrained by reason or redirected toward virtue. I hear everywhere this pernicious opinion, that men say they are compelled to vice. Others on the contrary, ignorant of their own nature, follow motions of this sort, thinking them to be precepts of the reason, and so, because anger or envy has persuaded them, they call it zeal for God. And as one state is more strife-ridden than another, so is one person more prone to virtue than another. This difference proceeds, not from a distinction between minds, but either from the influence of heavenly bodies or from forebears, or from education, or from the very habit of the body itself. Socrates' fable of the charioteers and horses, good and bad, is no old wives' tale.[94] For you may see some, born with such a moderate temperament, so tractable and easy to get along with, that they are trained toward virtue without any trouble, and even hurry on of their own accord without goading. But for others it happens that the much-sweating tamer is scarcely able to subdue the rebellious body, like an untamed, ferocious, bucking horse, even with the roughest rein or goad or spurs. If such falls, perchance, to your lot, do not straightway abandon your purpose; rather, cling the more sharply, so judging not that the way to virtue is closed to you, but that a richer material of virtue has been offered you. But if you are born with a good mind, in this you are forthwith no better than another, but happier; yet again, happier in such a way that you are under greater obligation. Yet who is so happy in disposition[95] that there are not very many things in which he does not need to struggle?

Therefore, the king ought especially to watch that which he feels is most disturbed. There are vices which appear to be more characteristic of certain nations, as they say that deceit is a familiar vice among some peoples, gluttony among others, lechery among still others. They accompany some bodily habit: as, for example, effeminacy and love of pleasure go along with the sanguine; anger, ferocity, evil-speaking, with the choleric; inactivity, sluggishness, with the phlegmatic; envy, sadness, bitterness, with the melancholic. Some of these qualities with age either slacken or weaken, as, for instance, in youth lust, prodigality, rashness; in old age, graspingness, moroseness, avarice. Also there are some which seem related to sex: for example, ferocity in man, vanity and desire for

[94] *Phaedrus*, 246a–b; 253cff.   [95] Disposition. Latin, *ingenio*.

revenge in woman. Meanwhile it happens that nature, making as it were pairs, compensates disease of mind with a diverse sort of endowment. This person is more prone to pleasure, but not at all irascible or envious. That person is of uncorrupted modesty, but prouder, more irascible, more concerned with material things. Nor is there lacking in those who are troubled by certain enormous and fatal vices theft, sacrilege, murder, which must be encountered with every effort, and against their reviling a brazen wall of definite purpose must be thrown up. On the other hand there are some passions so close to virtues that there is danger lest we be deceived by the doubtful distinction between them. These ought to be corrected, and suitably turned toward the nearby virtue. To take an example: someone is quite irascible; let him throw a rein over his mind, and he will be more eagerly active, he will walk erect, and be not the least bit sluggish. He will be free and simple. Another person is somewhat grasping; let him exercise his reason and he will be frugal. Let him who is rather given to flattery become friendly and agreeable. Let him who is inflexible become constant. Let him who is somewhat sad become serious-minded. Let him who is tactless become courteous. To the same end should other rather light diseases of the mind be directed. Only let us be careful not to cloak a vice of nature with the name of a virtue, calling sadness gravity, harshness severity, envy zeal, poverty frugality, adulation friendliness, scurrility urbanity. This, then, is the sole way to happiness: first, know yourself; second, do not submit anything to the passions, but all things to the judgment of the reason. Moreover, be sane, and let reason be wise, that is, let it gaze upon honest things.

Yet (you will say) what you advise is difficult. Who denies it? And yet there is a true saying of Plato's, "Those things which are beautiful are also difficult." [96] Nothing is harder than for a man to conquer himself, but there is no greater reward or blessedness. Jerome[97] expresses this thought very clearly, just as he does all others. Nothing is happier for a Christian to whom the Kingdom of Heaven is promised. Nothing is more burdensome for him who daily is in peril of his life. Nothing is stronger for him who conquers the devil. Nothing is more foolish for him who is overcome by the flesh. If you carefully

[96] *Republic*, 435c, 497d; *Hippias Major*, 304e; *Cratylus*, 384b; cf. *Adagia*, 2:1:12.
[97] Jerome, Epistle 125, *PL*, 22:1072.

weigh your strength, you will agree that there is nothing more difficult than to subject the flesh to the spirit. But if you are mindful of God as your helper, there is nothing easier. With a firm purpose, then, take upon yourself the proposal of perfect life; push that resolve once you have taken it up. The human mind has never commanded itself to do something strongly which it has not accomplished. The great part of Christianity is wholeheartedly to want to become a Christian. . . . There is no animal so wild that human effort cannot tame. . . . There will be no reason, will there, for the mind, the tamer of all things, itself to be tamed? You do everything to free your body from disease. Surely, then, you do not do those things which the pagans also have done, to rescue your body and soul from eternal death?

6. OF THE INNER AND OUTER MAN, AND OF THE TWO PARTS OF MAN FROM HOLY SCRIPTURE

. . . Now, indeed, the authority of the philosophers would be slight if they had not given all the same precepts as Holy Scripture, even though the words were different. Paul calls this reason of the philosopher sometimes "spirit," sometimes "inner man," sometimes "law of the mind." Its opposite, the passions, he sometimes calls "flesh," sometimes "body," sometimes "outer man," sometimes "law of the members." He says: "Walk in the Spirit, and you shall not fulfill the lusts of the flesh. For the flesh lusts against the Spirit, and the Spirit against the flesh . . . so that you do not the things that you would." [98] . . . Surely this is a new order of things: to seek peace in war, war in peace, life in death, death in life, freedom in slavery, slavery in freedom! . . . Hear what Paul says of freedom: "But if you are led by the Spirit, you are not under the law." [99] "We have not received the spirit of bondage again in fear, but you have received the spirit of adoption of sons of God." [1] . . . You read in Paul concerning "the outer man who is corrupted, and the inner man who is renewed from day to day." [2] Plato distinguished two souls in one man. [3] Paul in the same way makes two men in one man, fastened together in such a way that neither is going to be either in glory or in Gehenna without the other. They will not be separated: the death of one cannot be the life of the other. What Paul writes

[98] Gal. 5:16f.   [99] Gal. 5:18.   [1] Rom. 8:15.
[2] II Cor. 4:16.   [3] *Timaeus*, 69.

to the Corinthians is, I believe, also pertinent: "The first man was made a living soul; the last Adam a quickening spirit." [4]. . . . And that it might be more evident he set forth these things to apply not only to Christ and Adam, but to every one of us. "Like the earthly man, so are earthly men; like the heavenly, so are the heavenly. Therefore if we have borne the image of the earthly man, let us also bear the image of the heavenly. This indeed I say, brethren, because flesh and blood cannot inherit the Kingdom of God, nor will corruption possess incorruption." You see how evident it is that Paul, who elsewhere spoke of the "flesh" and the "outer or corruptible man," here calls him the "earthly Adam." This is surely that "body of death" about which Paul freely used to exclaim, "Unhappy man that I am: who shall deliver me from the body of this death?" [5] Then Paul, uncovering a far different fruit of the flesh and spirit, writes elsewhere: "For he that sows in his flesh, of the flesh also shall reap corruption; but he that sows in the Spirit, of the Spirit shall reap life everlasting." [6] . . .

This is indeed a new sort of remedy. Lest Paul might be proud, he is tempted by pride. That he may be firm in Christ, in himself he is forced to be infirm. For he bore the treasure of heavenly revelations in a vessel of clay, that the sublimity might be of the power of God, and not from himself. [7] This one example of the apostle reminds us equally of many others. When first we are disturbed by vices, immediately ought we to implore divine aid by repeated prayers. Then temptations for perfect men will become not only not dangerous but even necessary for the guarding of virtue. Finally, when all else has been subjugated, only the vice of vainglory lurks in the midst of the virtues. It is like that Herculean hydra, a lively monster, prolific in its wounds, which scarcely can be destroyed at the very end in spite of all careful labors. But "persistent labor conquers all things." [8]

In the meantime while the mind boils with violent disturbances, in every way press forward, push on, command and hold in check with tight bonds that Proteus of yours,[9] while

> "He changes himself into all wondrous shapes,
>   into flame and hideous beast and flowing river," [10]

until he returns to his natural appearance. The passions and

---

[4] I Cor. 15:45–50. [5] Rom. 7:24. [6] Gal. 6:8.
[7] II Cor. 4:7. [8] Virgil, *Georgics*, 1:145f.
[9] Cf. Horace, *Satires*, 2:3:71. [10] Virgil, *Georgics*, 4:441f.

desires of the foolish are like Proteus. When these passions drag the foolish now into brutal lust, now into savage anger, now into poisonous envy, now into one and another portents of vices, does not what the most learned poet said of Proteus beautifully apply to them:

> "Then will manifold forms baffle you, and figures of wild beasts.
> For of a sudden he will become a bristly boar, a deadly tiger,
> a scaly serpent, or a lioness with tawny neck;
> or he will give forth the fierce roar of flame." [11]

But remember here what follows:

> "But the more he turns himself into all shapes,
> the more, my son, should you strain his fetters." [12]

Surely we need not hark back again to the fables of the poets when the example of the holy patriarch Jacob teaches us to push constantly the nightly struggle, until the dawn of divine assistance shines forth, and to say, "I will not let you go unless you bless me." [13] . . .

Always after a temptation is overcome, an especial increase of divine grace is added to man, whereby he may be much better armed than before against the future attacks of the enemy. . . . "When you have chastised your flesh, and have crucified it, with the vices and concupiscences," [14] now when no one hinders, tranquillity and leisure will fall to your lot, that you may be free and may see the Lord, that you may "taste and see that the Lord is sweet." [15] . . .

Search yourself. If you are flesh, you will not see the Lord. If you see not, your soul will not be saved. Take care, then, that you be spirit.

7. Of the Three Parts of Man: Spirit, Soul, and Flesh

These were, if you please, quite sufficient, but that you may see and investigate a little more fully I should like briefly to refer you to Origen's section on man. [16] For he, following Paul, makes three parts, spirit, soul, and flesh, all of which the apostle

---

[11] *Ibid.*, 4:406–409.   [12] *Ibid.*, 4:411 f.   [13] Gen. 32:24 ff., 31.
[14] Gal. 5:24.   [15] Ps. 33:9, Vg.; 34:8, E.V.
[16] Origen, *Commentarius in epistolam ad Romanos*, 1:5, 10, *PG*, 14:850; 856.

writing to the Thessalonians has joined, "that your whole spirit, and soul, and body be preserved blameless for the day of our Lord Jesus Christ." [17] Isaiah, however, omitting the lowest part, recalls only two: "My soul will desire thee in the night, but likewise by my spirit within my breast, from early morning I will watch to thee." [18] Likewise Daniel: "Praise the Lord, ye spirits and souls of the righteous." [19] From these passages, Origen not absurdly derives the threefold portion of man. The body or flesh is our lowest part, upon which, through genital sin, that crafty old serpent inscribed the law of sin, and by which we are prompted to wickedness and vanquished, joined to the devil. The spirit represents in us the likeness of the divine nature, in which the blessed Founder, from the archetype of his own mind, engraved that eternal law of virtue with his finger, that is, his Spirit. By this we are bound to God, and are made one with him. Lastly, God founded the soul as the third and middle faculty between the other two, to hold the natural senses and impulses.

The soul, just as in a quarrelsome state, cannot refrain from acceding to one or the other of the parts. Hither and thither it is incited, [yet] it considers itself free to incline to which of the two sides it wishes. If, renouncing the flesh, it conducts itself toward the parts of the spirit, it will likewise become spiritual. But if it once abandons itself to the desires of the flesh, it will degenerate likewise into the body. . . .

Therefore the Spirit renders us gods; the flesh, animals; the soul makes us men. The spirit makes us pious; the flesh impious; the soul neither the one nor the other. The spirit seeks heavenly things; the flesh, delightful; the soul, necessary things. The spirit bears us off to heaven; the flesh drives us down to hell; to the soul nothing is imputed. Whatever is fleshly is wicked; whatever spiritual, perfect; whatever of the soul, mediate and indifferent.

Do you prefer, as they say, that Minerva point out the difference between these parts with a fatter finger? Let me demonstrate. You venerate your parents. You love your brother. You love your children. You love your friend. These things do not have as much to do with virtue as not to do with wickedness. Why should you not act as a Christian, because the heathen and even brute animals act according to the instinct of nature? What is of nature is not imputed to merit. But

[17] I Thess. 5:23. [18] Isa. 26:9.
[19] Dan. 3:86, Vg.; Song of the Three Children, v. 63, E.V.

in that place you have fallen upon the possibility that either
piety toward one's father ought to be condemned, love toward
one's children overcome, kindness toward one's friend
neglected, or God will be offended. What do you do? Does
your soul stand at the crossroads? The flesh beckons hither,
the spirit thither. The Spirit says: "God is stronger than your
parent. You owe your body only to your parent; to God you
owe everything." The flesh suggests: "Unless you obey him,
your father will disown you, men will call you unfaithful.
Think of property; think of reputation. God either will not
notice or will wink, or will certainly be easily placated."
Now the soul persists, now wavers. To whichever side she inclines herself, that will be the one to which she gives assent.
If, holding the spirit in contempt, she hearkens to the harlot
flesh, she is one body with it. [20] But if, spurning the flesh, she
rises to the spirit, she is transformed into spirit alone. To this
end accustom yourself to search yourself with care. Huge indeed
is the error of men who not rarely consider to be pure piety
what actually arises out of nature. Certain passions impose
themselves upon the unsuspecting, quite honorable in appearance, and as it were wearing the masks of virtues. . . .

Examine what this rule does. If one looks toward reputation,
or to gain, one is wise according to the flesh, not the spirit.
If one greatly indulges one's own nature, if one does what is
pleasing to the mind, one does not possess any reason for greatly
pleasing, nay, rather, one gives occasion for fear. Behold,
you are in danger. You pray, and judge one who does not pray.
You fast, and condemn your brother who is eating. Whoever
does not do what you do, you judge yourself better than he. [21]
Watch out lest your fasting pertain to the flesh. Your brother
needs your help, but you meanwhile mumble your little
prayers to God, pretending not to see your brother's need.
God will treat such prayers with disfavor. Why will God hear
you praying when you as a man do not hear a man?

Consider this also: You love your wife because she is your
wife, in name only. You do nothing great thereby, for you
and the pagans have this in common. Or you love her for no
other reason except for lustful pleasure. Your love tends
toward the flesh. But suppose you love her on account of this
most powerful fact that in her you have gazed upon the image
of Christ; then consider it piety, modesty, sobriety, chastity.

[20] I Cor. 6:16.
[21] Cf. Rom. 14:3.

Now you love not her in herself, but in Christ; indeed, you love Christ in her. So at last will you love spiritually. More of these matters, but in their proper place.

8. CERTAIN GENERAL RULES OF TRUE CHRISTIANITY

Now since we seem more or less to have shown the way to what has been proposed and, as it were, to have compared it to a sort of forest, we must hasten to what remains, lest this become, not a manual, but a huge tome. But we shall attempt briefly to put forward some rules as sort of wrestler's holds, by the application of which, just like the sons of Daedalus, you may easily be able to emerge from the errors of this world as if from a sort of inextricable labyrinth, and reach the pure light of spiritual life. Surely rules are not lacking to this discipline, and will the sole intention to live blessedly be aided by no precepts? It is, moreover, by all means a certain art and discipline of virtue which the Spirit, as promoter of holy efforts, infuses upon those who exercise themselves diligently therein. . . .

Now these rules will be taken partly from the person of God, of the devil, and of ourselves; partly from things, that is, virtues and vices, and what are joined to these; partly from the material of virtues and vices. These rules will conduce most powerfully against three evils, the remains of original sin. For even if baptism has wiped away the stain, yet some trace of the former disease persists in us, first for the guarding of humility, then for the substance and harvest of virtues. These are blindness, flesh, and infirmity. Blindness obscures the judgment of reason with a cloud of ignorance. For that purest light of the divine countenance which the Founder poured upon us,[22] after the guilt of the first parents somewhat obscured it, then corrupt upbringing, wicked intercourse, perverse passions, shadows of vices, habit of sinning, with such great rust enveloped it, that scarcely any trace of the divinely engraven law now appears. Therefore (as I began to say) blindness so acts that we are well-nigh blinded in our delight toward things, pursuing the worst instead of the best, placing the better things lower in our estimation than the less useful. The flesh incites the passions, so that, even if we know what is best, yet we will love things opposite. Infirmity so acts that we desert virtue once it has been snatched away, overcome as we are by boredom or temptation.

[22] Ps. 4:7, Vg.; 4:6, E.V.

Blindness obstructs judgment. The flesh corrupts the will. Infirmity shatters constancy.

The first thing, then, is for you to discern by investigation what things are to be shunned, and therefore blindness ought to be lifted, lest we wander mentally in the delight of things. The next task is for you to hate evil thoughts, love good ones; and in this the flesh ought to be conquered lest against the mind's better judgment we love things sweet instead of things salutary.The third is to persevere in things well begun. For this reason infirmity should be strengthened, that we may not more wickedly desert the way of virtue, than if we were not going to enter upon it. . . .

Against the Evil of Ignorance, the First Rule

But since faith is the sole door to Christ, the first rule ought to be that you rely upon Scripture to understand as well as possible concerning him and his Spirit. You should believe, not by the mouth alone, not coldly, not carelessly, not hesitatingly, as the generality of Christians does; but with all your heart fixed deep within and unmoved let your faith rest that there is not even one jot contained in the Scriptures [23] which does not greatly pertain to your salvation. Let nothing whatsoever move you because you see the better part of mankind so living as if heaven and hell were some sort of old wives' tales,[24] bugbears, or childish imaginings. But even though you believe, you will not make haste. And if to one the whole world be mad, the elements change, the angels revolt, the truth cannot lie; what God has foretold cannot fail to take place. If you believe that God exists, you must believe that he speaks the truth.

Thus straightway hold nothing to be so true, nothing so certain and undoubted of those things which you drink up with your ears, gaze openly upon with your eyes, touch with your hands, as what you read in Scripture which the will of heaven that is truth has inspired. The holy prophets made it known; the blood of many martyrs proved it; through the ages the agreement of pious men has subscribed to it; Christ himself in flesh and word has handed it down, and expressed it in his virtues; miracles have attested to it; and demons have confessed it,[25] for in the same degree do they believe as they fear it. Finally those things which are so becoming to symmetry

[23] Matt. 5:18.   [24] I Tim. 4:7.   [25] James 2:19.

of nature, which so agree among themselves, so also seize those who are attentive, so move and transform them. If these very great arguments agree in those matters alone, what evil, what madness is it, to hesitate in faith? Else let one make from past events a conjecture of future ones.

And how many incredible things of Christ were foretold by the words of the prophets! What of these has not taken place? Does God, who has not deceived in them, deceive in others? Finally, if the prophets did not lie, does Christ, the master of the prophets, lie? By these and like reasonings, if forthwith you arouse the flame of faith, and then ardently beseech God that he increase your faith,[26] I shall be amazed if you can be evil any longer. For who up till now is so wicked that he recoils not from vices, if only he deeply believe that by these momentary lusts, over and above that unhappy torture of a guilty mind, eternal torments are purchased? On the other hand, will not the pious in place of temporary and light vexations receive the hundredfold joys of a pure conscience, and, at the last, eternal life? [27]

Second Rule

If the first rule is to doubt nothing concerning the divine promises, then the next is to undertake the way of salvation, not with delay, not timidly, but with resolute purpose, with whole heart, with believing mind, and (so to speak) with the gladiator's pay, prepared to undergo loss either of property or of life for Christ's sake. "The sluggard wants, and doesn't want." [28] The Kingdom of Heaven belongs not to the lazy, but plainly rejoices to "suffer violence, and the violent bear it away." [29] When you hasten hither, let not the affection of loved ones hold you back, let not the allurements of the world recall you, let not domestic cares delay you. The shackles of worldly business are to be cut through, wherever they cannot be disentangled. Thus is Egypt to be forsaken, lest ever you should return in mind to the fleshpots.[30] Sodom must be forsaken quickly and at once, and it is not right to look back. . . . We are ordered to flee from Babylon,[31] not slowly and with delay to emigrate therefrom. See how many men are delaying from day to day, and hindering their flight from vices by counsels that are too slow. "When," they say, "I free myself from

26 Luke 17:5.   27 Matt. 19:29.   28 Prov. 13:4.
29 Matt. 11:12.   30 Ex. 16:3.   31 Cf. Jer. 50:8; 51:6.

these cares, when I finish this or that business." "Fool, what if today they should require your soul from you?" [32] Do you not know how business begets still other business? how vice invites vice? Why not rather do today what you should do earlier, for thus it will be easier to do? . . . Dare now to believe in Him with your whole heart, dare to distrust yourself, dare to lay your every care upon him, cease to lean upon yourself, and with full faith go forth from yourself unto him, and let him support you. . . .

Desire not to be divided among two, the world and Christ. "You cannot serve two masters." [33] "There is no agreement between God and Belial." [34] . . . God is too much a jealous lover of souls, and he desires to possess all for himself alone, which he has redeemed by his blood. [35] He suffers not fellowship with the devil, whom once he completely conquered by his death. Indeed there are two ways, one which through gratification of the passions leads to perdition, the other which through mortification of the flesh leads to life. [36] Which one do you hold fast unto yourself? There is no third way. Willy-nilly you must come to one or the other of these. Whoever you are, you ought to enter this path with skill, through which few mortal men walk. But Christ has trodden this path; since the beginning of the world men have trodden it, whosoever have been pleasing to God. This is indeed the inevitable necessity of Adrastean will. [37]

With Christ it is necessary for you to be crucified to the world, if you desire to live with Christ. [38] Why do we delude ourselves like fools? Why in a matter of such importance do we impose upon ourselves? One person says: "I am not a cleric; I am a dweller in the world. I cannot avoid making use of the world." Another thinks, "Even if I am a priest, I am not a monk;" he will see. And the monk finds how he may delude himself. "I am not so much a monk as such and such a one." Another says: "I am young, generous, rich, noble, even a prince. Nothing of what was said to the apostles applies to me." Poor man, does it therefore mean nothing to you for you to live in Christ? If you are in the world, you are not in Christ. If you mean by the world the earth, the sea, and this common air, and heaven, then everyone is in the world; but if you identify the world with ambition, delights, desire, lust—indeed, if you are a dweller in the world in this sense of the word, you are not

[32] Luke 12:20.   [33] Matt. 6:24; Luke 16:13.   [34] II Cor. 6:15.
[35] Cf. Rev. 5:9.   [36] Cf. Matt. 7:13f.   [37] Adagia, 2:6:38.   [38] Gal. 6:14.

a Christian. Christ has said to all men that he who does not bear his cross and follow in his steps is not worthy of him.[39] To die to the flesh with Christ means nothing to you, if to live by his Spirit is nothing to you. To be crucified to the world is nothing to you, if to live unto God is nothing to you. To be buried with Christ is nothing to you, if to rise again in glory is nothing to you. Christ's humility, poverty, tribulation, disregard of self, labors, agonies, sorrows, are nothing to you, if his Kingdom is nothing to you.[40]

What would be more wicked than to grant the reward to you in common with others, yet to cast the labors by which the reward is prepared upon a certain few? What would be more wanton than to wish to rule jointly with the Head, while you do not wish to suffer with him? Therefore, my brother, do not look around at what others do, and flatter yourself by comparison with them. To die unto sin, to die unto carnal desires, to die unto the world—this is indeed a hard thing and one known also to very few monks. And yet this is the common profession of all Christians. Once already in baptism you have sworn fealty to this. What can be more sacred or more religious than this vow? Either we must perish or, without exception, by this way proceed to salvation,

"Be we princes or needy husbandmen."[41]

But if it does not befall to all men to attain to perfect imitation of the Head, yet all must climb hither with hands and feet. He has a good part of Christianity who with certain mind has decided that he will become a Christian.

Third Rule

But lest you be deterred from the way of virtue by the fact that it is hard and sad, that it is necessary to renounce the conveniences of the world, that you must constantly fight against the three most wicked enemies, the flesh, the devil, and the world, let this third rule be set before you. The universal bugbears and apparitions, which immediately as it were rush upon you in the very jaws of hell, ought to be accounted as nothing, according to the example of Virgil's Aeneas.[42] But if, holding vain blandishments in contempt, you look at this thing more closely and fixedly, surely you will see that nothing else

39 Matt. 10:38.   40 Rom., ch. 6.
41 Horace, *Carmina*, 2:14:12.   42 Virgil, *Aeneid*, 6:236 ff.

is more favorable than the way of Christ, besides the fact that
it alone leads to happiness, even when consideration of reward
is left out.

What kind of life according to the world (I beg of you)
will you choose for yourself in which there are not very many
sad and hard things to be undergone and borne? Who unless he
be either inexperienced or surely very stupid does not realize
that the courtier's life is full of hardships? By the immortal
God, what's there but long and mean servitude that must
be endured to the end! With how great solicitude must the
grace of the prince be sought, must the favor of those who can
either harm or benefit be wooed! I recognize time and again the
appearance of feigning. The injuries inflicted by the stronger
must be spoken of in whispers. Indeed, what kind of evil is
there with which warfare is not crammed full? You can be
the best witness of either of these matters, for you have learned
both of them from your own danger. But now what does the
merchant neither do nor suffer,

"Fleeing poverty through sea, rocks, fire?" [43]

In marriage how great a weight of family cares, a misery that
they who are experiencing it do not see there? In public
duties that have to be met, how much anxiety, how much toil,
how much danger is there? Whatsoever you turn your gaze
upon, a huge crowd of misfortunes engulfs. The very life of
mortal men is beset with a thousand tribulations, which the
righteous and the wicked suffer in common. All these troubles
will for you serve to increase your merit if they discover you
in the way of Christ. But if not, nevertheless they must be borne,
both with greater trouble and no fruit. Those who fight for
the world: first how many years do they pant, sweat, rant?
Then for what fleeting nothings? Finally with what doubtful
hope? Add that in that direction there is no end of miseries;
the longer the labor has been, the more grievous it will be.
What is the end going to be of such an anxious, toilsome life?
Surely eternal punishment.

Go now and compare this life with the way of virtue,
which immediately ceases to be hard, becomes gradually
easier, becomes pleasant, through which with surest hope one
proceeds to the highest good. Would it not be as utter insanity
to prepare with equal toil for eternal death as for eternal
life? Yet do not they who prefer with the greatest labors to

[43] Horace, Epistles, 1:1:46.

go to everlasting labors act even more foolishly than those who, with moderate labors, prefer to go to everlasting rest? To these things, if the way of piety is much more toilsome than that of the world, yet this roughness of labor is smoothed by the hope of reward, nor is the divine anointment lacking which causes gall to turn to honey.[44] . . . What does Christ say? "Take my yoke upon you, and you will find rest for your souls. For my yoke is easy and my burden light." [45] In the highest things no pleasure is lacking where a peaceful conscience is present. No misery is absent where an unhappy conscience tortures. It is clear, then, that these facts are more than certain. But if there is doubt, even so take counsel with those who once turned to the Lord from the midst of Babylon,[46] and at least believe their experience: that nothing is more turbulent and unhappy than vices, nothing more advantageous and happy than virtue.

But act, make equal pay for equal labors. Yet how much more desirable is it to fight under the standards of Christ than under the banners of the devil? Nay, how much more desirable is it to suffer with Christ than to abound in delights with the devil? Now it will not be possible, will it, for even the most wicked, the hardest, and the most deceitful man to flee from God by veils and horses? The devil exacts such a wicked price, promises such futile things, and thus not rarely tricks the miserable ones. Or if he exceeds this, he ruins where he pleases, so that they lose their possessions by an illness greater than the labor by which they produced them. The merchant has mixed up right and wrong in his zeal for amassing property and has exposed reputation, life, soul to a thousand dangers. If indeed the dice of fortune should fall favorably, what else finally has he prepared for himself but the substance of miserable anxiety, to keep as a punishment if he loses? But if fortune is unfavorable, what is left but to become doubly miserable, both because he has been tricked out of the thing hoped for and because he remembers, not without pain, the complete exhaustion of his fruitless labor? No one struggles with certain purpose toward a good mind who does not reach his goal. "As Christ is not mocked, neither does he mock." [47]

Consider, when you flee from the world to Christ, that you do not give it up, if the world has for you anything attractive, but that you exchange lighter things for better ones. . . .

44 Cf. Plautus, *Cistellaria*, 1:1:69f.   45 Matt. 11:29f.
46 Lam., ch. 5.   47 Cf. Gal. 6:7.

Therefore do you hesitate to take hold of this way and to give up that one, even though the comparison is so evil—nay, so nonexistent—of God to the devil, of hope to hope, of reward to reward, of toil to toil, of solace to solace?

Fourth Rule

But that with a more certain course you may be able to strive toward happiness, let this be your fourth rule, that you set before you Christ as the only goal of your whole life, to whom alone you dedicate all zeal, all efforts, all leisure and business. Indeed, think of Christ not as an empty word, but as nothing else than love, simplicity, patience, purity—in short, whatsoever he has taught. Know the devil to be nothing else than whatsoever calls one away from those virtues. He who is impelled toward virtue alone advances toward Christ. He who is a slave to vices shackles himself to the devil. "Therefore when your eye is single, your whole body will be full of light." [48] Let it gaze toward Christ alone, your sole and highest good, so that you may love nothing, be in awe of nothing, seek after nothing, other than Christ himself, or for Christ's sake. Hate nothing, tremble at nothing, flee nothing, other than wickedness, or for the sake of wickedness. It will so come to pass that whatever you do, whether you are asleep or awake, [49] whether you are eating or drinking, finally your sports and leisure—let me speak more boldly—nay, also certain lighter vices, into which we sometimes fall as we hasten toward virtue, all these things will serve to increase your reward. . . .

The order of these things is virtually threefold. For certain things are so wicked that they cannot be honest—for example, to avenge an injury, to wish ill to a man. These are ever to be eschewed, however great may be the proposed pay or punishment. For there is nothing that can harm a good man except wickedness. Certain things, on the contrary, are so honest that they cannot be wicked. They are things of this kind: to wish well to all men, to help friends with honest reasonings, to hate vices, to rejoice in godly conversation. Some are mediate, such as health, beauty, strength, eloquence, learning, and such like. Of this type of thing nothing ought to be sought on its own account, nor ought they to be turned to either more or less, unless they conduce to some extent to the highest goal. . . .

But those things which are intermediate—not all in the

[48] Matt. 6:22; Luke 11:34.   [49] I Thess. 5:10.

same way—either help or hinder those going toward Christ. Hence, at the very moment they come to hand, they should be accepted or rejected. Knowledge provides more of a help toward godliness than does beauty, or strength of body, or wealth. And even though all learning can be referred to Christ, yet one way is more especially conducive than another.

From this end the usefulness or unusefulness of all means is to be measured. You love letters. Rightly, if for Christ's sake. But if you love them only that you may know, you have stopped at a point from which you ought to take a further step. But if you seek letters, that, aided by them, you may more clearly perceive Christ shining forth in sacred letters, that you may love him seen, that you may communicate him known and loved, or that you may enjoy him, then prepare yourself for the study of letters.[50] But not beyond what you think will be useful for a good mind. . . . It is better to be less wise and to love more than to be wiser and not love.

Therefore knowledge obtains the chief place among means; then come health, gifts of nature, eloquence, beauty, strength, rank, favor, authority, prosperity, reputation, birth, friends, family possessions. Whatever one of these will lead by the nearest course to virtue should be in the highest degree applied to ourselves, but only if they present themselves to us as we hurry along our way. But if not, one should not turn aside from the proposed course for the sake of these things. Suppose money comes your way: if it in no wise hinders you from a good mind, use it, prepare for yourself friends out of the mammon of wickedness. But if you fear the loss of a good mind, contemn filthy lucre, and, to imitate Crates the Theban, throw your heavy bundle into the sea rather than let it hold you back from Christ.[51] That will be easier for you to do if, just as we have said, you accustom yourself to admiring none of those things which are outside yourself, that is, which do not pertain to the inner man. It will so happen that you may not grow arrogant if these things should befall, nor be troubled in mind if they should either be denied or snatched away; surely, then, you should measure your happiness by Christ alone. But if they should happen apart from your effort, be more anxious, not more secure, pondering the fact that the means of exercising

---

50 Erasmus' discussion of the value of literary study in perfecting the Christian life comes principally from Augustine, *De doctrina Christiana*, 2:40, *PL*, 34:55.
51 Diogenes Laertius, 6:87; cf. Philostratus, *Vita Apollonii* 1:13.

virtue has been divinely given to you, but it is dangerous. But
if you hold fortune's kindliness in suspicion, imitate Prometheus. Do not take the unhappy box;[52] unencumbered and
bare, strive for that one and only good.

Those who seek money as a great thing, with immense
solicitude, and upon it establish the especial defense of life,
who think themselves blessed when their money is safe and
sound, who cry that they are miserable when it passes away—
such persons have fashioned for themselves too many gods.
You put money on a plane equal to Christ, if it can render you
happy or unhappy. What I have said concerning money, you
can apply to honors, pleasures, health—to the very life of the
body itself.

With such great ardor is it fitting for us to strive on to Christ
alone as our goal, that there will be no time to take care of any
of these things, either when they are given or when they are
taken away. As the apostle says, "The time is short; it remains
that they who enjoy this world be as if not enjoying it." [53]
I know the world laughs at this mind as foolish and insane,
but through this foolishness alone it has pleased God to make
safe those who believe.[54] "For that which appears foolish of God
is wiser than men." [55] Whatsoever you do, you will judge by
this rule. You will practice art rightly, if without fraud. But
whither do you look? That you may sustain your family. Yet
to what end? That you may win it to Christ? You hasten with
good reason. You fast—indeed a pious action in appearance.[56]
But to what do you refer your fasting? That you may save
food, or that you may consider yourself more religious? Your
eye is wretched. Yet you fast so as not to contract disease.
Why do you fear disease? Lest it deprive you of the enjoyment
of pleasure? Your eye is vicious. But you wish to be strong
that you may have sufficient zeal. But to what do you refer
your zeal? That you may appear to yourself as somewhat of a
priest. With what purpose do you seek the priesthood? Surely
you live for yourself, not for Christ. You have wandered from
the standard which it is fitting for a Christian to have fixed

[52] Hesiod, *Works and Days*, 5:83–89.   [53] I Cor. 7:29, 31.
[54] I Cor. 1:21.   [55] I Cor. 1:25.
[56] Of this Bataillon, 225n., says: "The opinion of Erasmus concerning
fasts and abstinences, expressed in distinct forms and with divers contexts
in innumerable passages of his works, caused great scandal and was one
of the points of attack congenial to his attackers." Cf. the Letter to
Volz (Allen, III, 858; 370, 373). See also *De interdictu esu carnium*, Opera
IX, cols. 1197–1214.

before him everywhere. You consume food, that you may be strong in body. But you wish to be strong in body for the reason that you may fulfill sacred studies, sacred vigils. You have attained your goal. You watch your health lest you become more ugly, lest you not suffice for lustful desire; you cut yourself off from Christ, making another god for yourself.

There are those who worship certain saints with certain ceremonies.[57] One person salutes Christopher each day, but not unless his image is visible. For what, then, is he looking? Surely for this reason, that he may persuade him to keep himself safe from evil death that day. Another adores one Roch, but why? Another mumbles certain little prayers to Barbara to keep the plague away, or to George, that he may not fall into the hands of the enemy. This one fasts for Apollo, that his teeth may not ache. That one visits the statue of the blessed Job, to prevent boils. Some assign a certain portion of their income to the poor, so that their merchandise will not be destroyed by shipwreck. A candle is burned to Hiero, that goods which have been lost may be recovered. To sum up, for everything we fear or desire, we set up a corresponding deity. And each nation has its own: among the Gauls, Paul is valued, while among us Hiero, and in such and such a place either James or John is held in esteem. This worship, if it may not, out of regard to bodily pains and pleasures, be referred to Christ, for that reason is not Christian because they are not free of the superstition of those who were wont to pledge a tenth part of their goods to Hercules in order to grow rich, or a cock to Aesculapius to recover from illness, or who were wont to sacrifice a bull to Neptune that they might sail without mishap. The names indeed are changed but both have a common end.[58]

You pray God that a premature death may not overtake you; and do not rather pray that he grant a better mind to you, that at whatever place death overtakes you, it will not catch you unawares. You do not think of changing life, and ask God that you may not die. Why, therefore, do you pray? Doubtless that you may sin as long as possible. You pray for goods and know not how to use godly things. Are you not praying for your own ruin? You pray for good health, and you

---

[57] Cf. *Praise of Folly*, tr. Hudson, 56 f.
[58] The passage beginning with "There are those who worship certain saints with certain ceremonies," and ending at this point, was included in the *Index expurgatorius* published at Antwerp (1571) 89 [Bataillon, 228].

abuse it: is not your piety impious? . . . I do not damn so much those who do these things with a simple sort of superstition as I do those who seek their own reward; they bring forth those things which perchance are tolerable in place of the highest and purest godliness, and for their advantage they encourage the ignorance of the masses, which I do not utterly contemn, but I will not bear the fact that they esteem middle things in place of the highest, least in place of greatest.

I shall praise them for seeking an unblemished life from Roch if they consecrate that life to Christ. But I shall praise them more if they pray nothing else than that love of virtue be increased along with hatred of vice. Of dying and living, let them give such matters into God's hands, and let them say with Paul, "For whether we live, we live unto the Lord; and whether we die, we die unto the Lord." [59] It will be perfect if they desire to be dissolved and to be with Christ; if they, in disease, loss, and other hardships of fortune, establish their glory and joy, because they are held worthy, who are conformed in this manner to their Head.[60] Therefore to do things of this sort is not so much to be reprehended as it is dangerous to persist in them and to rely upon them. I bear infirmity, but with Paul [61] I show forth a more excellent way.... If you will search diligently all your studies and actions, will you ever stop midway until you have reached even to Christ?...

Fifth Rule

Let us add likewise a fifth, subsidiary rule to this, that in this one respect you maintain perfect piety, if you try always to press on from visible things, which are for the most part either imperfect or intermediate, to things invisible, in accordance with the higher part of man. This precept pertains to the matter to such an extent that either by neglect of it or ignorance very many Christians are superstitious rather than godly, and, except for the name of Christ, are not very far away from the superstition of pagans.

Let us suppose, therefore, that there are two worlds, the one intelligible, the other visible. The intelligible (also called angelic) world is the one in which God dwells with the blessed minds; the visible world is the heavenly spheres and what is included in them. Then man, as it were, inhabits a third world as participant in both, the visible according to the body, the

[59] Rom. 14:8.   [60] Phil. 1:23.   [61] I Cor. 12:31.

invisible according to the soul. In the visible world, since we are
wayfarers therein, we ought never to be at rest, but whatever
appears to the senses, we should refer, with a certain suitable
comparison, either to the angelic world or (what is more
useful) to morals, and to its corresponding part in man. What
the sun visible here is in the visible world, that the divine mind
is in the intelligible world, and in your part corresponding to
it, namely, spirit. What is there, the moon, is in that assembly
of angels and of pious souls called the "Church Triumphant";
and in you, "spirit." Whatever the upper world does in the
world subject to it this God does in your soul. The sun sets,
rises, gives heat, tempers, quickens, produces, matures, attracts,
prolongs, purges, hardens, softens, illuminates, brightens,
gladdens. Therefore whatever you see in it; nay, whatever in
this grosser world, which is established out of elements, which
some have distinguished from the rest; finally, whatever you
see in the grosser part of yourself, may you accustom yourself
to refer this to God, and to your own invisible part. It will
so come to pass that whatever will in any way cast itself before
your senses will for you become the occasion of piety.

Since as often as this visible sun with new light pours itself
upon the earth it delights the bodily eyes, straightway consider
what that pleasure of the heavenly beings is for whom that
eternal Sun ever rises, never sets; how much that joy of the
pure mind is which the divine light shines upon. And when the
visible creation warns, pray in Paul's words that "He who
commands the light to shine forth upon the darkness may shine
in your heart, to give the light of the knowledge of the glory
of God, in the face of Jesus Christ." [62] Repeat passages like these
from the Holy Scriptures in which, here and there, the grace
of the divine Spirit is compared to light. Night seems sad and
abominable to you. Think of the soul destitute of divine light
and blinded by vices. And if within yourself you discover
anything of night, pray that the Sun of righteousness may rise
upon you.[63] So think that there are some invisible things, in
comparison with which things seen are scarcely even shadows,
representing to the eyes only a faint image of the former. Just
as the senses either strive after or bristle at something in
corporeal matters, in like manner it is even more fitting in inner
matters for the spirit to love or to hate. The suitable appearance
of the body is pleasing to the eyes: think what a noble thing the
appearance of the soul should be! Any deformed countenance

[62] II Cor. 4:6.   [63] Mal. 4:2.

appears unpleasant: remember what an odious thing a mind corrupted by vices is! And do the same concerning the remainder. For the soul possesses a certain charm or deformity which pleases respectively God and the devil; like to like; so does it also possess its own sort of youth, old age, disease, health, death, life, poverty, wealth, pleasure, pain, war, peace, cold, heat, thirst, drink, hunger, food. . . .

Now the apostle Paul opened certain fountains of allegory after Christ. Origen follows him, and in this part of theology easily obtains the principal place. But our theologians either almost despise allegory or actually treat it coldly, for they are either equal or superior to the ancients in the sharpness of their disputation. They ought not to be compared with the ancients [64] especially for two reasons as I contend: first, that the mystery, unseasoned by those powers of eloquence and charm of speaking in which the ancients excelled but we do not achieve, cannot fail to be regarded coldly. The other is that they, content with Aristotle alone, keep the Platonists and the Pythagoreans away from the games. Yet Augustine prefers these latter, not only because they have so many conceptions appropriate to our religion, but also because the very kind of figurative language itself, as I have said, abounding with allegories, more closely approaches the words of Holy Scripture. [65] It is not therefore astonishing if they who were able to enrich and deck out in flowing speech anything whatever—even lean and cold subjects—treat allegory more appropriately. Then the most learned folk of all antiquity were once wont to study in the poets and the Platonic books what was to be done in the divine mysteries. [66] Therefore I prefer that you read the commentaries of these writers, in order that I may lead you, not to scholastic disputation, but to a good mind.

But if you do not pursue the mystery, yet you will remember that there lies concealed within what at least is preferable to hope for unknown, than to find repose in the killing letter. [67] Nor is that only in the Old Testament, but also in the New.

[64] Cf. *Ratio verae theologiae*, Opera V, cols. 82f. For attacks on Scholastic theologians, see *Praise of Folly*, tr. Hudson, 77–85. See also Opera IX, cols. 80f., 917ff., 917–920.

[65] Cf. Augustine, *City of God*, 8.5ff., *PL*, 41:229ff.

[66] "The necessity for the study of rhetoric for the knowledge of the Scriptures and the preference which is given to the ancient theologians over the modern scholastics are ideas frequently repeated in Erasmus." Cf. *Ratio verae theologiae*, Opera V, cols. 75–138, esp. 80–82 [Bataillon, 246].   [67] II Cor. 3:6.

The gospel has its flesh and its spirit. For even if the veil was drawn away from the face of Moses,[68] nevertheless Paul sees through a glass and in an enigma,[69] and, according to John, Christ himself said, "The flesh profits nothing; it is the spirit that quickens."[70] To me it would have been religion to say that the expression "It profits nothing" was true enough of future events; yet for the present the flesh profits somewhat, but the spirit much more fully. Now the Truth said, "Profits nothing." And so it does not profit, for, according to Paul, the flesh is fatal unless it be referred to the spirit.[71] In other respects this flesh is useful in that it leads infirmity, as it were, gradually to the Spirit. The body cannot subsist without the spirit; the spirit needs nothing from the body. But if, with Christ as author, the spirit is such a great thing that it alone quickens,[72] we ought to tend in this direction, that in all letters, all acts, we respect the spirit, not the flesh. And if anyone will observe, he will notice that this is the one thing by which Isaiah, renowned among the prophets, calls us. Likewise Paul, among the apostles, in almost all of his letters, teaches the lesson that no confidence is to be placed in the flesh, but that in the spirit there is life, liberty, light, adoption, and those prized fruits which he enumerates.[73] Everywhere he contemns the flesh, condemns it, resists it. Attend, and you will discover by and by that our preceptor Jesus does this very thing. In lifting the ass from the pit,[74] in making the blind man see,[75] in picking corn,[76] in unwashed hands,[77] in eating with sinners,[78] in the parable of the Pharisee and the Publican,[79] in fasts,[80] in brothers according to the flesh,[81] in the boasting of the Jews because they are the sons of Abraham,[82] in gifts that are to be offered,[83] in prayers,[84] in broadened phylacteries,[85] and in many similar passages, he contemns the flesh of the law and the superstition of those who preferred to be Jews in the open rather than in secret. And when Jesus said to the Samaritan woman: "Woman, believe me, the hour is coming, when you shall neither on this mountain nor in Jerusalem adore the Father. But the hour is coming, and now is, when the true adorer shall adore the Father in spirit and in truth. For the Father also seeks such to

[68] Ex. 34:33; II Cor. 3:13ff. [69] I Cor. 13:12.
[70] John 6:64, Vg.; 6:63, E.V. [71] Cf. Rom. 8:6. [72] Cf. Rom. 8:11.
[73] Cf. Rom. 8:15. [74] Luke 14:5. [75] John 9:1. ff
[76] Matt. 12:1; Luke 6:1. [77] Matt. 15:20. [78] Matt. 9:10ff.
[79] Luke 18:10ff. [80] Matt. 9:14ff. [81] Matt. 12:46ff.
[82] Matt. 3:9. [83] Matt. 5:23f. [84] Matt. 6:5ff.
[85] Matt. 23:5.

adore him. God is a Spirit; and they that adore him, must adore him in spirit and in truth." [86] He meant the same thing by his act, when at the marriage feast he turned the water of the cold and insipid letter into the wine of the spirit, even to the contempt of life, inebriating the spiritual souls. [87] And think not that Christ holds these things in contempt which we have just recalled. Surely he had contempt for the eating of his flesh and the drinking of his blood, unless they be eaten and drunk in a spiritual manner. For whom do you think he spoke these words: "The flesh profits nothing; it is the Spirit that quickens"? [88] Surely not for those who think themselves safe from all evil by a gospel or a copper cross hanging from the neck, and consider *that* perfect religion, but for those to whom appeared the highest mystery of taking his body.

If such a great thing is nothing, nay, if it is pernicious, why should we have faith in any other carnal things unless the Spirit be present? Perhaps you sacrifice daily, and live for yourself alone, without having any concern for your neighbor's troubles. Then you are still in the flesh of the sacrament. But if in your sacrificing you give heed to what that taking of the sacrament means, surely the spirit is one and the same with Christ's Spirit; the body is a living member of the Church, identical with the body of Christ. If you love nothing except in Christ, if you think all your goods to be common to all, if the troubles of all men weigh upon you as much as your own—then you sacrifice with great fruit, and certainly in a spiritual manner.

If you feel yourself to be in some manner transfigured in Christ, and now less and less living in yourself, give thanks to the Spirit, who alone can quicken. Many are wont to count how much they frequent divine service everyday, and rely as it were wholly upon this thing; as if now they owe nothing further to Christ, when, having left the temples, they return to their former habits. [89] I praise them for embracing the flesh of piety, but I do not praise them for stopping at that point. Let what there is represented to the eyes take place within you. The death of the Head is represented. Examine yourself within your breast, [90] as they say, how near you are

---

86 John 4:21, 23f.
87 John 2:7. Cf. Gregory the Great, *Homilia in Ezechielem*, 6:7, *PL*,76: 831.
88 John 6:64,Vg.; 6:63, E.V.
89 Cf. *Coll.*, "The Youth's Piety," tr. N. Bailey, 51f. Cf. also *De amabile ecclesiae concordia*, Opera V, cols. 502–504 [Bataillon, 250].
90 The Latin has, "*Excute te intus in sinu, quod aiunt. . . ,*" a reminiscence

to being dead to the world. But if anger, ambition, greed, pleasure, envy, are in full possession of you, even if you take hold of the altar, you are yet far from holiness. Christ has been slain in your behalf; sacrifice also these animals; sacrifice yourself to him who once for you immolated himself unto the Father. If, indeed, you do not think upon these things, and have faith in him, God will hate your flabby and gross religion. You have been baptized, but think not that you are straightway a Christian. The whole mind savors of nothing except the world. You are openly a Christian, but in secret a Gentile of the Gentiles. Why so? Because you grasp the body of the sacrament; you are empty of the spirit. Do you wash the body while the soul remains in wickedness? The flesh is touched with salt: what then, if the mind remains unsalted? The body is anointed, yet the mind remains unanointed. But if you are buried with Christ within, and already practice walking with him in newness of life,[91] I acknowledge you as a Christian. You are sprinkled with consecrated water. Whither does it lead you when you do not cleanse inner filth from your mind? You venerate saints; you are glad to touch their relics. But you contemn what good they have left, namely the example of a pure life. No worship of Mary is more gracious than if you imitate Mary's humility. No devotion to the saints is more acceptable and more proper than if you strive to express their virtue. You wish to deserve well of Peter and Paul? Imitate the faith of one, the charity of the other—and you will hereby do more than if you were to dash back and forth to Rome ten times. You wish to do Francis the highest honor? You are elated; you are an admirer of money; you are contentious. Give away this wealth, restrain your inclinations, and, after the example of Francis, be more modest, contemn sordid gain, and gaze with eagerness upon the goods of the mind. Give up contention, and overcome evil with good.[92] The divine One will make more of this honor than if you were to light a hundred candles for him. Do you account it a great thing if, wrapped up in Francis' cowl, you are carried into the tomb? Like clothing will bestow no benefit upon you in death if your morals were unlike his in life. And although an example of universal piety be sought most fittingly from Christ, yet if the worship of Christ in his

of Neh. 5:13 (cf. Acts 18:6): *"Insuper excussi sinum meum. . . ,"* which is translated, "Shake out my lap." Erasmus is punning on the double meanings of *excutio* and *sinus*.
[91] Cf. Rom. 6:4.   [92] Rom. 12:21.

A.O.R.—22

saints delights you very much, imitate Christ in the saints, and
to the honor of each one change one vice, or be zealous to embrace a particular virtue. If this happens, I will not disapprove
those things which are now done in public.

You may embrace the ashes of Paul with the highest veneration—I don't condemn it—if your religion conforms to his.
If, however, you venerate dead, dumb ashes, and neglect his
living image, which shines forth, speaking and even breathing,
in Scripture, is your religion not a preposterous thing? You
worship the bones of Paul, preserved in nooks and niches, but
you do not worship the mind of Paul, hidden in Scripture? You
make much of a fragment of a body, seen through glass, yet
you do not marvel at the whole mind of Paul, shining through
Scripture? You worship ashes, to which the vices of the body
are ever reduced; why not rather worship the Scriptures, by
which the vices of souls are cured? Let the faithful wonder
at these signs, to whom they have been given. You will faithfully reflect upon His books, that, not doubting that God can
do all things, you may learn to love him above all else. You
give homage to the image of Christ's countenance, delineated
in stone or wood, or painted in colors;[93] much more religiously
ought you to honor the image of his mind, which the Holy
Spirit as artificer expressed in the words of the gospel. . . .

You gaze in dumb amazement at the tunic or sweat cloth
reputedly Christ's, yet half asleep you read the utterances of
Christ?[94] You believe it to be much more important that you
possess a small piece of the cross in your house. Yet this latter is
nothing in comparison with bearing the mystery of the cross
fixed in your breast. Otherwise, if these things make one religious, what is more religious than the Jews, of whom very
many were exceedingly impious, yet they saw Jesus living in
the flesh; they heard him with their ears; they touched him
with their hands? What did Judas do more happily, who
pressed the divine mouth with his own?[95] Without the spirit
the flesh cannot be of any benefit: indeed nothing of the Master
would have been of any benefit to the Virgin, because she bore
him from her flesh, unless also in the spirit she had conceived
his Spirit.

[93] Cf. *Modus orandi*, Opera V, col. 1121; see also Opera X, col. 1770
[Bataillon, 254].
[94] *Coll.*, tr. Bailey, "The Religious Pilgrimage," 244. See also Opera IX,
col. 1161 [Bataillon 255].
[95] Luke 22:47f.; cf. John 6:64, Vg.; 6:63, E.V.

This is very great, but hear something greater. Do you not read how foolish were the apostles, how grossly material was their wisdom, so long as they were enjoying the bodily fellowship of Christ? Who desired anything else for complete salvation than one so everlasting in his divinity and at the same time conquered in his humanity? And yet after sublime miracles, after teaching for so many years, expressed from the divine mouth, after so many proofs of resurrection, does he not at the last hour, as he is about to be received into heaven, prove to them their unbelief?[96]

What, then, is the cause? Surely the flesh of Christ stood in the way, and hence it is that he says, "If I go not, the Paraclete will not come to you; it is expedient for you that I go."[97] When the corporeal presence of Christ is useless to salvation, should we then dare to establish perfect piety in any corporeal thing? Paul had seen Christ in the flesh. What do you consider greater than this? Yet he contemns it, saying, "And if we have known Christ according to the flesh, but now we know him so no longer."[98] Wherefore did he not know? Because he had made progress toward the better graces of the spirit.

Perhaps I am arguing this thing more verbosely than is fitting to Him who taught the rules. But I am doing it more carefully, not without weighty cause, because by this very thing I know full well that this error is the common plague of all Christianity, which brings about a ruin even greater than this, because in appearance it is closest to godliness. . . .

On account of their ignorant superstition, or feigned piety, I ought the more frequently to witness, that I reproach not at all the bodily ceremonies of Christians, and the study of simple things, especially those which ecclesiastical authority has approved. For they are ever signs, supports of piety. These are quite necessary to children in Christ,[99] until they have advanced and arrived at the perfect man, yet it is not fitting that they be scorned by perfect men, lest by their example harm be done to the infirm. I approve what you do, if only its end be not vicious, if you do not set your goal there, when your steps should be directed to ends more proper to salvation. But to worship Christ in things visible,[1] for the sake of things visible, and in

---

[96] Mark 16:14.   [97] John 16:7.   [98] II Cor. 5:16.   [99] Cf. I Cor. 3:1.
[1] From "But to worship Christ in things visible . . ." to the end of the Fifth Rule was proscribed by the *Index expurgatorius*, Antwerp (1571) 89. Cf. Opera X, col. 1819 [Bataillon, 258].

these to place the highest part of religion, hence to please
oneself and damn others, to become stupid by these things and
then to die in them, and (as I once said) by these visible things
to be called away from Christ, which are really intended to
lead to him—this is certainly to revolt from the law of the gospel
which is spiritual and to sink back into a sort of Judaism,[2] perhaps no less dangerous than, without this superstition, to toil
in great and open vices of the mind. The latter disease indeed
is more dangerous. So it is, but the former is more unhealthful.
How copiously did that noble defender of the Spirit, Paul,
sweat, that he might move the Jews, taken away from faith in
works, to those things that are spiritual! And I see the generality
of Christians having revolved anew to this point. Why did I
say "generality"? It must be admitted that a good part of
both priests and doctors—and, of course, their flocks—who
profess the spiritual life in word and rite, are almost wholly
occupied by this error. If the salt be unsalted, whence will
the others be salted? I am ashamed to make reference to how
superstitiously very many of those folk observe foolish little
ceremonies,[3] instituted by mere men, yet not with this purpose
in mind; how hatefully they lash at the same sort of rites conceived by others; with how much security they put their trust in
these; with what great rashness they judge others; with what
great contention they protect themselves. When they have
done these things, do they think heaven belongs to them?
When they have become calloused in those actions, now do
they fancy themselves Pauls and Anthonys?[4] They begin
with great superciliousness to lay blame upon the life of another,
in accordance with that rule of the unlearned (as the comic
poet says), that they think nothing right except what they
themselves do.[5] Otherwise, when they have become old in
their habits, you will see them not yet savoring of Christ.
But they are like animals, reeking with various miserable vices,

2 "This idea, bound by Erasmus intimately with the Pauline teachings on
   the supremacy of the spirit, is the center and point of departure of the
   Christian philosophy of the *Enchiridion*, and is expressed in innumerable
   places in his works. . . . His opinions concerning the old law and his
   charge of Judaism against the Christianity of his age are embodied in
   various polemics." Cf. Opera IX, *passim*, and especially cols. 853–863,
   889–892 [Bataillon, 258].
3 *Ceremoniolas.* The criticism of external ceremonies (see also the Eighth
   Rule) is one of Erasmus' favorite topics and the occasion of innumerable
   polemics. Cf. Opera V, col. 113; IX, cols. 368, 382, 390, 1088f.,
   1152–1154, 1772, etc.
4 Cf. *Praise of Folly*, tr. Hudson, 93.   5 Terence, *Adelphi*, 98f.

morose in social intercourse, and scarcely bearable even to themselves. They are cold in charity, hot in anger, persistent in hatred, virulent in speech, unbridled in exercising jealousies. They are ready to struggle ever so much for mere vanity. They are foreign to the perfection of Christ. All this that they may not rob themselves of the common virtues which either natural reason or habits of life, or philosophers' precepts, impart to the Gentiles as well! Unruly, intractable, contentious, greedy for pleasures, inclined to vomit at divine words, agreeable to no one, evilly suspicious of others, flattering to themselves! Do so many years of labors finally end in this, that you are actually the worst and seem to yourself the best of men, that instead of a Christian you are a Jew, serving so much the dumb elements that you consider glory not to be in secret in God's presence, [6] but in the open among men? But if you have walked in the spirit, not in the flesh, [7] where are the fruits of the spirit? Where is charity? Where is joy of mind? Where is peace toward all men? Where is patience, long-suffering, goodness, kindness, gentleness, faith, modesty, continence, chastity? [8] Where is the image of Christ in your morals? . . . Surely you are one transgressing God's commandments on account of foolish man-made traditions. [9] Or is Christianity not the spiritual life? Hear Paul speaking to the Romans: "There is therefore no condemnation to them who are in Christ Jesus, who walk not according to the flesh. For the law of the spirit of life in Christ Jesus has delivered me from the law of sin and death. For what the law could not do in that it was weak through the flesh God, sending his own Son in the likeness of sinful flesh even of sin, condemned sin in the flesh, that the justification of the law might be fulfilled in us, who walk not according to the flesh, but according to the spirit. For they who are according to the flesh relish the things that are of the flesh; but they who are of the spirit, mind the things that are of the spirit. For the

6 Matt. 6:1 ff.   7 Rom. 8:1, 4.   8 Gal. 5:22f.

9 "There are many passages in which Erasmus criticizes those who, according to him, prefer human constitutions (rules of religious orders—to these he refers—episcopal constitutions, etc.) to the pure gospel teaching. This theme is repeated in distinct forms, and becomes intimately united with that of ceremonies in general, fasts and abstinences, clothing, celibacy, feast days, etc." See, for example, Letter to Volz (Allen, III, 373); cf. also Opera IX, cols. 1674, 1108; V, col. 107, etc. "It was natural that this theme so frequently, so distinctly, so fluctuatingly (as ever) treated by Erasmus, was the rock of offense of his attackers, and occupied a good part of almost all the polemics" [Bataillon, 262].

wisdom of the flesh is death; but the wisdom of the spirit is life and peace. Because the wisdom of the flesh is an enemy to God, for it is not subject to the law of God, neither can it be. And they who are in the flesh cannot please God." [10] What could be said more fully? What more aptly?

But men think that these things do not pertain to them at all. Deceived by their own vices, hastening to enjoy alien pleasures, they refer what Paul said about walking according to the flesh [11] solely to adulterers and fornicators; what he said concerning the wisdom of the flesh [12] (which is inimical to God) they twist into those who study secular literature (as they call it). They applaud themselves in both respects: that they are not adulterers, and are egregiously unlearned in all letters. On the other hand, to live in the spirit [13] they fancy to be nothing else than to do just what they themselves are doing. If these folk had observed Paul's language as diligently as they forcibly condemn Cicero's, [14] they would certainly have known only too well that the apostle calls "flesh" that which is visible, "spirit" that which is invisible. Indeed, he teaches that visible things ought everywhere to serve invisible, not the opposite. Preposterously you accommodate Christ to these things which really ought to be adapted to him. Or do you fiercely demand that the testimony, the word of the flesh, not pertain so much to lust or lechery? Listen to what the same apostle, acting as is his wont, writes to the Colossians: "Let no man seduce you, willing in humility and religion of angels, walking in the things he has not seen, in vain puffed up by the sense of his flesh, and not holding the Head, that is, Christ, from which all the body, by joints and bands being supplied with nourishment and compacted, grows unto the increase of God." [15] And lest you doubt that he speaks of those who, relying on certain bodily ceremonies, cry out against the spiritual zeal of others, attend what follows: "If then you be dead with Christ from the elements of this world, why do you yet decree as though living in the world?" [16] From these, therefore, calling us away a little later, he says, "Therefore if you be raised with Christ, seek the things that are above where Christ is sitting at the right hand of God; be wise in those things which are above, not in those things which are upon the earth." [17] Then, teaching precepts of the spiritual life, what

[10] Rom. 8:1-8.   [11] Rom. 8:1, 4.   [12] II Cor. 1:12.   [13] Gal. 5:25.
[14] Cf. *Praise of Folly*, tr. Hudson, 85. See also *Antib. lib.*, Opera IX, cols. 1711f. [Bataillon, 265].   [15] Col. 2:18f.   [16] Col. 2:20.   [17] Col. 3:1f.

final warning does he give? Surely not that we use such and such ceremonies? Surely not that we be clothed in such and such a manner? that we feed upon such and such foods? that we weary ourselves with so many psalms? None of these. What then? He says, "Mortify your members, which are upon the earth: fornication, uncleanness, lust, evil desire, and avarice, which mean enslavement to idols." [18] A little later he says, "Now likewise cast off all anger, indignation, malice." [19] Further on: "Strip off the old man, with his actions, and put on the new, him who is renewed in the knowledge of God, according to the image of Him who created him." [20] But who is the old man? To be sure, that Adam of the earth, earthly, whose conversation is upon the earth, not in heaven. [21] . . .

I shall not tarry over the fact that you do not omit vigils, fastings, silence, little prayers, and other observances of that sort. I shall not believe that you are in the Spirit, unless I see the fruits of the Spirit. Why shouldn't I affirm that you are in the flesh, when, after almost secular practice in these things, the works of the flesh, you have as yet to restrain them in yourself? Even womanish envy? Anger and military fierceness, passion for quarreling which is never satiated, rabid cursing, viperous venom of a backbiting tongue, a swollen mind, a stiff neck, a vanishing faith, vanity, deceit, flattery? You judge your brother in meat or drink, or worship. Yet Paul judges you according to your actions.

Does this separate you from worldly carnalities, that you labor in lighter matters, but yet with these vices? He who because of a stolen birthright, a ruined daughter, a betrayed parent, a magistracy, the favor of a prince, entertains anger, enmities, and emulations, is not more wicked, is he, than you who (I am ashamed to say) do all these things all the more harshly for no reason whatsover? A light cause for sinning does not remove guilt but exaggerates it. Nor does it matter how much you pray, but only with what intent. Nay—this is the important thing: the less time it takes anyone to be led away from honesty, the more wicked he is.

I do not now speak of those monks whose morals even the world detests, but rather of those whom the crowd admires, not as men, but as angels. Yet they who take note of vices, not men, must not be offended by this statement. But if they are good men, let them even rejoice to be warned by somebody in

[18] Col. 3:5. [19] Col. 3:8. [20] Col. 3:9 f.
[21] Cf. I Cor. 15:47; Phil. 3:20.

those things which pertain to salvation. Nor is it unknown to
me that most of them who have been helped by letters and
intelligence have acquainted themselves with the mysteries of
the spirit. As Livy says, "As often happens the larger party
prevailed over the better." [22] But if it is right to acknowledge
something else, do we not see also the strictest sort of monks
putting at the summit of religion either ceremonies or a certain
order of psalms, or bodily toil? If anyone investigates them or
interrogates them concerning spiritual matters, he will find
precious few who do not walk in the flesh. Hence comes this
very great infirmity of minds, trembling where there is no
fear, dozing where there is the highest danger. Hence that perpetual infancy in Christ, not to speak more gravely, because
we are perverted judges of things, the most of us do those things
which are but vain and worthless, while we neglect those
things which alone suffice. In our infancy we are always acting
under tutors, always under a yoke, never aspiring to liberty
of spirit, never growing toward fullness of charity. Paul cries
out to the Galatians, "Stand and be not again confined by the
yoke of bondage." [23] And in another place: "Therefore the law
was our tutor unto Christ, that out of faith we might be justified.
But when faith comes, we are no longer under a tutor. For all
of you are sons of God by the faith, which is in Christ Jesus." [24]
Not far below: "And so when we were children we were serving
under the elements of the world. But when the fullness of time
came, God sent his Son born of woman, born under the law,
that he might redeem those who were under the law, that we
might receive the adoptions of sons. Since then you are sons of
God, God sent the spirit of his Son into your hearts, crying,
Abba, Father. Therefore you are no longer a slave, but a
son." [25] Again in another place: "For you, brethren, have
been called unto liberty: only use not liberty for an occasion to
the flesh; but by charity of the Spirit serve one another. For all
the law is fulfilled in one sentence: You shall love your neighbor
as yourself. But if you bite and eat one another, take heed
that you be not consumed one by another." [26] Again to the
Romans: "For you have received the Spirit of adoption of
sons of God, whereby we cry, Abba (Father)." [27] To this
same matter pertains likewise what Paul writes to Timothy:
"Exercise yourself toward piety. For bodily exercise is profitable
to little, but piety is profitable for all things." [28] And to the

[22] Livy, *Annales*, 21:4:1.   [23] Gal. 5:1.   [24] Gal. 3:24–26.   [25] Gal. 4:3–7.
[26] Gal. 5:13–15.   [27] Rom. 8:15.   [28] I Tim. 4:7f.

Corinthians: "God is Spirit. Where the Spirit is, there is liberty." [29]

But why do we refer to one passage after another? In this is the whole Paul: that the flesh which is contentious is contemned, and he grounds us in the Spirit, which is the author of love and liberty. Flesh, bondage, uneasiness, contention, are comrades not divided among themselves. So are spirit, peace, love, and liberty. The apostle teaches these ideas in various passages. Surely we do not require a master of religion greater than he, when all divine Scripture especially agrees on this point? This was the greatest commandment in the Mosaic law; this Christ repeats and perfects in the gospel. For this end especially was he born and died, that he might teach us, not to act like Jews, but to love. After the Last Supper, how anxiously, with how much feeling, does he command his apostles to be sustained, not by food and drink, but by mutual love! [30] What else does he teach—indeed his fellow priest John asks— unless it be that we love one another? [31] Paul, when he is here and there (as I said) commending love, then writing to the Corinthians, places love above miracles, prophecy, and angels' tongues. [32]

Do not tell me therefore that charity consists in being frequently in church, in prostrating oneself before signs of the saints, in burning tapers, [33] in repeating such and such a number of prayers. God has no need of this. Paul [34] defines love as: to edify one's neighbor, to lead all to become members of the same body, to consider all one in Christ, to rejoice concerning a brother's good fortune in the Lord just as concerning your own, to heal his hurt just as your own; compassionately to rebuke the erring, to teach the ignorant, to lift up the fallen, to console the downhearted, to help the toiler; to support the needy, in the highest degree to bring all your wealth, all your zeal, all your care to bear on this that you may benefit as many as possible in Christ. Just as he neither was born for himself nor lived for himself, nor died for himself, but gave himself completely for our sake, so likewise we should look after the

[29] II Cor. 3:17.   [30] John 13:34f.
[31] Fellow priest. Latin, *symmystes*, from Greek, συμμύστης. John 15:12f.
[32] I Cor. 13:1f.
[33] "The devotion of burning candles to God and to the saints is one of the practices that Erasmus looked upon with little sympathy." Cf. Opera IX, col. 1156 [Bataillon, 276].
[34] Cf. I Cor. 8:1; Rom. 12:4ff.; Gal. 3:28; I Cor. 12:12ff.; I Cor. 12:26; I Thess. 5:14; Phil. 4:3; II Tim. 2:24.

welfare of our brothers, not of ourselves. But if this came to pass, then the life of the religious would be somewhat happier and easier than we on the contrary now see it—sad, toilsome, full of Jewish superstitions, not immune from any vices of the laity, but actually more infected with some of them. If Augustine now came to life once more, whom very many boast of as the author of their life, surely he would not recognize this sort of men. For he proclaimed that he was going to approve nothing less than this sort of life, and he established a way of life turning, not to the supersititions of the Jews, but to the rule of the apostles.[35]

But forthwith I hear certain slightly saner ones replying to me: "One must be watchful in least, lest gradually they swell into greater, vices." I hear and approve, but you ought to keep watch not a little more, lest you so attach yourself to the least that you straightway cut yourself off from the greatest. . . .

What therefore will the Christian do? Will he neglect the mandates of his Church? Will he contemn the honorable traditions of the majority? Will he damn godly customs? Indeed, if he is infirm, he will keep things as necessary, but if he is firm and perfect, he will observe so much more that his own knowledge may not offend his infirm brother, and kill him for whom Christ died.[36] One must not leave undone the former things, but it is necessary [also] to do the latter.[37] Bodily works are not condemned, but invisible works are preferred. Visible worship is not condemned, but God is pleased only by invisible piety. God is a Spirit, and is appeased by spiritual sacrifices.[38] It would be wicked for Christians to ignore what a certain pagan poet did not ignore. He teaches us concerning piety:

"If God, he says, is mind, in poems he's revealed;
    With a pure mind, then, you ought to worship him."[39]

Let us not despise the author, either as a pagan or as insignificant. His saying is worthy even of a great theologian and, as I have discovered, read by few, understood by fewer. Surely it is

---

[35] *Rule of Augustine.* See *Regula ad servos Dei, PL*, 32:1377ff. Saint Augustine, while a priest at Hippo, founded a religious community there. The Augustinian canons traditionally derive their rule from him.
[36] I Cor. 8:11.   [37] Cf. Matt. 23:3.   [38] John 4:24.
[39] A certain pagan poet. See Cato, *Distich.*, ed. Erasmus (Leyden, 1536) 11, or *Poetae Latin. minor.*, ed. Bährens, III, 216.

of this sort. Like affects like. You believe that God is greatly
moved by a slain bull or the smell of incense, as if he were a
body. He is mind, the purest and simplest mind of all. Therefore
he must be worshiped with a pure mind. You think burned
wax is a sacrifice. Yet David says, "A sacrifice to God is an
afflicted spirit." [40] And if he despised the blood of goats or of
bullocks, yet he will not despise a humble and a contrite heart. [41]
If you do what is required in the eyes of men, attend much more
to what the eyes of God require of you. The body is covered by
a religious cowl. [42] What, then, if the mind wears worldly
clothing? If the outer man be clad in a snow-white tunic, in
the same manner the white vestments of the inner man should
be as snow. [43] You keep silence in public; take all the more
care that the mind within be kept free. In the visible temple
you fall down on the knees of the body, but nothing is accomplished thereby if in the temple of the breast you stand up
against God. You venerate the wood of the cross. Follow rather
the mystery of the cross. You fast and abstain from those things
which do not pollute man; [44] yet you do not refrain from
obscene conversations, which pollute both your conscience and
the other person's? Is food taken into the body, and does the
soul gorge itself on swine's husks? [45] You decorate a stone building; you have sacred places for religion. What does it profit
if the temple of the heart, whose wall Ezekiel dug through, [46]
is profaned with Egyptian abominations? You keep the Sabbath
outwardly, and within all sorts of vices run riot. Your body
does not commit adultery, but you are greedy—your soul then
is the adulterer. You sing psalms with the bodily tongue, but
within listen to what your mind says! You bless with the mouth
and curse with the heart. [47] In the body you are contained in
a cramped little cell; in thought you wander throughout the
whole world. You hear the Word of God with bodily ears.
Rather should you hear it within. What does the prophet say?
"Unless you will hear within, your soul will weep." [48] What

40 Ps. 50:19, Vg.; 51:17, E.V.; cf. Isa. 57:15.
41 Heb. 9:12; Ps. 50:19, Vg.; 51:17, E.V.
42 For other statements of Erasmus' views on monastic clothing, see *Praise
of Folly*, tr. Hudson, 86. Also see Letter to Volz, Allen, III, 373. "The
theme of clothing appears again and again in Erasmus' polemics."
Cf. Opera IX, cols. 613–615, 645–648, 893f., etc. *Coll.*, "The Franciscans:
or, Rich Beggars," tr. Bailey, 184ff. [Bataillon, 283].
43 Cf. Eccl. 9:8; Dan. 7:9; Matt. 17:2.   44 Matt. 15:11.
45 Luke 15:16.   46 Ezek. 8:8ff.; 12:7.   47 Ps. 61:5, Vg.; 62:4, E.V.
48 Jer. 13:17.

ADVOCATES OF REFORM

do you read in the Gospel? "Seeing, they see not, and hearing, they do not hear." [49] And again the prophet: "You hear with the ear, and perceive not." [50] Blessed are they who hear the word of God within. Happy, they to whom the Lord speaks the word inwardly, for their souls will be saved. The daughter of the king was ordered by David to incline this inward ear, she whose every ornament was within in golden borders. [51]

Finally, what does it mean not to do the evil things which by affection you lust after? What does it mean to do good deeds in public, by which various things are brought to pass within? Is it a great matter that you visit Jerusalem in the flesh, [52] when inwardly you are a veritable Sodom, an Egypt, a Babylon? It is not great to have trod in Christ's footsteps with carnal feet, yet it is the greatest thing to follow in Christ's footsteps in the affection. If it is a wonderful thing to have touched the Lord's sepulcher, will it not be wonderful also to have expressed the mystery of the sepulture? You reproach your own sins before a human priest: see how you will reproach them before God! [53] For to reproach before him is to hate within. Perchance you believe that by wax seals, or trifling coins, or paltry little pilgrimages, your guilt can be washed off all at once. [54] You have wandered completely from the path. Within, the wound has been inflicted; within, it is necessary to attack the poisoner. The affection was corrupt: you loved what deserved to be hated; you hated what ought to have been loved. Sweet was bitter to you, and bitter sweet. [55]

I tarry no longer over what you show outwardly. But if, to turn the tables, you begin to hate, to flee, to tremble at what you used to love, if what once tasted like gall becomes sweet to your affection, I hereby accept proof of your sanity.

[49] Matt. 13:13; Luke 8:10.   [50] Isa. 6:9f.; Jer. 5:21; cf. Acts 28:26.
[51] Ps. 44:11, 14, Vg.; 45:10, 13, E.V.
[52] *Praise of Folly*, tr. Hudson, 70. *Coll.*, "Rash Vows," tr. Bailey, 34–36; "Religious Pilgrimage," 238ff. Cf. Opera IX, cols. 368, 930 [Bataillon, 286].
[53] Erasmus on confession: *Exmologesis, sive modus confitendi*, Opera V, cols. 146–170. "A whole chapter of censurable propositions respecting confession taken from Erasmus' works was presented by the Spanish friars in their charges." Opera IX, cols. 1062–1064 [Bataillon, 286].
[54] Indulgences and purgatory are another frequent theme in Erasmus. Cf. *Praise of Folly*, tr. Hudson, 56. Also *Coll.*, "The Religious Banquet," tr. Bailey, 82–107, especially 99. "Erasmus has no sympathy in his religious treatises for pontifical indulgences." Cf. *Exmologesis, sive modus confitendi*, Opera V, col. 167. See also Opera IX, col. 1090 [Bataillon, 287].
[55] Isa. 5:20.

Mary Magdalene loved much; hence many sins were forgiven her.[56] The more you love Christ, the more you will hate your vices, for the hatred of sin follows the love of godliness, just as the shadow the body. . . .

You, therefore, my brother, advance not much by sad labors, but with moderate exercise, quickly, abundantly, vigorously, escape into Christ, embracing diligently this rule that you desire not to crawl upon the ground with unclean beasts, but always relying upon those wings which Plato thinks are sprouted in minds through the heat of love,[57] anew choose to put them forth, from the body to the spirit, from the visible world to the invisible, from letter to mystery, from things sensible to things intelligible, from things compound to things simple, just as if by the rungs of Jacob's ladder.[58] Thus to him who comes nigh unto the Lord, He in turn will come nigh unto him,[59] and if you will make a strong effort to surmount your blindness and the clamor of your senses, he will come forth fitly from his inaccessible light,[60] and that unthinkable silence in which all tumult of the senses disappears and even the images of all intelligible things keep silence.

Sixth Rule

And since from the time of writing one thing after another has come to mind, I shall subjoin likewise a sixth rule, indeed related to the above rules, yet as necessary to salvation for all as it is observed by few. This rule is that the mind of him who pants after Christ should disagree first with the deeds of the crowd, then with their opinions; nor should one seek the example of godliness from any other place than Christ himself. For this is the sole archetype. If anyone departs from it even a finger's breadth, he departs from the right, and runs outside the way. . . . For whatever has deeply stuck in the mind by persuasion one expresses in his moral actions. And to that end the especial care of Christians ought to be directed: that children from the very time of swaddling clothes, among the caresses of nurses and the kisses of parents, in the tutelage of teachers, should imbibe persuasions worthy of Christ. On that account nothing settles more deeply in the mind or nothing sticks to it more tenaciously than what is taught in the rude years.[61] . . .

[56] Luke 7:37, 47.
[58] Gen. 28:12.
[60] I Tim. 6:16.

[57] *Phaedrus*, 245d–251b.
[59] James 4:8.
[61] Quintillian, *Inst. or.*, 1:8:4.

Far, far from the infant's tiny ears [62] keep those little love ditties which Christians sing at home and in public, fouler than even the pagan multitude allowed. Let them not hear their darling mother bewailing the loss of something. When a sister has been lost, let them not hear her bewailing her sad fate. Let them not hear the father upbraiding slothfulness in his son because he did not return an injury with interest, or because he does not express admiration for those who have done something very great in some manner or other. The genius of man, descending downward to vices, at once seizes upon a pernicious example, just as naphtha sets fire to something beside it. Yet this same thing should at some age be carried out so that all vulgar errors be uprooted from the depths of the mind, and in their place salutary opinions be sown, and hereafter strengthened, that they may be torn loose by no forces whatsoever. Let him who does this follow virtue of his own free will without haggling and thereupon he will judge those so acting to be deserving of pity, not of imitation. . . .

Beware lest you ponder thus: "Someone else does this. By these footsteps those greater than I have entered. This philosopher or that theologian held such an opinion. So do the great men live. This was established by the king. This both bishops and supreme pontiffs practice." Surely these are not the crowd. Let big names move you not at all. I do not lay store by the crowd, but I measure by the heart. The crowd consists of those who in that Platonic cave,[63] chained to their passions, admire as the truest things what are really empty images of things. Would it not be preposterous for one not to fit the stone to the rule, but the rule to the stone? [64] Would it not be even more absurd if one labored to bend, not men's morals to Christ, but Christ to men's life? Do not think therefore because the leaders and the greater part of men habitually do something that it is right. But what is done is right only if it squares with the rule of Christ. Indeed you ought to be suspicious of anything when it pleases the majority. The flock is tiny,[65] and always will be, whose heart is possessed by Christian simplicity, poverty, truth. It is tiny but blessed, for to it alone belongs the Kingdom of Heaven. The way of virtue is narrow, and trodden by few, but no other leads to

[62] Cf. Virgil, *Aeneid*, 6:258.
[63] Plato, *Republic*, 514a–517c. Cf. *Praise of Folly*, tr. Hudson, 64.
[64] Cf. *Adagia*, 1:5:93, *Lesbia regula*; Aristotle, *Eth. Nic.*, 1137b.
[65] Luke 12:32.

life.[66] Does a prudent builder seek his pattern from the most commonly practiced or from the best work? Painters set before themselves nothing but the best paintings as their models. Our pattern is Christ, in whom alone are all the blessed ways of living. Him without exception it is meet to imitate. Otherwise among tested men it is advisable to summon anyone as an example, to the extent that he corresponds to the archetype of Christ. As far as morals are concerned, however, consider nothing ever to have been more corrupt than the opinion of them held by the generality of Christians, not even excepting those current among pagans.

Otherwise concerning faith they will themselves see what they believe. This is most indubitably so, that faith without morals worthy of faith is of no help,[67] in fact piles up their damnation. Unroll the ancient records and compare them with the customs of today. When was true honesty thought more contemptible? When were riches, wherever acquired, held in higher esteem? In what age was ever truer that saying of Horace:

"Of course a wife and dowry, credit and friends,
Birth and beauty, are the gift of Queen Cash"[68]? . . .

Elsewhere he says,

"And yet birth and worth, without substance, are
More paltry than seaweed."[69]

Who does not read seriously that satiric irony:

"O citizens, citizens, money you first must seek;
Virtue after pelf"[70]?

When was luxury more unfettered? When were fornication and adultery either more widely open to view or less punished, or less ashamed? While princes condone their own vices in others and everyone feigns a brilliant appearance, what has departed in the morals of the courtiers? To whom does poverty not seem the final evil and disgrace? Once upon a time in the games of the pagans it was customary to fling defamatory taunts even from wagons against fornicators, filthy persons, boastful ones, admirers of money;[71] the crowd used to applaud

---

[66] Cf. Matt. 7:14.   [67] Cf. James 2:14.   [68] Horace, *Epistles*, 1:6:36 f.
[69] *Satires*, 2:5:8.   [70] *Epistles*, 1:1:53 f.
[71] Horace, *Ars poetica*, 276; cf. *Satires*, 1:4:1–5. Cf. also *Scholia* on Lucian, vi, 388. For this footnote and the following one I am indebted to Professor Merriman of Trinity College, Hartford, Connecticut.

when vices were cleverly disguised; but now when these are evilly praised the leaders of the Christians applaud. The audiences of the Athenian theater did not tolerate the actor in a certain play of Euripides, acting the role of a greedy man who preferred money alone to all the other goods of human life. Obviously the audience was going to hiss the actor and the whole play off the stage and cast him out. Nor was the poet able, when he rose up, to entreat them to remain even a little while to watch how that admirable character was going to turn out.[72] How many examples there are among them who from a well-administered state, save for honest opinion, have returned nothing to their poor family, but considered faith preferable to money, virtue to life? Who could neither become accustomed to prosperous things nor be broken by adverse ones? Who have placed honest dangers before pleasure? Who with a conscience only of right purpose have desired neither honors nor wealth nor the other advantages of fortune? And I need not remind you of the sanctity of Photion, of poverty better than the riches of Fabritius, of the magnanimity of Camillus, of the severity of Brutus, of the modesty of Pythagoras, of the unassailable continence of Socrates, of the integrity of Cato, and of a thousand most beautiful ornaments of all the virtues, which one from time to time reads about in the annals of the Lacedemonians, the Persians, the Athenians, or the Romans—indeed to our great shame. Saint Augustine, as he testifies concerning himself in the pages of his *Confessions*,[73] should have put on Christ much sooner, for he held money in contempt, had no use for honors, was not moved by glory, yet denied the reins to pleasures to the extent that as a young man he was content with one mistress, to whom he preserved conjugal fidelity. One would not find these minds, these examples, by chance among the nobility, among ecclesiastics, and I add, among monks. But if anyone of this sort should exist in that very place like an ass among apes,[74] he will be pointed out and laughed at; everybody with one voice will call him mad, dull-witted, a hypocrite, unschooled in affairs, melancholic, insane, and will even judge him not to be a man. As Christians we so venerate the teaching of Christ, we so express ourselves, that nothing be held more senseless, more debased, more to be ashamed of by the crowd, than truly and wholeheartedly to

[72] Seneca, *Epistulae morales*, 115:14–16.
[73] Augustine, *Confessions*, 4:2; 6:15, *PL*, 32:693f., 731f.
[74] *Adagia*, 1:5:41.

be Christian. As if either Christ in vain dwelt upon the earth or Christianity is now something else than it once was, or does not pertain to all equally! From these opinions therefore I wish you to desist with your whole mind and to measure the worth of all things by communion with Christ alone.

Who asserts to the crowd that he is not excellent, and to be placed among things especially good, and to be a descendant of more famous forebears? They call this nobility! May nothing move you when you hear the prudent of this age, serious men, armed with the highest authority, absolutely seriously poring over the branches of a genealogical tree, with eyebrows knit as if it were something especially difficult, and babbling great nothings with great effort; while you see others so puffed up over grandfathers' and great-grandfathers' pictures that they judge the rest of us scarcely to be men in comparison with themselves. But pursuing their error with a Democritic laugh, consider the sole and highest nobility to consist in being reborn in Christ, being engrafted into his body, being made one body and one spirit with God.[75] Let others be sons of kings; let the greatest things for you be both to be and to call yourself a son of God. Let them please themselves about dwelling in the halls of princes; choose for yourself with David "to be a humble person in the house of God."[76] Attend whom Christ chooses: the infirm, foolish, ignoble—according to the world.[77] In Adam all of us are born ignoble; in Christ we are all one.[78] True nobility means to despise empty nobility. True nobility means to be a servant of Christ. Think these whose virtues you emulate to be greater than you. Hear what the best judge of nobility said in the Gospel against the Jews, who boasted about their descent from Abraham. What sort of ancestor? Not famous, not wealthy, not a victor over kings, but one divinely commended because of divine virtues. Who does not judge this remarkable, worthy of glory? Hear what they heard: "You are of your father the devil; and the works of your father you will do."[79] Behold Paul likewise, judging nobility according to the Master's rule, saying, "Not all who are of Israel by circumcision are Israelites, nor are all who are of the seed of Abraham children."[80] Shameful ignobility is it to serve wickedness, to have no acquaintance with Christ, who knows only those who do the will of his Father who is in heaven.[81] Wickedly false is he

75 Cf. Rom. 12:5.　　76 Ps. 83:11, Vg.; 84:10, E.V.
77 I Cor. 1:27 f.　　78 Cf. I Cor., ch. 15.　　79 John 8:44.
80 Rom. 9:6 f.　　81 Matt. 7:21.

who has the devil for his father, who does the devil's work, unless
Christ has lied.[82] But the Truth knew not how to lie. It is
the highest nobility to be both a son and an heir of God, a
brother and a coheir of Christ.[83] They will see their badge,
what they want for themselves; the badge of Christians is
common to all: the most illustrious cross, the crown of thorns,
the keys, the lance, the wounds of the Lord, which Paul gloried
to bear in his body.[84] . . .

Think not yourself a whit better if you surpass either Midas
or Croesus in wealth, but more bound, more impeded, more
burdened. He has fully enough who can strongly despise such
things. He has enough to look forward to for himself to whom
Christ has promised nothing to be lacking. He will not hunger
who sagely savors the manna of the divine word. He will not
go bare who puts on Christ.[85] Consider this alone a loss, how
many times one has departed from piety, and has increased
in vices. Think it a huge gain, when the mind by accession of
virtue has been made better. Consider that you lack nothing
if you possess Him in whom are all things.

What is this that the miserable call pleasure? Surely nothing
less than what is said. What therefore? It is utter insanity, and
plainly (as the Greeks used to say) the laughter of Ajax, sweet
poison, smooth ruin.[86] The true and only pleasure is the joy
of a pure conscience. The most elegant banquets are enjoyed
in the study of the Holy Scriptures. The most pleasing songs are
the psalms of the Holy Spirit. The most joyous fellowship is
the communion of saints. The highest delights are in the enjoyment of truth. Only purify your eyes, your ears, your palate,
and Christ will begin to become sweet to you. When he has truly
been tasted, even if Milesians, Sybarites, debauchees,[87]
Epicureans—in short, all the master craftsmen of pleasures—
heap up in one place all their delights, in comparison with
Christ they will seem but vomit. That is not really sweet which
tastes so, but which tastes sweet to a healthy man. If to a fevered
man water tastes like wine, no one calls that pleasure, but
disease. You are mistaken if you do not believe tears to be far
more joyful to godly men than laughter, jeers, pranks to the
ungodly; what fasting is not sweeter to the former than their

---

[82] John 8:44.   [83] Rom. 8:16 f.   [84] Gal. 6:14, 17.
[85] Cf. Rom. 13:14.   [86] *Adagia*, 1:7:46.
[87] Debauchees. Latin, *asoti*, from Greek, ἄσωτος, found only in Cicero.
   See *De finibus*, 2:8:23; *De Deorum natura*, 3:31:77; cf. Aristotle, *Eth. Nic.*,
   1107b, 1120a, etc.

heath cocks, pheasants, partridges, sturgeon, or flatfish to the latter;[88] that the frugal little meals of the former furnished with their cabbages and Pythagorean beans[89] are not far more elegant than the sumptuous delicacies of the latter. . . .

Take, for example, power and weakness, courage and cowardice: what does popular error think them to be? Do they not call him powerful who can easily harm whomever he will? Although to be able to do harm, to inflict evil, is a power excessively hateful, it is common to the latter, along with flies and scorpions, and the devil himself.

God alone is truly powerful, who can neither do harm if he wishes nor wishes to do so if he could, for his very nature is to do good. But how, then, does this powerful One harm man? Will he snatch money away, will he strike the body, will he take away life? If he does this to a pious man, he has given good for evildoing, but if he has done it to a wicked man, God has furnished the occasion but man has harmed himself. For no one is harmed except by himself.[90] No one prepares to harm another, unless he has already far more gravely harmed himself. You prepare to cause me a loss of money; when charity is lost, you have already given yourself the gravest loss of all. You cannot inflict a wound upon me unless you have already received at your own hands a much more frightful hurt. You will not deprive me of the life of the body, unless already you have safely slain your own soul. Yet does not Paul boast that he can do all things in Christ,[91] for he is feeble in inflicting injury but exceedingly strong in bearing it? The crowd considers him strong and courageous who is fierce and of weak mind, who boils over with anger at any injury however slight, who returns reproach for reproach, evil deed for evil deed. On the other hand, they call him who disregards or conceals an injury which he has sustained cowardly, pusillanimous, spiritless. Nay, what is more foreign to greatness of mind than to be driven by a mere word from a state of mind; hence not to be able to contemn folly as alien, so that you do not think yourself to be a man unless you heap curse upon curse? Yet how much more manly, with full and lofty purpose, is it to be able to ignore an injury, and besides that to return good for evil? . . .

[88] *Coll.*, "The Religious Banquet," tr. Bailey, 99.
[89] *Leguminibus Pythagoricis.* Beans were reputedly not eaten by the Pythagoreans. See Cicero, *Div.*, 1:30:62; 2:58:119; Horace, *Satires*, 2:6:63; but cf. Aulus Gellius, *Noctes Atticae*, 4:11:4.
[90] John Chrysostom, *Expositio in Psalmum CXXXIX*, PG, 55:420 [Bataillon, 314]. Cf. chapter 13, n. 68.   [91] Phil. 4:13.

Let us examine likewise that which the world calls glory, ignominy, and shame. You are praised. Why and by whom? If on account of wickedness by wicked folk, this indeed is false glory and true ignominy. You are abused, mocked. For what reason, and by whom? On account of piety, innocence, by evil folk. This is not ignominy, for there is no truer glory. Be sane, even if the whole world hisses and hoots at you.[92] What Christ approves cannot but be glorious. And if he applaud or acclaim anything of mortals as "Well done!",[93] one cannot but be ashamed of what displeases God.

Vulgarly they call it prudence to prepare something strenuously, to establish firmly what has been brought forth, and even to look forward into the future. For so we hear them speaking earnestly from time to time. Man is temperate, sagacious, prudent, foresighted, about those things which make life more luxurious for a short time. By this is meant the world, which is both false and his father.[94] Yet what does the Truth say? "Fool, this night your soul will be required of you."[95] He had filled the barns with the harvest, he had furnished all the storehouses with provisions, he had laid up in his house very much money. He thought that nothing remained. . . . All he needed to do (so he thought) was to enjoy the produce of his fields.[96] Yet the gospel calls this foolishness. What indeed is more foolish, more senseless, than to gape at shadows and lose the true things; we laugh at this when we see it in Aesop's dog.[97] And in the morals of Christians ought it not the more to be laughed at or rather wept over? . . .

Consider another error. They call a person skilled and dexterous who, laying hold of every little rumor, knows everything that goes on in the world. What fortune of commerce, what the king of the Britons busies himself about, what's new at Rome, what rising among the Gauls, how the Dacians and Scythians are getting along, what the princes are deliberating about—in short, him who is practiced in chattering about all sorts of business, among all kinds of men, they call wise. What is more unthinking, more ignorant, than to inquire into those things which take place far away and have nothing to do with you, yet not to ponder over all those things which you carry in your breast, and pertain to you alone? You tell me about British troubles; tell me rather what is stirred up in your breast—

---

[92] *Explodat exsibiletque.* Cf. Cicero, *Paradoxa Stoicorum*, 3:26; Suetonius, *Augustus*, 45.   [93] Matt. 25:21, 23.   [94] Cf. John 8:44.
[95] Luke 12:20.   [96] Luke 12:16 ff.   [97] *Aesop's Fables* (ed. Halm), 233.

anger, envy, lust, ambition. How nearly already have these vices been brought under the yoke! What hope of victory! How great a part of the war has already been won! How well-trained is your reason! In these things, if you have been vigilant, if you have kept ears and eyes equally alert, if you have been sagacious and circumspect, I will pronounce you expert. And that which the world is wont to cast upon us I shall cast back to it. Fruitless is the wisdom of him who has no knowledge of himself.

Toward this end if you care for all mortals, you will drive out joys, hopes, fears, zeal, purposes; you will find all these full of error; while they call good evil and evil good, while they make sweet of bitter things, bitter sweet,[98] while they make light darkness, and darkness light. And this indeed is by far the greatest disturbance of men. Yet you ought at the same time both to contemn these, lest you should wish to be like them, and to feel pity, that you desire them to become like you; (to use Augustine's words) it is sometimes fitting to weep for those deserving of laughter, sometimes to laugh at those deserving of weeping.[99] "Do not be conformed in evil to this world, but be reformed in the newness of your mind, that you may prove, not what men admire, but what is the good, and the acceptable, and the perfect will of God."[1] You are closest to danger and are plainly beginning to slip, if you begin to look about at what many folk are doing, if you begin to clutch at what they believe. You are the offspring of life and light;[2] "let the dead bury their dead";[3] "the blind leaders of the blind fall at the same time into the pit."[4] Beware also lest you move the eyes of your heart away from your example, Christ. You will not err if you follow the leadership of the Truth. You will not cast yourself among the shadows while you walk after the light. When the light shines through, if you distinguish the counterfeit good from the true, the true evils from the false, you will shudder, you will not imitate the blindness of the multitude,[5] burning with desire for some Euripus or other[6] with each of the passions in turn—anger, envy, love, hate, hope, fear, joy, pain—for the inanest mockery of things. Brahmans,[7] Cynics, Stoics are wont to

98 Isa. 5:20.
99 Cf. Augustine, Sermon 175, PL, 38:945f.(?) [Bataillon, 319].
1 Rom. 12:2.   2 Cf. Eph. 5:8; John 12:36.   3 Matt. 8:22; Luke 9:60.
4 Matt. 15:14.   5 Cf. Isa. 59:9 f.   6 Adagia, 1:9:62.
7 Brahmans. Latin (1515 ed.), Bragmani; ed. Holborn (1933), Brachmani. From Greek βραχμᾶνες. See Strabo, Geography, 15:1:59 (c. 712); Loeb, Vol. vii, 98/99; Tertullian, Apology, 42:1; Ammianus Marcellinus, 23:6:33; 28:1:13.

protect their doctrines with the teeth, and when the world loudly contradicts them, when everyone hisses and hoots at them, yet they pertinaciously urge what they have once persuaded themselves to be true. Dare likewise to fix the rules of your own sect deep within; dare, securely and completely, to go over to the views of your Maker.

Opinions Worthy of a Christian

Let these always before you stand as the paradoxes of true Christianity: That no Christian think himself to have been born for himself, nor wish to live for himself, but all that he has, or is, he credit not to himself, but that he give credit to God as Author for all his goods, and that he consider them to be the common property of all. Christian charity recognizes no property.[8] Let him love the pious in Christ, the impious for Christ's sake, who already so loved us as yet enemies that he gave himself wholly for our ransom. The pious he embraces because they are good; the impious none the less, that he may render them good. He certainly hates no man, not any more than a faithful doctor hates a sick person, but he is unfriendly toward vices. The graver the disease, the greater the care that pure charity will bring to it. A man is an adulterer, he commits sacrilege, he is a Turk—let the act of adultery be execrated, not the man; let the sacrilege, not the man, be despised. Let him kill the Turk, not the man.[9] Let him put forth effort that the impious man he has made of himself may perish; but that the man whom God has made may be saved. Let him sincerely desire well of all men and let him pray well, let him do good.[10] Nor let him harm the deserving, and benefit the undeserving. Let him manifest as much joy over the good fortunes of all men as he does over his own. Let him be grieved over the ill fortunes of all men, not differently than he is over his own. Doubtless this it is that the apostle urged, to weep with those who weep, to rejoice with those who rejoice.[11] Nay, let him bear more heavily another's evil than he does his own.

Let him be happier about his brother's good fortune than his own. It is not the Christian's way to reason thus: "What

---

[8] *"Proprietatem Christiana caritas non novit."* This phrase was censured by the Spanish friars. See *Apologia adversus Monarchos Hispanos, Opera* IX, cols. 1090 f. [Bataillon, 322].

[9] "Kill the Turk, not the man." This is an idea expressed by Erasmus, among other places, in the Letter to Volz (Allen, III, 364 f.) [Bataillon, 323].   [10] Matt. 5:44.   [11] Rom. 12:15.

have I to do with him? I know not whether he be white or black, he is unknown, he is a stranger, he never deserved anything well of me. . . ." At least remember that Christ gave none of these things to you out of merit, for he wanted his benefit toward you to be reciprocated, not to himself, but to your neighbor. See what your neighbor lacks, and what you can do for him. Consider this: he is your brother in the Lord, coheir with you in Christ,[12] a member of the same body, redeemed by the same blood, a comrade in the common faith, called to the same grace and happiness in the future life. It is just as the apostle says: "One body, and one Spirit, as you are called in one hope of your vocation. One Lord, one faith, one baptism. One God and Father of us all, who is above all, and through all, and in us all."[13] . . .

No man savors Christianity just because he is a noble rather than a member of the town mob, a rustic instead of a city dweller, a patrician instead of a plebeian, a magistrate instead of a private citizen, a rich man instead of a pauper, a famous man rather than an obscure one, a strong rather than a weak, an Italian rather than a German, a Gaul instead of a Briton, a Briton instead of a Scot, . . . and not to refer to all nugatory differences, it is worse to be unlike in unlike things.

Where is love, which even loves the enemy when the name is changed, when the color of clothing is somewhat different, when the belt, or shoe, and such absurdities of men make me hateful to you? Why not banish all this childish trumpery and whatever else pertains to the matter? Then we can accustom ourselves to hold before our eyes the truth which Paul[14] in many places drives home, that we are all, in Christ as Head, members of one body, animated by the same Spirit, if we live in him, so that we may not envy happier members, and may willingly help weaker ones; that we may know that we have received benefit when we benefit our neighbor, and also know that we have been injured when harm has been done to our brother. Nor should anyone strive for himself alone, but, to the best of his ability, contribute to the common store what he has received of God, that all things may flow back whence they flowed forth, namely, to the Head.

This, indeed, is what Paul writes to the Corinthians: "For as the body is one, and has many members, and all the members

12 Rom. 8:16 f.   13 Eph. 4:4-6.
14 Cf. Rom. 12:5; Eph. 4:4.

of the body, whereas they are many, yet are one body; so also is Christ." [15] . . .

And elsewhere he bids all to bear one another's burdens, since we are all members of one another. [16] See, therefore, whether they belong to this body, whom now and again you hear speaking in this way: "My property came to me by inheritance; I do not possess it by fraud. Why shouldn't I enjoy it according to my own inclination, and abuse it? Why should I give anything to them to whom I owe nothing? I squander, I lose it, yet what is lost is mine. It makes no difference to others." Your fellow member opens wide his mouth with fasting, while you reek with the flesh of partridge. Your unclothed brother horrifies you, yet your clothing is rotting with moths and decay. You gamble away a thousand pieces of gold in one night, while some poor girl, plunged into dire need, prostitutes her body and loses her soul, for which Christ poured out his soul. You say: "What has that to do with me? My own concerns take up all my thoughts." And afterwards will you see yourself a Christian with this mind, who may not even be a man? You hear in the crowd the reputation of such and such a person being injured; yet you remain silent or perhaps you smile at the detractor. "I would have suppressed," you say, "what was said, if any of it had pertained to me. Yet I have nothing in common with him who was harmed." Therefore you have nothing in common with the body if you have nothing in common with a member of it. Nor is there anything in common with the head, if there is nothing in common with the body.

They say, "It is lawful to repel force with force." I do not tarry over what the imperial laws permit; I wonder at this— whence these voices penetrated into the ways of Christians. "I have harmed someone, but I was provoked to it. I preferred to give evil rather than to receive it." Granted that human laws do not punish what they have permitted. Yet what is Christ your leader going to do if you defraud his law, which is given in Matthew's Gospel?: "But I say to you, not to resist evil; but if any man strike you on your right cheek, turn to him the other also." [17] . . . You reply: "These words which he has spoken do not apply to me. He spoke to the apostles, the perfect." Have you not heard that you are the sons of your Father? If you do not desire to be a son of God, the law means nothing to you. Yet there is no good man, indeed, who does not want

---

[15] I Cor. 12:12. [16] Gal. 6:2; Eph. 4:25. [17] Matt. 5:39–41, 44 f.

to be perfect. Understand that rule, if you do not desire reward, as not enjoined upon you. There follows: "If you love those who love you, what sort of recompense will you have?" [18] None to speak of. Nor does virtue consist in doing this, but it is a crime not to do it. Nothing is owed to anyone where like repays like. . . .

You believed that only to monks was property forbidden and poverty imposed? You have erred, for it pertains to all Christians. [19] The law punishes you if you take unto yourself what belongs to another. It does not punish you, if you take your possessions away from a needy brother. Yet even so Christ will punish you. . . .

Therefore, most dearly cherished brother, holding the crowd with its opinions and actions in complete contempt, embrace wholly and entirely the Christian sect, neglecting out of the love of piety in equal measure whatever is brought before the senses either to be shunned or sought. . . . Accommodate yourself outwardly to all, that inwardly your resolution may remain unmoved. Outwardly let friendliness, affability, courteousness, pleasantness attract your brother, that he may blandly agree to be invited to Christ, not be deterred by harshness. Finally, you should express what you feel, not so much by angry words, as by your actions. Nor, again, should indulgence be shown to the crowd's infirmity, with the result that there you dare not strongly defend the truth. All men should be amended, not deceived, in humaneness.

Seventh Rule

But if through the childishness and imbecility of our minds, we are not permitted to aspire to these spiritual things, yet must the works be accomplished with the more alacrity, that we may at least stand in their neighborhood. On the other hand, true and quick is the way to happiness, if once we so turn our whole mind to the admiration of things heavenly that, just as a body takes unto itself a shadow, so the love of Christ, the love of things eternal and honorable, draws the mind by its very nature to the shunning of transient things and the hatred of wicked things. This is true whether necessarily the one follows

[18] Matt. 5:46.
[19] These two sentences were proscribed in the *Index expurgatorius* of Antwerp (1571), 89. The passage was also censured by the Spanish friars. Cf. *Opera* IX, col. 1090f. [Bataillon, 336].

the other, and the one increases or decreases with the other. The more you advance in the love of Christ, the more you will hate the world. The more you marvel at things invisible, the more vile will be changing and momentary ones. . . .

Wherefore youths ought especially to be warned to prefer the word of many great writers as to the nature of sin rather than to learn what it is from their own unhappy experience. They ought also to be taught not to contaminate their life with vices before they plainly understand what life is. If Christ is worthless to you, with whom you so much agree, at least let the reason for your opinion abstain from base considerations. And although it is utterly perilous in this condition to hesitate for long at the crossroads (as they say),[20] yet for those who are not yet able to rise up to heroic virtue it is not a little better to remain in social virtue rather than to go precipitously into every sort of immorality. The goal of felicity is not here, but hither is the better way to felicity. Yet meanwhile we ought ever to pray to God that he may deign to draw us to better things.[21]

Eighth Rule

If the storm of temptations more frequently and heavily assails you, do not begin to be profoundly dissatisfied with yourself, as if on this account it is not a matter of heartfelt concern for your God that you are insufficiently pious or even less perfect. Nay, give thanks rather that he is teaching the future heir, that he is flaying the dearly beloved son, that he is searching out the friend. [22] The greatest argument for man's having been cast out from the divine mercy is when he is pressed by no temptations. Paul the apostle comes to your mind who deserved to be admitted into the mysteries of the third heaven, yet his ears were boxed by the angel of Satan.[23] Let Job the friend of God assist you; let Jerome, Benedict, Francis, and with them innumerable other fathers, help you, plagued as they have been by the greatest vices. Why are you dejected in mind, if what you suffer is common to so many very great men? Strive all the more, that with them you may conquer. "God will not forsake you, and will not let you be tempted more than you are able to bear." [24]

[20] *Adagia,* 1:2:48.   [21] Cf. II Thess. 1:11.
[22] Cf. Rom. 8:17; Heb. 12:6 f.; Rev. 3:19.   [23] II Cor. 12:2, 7.
[24] I Cor. 10:13.

Ninth Rule

Canny generals are accustomed, even in times of peace, to set guards. In like manner you too ought always to have a mind vigilant and circumspect to the future assaults of the enemy. "For he ever goes about, seeking whom he may devour." [25] Against him put yourself in greater readiness, that you may immediately and stoutly repulse his onslaught, and hiss him away, crushing straightway the head of the plague-bearing serpent. [26] For he is never either easily or completely conquered. For this reason it is of the greatest importance to dash the children of Babylon, as they were born in that very place, upon the rock that is Christ before they grow large. [27]

Tenth Rule

But the tempter is best repelled by these means: if you either vehemently put out of mind and immediately as it were spit upon the suggester, or earnestly pray, or wholeheartedly betake yourself to some holy task, or answer the tempter with words chosen from Holy Scripture, just as we have admonished above. In this matter it is not of any moderate profit against every sort of temptation to have some particular sentences ready, especially those by which you may at any time sense that your mind is being violently stirred up.

Eleventh Rule

A most powerful double danger grips pious men: on the one hand lest they succumb to temptation; on the other, lest after victory they become haughty in consolation and spiritual joy. That, therefore, you may be safe, not only from nightly fear, but also from the noonday demon, [28] let it come to pass that when the enemy incites you to wicked actions, you may not gaze back upon your own foolishness, but ever remember that in Christ you can do all things, [29] for he said, not to his apostles only, but also to you and to all his members, "Have confidence; I have overcome the world." [30] Again, when either

---

[25] I Peter 5:8.   [26] Gen. 3:15.
[27] Cf. Ps. 136:8 f., Vg.; 137:8 f., E.V. See Augustine, *Enarrationes in Psalmos*,
    tr. H. Walford, Vol. VI, 175 f.   [28] Cf. Ps. 90:5 f., Vg.; 91:5 f., E.V.
[29] Phil. 4:13.   [30] John 16:33.

after the defeat of the tempter, or in any sort of pious task, you feel your mind, your inner shrine, flooded with sensual pleasure, then particularly beware lest for that reason you arrogate anything to your own merits, but give all credit to the gratuitous beneficence of God. Straightway restrain yourself by the words of Paul: "What do you have that you did not receive? And if you received it, why do you boast, as if you had not received it?" [31] Therefore against this double evil there will be a double remedy. In conflict, distrustful of your strength, flee unto Christ your Head; and place all hope of victory in his benevolence alone. In spiritual consolation, give thanks at once to him for his beneficence, humbly recognizing your unworthiness.

Twelfth Rule

When you fight with the enemy, it is not enough for you if you decline his blow, or even repel it, unless you cast the seized spear back upon the author himself, slashing him with his own sword. So act, if you are incited to evil, not only that you sin not, but also that you thereby grasp for yourself the occasion for virtue. How elegantly the poets wrought, that Hercules, when beset by the perils thrown against him by the angry Juno, increased in purpose and steadfastness!. . . In the same manner you should see to it that you are not made worse by the incitements of the enemy, and also may the better evade them. . . . If you are incited to greed and grasping, increase your alms. If you are stirred up to vainglory, so much the more abase yourself in everything. So will it come to pass that any one temptation will become for you a sort of renewal of your holy intention and an increase of your piety. For no other strategy is quite so effective for the destruction and ruin of our enemy. He will then be afraid of provoking you anew, lest he who enjoys being the author of impiety furnish the occasion of piety.

Thirteenth Rule

But always struggle with this mind and this hope if you would depart victorious: treat each battle as if it were the last. For it can happen that divine kindness may bestow this sort of reward for your virtue, that the enemy, once shamefully overcome, may never afterward again seek you. This has

[31] I Cor. 4:7.

happened to a few pious men. Origen did not foolishly believe, when Christians are victorious, that the enemy's forces are diminished; when once strongly repelled, that the devil is never again permitted to molest a man.[32] Therefore, in the struggle dare to hope for everlasting peace. Yet again, when you conquer, so conduct yourself as if you were at once going to return to the fray. We ought always to expect one temptation after another; nor should we ever be separated from our arms, ever give up our post, ever slacken our guard, so long as we fight in the garrison of this body. Ever ought we to hold that prophetic word in our hearts: "I shall stand upon my watch."[33]

Fourteenth Rule

We should especially be on our guard not to contemn lightly any vice whatsoever. For no enemy ever was victor more often than he who was held in contempt. In this matter I find that not a few mortals miserably deceive themselves. For they deceive themselves when they connive in one vice or another, which each one thinks venial for his own morals, yet they incessantly curse the remaining vices. The better part of those whom the crowd calls unblemished and incorrupt certainly do detest theft, pillage, homicide, adultery, incest. Yet simple fornication and moderate enjoyment of pleasure, as lightly committed, they in no wise eschew. One person, sufficiently incorrupt as far as other vices are concerned, is somewhat of a drunkard or somewhat intemperate in eating. Another has a rather unbridled tongue. Another is somewhat vain and boasting. What vice will we lack, if each one of us is deluded by his own in this way? The point is not that those who enjoy any vice indeed possess the remaining virtues, but rather certain likenesses of virtues which either nature or education or finally habit has imparted likewise to the minds of pagans. Yet he who curses one particular vice with Christian hatred must detest all vices. Once true charity has occupied his mind, he pursues the whole army of evils with equal detestation and does not delude himself in venial vices, lest gradually from the least vices he will slip into the greatest, and while he is negligent toward light ones, he will perish at the hands of the highest vices. And if perchance you are as yet unable to root out the whole tribe of vices, yet daily we ought to pluck out something of our sins, and always at the same time replace them with

32 Origen, *Contra Celsum*, 8:44, *PG*, 11:1581 ff.   33 Hab. 2:1; Isa. 21:8.

good habits. In that manner that huge mound of Hesiod will decrease and increase.[34]

Fifteenth Rule

If the labor which it is necessary for you to undergo in the conflict of temptations terrifies you, this is the remedy. Do not compare the hardship of the combat with the pleasure of the sin. But compare the present bitterness of the battle with the future bitterness of sin which follows the vanquished; then compare the present sweetness of guilt, which allures you, with the future sweetness of victory and tranquillity of mind, which will follow your strenuous fighting, and you will soon see how unequal the comparison is. But in this the insufficiently cautious are deceived, because they compare the bitterness of battle with the delights of sin, nor do they pay attention to the consequences of either. The vanquished will experience a much graver and longer lasting annoyance in the coming contest than the conqueror felt; the victor will enjoy a far greater and more persistent pleasure than the one which dragged him into sin was for the vanquished. That is something easy to judge for the man who makes a danger of both things. But no Christian ought to be so sluggish that, when he undergoes daily temptation, he does not at least take care to find out what it is to conquer temptation. The more frequently he does this, the sweeter the victory will become.

Sixteenth Rule

If ever you might happen to receive a deadly blow, beware lest at the very outset having thrown away your shield, having forsaken your arms, you give yourself up to the enemy. Not a few persons, quite insane and effeminate by nature, once overthrown, cease to struggle, abandon themselves completely to their passions, and never think of regaining their liberty. Far too dangerous is this timidity, which, while it is not yet joined to an abandoned nature, yet is wont to lead to what is most abandoned of all, that is, despair. Against this the mind ought to be fortified with this rule, that, having lapsed into sin, we not despair, but imitate skilled soldiers. For they are seldom driven to flight by disgraceful defeat and painful wounds, but are spurred to fight more stoutly

[34] Hesiod, *Works and Days*, 361 f.

than before, and recoup themselves. It is the same with us. When we have been led into a capital disaster, let us hasten to restore our courage, and when we have fallen into disgrace, to restore ourselves with new eagerness of virtue. It is easier to doctor one wound than many, and a recent one than one already far gone and putrid. Quicken yourself with that most famous verse which Demosthenes is said to have made use of: "A fleeing man will fight again." [35] Think of David the prophet, King Solomon, Peter the prince of the Church, Paul the apostle, such great lights of holiness, in whom nevertheless wickedness entered. God perchance has permitted them to fall for this reason, that you in your fallen state may not despair. Stand up on your feet then, immediately and with great resolve, and return to the fray more ardently and more cautiously. It happens meanwhile that the capital sins committed by pious men redound to their piety, while they who more wickedly erred love their own wickedness the more ardently.

Seventeenth Rule

But against some inroads of the tempter certain remedies are more appropriate; against others, other remedies are more effective. Yet there is a unique remedy, by far the most efficacious of all, against every kind either of adversity or of temptation—the cross of Christ, which is itself at once the example for those who err, the refuge for those who toil, and the armament for those who fight. This one weapon ought to be cast against all the javelins of the most worthless one. Accordingly, it is fitting to be diligently practiced in this, not indeed in the fashion of the crowd, to which daily someone reads the story of our Lord's Passion, or who adore the image of the cross, or fortify the whole body on all sides with a thousand signs of him, or keep in their home a piece of the holy cross, or so meditate at certain hours upon the punishment of Christ that they suffer with him as with a just man suffering undeservedly, and weep for him with human affection. The true fruit of that tree is not here, but for the moment let it be milk for infant souls. [36] . . . Who indeed truly loves him who rejoices to be so unlike him? But if you would meditate with greater fruit upon the mystery of the cross, you need to prepare for it some plan and some godly art of fighting for life and death, and to be diligently

---

[35] *Adagia*, 1:10:40; cf. Aulus Gellius, *Noctes Atticae*, 17:21:31.
[36] I Cor. 3:1 f.

practiced in it, that when the occasion demands it may be in readiness. This preparation can be of this sort, that when each individual passion has to be crucified, you apply that part of the cross which corresponds most closely to it. For there is no temptation or adversity at all which does not have its own proper remedy in the cross. For example, when ambition of this world tickles you, . . . think, O infirm member, how great is Christ your Head, and to what depths he cast himself down for your sake. When the evil of envy attacks your mind, remember in what a kindly and sincere manner he expended himself completely for our benefit, and also how good he was to the worst of us. When you are stirred up by gluttony, reflect upon that drink of gall and vinegar.[37] When you are tempted by foul pleasure, recall how far the entire life of the Head was from pleasure, how full it was of all sorts of discomforts, punishments, misfortunes. When anger stirs you up, he will straightway assist you who like a lamb remained dumb before his shearer and did not open his mouth.[38]

If poverty evilly consumes you, or avarice disturbs you, straightway let that God of all things come into your mind, who became needy for your sake,[39] so that he had not a place to lay his head.[40] And for the same reason, if you have acted likewise in other temptations, not only will it not be harsh to have resisted your passions, but even sweet, because you know in this way you have conformed yourself to your Head, and have rendered thanks as it were to him for his immense pains, which he endured for your sake.

Eighteenth Rule

And indeed this sort of remedy, even though it is the by far the most effective one for those who have been proceeding at a moderate pace along the way of life, yet will also benefit the weaker folk somewhat if, when their passions are stirred to impiety, they immediately recall before the eyes of the mind how loathsome, how execrable, how deadly a thing sin is, and on the contrary how great is the dignity of man. We consult among ourselves for a little while in futile calculations concerning this greatest of all things, and before we bind ourselves to the devil by our assent, as if by our signature, we do not reckon within our minds by what a great artificer we were

[37] Matt. 27:34, 48.　　[38] Isa. 53:7; Acts 8:32.
[39] II Cor. 8:9.　　[40] Matt. 8:20.

established, in what an excellent state we were constituted, by what an immense price redeemed,[41] to what great happiness called. Man is a noble animal, for whose sake alone God fashioned this wonderful machine of the world. He is likewise a fellow citizen of the angels, a son of God, an heir of immortality, a member of Christ, a member of the Church. Our bodies are temples of the Holy Spirit,[42] our minds at one and the same time the likeness and shrine of divinity. Yet on the contrary sin is the foulest plague and pestilence of both body and mind. When innocence blooms again in native splendor, the contagion of sin dwindles away even in this age. Sin is the deadly poison of the uncleanest serpent, the contract of the devil, and of a bondage not only exceedingly wicked but also most miserable. When you have deliberated these and like considerations, ponder also whether it is advisable for the sake of a counterfeit, fleeting, poisoned little delight of sin, to fall from such dignity into such indignity, whence through your own effort you cannot free yourself.

Nineteenth Rule

Compare, then, those two authors so unlike each other, God and the devil, one of whom you make an enemy for yourself by sinning, the other you establish as your lord. Through innocence and grace you are received into the number of the friends of God,[43] you are adopted into the privilege and inheritance of sons.[44] Through sin you are made both a servant and a son of the devil.[45] The one is that fountain eternal, that Mount Ida of highest beauty, of the highest pleasure, of the highest good, uniting itself to all. The other is the father of all evils, of extreme wickedness, of the highest unhappiness. Remember the benefits of the one upon you, the evil actions of the other. In what goodness did the former establish you? With what mercy has he redeemed you? With what liberality has he enriched you? With what gentleness has he daily sustained you in your backsliding? With what joy has he received you when you recover your senses? Opposite all these things is the devil: with what great envy does he lay traps against your salvation? In what miseries does he implicate you? And what else does he daily attempt unless it be to drag with him into eternal ruin the whole of mankind? When these considerations have been

41 I Cor. 6:20.   42 I Cor. 3:16; II Cor. 6:16; Eph. 2:21.
43 John 15:14f.   44 Gal. 4:7.   45 John 8:34; II Peter 2:19.
A.O.R.—24

promptly and rightly pondered, take counsel with yourself as follows: Oblivious of my origin, oblivious of such great benefits, because of a paltry morsel of false pleasure, shall I ungratefully desert such a noble, loving, and deserving parent, and enslave myself, moreover, to the most wicked, cruelest of masters? Shall I not at least be superior to him, because I was superior to a well-deserving manikin? Shall I not flee him who flee a man desiring to inflict evil?

Twentieth Rule

Nor, indeed, are the rewards less unequal than the authors thereof unlike. For what are more unequal than eternal death and immortal life; than endlessly to enjoy the highest good in the fellowship of the citizens of heaven and endlessly to suffer the extreme evils in the most unhappy society of the damned? And he who doubts concerning this is not even a man, let alone a Christian. Who does not think this even a more insane insanity? Now indeed on this account, both piety and impiety have in this interim life their quite different fruits. For out of piety the secure tranquillity of the mind is bestowed as well as the blessed joy of the pure mind. When once anyone tastes of it, he will agree that this world possesses nothing so precious, nothing so pleasurable, with which he wishes to exchange it. Conversely, impiety is followed first by a thousand other evils, then by that most miserable punishment of a guilty mind. For the former is the hundredfold increase of spiritual joy which Christ promised us in the gospel,[46] an earnest of everlasting happiness. These are those wonderful gifts spoken of by the prophet, which "neither eye has seen nor ear heard, nor has ascended into the heart of man, which God has prepared for those that love him," [47] without doubt in this life. In the meantime, the worms of the impious do not die,[48] and they suffer their hell among the inhabitants of the upper world.[49] Nor is the flame other than that in which the rich man mentioned in the Gospel was punished.[50] Nor are the punishments of hell

[46] Matt. 19:29.   [47] I Cor. 2:9; Isa. 64:4.   [48] Cf. Isa. 66:24.
[49] From "In the meantime the worms of the impious" to "which accompanies the habit of sinning" was prohibited in the *Index expurgatorius*, Antwerp (1571), 89. Bataillon, 376, points this passage out as very important on Erasmus' implied denial of hell-fire and torment. See Letter to Beda of 15 June, 1527, Allen, VI, 105. Cf. Opera IX, cols. 1091 f., 699 f.
[50] Luke 16:24.

(of which the poets have written much) anything else than ever-lasting vexation of mind, which accompanies the habit of sinning. Therefore let him who wishes the very diverse rewards of the future age rise up; for virtue has its connection with itself, on account of which it ought abundantly to be sought; it has its adjoining sin, whose cause ought to be shunned.

Twenty-first Rule

Think upon these things: how wretched, how fleeting is the present life; how insidious death bears down on all sides; how it tramples underfoot the unwary. And since no one is secure from the moment of life, how huge the danger to defer the time of trial of that life in which, if sudden death (as often happens) should strike you, you will perish in eternity.

Twenty-second Rule

Then impenitence ought always to be feared, the last of evils. For he who carefully considers this will see of how many people, how few truly and wholeheartedly come to their senses from sins, especially of those who protract the cords of iniquity to the very end of life.[51] Slippery and easy indeed is the fall into wickedness. But

> "hence to recall the step and to go forth to the upper air—this is effort, this is toil."[52]

Or warned, as it were, by the fall of Aesop's goat before you go down into the pit of sin, ponder that it is not easy to climb out once more.[53]

9. REMEDIES AGAINST CERTAIN SPECIAL VICES, AND FIRST AGAINST LUST

Up to this point we have demonstrated in one way or another the common remedies against every sort of vice. Now we shall try to take up certain ones, and to state by what means you ought to meet each sin; and, first, the sin of lust, than which evil no other assails us earlier, nor goads us more sharply, nor extends more widely, nor drags more persons to perdition.

[51] Cf. Isa. 5:18.   [52] Virgil, Aeneid, 6:128.
[53] Aesop's Fables (ed. Halm), 45.

If at any time therefore foul lust stimulates your mind, straightway remember to come against it with these arms. First, think
how unclean, how filthy, how utterly unworthy of man that
pleasure is which puts our divine essence on a level not only
with cattle, but also with swine, goats, dogs, and the brutest
of the brutes; nay, which casts it beneath the condition of beasts.
Yet we were destined for fellowship with the angels, for communion with Divinity! . . . The rumor of no vice stinks worse
than that of lust. It exhausts one's patrimony. . . . It violently
injures health. It gives birth to innumerable diseases of the
foulest sort. It destroys the flower of youth before its time. It
speeds the coming of wicked old age. It takes away one's natural
vigor, it dulls sharpness of mind, and, as it were, sows the
mind with wealth. It calls man, great as he is, once for all from
honest pursuits, and immerses him in filth, so that it pleases
him to think about nothing except dirty, low, foul things.
And it deprives man of the use of reason, that which is proper
to him. It makes adolescence unhealthy and infamous, hateful
and wicked, and makes old age miserable. . . .

Stir yourself toward continence, by so many examples of
youths, so many examples of charming virgins, and by comparable evidence let your sloth be reproached. Can you do less,
because such and such persons, by sex and age, so born, so
educated, could and can attain such continence? Like them,
cherish this virtue, and you will be no less strong in it than they.
Think what an honorable, what a pleasing, what a fragrant
thing purity of body and mind is! This especially makes us
friends of the angels,[54] capable of receiving the Holy Spirit.
Indeed, from no vice does that Spirit, the lover of purity, spring
back so rapidly as from immodesty. Nowhere does he rest and
take so much delight as in virginal minds. . . .

10. AGAINST THE PROVOCATIONS OF AVARICE

If you should feel yourself either by nature somewhat
inclined to the vice of avarice, or instigated thereto by the devil,

[54] "There are many passages of Saint Jerome in which are expounded
ideas similar to this." See, for example, *S. Hieronymi Lucubrationes omnes . . .
per Des. Erasmum Roterdamum . . . emendatae*, Leyden, 1530, t. IV, 87:
"Virginity is always connected with the angels. Indeed, to live in the
flesh apart from the flesh is not earthly life but heavenly. Whence to
acquire angelic life in the flesh is greater than to have merit" [Bataillon,
381].

recall to mind once more according to the abové rules the dignity of your condition, that you have been created to such a great end, redeemed in this, that you may ever enjoy that highest good. But God made this entire machine of the world, that all things might serve your ends. How sordid then, how narrow-minded, not to use it, but in such a high degree to be captivated by things dumb and worthless! Banish men's error— what will gold and silver be but red and white earth? Should you, a disciple of Christ, called to a far better possession, be deprived of this, which even some of the pagan philosophers held in contempt, that you may admire something truly great? The great thing is, not to possess riches, but to contemn riches. But the generality of so-called Christians loudly contradicts me, and rejoices in most craftily deceiving itself. "Necessity itself," they say, "urges us to do the thing; for if there were no necessity, one couldn't live at all; if it is more restricted, one lives too uncomfortably, but if more elegant and richer, necessity occasions the most convenience of all." It is consulted as to health; it is looked out for with respect to children; it is accommodated to friends; and finally contempt and better reputation are excluded, since matters have come to such a pretty pass. [55] Among so many thousands of Christians, you may find scarcely one who does not harbor and express sentiments such as these. But to answer them point by point, first because they have cloaked their desire with the name of necessity, let me throw back at them in turn the Gospel parable concerning the lilies and the birds living for each day, to the imitation of which Christ urges us. [56] Let me throw back at them the fact that he did not permit the disciples to carry a scrip or a purse. [57] Let me throw back at them the fact that, when we have forsaken all else, he bids us seek before all things the Kingdom of God, and promises us that all these things will be added unto us. [58] When will the necessities of life ever not suffice for those who study godliness with all their heart? . . .

11. AGAINST AMBITION

If ever ambition tempts your mind with its enchantments, you will fortify yourself against it with these remedies. Immediately, according to those things which we have set forth above, let this be held fast: that that alone is honor which arises from

[55] *Cum res bene habet.* Cf. Cicero, *De oratore,* 1:25:114.
[56] Matt. 6:26, 28.   [57] Luke 10:4.   [58] Matt. 6:31–34.

true virtue, yet which ought meanwhile to be avoided, just
as by word and example Christ Jesus has taught us. Only
one sort of honor ought to be sought by the Christian man,
namely, to be praised, not by men, but by God. For as the
apostle says, "He whom God commends is approved." [59] But
honor, if it is bestowed by men on account of something dishonest, as for example by wicked men, is not honor at all, but
rather a huge scandal. If it is bestowed on account of something
in between—say, beauty, strength, wealth, birth—then it will
not rightly be called honor. No one would merit honor by
that thing which does not merit to be praised. If it be bestowed
on account of something honest, it will indeed be honor, yet
he who merits it will not seek it, content doubtless with this
very virtue and with his consciousness of right. See, therefore,
how ridiculous are these honors, with desire for which the crowd
burns so much. First of all, by whom are they at last given?
Surely by those who possess no discrimination as to what
is honest and dishonest. On what account? Very many on
account of things in between, sometimes on account of wicked
things. To whom? To an undeserving person. Whoever therefore holds forth honor either does it out of fear, and ought in
turn to be feared, or that you may benefit, and mocks you;
or because he admires things not at all and considers them
worthy of no honor, and he ought to be pitied; or because he
judges you endowed with those things to which honor is due,
but if he estimates falsely, take care that you become that which
he thinks you to be. If, on the other hand, he estimates truly,
refer all your honor to Him to whom you owe those things
through which honor is bestowed. The more it does not agree
with you to arrogate honor to yourself, the more you ought not
to arrogate virtue to yourself. Besides, what would be more
insane than to measure your worth by the opinion of mere
men? As soon as it pleases them, once this very sort of honor
which they bestow is in hand, they withdraw it, and strip you
of your honor. In the same manner nothing is more foolish
than to exult over such great honors when they befall, or to
become angry when they are withdrawn. Even by this evidence
you will know they are not true honors, because they are held
in common with the worst and the most wicked ones. Surely
they befall none scarcely any more copiously than those who
are most unworthy of true honors. Think how blessed is the
tranquillity of a modest and private life, removed from all

[59] II Cor. 10:18.

clamor of pride. On the other hand, how thorny, how full of cares, perils, pains, is the life of the powerful! How difficult in favorable circumstances not to forget one's own! How hard, standing on the slippery path, not to fall! How complete the crash from the heights! Every honor is joined with the highest burden. How severe the judgment of the supreme judge will be upon those who put themselves ahead of the rest in the enjoyment of honors! Indeed, mercy will succor him who humbles himself in his weakness. [60] But he who stands up to be looked upon denies to himself the help of divine grace. Let the example of Christ the Head ever inhere in your mind. What is more ignoble, despised, dishonored than he according to the world? How he fled even the honors offered, [61] who was greater than any honor whatsoever! How he laughed in derision, sitting upon an ass! How he condemned, clad in a mantle and crowned with thorns! What an inglorious death he chose! But him whom the world held in contempt, the Father has glorified. Let your glory be in the cross of Christ, [62] in which likewise is your salvation. Of what value are human honors to you, if God casts you out, and despises you, and the angels curse you?

12. AGAINST ELATION AND THE SWOLLEN MIND

You will not be puffed up in mind, if according to that well worn proverb you know yourself, [63] that is, if there is anything great in you, anything beautiful, anything famous, you will take it to be the gift of God, not your own good. On the contrary, whatever is low, sordid, mean, all that you should refer to yourself alone. Remember in what great filth you were conceived, in what depraved circumstances you were born, how naked, how poor, how brute, how pitiful you were when you crawled forth into this light of day! To how many diseases, misfortunes, hardships, has this little body been exposed from all sides! What a little thing could suddenly make it enormous, huge, swollen with immense wind! Weigh also what sort of thing it is whereby you flatter yourself. If it is intermediate, folly; if wicked, madness; if honest, ingratitude. You will recall no other proof of stupidity and unwisdom to be more certain than if anyone violently flatter himself. For this reason no sort of folly is more deplorable. If the mind swells up, and if a little man submits himself to you, think how much

60 Cf. Luke 14:11.   61 Cf. John 6:15.
62 Cf. Gal. 6:14.   63 Adagia, 1:6:95.

greater, how much more powerful God is, who threatens your head, who depresses every proud neck, and who brings all hills down into the plain; [64] who spared not the proud angel. [65] Those matters also will serve you, even if they are of lesser weight, if you ever compare yourself with your betters. You pride yourself on your bodily beauty; compare yourself with those who exceed you in beauty. You are proud of your teaching; turn your eyes toward those to whom you see you have taught nothing. Then if you consider not how much good is present, but how much is lacking, [say] with Paul, "forgetting those things which are behind, press toward those things which remain in front." [66] . . .

13. Against Anger and Desire for Revenge

When fierce sorrow of mind goads you to revenge, remember that there is nothing less like anger than what it falsely imitates, namely, fortitude. Nothing is quite so womanish, nothing has so much the quality of a feeble and degraded mind, as to take delight in revenge. [67] You are zealous to appear brave by not suffering an injury to go unavenged, yet in this same way you display your childishness, for you are not able to temper your mind (an act proper to a man). How much stronger and more generous it is to reject another's folly than to imitate it! Yet someone has done harm, he is violent, he insults you. The more wicked he is, the more you should beware lest you become like him. What evil is this madness, that you avenge the depravity of another only to become more depraved yourself? If you hold abuse in contempt, all men will know you have been undeservedly abused. But if you are aroused, you will furnish a better reason for being inflicted with it. Then reflect upon what a thing it is, if an injury has been received, that it is in no wise removed by revenge, but is rather spread thereby. For what will be the end of mutual injuries if anyone continues to retaliate his own pain by revenge? Enemies increase on both sides; the pain becomes very raw. The more inveterate it is, surely the more incurable it becomes. Yet by leniency and tolerance sometimes even he who has done the injury is cured, and, having returned to himself, from an enemy becomes the surest of friends. . . .

---

[64] Luke 3:5; cf. Isa. 40:4.   [65] II Peter 2:4.
[66] Phil. 3:13.   [67] Cf. Juvenal, *Satires*, 13:191.

No Christian therefore is harmed, except by himself[68]; he is harmed by no injury except at his own hand. And these things, even if they are lighter, help in not succumbing to despair, if according to the conveniently collected evidence of the rhetoricians you at one and the same time lessen your own trouble and avert another's injury by these means. . . . God will not reject the law which he himself established. That you may be absolved from guilt, you dash to Rome, you sail to the shrine of Saint James, you buy the most ample indulgences. Certainly I do not condemn what you do, but that you do all things; yet there is no more useful method by which after the offense you may become reconciled to God than if you, offended, are reconciled to your brother. Pardon your neighbor for a light sin (for whatever man sins against man is light) that Christ may forgive you for your countless thousands of sins.[69] "Yet it is hard," you say, "to restrain a mind on fire." It will not be of help to you, how much harder things Christ bore for your sake? What were you, when for your sake he expended his precious life? Were you not an enemy?[70] With what gentleness does he daily tolerate you, daily repeating old offenses? Finally with what mildness has he endured insults, chains, lashes, and at last the most ignominious death of all? Why do you boast of the head, if you do not take care to be in the body?[71] You will not be a member of Christ unless you follow in the footsteps of Christ. . . . You wish to indulge praiseworthy anger? Be angry toward vice, not man. . . .

You see, dearly beloved friend, what an immense sea of remaining vices lies open to be discussed in similar fashion. But in mid-passage let us strike sail; that which remains will be left to your skill. Nor was it our intention, and indeed how infinite it would be, to begin to dissuade from individual types of vices as it were by individual exhortations, and to urge virtues opposed to these. I have wanted very much (what I believed was going to be sufficient for you) to impress upon you the reason and art of this new warfare, by which you might be able to fortify yourself against the evil attacks of your past life. Therefore what we have done by way of example in one case or another, that you yourself ought to do, first in single instances, then especially in these toward which you know that you, either by vice of nature or of habit, have been par-

---

[68] Cf. *Coll.*, "The Religious Banquet," tr. Bailey, 94: "No man is hurt but by himself." See above, Sixth Rule, n. 90.
[69] Matt. 6:14.   [70] Rom. 5:10.   [71] Cf. Eph. 4:15 f.

ticularly stirred up. Against this certain decrees ought to be inscribed in the tablet of our mind, and, lest they become old from disuse, ought repeatedly to be renewed; as, for example, against the evil of detraction, of slander, envy, gluttony, and others of that sort. These alone are enemies of Christian soldiers, against whose attack the mind ought to be fortified well in advance by prayer, the words of the wise, the teachings of Holy Scripture, the examples of pious men and especially of Christ.

CONCLUSION [72]

Even if I did not doubt that the reading of Scripture is going to supply you abundantly with all these things, yet brotherly charity has urged me that I at least promote and aid your pious proposal to the best of my ability with this little extemporaneous treatise. I have written this more speedily because I was afraid you might fall among the superstitious kind of religious, who, partly serving their own advantage, partly out of great zeal but not according to knowledge, "wander about seas and deserts [73]"; if in any place they stumble upon a man returning from vices to a better life, they try by the most outrageous incitements, threats, blandishments to drag him into the monastic life, as if outside of the cowl there were no Christianity. [74] Then when they have filled his heart with mere scruples and inextricable thorns, they truss him up with various paltry human traditions, and clearly drive the poor wretch into a sort of Judaism, and teach him not to love but to fear.

Monasticism is not godliness, [75] but a kind of life, either useful or useless to anyone depending on one's habit of body and of temperament. Certainly just as I do not urge you to it so I do not urge you against it. Yet this warning I do give, that you do establish godliness neither in food, nor in worship,

[72] See first n. 1.   [73] Matt. 23:15.
[74] This section against the monastic life was denounced by Zúñiga (1522), who was answered by Erasmus, *Apologia ad blasphemias Stunicae*, Opera IX, cols. 364f. See also *Index expurgatorius*, (Madrid, 1584), fol. 108ᵛ.
[75] Bataillon, p. 413: "The most famous passage in the entire *Enchiridion*. Before the publication of the Spanish translation it aroused the anger of the Spanish religious, some of whom attempted to hinder the publication of it. On their side the Erasmians—Luis Coronel, for example—hastened to defend it." See Letter of Erasmus to Beda, 15 June, 1525, Allen, VI, 105; also *Responsio adversus febricitantis cujusdam libelium*, Opera X, cols. 1674f., 1677. For Erasmus' reply to Beda's attack on the passage, see *Supputatio errorum in censuris Beddae*, Opera IX, cols. 700f. See further, Allen, VII, 139.

nor in any other visible thing, but in those things which we have mentioned.[76] In whatsoever things you gaze upon the true image of Christ, join yourself with these. Indeed where men are lacking whose conviction would render you better, separate yourself as much as you can from human intercourse and take into your fellowship the holy prophets, Christ, and the apostles. Especially make yourself familiar with Paul. Him you ought to hold ever in your heart, "day and night he should dwell in your hand,"[77] and his words you should commit to memory. In this interpretation we have struggled long and zealously. This is indeed a bold action, but nevertheless relying upon divine help, we shall carefully devote our attention, that after Origen, Ambrose, Augustine, and so many more modern interpreters, we may not seem to have undertaken this labor quite without cause or without fruit. And that certain detractors may know, who judge that the highest religion knows nothing of belles-lettres, we have embraced since our youth the more polished of ancient literature; not without many vigils we have acquired a fair knowledge of both Greek and Latin; we have not undertaken their study for empty fame or childish pleasure of mind, but long ago put our mind to it that we might with exotic riches abundantly adorn the Lord's temple (which some persons have too much dishonored out of their own ignorance and barbarousness). By these efforts the generous natural qualities can be kindled to the love of divine Scripture. But having for a few days neglected this very important matter, we have taken upon ourselves this labor in your behalf, that we may point out to you as it were with a finger the way which by a short cut leads to Christ. I pray that Jesus will prosper your undertaking, that he may kindly deign to favor your salubrious project, verily that he may increase and perfect his gift in transforming you, to the end that you may quickly grow great in him, and may hasten to perfect manhood. In him, farewell brother and friend, ever beloved to my mind, yet now even dearer than before, and more pleasing.

At St. Omer, the year of our Lord Jesus Christ[78] 1501.

76 From "Yet this warning" to "which we have mentioned" was censored by the Spanish monks. See *Apologia adversus Monachos Hispanos*, Opera IX, cols. 1068–1070, especially Obj. and Resp. 44 [Bataillon, 413].
77 Horace, *Ars poetica*, 269.
78 The first edition of the *Lucubratiunculae* (Martinus, Antwerp, 1503) and its reprints add at this point: "*ex monasterio Bertinico*" [Holborn, 136 n.].

BIBLIOGRAPHIES

BIBLIOGRAPHY ON JOHN WYCLIF

For a detailed bibliography, cf. *The Cambridge Medieval History*, VIII, Chapter XVI, 900–907 (Cambridge University Press, New York). Latin works in the process of publication by the Wyclif Society, London, 1884–1930.

J. C. Carrick, *Wycliffe and the Lollards* (New York, 1908).

M. Deanesly, *The Lollard Bible and Other Medieval Biblical Versions* (Cambridge, 1920).

Aubrey Gwynn, *The English Austin Friars in the Time of Wyclif* (Oxford University Press, London, 1940).

John T. McNeill, "Some Emphases in Wyclif's Teaching," in *The Journal of Religion* (Chicago, 1927), VII.

B. L. Manning, *The People's Faith in the Time of Wyclif* (Cambridge, 1919).

F. D. Matthew, ed., *The English Works of John Wyclif* (London, 1880).

O. Odložilík, "Wycliffe's Influence Upon Central and Eastern Europe," in *Slavonic Review* (London, 1928), VII.

R. L. Poole, *Wycliffe and Movements for Reform* (London, 1911).

S. H. Thomson, "The Philosophical Basis of Wyclif's Theology," in *The Journal of Religion* (1931), XI.

"The Order of Writing of Wyclif's Philosophical Works," in *Českou Minulostí* (Prague, 1929).

G. M. Trevelyan, *England in the Age of Wycliffe* (4th ed., London, 1909).

Herbert B. Workman, *John Wyclif* (London, 1926), 2 vols.

BIBLIOGRAPHY BEARING ON CONCILIARISM

For a detailed bibliography, cf. *The Cambridge Medieval History*, VII (Chapter X, 865–868) (Cambridge University Press, New York).

F. M. Bartoš, *Čechy v době Husově* (Jan Laichter, Prague, 1947).

F. Bliemetzrieder, *Das Generalkonzil im grossen abendländischen Schisma* (Paderborn, 1904).

   Literarische Polemik zu Beginn des grossen abendländischen Schismas (Vienna, 1909). Contains Conrad of Gelnhausen's *Epistola concordiae*.

J. L. Connolly, *John Gerson, Reformer and Mystic* (Librairie Universitaire, Louvain, 1928).

D. E. Culley, *Konrad von Gelnhausen* (a Halle dissertation, 1913).

H. Finke, *Acta concilii Constanciensis* (Regensbergsche Verlagsbuchhandlung, Münster, 1896–1928), 4 vols.

A. Gewirth, ed. and tr., *Marsilius of Padua; The Defender of Peace* (Columbia University Press, New York, 1951), I.

E. Goeller, *König Sigismunds Kirchenpolitik* (Freiburg im Breisgau, 1902).

Johann Haller, *Papsttum und Kirchenreform* (Berlin, 1903).

H. von der Hardt, *Magnum oecumenicum Constantiense concilium de ecclesiae reformatione* (Frankfurt and Leipzig, 1697–1700), 6 vols. Contains the writings of Henry of Langenstein, John Gerson, and Peter d'Ailly.

H. Heimpel, *Dietrich von Niem* (*c. 1340–1418*) (Regensbergsche Buchhandlung, Münster and Regensberg, 1932).

E. F. Jacob, *Essays in the Conciliar Epoch* (Manchester University Press, Manchester, 1943).

E. J. Kitts, *In the Days of the Councils* (London, 1908).

A. Kneer, *Die Entstehung der konziliaren Theorie* (Rome, 1893).

John T. McGowan, *Pierre d'Ailly and the Council of Constance* (Catholic University of America Press, Washington, 1936).

E. du Pin, *Gersoni opera omnia* (Antwerp, 1706), 5 vols.

L. Salembier, *Le grand schisme d'Occident* (Paris, 1922, 5th ed.).

J. B. Schwab, *Johannes Gerson* (Würzburg, 1858).

P. Tschackert, *Peter von Ailli* (Gotha, 1877).

Noël Valois, *La France et le grand schisme d'Occident* (Paris, 1896), 4 vols.

BIBLIOGRAPHY CONCERNING JOHN HUS

F. M. Bartoš, *Čechy v době Husově* (Jan Laichter, Prague, 1947).

Co víme o Husovi nového (Pokrok, Prague, 1946).

Husitství a cizina (Čin, Prague, 1931).

Knihy a zápasy (Husova českosl. ev. Fakulta bohoslovecká, Prague, 1948).

Jan Herben, *Huss and His Followers* (London, 1926).

E. J. Kitts, *Pope John the Twenty-third and Master John Hus of Bohemia* (London, 1910).

Kamil Krofta, "Bohemia in the Fifteenth Century" in *The Cambridge Medieval History* (Cambridge University Press, New York, 1936), VII.

V. Kybal, *Matěj z Janova* (Prague, 1905).

ed., Matthew of Janov's *Regulae veteris et novi testamenti* (Innsbruck, 1908–1913), i-iv; O. Odložilík, ed. (Prague, 1926), V.

Johann Loserth, *Wiclif and Hus* (London, 1884); *Hus and Wiclif* (Munich, 1925, 2d ed. rev.).

F. Lützow, *The Life and Times of Master John Hus* (London, 1909).

Matthew of Cracow, *De squaloribus Romanae curiae*, ed. C. W. F. Walsh, in *Monumenta medii aevi* (Göttingen, 1757), I, i.

V. Novotný, *Náboženské hnutí české ve 14. a 15. století* (Prague, 1915), I.

ed., *Korespondence a dokumenty M. Jana Husi* (Prague, 1920).

and V. Kybal, *M. Jan Hus, život a učení* (Prague, 1919–1931), I, i-ii, II, i-iii.

D. S. Schaff, tr., *John Hus' De ecclesia* (New York, 1915).

John Hus (New York, 1915).

R. W. Seton-Watson, *A History of the Czechs and Slovaks* (Hutchinson & Co., London, 1943).
Matthew Spinka, *John Hus and the Czech Reform* (University of Chicago Press, 1941).
S. H. Thomson, *Czechoslovakia in European History* (Princeton University Press, Princeton, 1943).

BIBLIOGRAPHY CONCERNING DESIDERIUS ERASMUS

P. S. Allen, *et al.*, *Erasmus* (Oxford University Press, London, 1934). eds., *Opus epistolarum Des. Erasmi Roterodami* (London, 1906-1947). ed., *Erasmi Roterodami Compendium vitae* (Basel, 1935).
M. Bataillon, *Érasme et l'Espagne* (E. Droz, Paris, 1937).
W. E. Campbell, *Erasmus, Tyndale, and More* (Eyre & Spottiswoode, Ltd., London, 1949).
J. Clericus, ed., *Des. Erasmi Roterodami opera omnia* (Leyden, 1703–1706), 10 vols.
W. K. Ferguson, *Erasmi opuscula* (M. Nijhoff, The Hague, 1933).
L. Gautier-Vignal, *Érasme, 1466–1536* (Payot, Paris, 1936).
Hajo Holborn and A-M. Holborn, *Desiderius Erasmus Roterdamus ausgewählte Werke* (C. H. Beck, Munich, 1933). Contains *Enchiridion*.
A. Hyma, *The Christian Renaissance* (New York, c. 1925).
The Youth of Erasmus (University of Michigan Press, Ann Arbor, 1930).
J. J. Mangan, *Life, Character, and Influence of Desiderius Erasmus of Rotterdam* (New York, 1927), 2 vols.
K. A. Meissinger, *Erasmus von Rotterdam* (Albert Nauck & Co., Berlin, 1948), 2d ed.
Paul Mestwerdt, *Die Anfänge des Erasmus. Humanismus und Devotio moderna* (Leipzig, 1917).
A. Renaudet, *Études Érasmiennes (1521–1529)* (E. Droz, Paris, 1939), *Érasme, sa pensée religieuse et son action d'après sa correspondence, 1518–1521* (Paris, 1926).
Otto Schottenloher, *Erasmus im Ringen um die humanistische Bildungsform; ein Beitrag zum Verständnis seiner geistigen Entwicklung* (Aschendorff, Münster, 1933).
Preserved Smith, *Erasmus* (New York, 1923).
C. R. Thompson, *Inquisitio de fide* (Yale University Press, New Haven, 1950).

INDEXES

NAMES AND SUBJECTS

BIBLICAL REFERENCES

Printed in the United States
51296LVS00004BA/1-75